Springer Texts in Business and Economics

More information about this series at http://www.springer.com/series/10099

Sibabrata Das · Alex Mourmouras
Peter C. Rangazas

Economic Growth and Development

A Dynamic Dual Economy Approach

Springer

Sibabrata Das
International Monetary Fund
Washington, DC
USA

Alex Mourmouras
Asia and Pacific Department
International Monetary Fund
Washington, DC
USA

Peter C. Rangazas
Indiana University-Purdue University
Indianapolis (IUPUI)
Indianapolis, IN
USA

Additional material to this book can be downloaded from http://extras.springer.com.

ISSN 2192-4333 ISSN 2192-4341 (elctronic)
Springer Texts in Business and Economics
ISBN 978-3-319-35795-9 ISBN 978-3-319-14265-4 (eBook)
DOI 10.1007/978-3-319-14265-4

Springer Cham Heidelberg New York Dordrecht London

Softcover reprint of the hardcover 1st edition 2015

Printed on acid-free paper

Springer International Publishing AG Switzerland is part of Springer Science+Business Media (www.springer.com)

Contents

Overview

1

Among the most enduring questions in economics are those related to growth and development. Since 1776, when Adam Smith published *An Inquiry into the Nature and Causes of the Wealth of Nations*, economists have been assessing the factors determining a nation's standard of living and rate of economic progress. More than two centuries of research have improved our understanding of the roles of investments in physical and human capital, advancing technologies, openness, and sound institutions in transforming relatively poor economies into economic powerhouses. This book is an introduction to some of the newer features of growth theory that were developed after 1950. We show how the theory can be blended with historical data and case studies to think about the sources of economic prosperity.

Our coverage is selective and the book is no means a broad survey. We concentrate on transitional growth from a two-sector perspective. Most economists believe that this is the right approach for studying early growth. However, we also believe that the importance of transitional growth in explaining the complete growth experience of countries over very long periods of time has been underestimated. One of the primary objectives of the book is to make a case for transitional growth and its implications. For these reasons, we do not cover *endogenous growth theory*, which is an attempt to explain long-run technological change. For those who have an interest in endogenous growth theory, Aghion and Howitt (2008) is an excellent text for advanced undergraduates and beginning graduate students that discusses the topic in detail.

We begin with a single, relatively simple, theoretical framework that extends the Solow model to include endogenous theories of saving, fertility, human capital, and policy formation. The analysis is then expanded to include two sectors of production. We study the structural transformation of developing economies as they shift from traditional production in largely rural areas to modern production in largely urban areas during the early take-off period of modern growth. The two-sector growth model is used to explain the commonly observed differences in saving, worker productivity, and fertility across rural and urban sectors. We examine the effects of policies that reallocate resources across these sectors, such as taxation, migration restrictions, international trade, and the urban bias in the provision

S. Das et al., *Economic Growth and Development*,
Springer Texts in Business and Economics, DOI 10.1007/978-3-319-14265-4_1

of public services. How policies affect the pace of the structural transformation is a critical feature of development as it plays an important causal role in determining an economy's aggregate growth rate.

The extensions to the standard one-sector growth model mentioned above add significant complexity to the analysis. We maintain tractability by using specific functional forms that make the main points more transparent. The use of specific functional forms also allows us to calibrate the models and assess the quantitative importance of various sources and mechanisms of growth. We believe this approach makes the book suitable for advanced undergraduates, beginning graduate students, and policy makers specializing in the macroeconomic analysis of development. The mathematics used in most of the text requires only undergraduate calculus and an exposure to optimization theory that can be found in intermediate microeconomics or an undergraduate mathematics-for-economist course. The more technical material is contained in starred sections and in the appendices at the end of chapters. End-of-chapters *Questions* are provided that help further focus the main points for less advanced students, and *Problems* are provided for more advanced students who want to work on model-building skills.

1.1 Why a Two-Sector Approach

Given the predominance of one-sector models in growth theory, it is natural to ask whether a two-sector model is needed. As mentioned, many economists believe accounting for two sectors is essential, especially for understanding the early stages of development. Lewis (1954) noted that developing economies exhibit a *dualism*, where two economies with fundamentally different structures operate within a single country. One economy operates in a *traditional* sector using elementary production technologies that rely heavily on raw labor, natural resources, and land. The other economy operates in a *modern* sector using advanced technologies that rely heavily on skilled labor and physical capital. The precise interpretation of the two sectors is left open and depends on the particular application of the framework.

In some applications, the traditional sector is thought of as rural in location and the goods produced are assumed to be agricultural. The modern sector is urban in location and produces manufacturing goods. In other applications, the same goods are produced in each sector but using different production technologies and inputs. For example, agricultural products can be produced using traditional or modern methods. As the economy evolves, the traditional ways of producing disappear, but not the products themselves.

The existence and effectiveness of markets also may differ across the two sectors as the markets for labor and capital in the modern sector will generally be more developed than the markets for labor and land in the traditional sector. Under this interpretation, the decline in the traditional sector represents the spread of markets for labor and land (as land is enhanced and developed, essentially becoming part of the reproducible capital stock).

In most developing countries, these different interpretations of the two-sector framework strongly overlap. The traditional sector is predominately rural and agricultural and is operated without much reliance on formal markets for labor and land. In the early stages of growth, the traditional sector is very large, and this is where the dual economy approach has the greatest potential to improve our understanding of development.

When the two sectors are given an explicit geographic interpretation, the households living and producing in the two locations may differ in their behavior because of differences in their economic environments and their initial conditions. Household behavior that may differ across sectors includes saving, work effort, human capital investment, and fertility—all of which relate to aggregate economic growth in important ways.

For example, Lewis thought that a dual approach was necessary to explain how saving rates and capital accumulation increased over the course of development. He conjectured that the income of capital owners in the modern sector would rise relative to incomes of workers and land owners as "surplus" labor from the traditional sector is pulled into the modern sector with little upward pressure on wages. Lewis believed that the relative expansion of capital income was important for growth because capital owners were viewed as saving a larger fraction of their income than land owners and workers. Thus, growth was accelerated by an increase in the economy's saving rate as the modern sector expanded and the traditional sector contracted.

Carter et al. (2003) argue saving rates expand with development for a different reason, but one that is also related to the presence of a dual economy. Residual income from inherited farms finances the consumption of the elderly and reduces the need for retirement saving during working years. As the economy goes through the structural transformation away from traditional family farming, the reliance on income from inherited family farms declines and the retirement saving out of earnings rises.

The difference in saving rates across the two sectors is only one possible feature of dual economies that affects aggregate growth. There is now a substantial body of evidence suggesting that there are large gaps in worker productivity across sectors in the early stages of development (Gollin et al. 2002, 2004, 2014). These productivity gaps suggest that labor may be inefficiently allocated and that TFP and aggregate economic growth increase as labor migrates from the low-productivity traditional sector to the high-productivity modern sector.

It is commonly observed that fertility is much higher in the traditional sector than in the modern sector (e.g., Greenwood and Seshadri 2002). This fact suggests that the movement of households from the traditional sector to the modern sector lowers the economy's fertility rate. A reduction in the economy's fertility creates another link between the transformation of the dual economy and economic growth. Reductions in population growth allow for greater accumulation in physical capital *per worker*, for a given saving rate.

Years of schooling for children of households in the modern sector are typically higher than those in the traditional sector (Cordoba and Ripoll 2006; Vollrath 2009). There is some suggestion that the "quality" of schooling is also different across the two sectors, as students in the rural schools of developing countries are less well equipped and have fewer days of attendance over the course of a school year (e.g., Banerjee and Duflo 2011, Chap. 4). Thus, growth of the modern sector may increase human capital, yet another important cause of economic growth. Recent theories connect the rise in schooling and the decline in fertility associated with development (Galor 2005, 2011). Some of the theories relate both behaviors to the dual structure of economies (Greenwood and Seshadri 2002; Doepke 2004; Cordoba and Ripoll 2006; Mourmouras and Rangazas 2009a).

A country's fiscal policy is also affected by its dual structure. Countries with larger traditional sectors have a more difficult time collecting taxes and providing essential public infrastructure to private producers (Mourmouras and Rangazas 2009b). Similar to private capital accumulation, the structural transformation of an economy away from the traditional sector and toward the modern sector may accelerate the growth in productive public capital per worker. There are also many political economy issues associated with how policies are affected by the relative influence of landowners who dominate the traditional sector versus capitalists who dominate the modern sector (e.g., Galor et al. 2009) or rural versus urban households, who may receive different levels of attention from government officials (e.g., Mourmouras and Rangazas 2013).

A final connection between the dual economy and aggregate economic growth focuses on the role of cities in the urban sector (Henderson 2010). There are theories and evidence supporting the idea that producing in larger cities can raise worker productivity through knowledge and information spillovers. These externalities are believed to be positively associated with the population density of the city, at least up to the point where various negative effects of crowding begin to dominate. The premise is that the more people who work in a concentrated area, the greater the flow of ideas and the better the match between employers and employees. Raising the stock of knowledge, and matching skills and tasks more effectively, raises worker productivity in the city. Thus, the concentration of workers in larger cities may increase economic growth apart from the other mechanisms described above.

1.2 Early Theory

The recent literature on two-sector models and the structural transformation relates back to the earlier work on dual economies, although there are substantial differences between the older and more modern approaches. Lewis (1954) and Ranis and Fei (1961) pioneered the analytical treatment of dual economies and the structural transformation. Important assumptions in their analysis included the following: (i) an exogenous institutional wage in the agricultural sector, (ii) the institutional wage is paid out of the average product of labor (which includes land rents) and (iii) a "surplus" of labor in the agricultural sector with the marginal product of labor in agriculture lower than the marginal product of labor in industry (which equals the institutional wage and average product of labor in agriculture). There are no wage gaps in their models, as the institutional wage also determines the wage paid to labor in industry. In the early stages of development, with most of the labor in traditional agriculture, the marginal product of labor in agriculture was thought to be, not just low, but actually zero. This was Lewis's extreme interpretation of "surplus" labor.

The empirical relevance of surplus labor, even in the poorest developing countries, was challenged early on by Schultz (1964). He used the natural experiment of an influenza epidemic in India as a test of the idea. The epidemic caused a sharp decline in the agricultural labor supply and total agricultural output fell accordingly—a clear contradiction to the surplus labor assumption. The surplus labor assumption certainly is not relevant to labor scarce countries, such as the USA in the nineteenth century, because migrant workers from other sectors of the economy were typically hired during harvest times.

The assumption of an exogenous institutional wage that determines wages across the economy is also problematic. As mentioned above, not only are there large productivity gaps across sectors, but there are large annual wage gaps as well. Explaining the presence of these large wage gaps has become the main focus of the recent literature on dual economies.

The earlier dual theories were naturally not unified in the sense that models are today. They ignored human capital altogether. The theories did recognize the importance of population growth and physical capital formation for the economic transformation, but these variables were treated exogenously. Schultz (1964) was the first to stress the importance of human capital in causing the movement away from traditional agriculture. Eaton (1987) and Drazen and Eckstein (1988) modeled the interaction between a dual structure and physical capital formation. Galor and Weil (1996, 2000) insisted that fertility and population growth must be given a central role in theories of long-run development. This book incorporates all these features from the recent literature into a dual economy approach.

To see how a unified approach to modeling the dual economy is able to generate connections between key features of development, consider the treatment of implicit claims on land. In the older theories, there were implicit claims on land rents that allowed "wages" to exceed the marginal product of labor in the traditional sector, resulting in an inefficient allocation of labor. The older theories were static models, with no markets for land, and the total output was simply assumed to be split across the workers.

In the newer theories, inefficiencies in the allocation of labor are also linked to land rents. The current generation of landowners desires to bequeath land to the next generation if they are willing and able to maintain the tradition of family farming (a preference that is more likely to be operative when land markets are incomplete). Workers in the traditional sector accept lower wages (which do equal their marginal product) in the traditional sector because if they move off the farm they lose their claims to land in the future, i.e., they will not inherit the land from their parents or tribal elders. Thus, expectation of future rents from an intergenerational transfer of land creates both wage and productivity gaps across sectors. Moreover, the expectation of future land rents also lowers saving and raises fertility. The observed sector differences in wages, productivity, saving, and fertility are all explained in the same way.

1.3 Outline

We hope this book encourages readers to think about the connections mentioned above and to explore new connections between the structural transformation and economic growth. Chapter 2 presents a standard one-sector model of physical capital accumulation where saving is motivated by the need to finance retirement consumption, based on the seminal work of Diamond (1965). The model is then extended to include intergenerational transfers that take the form of both physical assets and investment in children's human capital. Calibration exercises show that one can explain very little growth in US history unless human capital is included. This result receives further support when we move to a two-sector setting. Chapter 3 extends the one-sector model to include endogenous human capital, fertility, and policy formation. In this chapter, large income differences across countries are explained by a combination of a poverty trap that keeps human capital low and fertility high, and anti-growth fiscal policies. We discuss the limitations of outside aid in addressing both these sources of poverty.

Chapter 4 provides an introduction to a two-sector model with complete markets across the economy. We use the model to examine the origins of modern growth, asset bubbles, how the structural transformation affects physical capital accumulation, the impact of opening the economy to the trade of goods on economic growth and welfare, and how health considerations help explain the relatively constancy of caloric intake and the decline in household budget shares spent on food over the course of development.

Chapters 5, 6, and 7 introduce market imperfections and cultural attitudes that create the dualism observed in many developing countries. The dual structure leads to differences in household behavior and to policy conflicts. Chapter 5 focuses on gaps in worker productivity and fertility. Chapter 6 focuses on how differences in saving behavior and the internal migration of workers affect physical capital accumulation per worker in the modern sector. Chapter 7 combines the material in Chaps. 5 and 6 to provide a complete dynamic analysis of a dual economy. The model is used to simulate transitional growth over two centuries. The simulated growth and predictions about other features of development are compared to real-world data.

Chapter 8 introduces fiscal policy in a two-sector setting to examine the connection between government provision of goods and services and urbanization. We find that it can be efficient for fiscal policy to be "biased" toward the modern sector, as the bias encourages internal migration that raises worker productivity throughout the economy. However, the rural sector cannot be completely ignored. Some rural development is needed to maintain a reasonable pace of migration to the city in order to prevent crowding of government services. We also find that internal migration restrictions is not an efficient way to pace the structural transformation as they make modern urban sector households better off at the expense of rural households. Chapter 9 provides a conclusion.

To further summarize our focus, below we list some of the important stylized facts we attempt to explain and some of the economic policies we examine.

1.4 Stylized Facts Associated with Economic Development

1. Relatively trendless economic growth rates and interest rates for long periods
2. Rising investment rates in physical capital and, especially, in human capital
3. Increasing, and then decreasing, fertility and population growth rates
4. Large gaps in wages, hours worked, fertility, and savings rates between the urban/manufacturing sector and the rural/agricultural sector
5. Gradual migration of labor from the rural/agricultural sector to the urban/manufacturing sector over long periods of time (the *Structural Transformation*)
6. An increase in the relative size of government (*Wagner's Law*)
7. The presence of an urban bias in the provision of government infrastructure and services
8. Declining family budget shares spent food, approximately constant caloric intake, and rising body mass and health
9. Persistent poverty traps that delay and limit modern growth in many countries
10. The absence of a robust correlation between foreign aid flows and economic growth in recipient countries
11. The absence of convergence in per capita income across countries of the world
12. The difference in growth rates across Asia and Africa since WWII.

1.5 Policies Examined

1. Domestic fiscal policy such as taxation, government consumption, and infrastructure investment; including a theory of their formation as well as their effects on economic growth
2. Opening the economy to both the trade of goods and the trade of assets, including how domestic fiscal policy responds to openness and an analysis of the *De-Industrialization Hypothesis*

3. Human capital policies such as child labor and mandatory schooling legislation, as well as more recent policy attempts to increase human capital such as compensating families for the forgone earnings of older children that attend school and explicitly restricting family size
4. Restrictions on the domestic migration of labor from rural to urban sectors
5. The use of conditional and unconditional foreign aid to developing countries.

References

Aghion P, Howitt P (2008) The economics of growth. MIT Press, Cambridge, Mass

Banerjee A, Duflo E (2011) Poor economics. Public Affairs, New York

Carter S, Ransom R, Sutch R (2003) Family matters: the life-cycle transition and the unparalleled fertility decline in antebellum America. In: Guinnane T Sundstrom W, Whately W (eds) History matters: essays on economic growth, technology, and demographic change. Stanford University Press, Stanford, California

Cordoba J, Ripoll M (2006) Agriculture, aggregation, wage caps, and cross-country income differences. Working paper 246, University of Pittsburgh, Department of Economics

Diamond P (1965) National debt in a neoclassical growth model. Am Econ Rev 55(5):1126–1150

Doepke M (2004) Accounting for fertility decline during the transition to growth. J Econ Growth 9 (3):347–383

Drazen A, Eckstein Z (1988) On the organization of rural markets and the process of development. Am Econ Rev 78(3):43–431

Eaton J (1987) A dynamic specific factors model of international trade. Rev Econ Stud 54:325–338

Galor O (2005) From stagnation to growth: unified growth theory. In: Aghion P, Durlauf S (eds) Handbook of economic growth. North Holland, Amsterdam

Galor O (2011) Unified growth theory. Princeton University Press, Princeton, New Jersey

Galor O, Weil D (1996) The gender gap, fertility, and growth. Am Econ Rev 86:374–387

Galor O, Weil D (2000) Population, technology, and growth: from malthusian stagnation to modern economic growth. Am Econ Rev 90(4):806–828

Galor O, Moav O, Vollrath D (2009) Inequality in land ownership, the emergence of human capital promoting institutions, and the great divergence. Rev Econ Stud 76(1):143–179

Gollin D, Lagakos D, Waugh M (2014) The agricultural productivity gap. Quart J Econ 129 (2):939–993

Gollin D, Parente S, Rogerson R (2002) The role of agriculture in development. Am Econ Rev 92 (2):160–164

Gollin D, Parente S, Rogerson R (2004) Farmwork, homework, and international income differences. Rev Econ Dyn 7(4):50–827

Greenwood J, Seshadri A (2002) The US demographic transition. Am Econ Rev 92(2):59–153

Henderson V (2010) Cities and development. J Reg Sci 50(1):515–540

Lewis A (1954) Development with unlimited supplies of labor. The Manchester Sch 22:92–139

Mourmouras A, Rangazas P (2009a) Reconciling Kuznets and Habbakuk in a unified growth model. J Econ Growth 14(2):149–181

Mourmouras A, Rangazas P (2009b) Fiscal policy and economic development. Macroecon Dyn 13 (4):450–476

Mourmouras A, Rangazas P (2013) Efficient urban bias. J Econ Geogr 13(3):451–471

Ranis G, Fei J (1961) A theory of economic development. Am Econ Rev 51(4):533–565

Schultz T (1964) Transforming traditional agriculture. Yale University Press, New Haven

Vollrath D (2009) How important are dual economy effects for aggregate productivity? J Dev Econ 88(2):325–334

Part I
Introduction to Economic Growth

Neoclassical Growth Theory

2

This chapter discusses the one-sector neoclassical growth model—the foundation for all the growth theory in the book. The primary focus of the chapter is growth via capital accumulation. We think of *capital* as man-made durable inputs to the production process. The first type of capital we include is *physical capital*. For our purposes, physical capital can be primarily thought of as plant and equipment that is produced in one period and then used in production in the following period.[1] To model production, we introduce *firms*, economic institutions that combine physical capital and labor to produce goods and services.

Physical capital introduces two fundamental features to the economy. First, the presence of physical capital allows the economy to expand its productive capacity over time—that is to experience economic growth through investment and capital accumulation. Second, the production of output generates *endogenous* income flows to households that own and rent physical capital to firms. In addition, physical capital will raise the productivity of the labor input and thereby raise the wage received by workers.

The accumulation of capital must be financed or funded by household saving. We use the life-cycle theory of household consumption as the basis for explaining saving behavior. In the pure life-cycle theory, households save to finance retirement consumption. Later in this chapter, we extend the life-cycle theory of the household to include transfers of assets across generations—including investments in children's *human capital* by their parents. Human capital, a second type of man-made durable input, is defined to be the embodied knowledge, skills, and health that affect a worker's productivity. Investments in human capital, just as with physical capital, allow an economy to experience economic growth.

---

[1] Definitions of physical capital will vary depending on the purpose at hand. In some cases, physical capital is defined to include inventories, software, land, and other inputs that extend beyond plant and equipment.

S. Das et al., *Economic Growth and Development*,
Springer Texts in Business and Economics, DOI 10.1007/978-3-319-14265-4_2

Finally, we illustrate how the model with capital can be "estimated," or more precisely *calibrated*, to make quantitative analysis possible. In particular, we examine how well our simple models can replicate the economic growth in the USA from 1870 to 2000.

2.1 Firms, Production, and the Demand for Capital

The first step in developing a general equilibrium model of output and income is to introduce a production technology. We assume that production takes place in "firms"—organizations that hire labor and rent capital in order to produce output. Each firm's production knowledge or "technology" is represented by a *Cobb–Douglas production function*,

$$Y_t = AK_t^{\alpha} M_t^{1-\alpha}, \tag{2.1}$$

where Y denotes output, K denotes the capital stock rented, M denotes the hours of work hired, and where A and α are technological parameters. The production function is a technological "recipe" that relates the inputs hired and used by the firm to the output that the firm is capable of producing. The parameter A is sometimes referred to as *total factor productivity* (TFP). It captures a wide variety of unmeasured variables that affect the productivity of labor and capital; from climate and geography that determine natural resources available and the health environment of households to laws and regulations that restrict the way that production is carried out. The parameter α measures the relative importance of physical capital in the production process. This interpretation of α will become more clear as the theory of the firm is developed below.

The output produced by firms is a single "all-purpose" good that can either be consumed or invested as a physical asset (somewhat like corn that can be either consumed or stored and invested as a physical asset to plant and produce more corn in the future). This abstraction avoids the complication of having two distinct sectors of production, one producing consumer goods and the other capital goods. For some purposes, one may require this more elaborate two-sector model, but this is not the way to begin an analysis of a growing economy.

The Cobb–Douglas production function is a special case of what is called a "neoclassical" production function. All neoclassical production functions have three general properties: (i) positive marginal productivity, (ii) diminishing marginal productivity, and (iii) constant returns to scale. Economists believe that these properties are common to most production processes.

The marginal product of an input is the increase in output that results from an increase in the use of the input. Formally, it is the derivative of the production function with respect to a particular input, holding other inputs constant. For a Cobb–Douglas production function, the marginal product of labor and the marginal product of capital are $\frac{\partial Y_t}{\partial M_t} = (1-\alpha)AK_t^{\alpha}M_t^{-\alpha}$ and $\frac{\partial Y_t}{\partial K_t} = \alpha AK_t^{\alpha-1}M_t^{1-\alpha}$. The marginal productivity of increasing the level of either input is always positive—more output results when the firm hires either more labor or more capital.

Diminishing marginal productivity means the additional output, associated with adding an additional unit of an input, decreases as more of that input is used. So while output increases as the firm uses more of an input, the size of the increase gets smaller as the amount of the input used in production increases. This assumption is based on the intuitive notion of "input crowding." The increasing scarcity of the input held fixed, limits the production that results from adding more of the other input. For example, if there is given amount of capital, as more workers are hired the amount of capital that each worker can use decreases—serving to limit the rise in output. Note that the marginal product of labor expression above is decreasing in M_t, for a fixed value of K_t. The same reasoning applies to the marginal product of capital.

Constant returns to scale means that if *both* inputs were increased in the same proportion, then the ability to produce output would also increase by that proportion. This property makes sense because if the firm can simply duplicate its current plant, equipment, and workforce, it should be able to duplicate or double its output as well.

Finally, note that the properties we just established imply that the marginal product expressions can be simplified by combining M_t and K_t into the *capital–labor ratio*, also known as *capital intensity*, $k_t \equiv K_t/M_t$. The simplified expressions for the marginal products are, $\frac{\partial Y_t}{\partial M_t} = (1-\alpha)Ak_t^{\alpha}$ and $\frac{\partial Y_t}{\partial K_t} = \alpha A k_t^{\alpha-1}$. The marginal product of labor is increasing in capital intensity. The more capital per worker, the more productive an additional worker is. The marginal product of capital is decreasing in capital intensity. Higher capital intensity means that there are fewer workers available to work with any additional capital bought to the workplace.

The fact that the marginal products of capital and labor are both functions of the capital–labor ratio, k, and not the levels of K and M, is a consequence of the constant returns to scale assumption. This property implies that the *scale* of a firm is indeterminate, i.e., the optimal size of a firm cannot be pinned down by the theory. Firms are indifferent about the level of production, but they do want to hire capital and labor in a particular ratio that depends on the relative market prices of the inputs.

From the point of view of microeconomics, the indeterminacy of firm size can be seen as a disadvantage. One is forced to simply assume that firms are of a given size and that there are enough of them competing to justify the *perfect competition* assumption that is discussed below and used throughout the book. From a macroeconomic point of view, the indeterminate size of firms can be seen as a convenient simplification. The key expressions that characterize the production side of the economy apply both to the individual firm and to the collection of firms as a whole. This is why in many macroeconomic models, the distinction between the individual firms and production in the economy as a whole is not emphasized.

What makes (2.1) special in the class of neoclassical production functions is that the Cobb–Douglas functional form implies that the *shares* of national output that are paid to capital owners and workers are the *constant* output elasticity values α and $1-\alpha$. Data show that over the last century, income shares have in fact stayed roughly constant within and across countries. For this reason, many economists view the Cobb–Douglas functional form as a reasonable approximation to an economy's aggregate production technology. To explicitly see that (2.1) has the constant income share property, we next need to think about how capital owners and workers are paid.

We assume that markets are perfectly competitive in our production economy. As discussed in elementary economics, the notion of competitive markets applies not only to the markets for goods but also to the factor markets for labor and capital. The competitive assumption applied to the factor markets means that firms demand inputs to maximize profits taking as given the market prices of the inputs: the wage rate paid to labor (w) and rental rate for physical capital (r). No single firm is large enough to be able to influence market prices when they unilaterally change their production or input levels. The price of the economy's single output good is taken to be one. So we can think of output and revenue as being the same. Therefore, profit can then be written as $Y_t - w_tM_t - r_tK_t$.

Maximizing profits requires that firms hire capital and labor as long as the marginal benefit (marginal product) exceeds the marginal cost (factor price). Formally, the necessary conditions for profit maximization are

$$\alpha A k_t^{\alpha-1} = r_t \tag{2.2a}$$

$$(1-\alpha) A k_t^{\alpha} = w_t. \tag{2.2b}$$

Equation (2.2a, b) say that, in order to maximize profit, the marginal product of each input must be equated to its market price, just as in the theory of competitive factor markets from intermediate microeconomics.

From the perspective of an individual firm, that takes factor prices as given, it appears that there are two independent equations, (2.2a, b), to determine one unknown, k. In general, this situation leads to inconsistent solutions for k—i.e., different solutions for k from each equation. This is not the case here because of an important implication of competitive markets: economic profits are driven to zero. Competition between firms for the available resources will force factor prices to satisfy these equations, which in turn implies that economic profits are zero. Thus, (2.2a, b) also play a role in determining the market factor prices and not just k.

To think about this last point further, first notice that we can write the production function as $Y_t = Ak_t^{\alpha}M_t$. Next, multiply each side of (2.2a, b) by M_t to get

$$\alpha Y_t = r_t K_t \tag{2.3a}$$

$$(1-\alpha) Y_t = w_t M_t \tag{2.3b}$$

Equation (2.3a) shows that the share of output and revenue paid to owners of capital (by each firm and in the economy as a whole) is the constant, α, an interpretation that was suggested above. Moreover, if αY_t goes to capital owners as a gross rent to capital, there is just enough revenue left over, $(1-\alpha)Y_t$, to pay workers the competitive wage, implying that economic profit is zero.

The connection made in (2.3a, b) allows us to refer to α and $1-\alpha$ as the capital and labor shares. The fact that the Cobb–Douglas technology, combined with competitive markets, implies constant factor shares is a strong prediction of the model. Remarkably, this prediction is approximately consistent with empirical evidence that shows little trend in factor shares as a country develops.

The two Eqs. (2.2a, b) are then profit-maximizing conditions that determine two variables: the firm's demand for capital relative to labor and, via the zero profit condition, one of the factor prices. To determine the remaining factor price, we need the final requirement of a competitive equilibrium: *market clearing*. The firm's demand for capital per worker must equal the supply of capital per worker coming from households. We will think of the rental rate on capital as the "price" that clears the capital market. Then interpreting (2.2a, b) as determining the demand for capital and the competitive wage rate that generates zero profit, we have three conditions to determine the three unknowns: r_t, w_t, and k_t.

The first step in developing the market clearing condition is to be more explicit about what we mean by the *demand* for capital in the production economy. Start by thinking of the capital–labor ratio on the left-hand side of (2.2a) as the capital–labor ratio *demanded* by firms at different rental rates for capital. Call the firm's demand for k, k_t^d. In period t, firms will enter the capital market to rent capital that they can use in production. Solving (2.2a) for k, we can write the demand for capital in period t as

$$k_t^d = \left[\frac{\alpha A}{r_t}\right]^{1/(1-\alpha)}. \tag{2.4}$$

Equation (2.4) indicates that as the rental rate required by the market rises, the firm's demand for capital declines. This is because, as the cost of capital rises, firms will shift toward using less capital and more labor in production.

The theory thus far gives us the firms' demand for capital intensity. Now we need to develop a theory for the supply of capital in period t. In other words, we need to discuss who owns the capital and how much capital they are willing to supply to the market.

2.2 Household Saving and the Supply of Capital

In our model, households purchase capital as an asset, a type of saving used to finance retirement consumption. The capital generates funds for retirement consumption purchases when the households rent the capital to firms. So, the supply of capital referred to at the end of Sect. 2.1 results from older households attempting to generate income for retirement consumption.

To capture a retirement motive for saving in the simplest way possible, we assume households live for two periods: one when they are young and working and one when they are old and retired. This means that in any one period, there are two household types from distinct generations: a young working household and an old retired household. Macroeconomic models where different generations operate as distinct decision makers in each period are called *overlapping generations* models.

Including the saving behavior of households is an important extension to the Solow model of capital accumulation that you may have seen in undergraduate macroeconomic courses. In the Solow model, saving is treated as an exogenous variable. The economy's saving rate is simply assumed to be a constant fraction of total income with no explanation provided.

2.2.1 The Supply of Labor and Capital

As just mentioned, the supply of capital that is rented to firms is owned by old retired households. They rent the capital to firms to generate income that finances their retirement consumption. Once the firms complete production using the capital, the retired households sell the capital to the young working households that are looking to save assets to finance their future retirement consumption. The sale of capital provides further resources for retirement consumption of the current old households.

Formally, the currently old households, who own the capital, purchased the capital as an asset during their working lives in the previous period. In period $t-1$, each young household supplied one unit of labor to firms and earned the wage, w_{t-1}. For now, there is no variation in household labor supply. We model the choice of how much to work in Chap. 5. With each household supplying one unit of labor, the aggregate supply of labor in each period is then just the number of young households. In period $t-1$, the total supply of labor to all firms is the total number of young households from that generation, $M_{t-1}^{s} = N_{t-1}$.

The capital supplied per unit of labor results from the household's saving behavior, s_{t-1}. Young households save in period $t-1$ by purchasing output and treating it like a physical asset that generates income during retirement by supplying or renting it to firms for use in production during period t. The firms use this physical capital to produce output and generate revenue in period t. The firms then return the capital, that has been depreciated by use in production, back to households and pay them the rental rate r_t. So, for every unit of capital that households purchase and rent to firms, they receive back in period t, $1-\delta+r_t$, as their return to saving, where δ is the fraction of capital that depreciates from use. We somewhat loosely refer to $r_t-\delta$ as both the "return to capital" and the "interest rate" on household saving.

The total supply of new capital to the market in period t is the total saving of young households in period $t-1$, $s_{t-1}N_{t-1}$. To match the demand concept in (2.4), we need an expression for the capital supplied *per worker* in period t. The supply of capital per worker in period t is $k_t^s \equiv s_{t-1}N_{t-1}/M_t^s = s_{t-1}N_{t-1}/N_t = s_{t-1}/n$, where n is the average number of children born in each young household. In Chap. 3, we make fertility endogenous by allowing parents to choose the number of children, but for now we treat n as an exogenous constant. The number of children each household has determines the relative population size of different generations. For example, if $n = 1$, then generations are of equal size and $N_t = N_{t-1}$. If $n > 1$, $N_t > N_{t-1}$ and there is positive population growth over time. Note that the rate of population growth is $(N_t/N_{t-1}) - 1 = n - 1$.

2.2.2 Household Saving

We now develop a theory of household saving. Households do not directly benefit from saving but rather use saving to create their desired lifetime consumption path. The consumption path that households prefer depends on their attitudes about consuming now rather than later in life. Household preferences are represented by a utility function. The utility function captures the household's preference for consuming at different points in their lifetime.

We assume that household preferences are represented by a *constant elasticity of substitution* (CES) utility function,

$$u_t = U(c_{1t}, c_{2t+1}) = \frac{(c_{1t}^{1-1/\sigma} - 1) + \beta(c_{2t+1}^{1-1/\sigma} - 1)}{(1 - 1/\sigma)}.$$

For a generation t household, consumption in the first and second periods, c_{1t} and c_{2t+1}, determine the value of lifetime utility. The CES utility function has the standard properties that the marginal utility of consumption in each period is positive but diminishing (try taking the first and second derivative with respect to consumption in any one period).

The two parameters used to reflect individual preferences about the timing of consumption are the pure time discount factor (β) and the intertemporal elasticity of substitution (σ). Typically, one assumes that $\beta < 1$ because people are generally viewed as being "impatient," i.e., they weigh utility gained from current consumption higher than utility gained from future consumption. The intertemporal elasticity of substitution is a measure of the individual's willingness to substitute current for future consumption when the relative price of future consumption falls, but this will not be made clear for a while. Subtracting 1 from each consumption term is done for purely technical reasons. It allows the commonly used logarithmic utility function, $\ln c_{1t} + \beta \ln c_{2t+1}$, to appear as a special case when $\sigma = 1$.

Households face constraints that restrict the consumption paths they can afford. In each period, there is a budget constraint that must be satisfied. In the first period of life, a generation t household has its wage (w_t) as a source of funds that can be used to purchase output for consumption (c_{1t}) or for saving (s_t). This gives the first-period budget constraint, $c_{1t} + s_t = w_t$. In the second period, consumption

(c_{2t+1}) is financed by the saving from the first period, $c_{2t+1} = R_t s_t$, where $R_t = 1 + r_{t+1} - \delta$ is the return from owning physical capital or what sometimes is called the "interest factor." The two single period budget constraints can be combined to form a single lifetime budget constraint that says the present value of consumption must equal the first-period wage, $c_{1t} + c_{2t+1}/R_t = w_t$.

Households maximize lifetime utility subject to the lifetime budget constraint. The solution to this problem gives us the optimal consumption and saving behavior of a household

$$c_{1t} = \Psi_{1t} w_t \tag{2.5a}$$

$$c_{2t+1} = \Psi_{2t} w_t \tag{2.5b}$$

$$s_t = \Psi_{1t} \beta^{\sigma} R_t^{\sigma-1} w_t, \tag{2.6}$$

where $\Psi_{1t} \equiv \frac{1}{1+\beta^{\sigma} R_t^{\sigma-1}} < 1$ and $\Psi_{2t} \equiv \frac{\beta^{\sigma} R_t^{\sigma}}{1+\beta^{\sigma} R_t^{\sigma-1}}$.

All choices are fractions of the wage rate that depends on the return to capital. The return to capital affects the fraction differently depending on the value of σ.

The effect of a change in R_t can be conceptually decomposed into an *income* effect and a *substitution* effect. The income effect refers to the fact that a higher return to capital increases the purchasing power of savers that own capital. Greater purchasing power increases the demand for consumption in both periods but lowers saving. The substitution effect refers to the fact that a higher return to capital raises the cost of consuming in the first period relative to consuming in the second period. This is because the forgone interest income from consuming, and not saving, in the first period has increased. The substitution effect from an increase in the return to capital lowers current consumption but raises saving and future consumption. Thus, the overall effect of an increase in the return to capital on current consumption and saving is ambiguous. The relative strength of the income and substitution effects is determined by σ. The greater the value of σ is, the stronger the substitution effect is and the weaker the income effect is. When $\sigma = 1$, the income and substitution effects cancel exactly and the saving rate become a constant fraction of wages, $\frac{\beta}{1+\beta}$. This convenient special case is similar to the Solow model in that the saving rate is a constant.

2.2.3 Supply of Capital Per Worker

Using Eq. (2.6), dated for a generation $t - 1$, and the definition of k_t^s that was introduced previously, we can now write the economy's supply of capital per worker as

$$k_t^s = \frac{w_{t-1}}{n}\left[\frac{1}{1+\beta^{-\sigma}(1+r_t-\delta)^{1-\sigma}}\right]. \tag{2.7}$$

The economy's supply of capital per worker next period is based on the saving per worker this period and the growth of the economy's workforce. An increase in this period's wage raises saving because a portion of the higher wage is consumed and a fraction is put aside to allow consumption in the future to rise as well. The interest rate has an ambiguous effect on saving because of conflicting income and substitution effects (with the relative strength of the substitution effect determined by σ).

The extent to which saving and capital supplied this period raises the capital–labor ratio next period depends on the growth in the workforce. Greater fertility implies a higher rate of population growth and a faster growing workforce. As the workforce next period rises relative to the current workforce, less saving and capital will be available per worker in the future. Thus, higher rates of population growth lower the capital–labor ratio by forcing the available capital to be spread over a larger workforce.

2.3 Competitive Equilibrium in a Growing Economy

Before moving to the determination of the market clearing condition in the capital market, let us summarize the key actions taken in period t by each agent.

Firms	hire labor, pay each worker w_t and rent physical capital per worker, k_t^d, pay owners r_t per unit supplied
Young households	supply one unit of labor, receive w_t, and purchase $s_t = nk_{t+1}^s$ units of physical capital
Old households	supply $s_{t-1} = nk_t^s$ units of physical capital and receive r_t per unit supplied

A market clearing equilibrium in the capital market requires that the firms' demand for capital per worker equals the supply of capital per worker by old households, i.e., $k_t^d = k_t^s$ for all values for t. As in other competitive markets, the market price is the mechanism for bringing the two sides of the market together. In the capital market, the market price is the rental rate on capital that is paid by those demanding capital and received by those supplying the capital. Market clearing requires finding a value of r_t that equates (2.4) and (2.7) in every period, as sketched in Fig. 2.1.[2]

[2] You can think of the value of r_t as actually determined in period $t-1$. In that period, households make their saving decision based on the firms' commitments to rent capital in period t and pay the rental rate r_t. In other words, r_t is determined in period $t-1$ based on the savings behavior of households and the *planned* investment demands of firms.

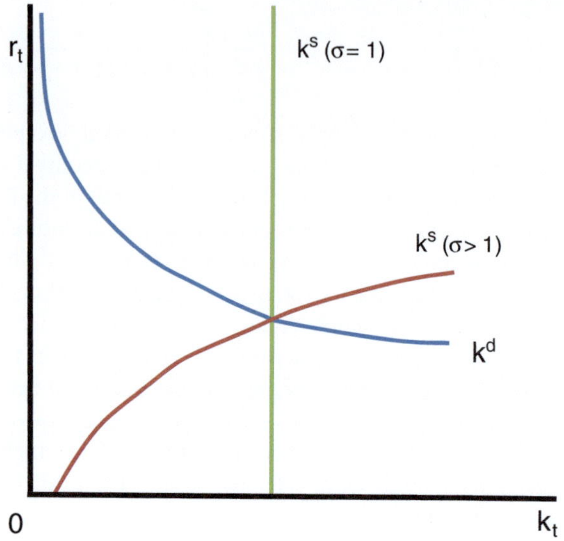

Fig. 2.1 Market clearing equilibria in the capital market

The period t equilibrium is sketched for two different "supply curves." The vertical supply curve assumes $\sigma = 1$ (exactly offsetting income and substitution effects) and the upward sloping supply curve assumes $\sigma > 1$ (a dominant substitution effect). Note that once the equilibrium values of r_t and k_t are determined, then the equilibrium value of w_t is determined by (2.2b).

The figure above is the standard demand–equals–supply way of thinking about how equilibrium is determined. While intuitive, it has limitations as an analytical tool. The problem is that it is a static snapshot of a dynamic economy. In general, a production economy will experience capital accumulation over time. In other words the k_t determined in the figure will be larger than k_{t-1}. This implies that, using (2.2b), w_t will be larger than w_{t-1}. The increase in wages over time will cause the supply curve in the figure to shift to the right each period. Thus, the diagram reveals that growth in the economy is due to the effect of capital on wages. As the capital stock increases, wages increase. The increase in wages increases saving and leads to further capital accumulation. However, there are important details of the growth process that are not revealed by this essentially static depiction.

Fortunately, there is a nice way of displaying the dynamics of the economy more explicitly. One can substitute the factor price equations from (2.2a, b) into (2.7) and impose the equilibrium condition $k_t^d = k_t^s$ to get

$$k_t = \frac{(1-\alpha)Ak_{t-1}^{\alpha}}{n}\left[\frac{1}{1+\beta^{-\sigma}(1+\alpha Ak_t^{\alpha-1}-\delta)^{1-\sigma}}\right]. \tag{2.8}$$

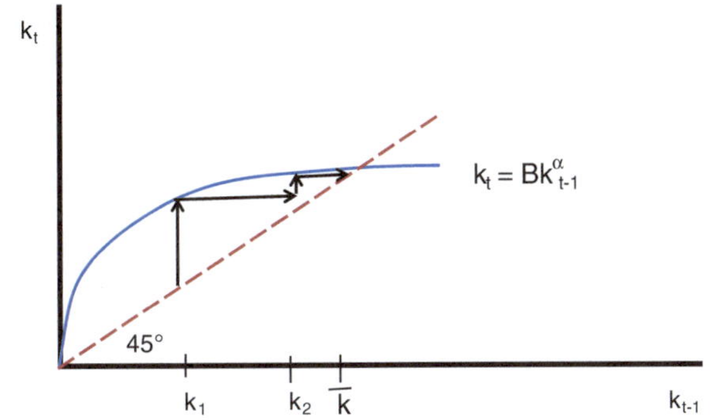

Fig. 2.2 Transitional growth

Mathematically, Eq. (2.8) is known as a *difference equation*, which is the discrete-time analog to the differential equation in continuous time. This equation highlights the underlying dynamics of the model that is driven by changes in the capital–labor ratio over time. In economics, Eq. (2.8) is referred to as a *transition equation* because it describes how the economy evolves over time.

Viewing (2.8), note that the variable we need to solve for, k_t, appears on both sides of the equation. In general, there is no way to use algebra to solve for the unknown value of k_t in terms of the parameters and the known value k_{t-1} (the value of k in the initial period is given as an initial condition of the economy). In this case, one needs to use a numerical approach to find an approximate solution to (2.8). The numerical approach will be discussed in Sect. 2.5.

The dynamic structure of the economy becomes more transparent when we assume $\sigma = 1$. In this special case, (2.8) simplifies to

$$k_t = Bk_{t-1}^{\alpha}, \tag{2.8'}$$

where $B \equiv \frac{\beta}{1+\beta}\frac{(1-\alpha)A}{n}$.

In this case, we have an explicit algebraic solution because the expression involving k_t on the right-hand side of (2.8) vanishes. As mentioned previously, this special case is similar to the Solow model because the saving rate of young households is a constant, with no dependence on the return to capital.

The dynamic features of (2.8′) can be easily sketched by plotting k_t against k_{t-1} as in Fig. 2.2.

Imagine that the economy begins at $k_{t-1} = k_1$. To find out what the capital–labor will be in period 2, move vertically up to the transition equation to find k_2. In period 2, k_2 will now be the initial capital–labor ratio, move horizontally from the transition equation to the 45-degree line and then back down vertically to the horizontal axis. The process then repeats itself until one reaches $k_t = \bar{k}$, where the transition equation crosses the 45-degree line.[3] At this point, the capital–labor ratio remains constant from period to period and the economy is said to have reached a

[3] The economy never literally reaches the steady state, although it will get arbitrarily close.

steady-state equilibrium. An algebraic solution for the steady state is found by setting $k_t = k_{t-1} = \bar{k}$ in (2.8) and then solving the equation for $\bar{k}$. The transition equation given by (2.8) is simple enough to allow an explicit solution for the steady-state capital–labor ratio, $\bar{k} = B^{\frac{1}{1-\alpha}}$.

The transition diagram reveals an important prediction about economic growth via capital accumulation. In the early stages of growth, period-to-period changes in k_t are relatively large and the economy grows fast. Over time, the increases in k_t get smaller and the economy's growth rate slows down, until growth ceases altogether in the steady state. From the static demand and supply figure, we know that growth occurs due to the effect of capital accumulation on wages and saving. What the transition diagram makes clear is that the effect of capital accumulation on wages becomes weaker over time. There is a diminishing effect of k_t on w_t because α is less than one. When an economy is undeveloped and capital is scarce, the creation of new physical capital significantly raises worker productivity and wages. However, as the economy industrializes, the impact of further capital accumulation weakens.[4]

Notice two things about the steady state. First, as k_t grows in approaching the steady state, we know from (2.2a, b) that interest rates will be falling and wages will be rising. Once the steady state is obtained, because k_t is constant, interest rates and wages must also be constant. Thus, the steady state is characterized by constant interest rates and *zero* growth in labor productivity, real wages, and consumption. In many developed countries, the *average* values of interest rates and returns to capital have been relatively constant over long periods of time—suggesting that we might view the average position of the economy as being a steady state (with some annual business cycle fluctuations around the economy's typical or average position). However, these same economies are observed to experience *positive* growth rates in labor productivity and real wages *on average*. According to our model, if interest rates show no downward trend, then this positive growth cannot come from increases in the capital–labor ratio. Where does persistent, long-run growth come from after the steady-state capital–labor ratio is obtained?

2.3.1 Steady-State Growth—Technical Progress

One explanation for persistent economic growth is technical progress—that is increasing knowledge that improves productivity. Technical progress can be thought of as improved production designs or improved factories and equipment. To grow in the steady state with the same amount of capital per worker, we have to get smarter about how we use and design the capital. They are some attempts to explicitly model the research and development process that leads to technical

[4] The weakening effect of the capital–labor ratio on wages stems from the diminishing marginal product of capital. As capital accumulates relative to labor, the effect of further capital accumulation on output and wages gets smaller. Formally, note that the effect of an increase in k on the marginal product of labor is $(1-\alpha)\alpha Ak^{\alpha-1} = (1-\alpha) \times$ marginal product of capital.

process, but economists often treat technical progress as an exogenous variable, as we do here.

Think of technology as the current stock of *disembodied* blueprints for production methods and machine designs. The state of technology in period t affects the productivity of the workforce. We assume that there is an index number, D_t, that measures the extent to which the state of technology influences the *effective* workforce. The effective workforce in period t is defined as $H_t = D_t M_t$, which replaces M_t as an input in the Cobb–Douglas production function. When D_t increases, it raises the effective workforce proportionately. For example, if D_t doubles, and the number of workers remains the same, the effect on production will be the same as doubling the number of workers. We further assume that technical progress is such that D_t increases from one period to the next at the constant rate, d. Thus, $H_{t+1}/H_t = n(1+d)$, the effective workforce increases due to both population growth and technical progress.

We can model the firms as choosing H_t and paying a wage rate per unit of *effective* labor, w_t. The total wage payment received by an actual worker will now be $w_t D_t$. The factor price equations given by (2.2a, b) remain the same, except we now must interpret k as the capital-to-effective-labor ratio, i.e., $k = K/H$.

Now let us think about how the equilibrium and transition equation are altered by technical progress. The firm's demand for the capital, which we can think of as a demand for the ratio of capital to effective labor, will take the same form as (2.2a). On the household side, we need only adjust the saving function for the new concept of household wages to get $s_t = \Psi_{1t}\left(\beta^{\sigma} R_t^{\sigma-1} w_t D_t\right)$. The supply of capital per effective worker is defined as $k_t^S \equiv s_{t-1} N_{t-1}/D_t N_t$. Using the household saving function, the supply of capital per effective worker can be written as $k_t^S = \frac{w_{t-1}}{n(1+d)}\left[\frac{1}{1+\beta^{-\sigma}(1+r_t-\delta)^{1-\sigma}}\right]$. Finally, using the factor price equations, the adjusted transition equation becomes

$$k_t = \frac{(1-\alpha)Ak_{t-1}^{\alpha}}{n(1+d)}\left[\frac{1}{1+\beta^{-\sigma}(1+\alpha Ak_t^{\alpha-1}-\delta)^{1-\sigma}}\right], \tag{2.9}$$

which has the same form as (2.8), except for the presence of 1 + d in the denominator of the expression on the right-hand side of the equation.

Thus, the transitional dynamics of the economy are the same as before. However, now there is an *endogenous* source of growth (increasing physical capital intensity) and an *exogenous* source of growth (technical progress). When the steady state is reached, the transitional growth from increasing physical capital intensity is over and interest rates become constant. However, there will continue to be positive economic growth from exogenous technical progress. Labor productivity, real wages per worker $(w_t D_t)$, and the standard of living (measured by consumption per household) all increase at the rate $d > 0$ in the steady state.

2.4 Intergenerational Transfers

In his presidential address to the American Economic Association, Becker (1988) encouraged economists to pay greater attention to the role of the family in their thinking about macroeconomic issues. Becker pointed out how intergenerational transfers between family members are likely to influence economic growth and alter the effects of important fiscal policies such as social security and government borrowing. Understanding the causes and consequences of intergenerational transfers is one of the most important motivations for taking an overlapping generations approach that recognizes the generational structure of the economy.

We define intergenerational transfers to be a private transfer of resources from one generation to another generation. The transfers take two distinct forms: *human capital* investments (x) and transfers of physical or financial assets (b). The financial assets are identical to the assets used for life-cycle saving, but instead of being used to increase future income for the household, they are used to increase the future income of the household's children.

Human capital investments are *in-kind* transfers of goods and services designed to raise the recipient's productivity by increasing knowledge, skills, or health. The effect of these in-kind transfers on the child's market productivity is given by a human capital production function $H(x_{t+1})$. Here, we are treating effective labor supply as an endogenous function of parental investments. To focus on the human capital component of effective labor supply, we temporarily ignore the exogenous component of effective labor supply, D_t.

The only assumption about the human capital production function that we will use in this section is that the derivative of H with respect to x is positive but diminishing $(H' > 0, H'' < 0)$, i.e., H is increasing and strictly concave in x. This assumption means that while spending more on children's education this period will always increase their knowledge and productivity next period, when they enter the labor force, the marginal return to additional educational spending decreases with the level of expenditures. In other words, there are natural limits to the rate at which a child can accumulate skills and knowledge.

The distinction between the two types of transfers is important since there are situations where human and financial investments of equal dollar amounts are not equivalent in their effect on the recipient's behavior and wealth. For example, a dollar spent on a dependent child's primary and secondary education is generally not going to have the same economic effect as a dollar invested in a financial asset that is ultimately bequeathed to the child. In other circumstances, the distinction may be less clear. Is the payment of a child's college tuition by a parent equivalent to a cash transfer to the child? The answer is not obvious and will depend on the preferences and constraints of *both* the parent and the child. It may also be true that parents value the two transfers differently. For example, parents may value education for its own sake, beyond its effect on the child's future labor productivity in the market.

The accounting relationship between intergenerational transfers and the accumulation of wealth is made precise by examining the household budget constraints in our two-period model. Households have n children, an exogenous variable in this chapter, in the first period of adulthood. During the first period, along with the typical life-cycle consumption and saving choices, parents make human capital investments in their children and save to make financial transfers to their children when they become young adults in the next period. The first-period budget constraint is

$$c_{1t} + s_t + n(x_{t+1} + b_{t+1}) = W_t, \tag{2.10}$$

where $W_t \equiv w_t H_t + R_{t-1} b_t$ is initial wealth and recalls that $w_t H_t$ now represents lifetime earnings with w_t interpreted as the wage per unit of *effective* labor supply.[5] The other term on the right-hand side of the initial wealth expression is the physical or financial asset, plus interest, that the household receives from its parents during the first period of adulthood. The second-period constraint remains the same as before and given by

$$c_{2t+1} = R_t s_t. \tag{2.11}$$

In addition to the budget constraints, one important additional constraint is needed. It is assumed that parents cannot accumulate debt that their children are legally bound to pay (a legal restriction that exists in most societies). This means there is a nonnegativity constraint on financial transfers

$$b_{t+1} \geq 0. \tag{2.12}$$

We next turn to two different approaches to modeling *why* parents make intergenerational transfers. The first approach assumes parental altruism, parents care about the welfare of their children. The altruistic approach provides an interesting and rich theory, but also one that is technically demanding. Less advanced students should skip to Sect. 2.4.3, where a second theory of transfers is presented. This theory assumes that parents receive utility, a "warm glow," directly from the transfers they make to their children.

[5] Note that the acquisition of financial assets occurs in the first period of adulthood and the financial transfers are made in the second period of adulthood. Thus, the transfers are made when both generations are alive. Transfers of this type are called *intervivos* transfers, as opposed to *bequests* that are transferred at death. In our model, where we assume (i) perfect certainty, (ii) perfect life-cycle credit markets, and (iii) no strategic interactions between generations, the timing of financial transfers is irrelevant. However, the timing of transfers can matter when these conditions are not met [see, e.g., Bernheim et al. (1985) and Cox (1987)].

2.4.1 Altruism*

One natural way to explain *why* intergenerational transfers occur is to assume that parents are altruistic, i.e., that they care about their children's welfare as adults. An important way of modeling altruism assumes that parents care about their adult children's lifetime utility. We call this type of altruism *Barro–Becker* altruism named after the two economists who introduced the concept (Barro 1974; Becker 1974). As we shall see, this particular way of modeling altruism has very interesting implications, ones that have had a major effect on the development of macroeconomic theory.

Barro–Becker altruism implies a utility function for the generation t parent of the form, $U_t + \beta V_{t+1}(W_{t+1})$, where U_t is utility from the consumption of the generation t household, which we take to be of CES form throughout, and V is the *maximum attainable utility* of the next generation. The function V_{t+1} depends on W_{t+1} because it is the utility attained when adult children maximize their utility subject to their initial wealth and market prices.[6] We assume that parents cannot directly affect the choices of their adult children, but they can have a significant effect on their children's initial wealth and therefore on V. The value function is discounted by parents because the adult utility of their children is generated in the future and the parents have a positive rate of time preference. It is also possible that parents care more or less about their adult children's welfare than their own. In this case, the generational discount factor would differ from the pure time discount factor, but the qualitative conclusions would be the same.

We are now ready to formally lay out the optimization problem for the altruistic household. The generation t altruistic household chooses life-cycle consumption and intergenerational transfers to maximize

$$U_t + \beta V_{t+1}(W_{t+1}), \tag{2.13}$$

subject to $W_{t+1} \equiv w_{t+1}H(x_{t+1}, \cdot) + R_t b_{t+1}$ and the generation t lifetime budget constraint, formed by combining (2.10) and (2.11), along with (2.12). The problem can be solved in two steps. First, for *given* values of the transfer variables, the solution for life-cycle consumption follows as before

---

[6] In microeconomics, the maximum attainable utility function is called an *indirect utility function*. In the pure life-cycle version of our model, with no altruism, an indirect utility function is easily obtained. Take the optimal consumption choices of the household (2.5a, b) and substitute them back into the CES utility function. For example, if we do this for the case of $\sigma = 1$, we get the very simple indirect utility function $U_t^* = \beta \ln \beta + (1+\beta) \ln \frac{1}{1+\beta} + (1+\beta) \ln w_t + \beta \ln R_t$. With altruism, things are not nearly so simple. This is because generation t's utility depends on generation $t+1$'s utility, which depends on generation $t+2$'s utility, and so on. As we shall see, in this case V_t cannot be found directly. Instead, it is implicitly defined by a difference equation in the function V_t—what is known as a *Bellman equation*. In this case, V_t is called a *value function* and solving for this function is tricky business. Stokey and Lucas (1989) provide a general discussion of the conditions under which the value function exists, is unique, and is differentiable with respect to initial wealth.

$$c_{1t} = \Psi_{1t}(W_t - n(x_{t+1} + b_{t+1})) \tag{2.14a}$$

$$c_{2t+1} = [\beta R_t]^{\sigma} c_{1t}. \tag{2.14b}$$

The life-cycle consumption choices can then be substituted back into (2.13), making it solely a function of the intergenerational transfer choices.

Second, (2.13) can be maximized with respect to the transfer choices. The first-order conditions for the transfer choices are

$$n(W_t - n(x_{t+1} + b_{t+1}))^{-1/\sigma} \Psi_{1t}^{-/\sigma} = \beta V'_{t+1} w_{t+1} H'_{t+1} \tag{2.15a}$$

$$n(W_t - n(x_{t+1} + b_{t+1}))^{-1/\sigma} \Psi_{1t}^{-1/\sigma} \geq \beta V'_{t+1} R_t \tag{2.15b}$$

The left-hand side of each equation is the marginal cost of making a transfer to children measured in terms of forgone consumption and utility of the parent. The right-hand side is the marginal benefit of the transfer measured in terms of the resulting rise in lifetime wealth and utility of the adult child. The inequality in (2.15b) includes the possibility that a nonnegative financial transfer may not be optimal. If not, (2.12) binds and (2.15b) becomes a strict inequality.

Note that solving this maximization problem gives us the maximum attainable utility, or *value function*, of the current generation,

$$V_t(W_t) = \max\{U_t + \beta V_{t+1}(W_{t+1})\}.$$

This equation implicitly defines the value function and is known as the *Bellman equation*. The Bellman equation allows us to obtain the following result (see Appendix A)

$$V'_{t+1} = (W_{t+1} - n(x_{t+2} + b_{t+2}))^{-1/\sigma} \Psi_{t+1}^{-1/\sigma} = c_{1t+1}^{-1/\sigma}, \tag{2.16}$$

The derivative of the value function is just the marginal utility of consumption. Using (2.16), the first-order conditions given by (2.15a, b) can be presented and discussed intuitively for the two possible cases,

unconstrained transfer equations

$$w_{t+1} H'(x^*_{t+1}, \cdot) = R_t \tag{2.17a}$$

$$c_{1t+1} = [\beta R_t / n]^{\sigma} c_{1t} \tag{2.17b}$$

or

constrained transfer equations

$$b_{t+1} = 0, \tag{2.18a}$$

$$c_{1t+1} = [\beta w_{t+1} H'(x_{t+1}, \cdot)/n]^{\sigma} c_{1t}. \tag{2.18b}$$

If the optimal financial transfers are positive, then human capital investments are unconstrained. This allows the investments to be *productively efficient* in the sense that the return on human investment is equated to the return on physical investment. Parents invest in their children until the rate of return to human capital is driven down to the rate of return on physical capital. At that point, any further intergenerational transfers are in the form of physical or financial assets.

In the efficient case, human capital investment is completely determined by (2.17a), independent of consumption choices and household wealth. In addition, when the generations are linked by financial transfers, one gets the familiar Euler condition, (2.17b), where the growth of consumption over time (actually over generations in this case) is determined by the return to capital—perfectly analogous to the optimal pattern of life-cycle consumption growth in (2.14b).

Desired financial transfers may also be negative, i.e., parents may want to leave debt for their children to repay. In this case, (2.12) binds and there is a strict inequality in (2.15b). Now the human capital investment decision cannot be separated from the household's consumption choices; (2.14a, b), and (2.18b) must be solved simultaneously. Under these circumstances, the *wealth* of the current generation becomes a determinant of human capital investment. Combining (2.15a, b) shows that this situation is *productively inefficient*, because the rate of return on human capital investment exceeds the rate of return on financial assets. However, the current generation cannot "afford" to invest more in their children's education, which is why they want to raise both their own consumption and human capital investment in their children by leaving debt for their children to pay. The legal restrictions forbids this, so they are forced to set $b_{t+1} = 0$. If parents could invest more, by setting $b_{t+1} < 0$, then x_{t+1} would rise and H' would fall until (2.15a) is satisfied. This situation implies that the ratio of consumption of the next generation to the consumption of the current generation would also fall.

2.4.2 Explicit Household-Level Solutions in Some Special Cases*

To go further in uncovering the behavioral implications of adding altruistic transfers, we now solve the model for some special cases. For most of the special cases, we also assume that the economy is in a steady state with zero technical progress, so that $r_t = r$ and $w_t = w$. This assumption serves to simplify the notation considerably.

2.4.2.1 Exogenous Human Capital

To isolate the role of financial transfers, assume that human capital is exogenous and constant, and, for simplicity, set $H = 1$. Under this assumption, a household can only help its descendants by giving them financial transfers. In this case, the *constrained* solution, with $b_{t+1} = 0$ for all t, reverts back to the pure life-cycle solution—with no links between the generations. To solve the *unconstrained* case, with $b_{t+1} > 0$ for all t, we begin by writing out the lifetime budget constraints for the first two generations

$$c_{1t} + \frac{c_{2t+1}}{R} + nb_{t+1} = w + Rb_t \tag{2.19a}$$

$$c_{1t+1} + \frac{c_{2t+2}}{R} + nb_{t+2} = w + Rb_{t+1}. \tag{2.19b}$$

Solving for b_{t+1} in (2.19a), substituting into (2.19b), and rearranging gives

$$c_{1t} + \frac{c_{2t+1}}{R} + \left(\frac{n}{R}\right)\left[c_{1t+1} + \frac{c_{2t+2}}{R}\right] + \left(\frac{n}{R}\right)nb_{t+2} = Rb_t + w + \left(\frac{n}{R}\right)w. \tag{2.20}$$

Notice that we could solve (2.20) for b_{t+2} and substitute the solution into the generation $t+2$ version of (2.19a, b) to get a version of (2.20) for *three* generations of the family.

Proceeding in this way, by successively substituting into the lifetime budget constraints of future generations, produces a budget constraint for the entire "family dynasty,"

$$c_{1t} + \frac{c_{2t+1}}{R} + \left(\frac{n}{R}\right)\left[c_{1t+1} + \frac{c_{2t+2}}{R}\right] + \left(\frac{n}{R}\right)^2\left[c_{1t+2} + \frac{c_{2t+3}}{R}\right] + \cdots = W_\infty, \tag{2.21}$$

where $W_\infty \equiv Rb_t + w + (\frac{n}{R})w + (\frac{n}{R})^2 w + \cdots$. Thus, W_∞ is the wealth of the entire family dynasty, a well-defined value provided that rate of return on assets exceeds the sum of population growth and the growth rate in wages (zero in this case) over time.

The left-hand side of (2.21) can be simplified by using the Euler equation for life-cycle consumption, (2.14b), to get

$$\Psi_1^{-1}c_{1t} + \left(\frac{n}{R}\right)\left[\Psi_1^{-1}c_{1t+1}\right] + \left(\frac{n}{R}\right)^2\left[\Psi_1^{-1}c_{1t+2}\right] + \cdots = W_\infty. \tag{2.22}$$

Next, use (2.17b), the Euler equation that applies to generations, to express consumption for *each* generation in terms of consumption for the *first* generation to get

$$\Psi_1^{-1}c_{1t}\left\{1 + \left(\frac{n}{R}\right)\left[\frac{\beta R}{n}\right]^\sigma + \left(\frac{n}{R}\right)^2\left[\frac{\beta R}{n}\right]^{2\sigma} + \cdots\right\} = W_\infty. \tag{2.23}$$

The geometric sum in the curly brackets is finite provided $\beta^\sigma(\frac{n}{R})^{1-\sigma} < 1$ or $\beta^{\sigma/(1-\sigma)} \leq \frac{R}{n}$. If $R > n$, then this condition holds if $\sigma \leq 1$ and $\beta \leq 1$ Under these conditions, Eq. (2.22) then gives us the solution

$$c_{1t} = \Psi_1 \left(1 - \beta^{\sigma} \left(\frac{n}{R} \right)^{1-\sigma} \right) W_{\infty}, \tag{2.24}$$

which says the consumption of the current generation is a function of its wealth *and* the wealth of all future generations as well. Once the current generation makes its consumption choice, then by using (2.17b), we can find the consumption of *every* member of the family dynasty. Thus, the current generation determines the family consumption path into the indefinite future. In this sense, the current generation behaves "as if" it is "infinitely lived."

The *infinitely lived agent* model is perhaps the dominant model for studying macroeconomics because it allows one to avoid treating each generation as a distinct household. Being able to ignore the generational structure of the economy is a very handy simplification, especially when you have many generations coexisting in the same period. In Problem 10, you will see that the infinitely lived model allows the entire economy's behavior to be determined by a single *representative agent*.

However, the assumptions that must hold for the infinitely lived agent to be valid are strong. In particular, intergenerational transfers must be strictly motivated by Barro–Becker altruism and financial transfers must be nonzero for all generations. Evidence presented in Sect. 2.6 suggests that these assumptions do not generally hold. Still, for some purposes, the convenience of the infinitely lived agent model may be useful without doing obvious harm to the analysis. For example, to study business cycles, each period must represent a year or even a quarter of a year. Thus, you cannot aggregate time as we have in the two-period life-cycle model. If each period corresponds to a year, then the life cycle of an adult must contain 50–60 periods. This, in turn, means that *many* generations will be present in *each* period of the model. It simplifies the analysis greatly if this generational structure can be ignored. In addition, business cycles do not cause resources to be shifted across generations in any obvious systematic fashion. Here, the argument for the infinitely lived agent model is convincing. For other issues, long-run issues that involve significant transfers of resources across generations, use of the infinitely lived agent model can be very misleading.

It is possible to derive an explicit solution for the optimal financial transfers. This solution adds additional insights and gives a sense of the dramatic implications of assuming intergenerational altruism. Using (2.14b), (2.19a), and (2.24), we get

$$nb_{t+1} = W_t - \left(1 - \beta^{\sigma} \left[\frac{n}{R} \right]^{1-\sigma} \right) W_{\infty}. \tag{2.25}$$

Holding W_{∞} constant, an increase in W_t will raise transfers to children one for one. Note if W_{∞} is constant and W_t increases, then the wealth of future generations must have fallen in present value by the amount that W_t rose (so as to maintain W_{∞}). In this thought experiment, the rise in the wealth of the current generation is entirely at the expense of future generations. The current generation acts to exactly offset the exogenous reallocation of the dynasty's wealth by transferring the entire increase in W_t back to future generations. It does this by increasing transfers to its children. Thus, any exogenous reallocation of dynasty wealth is completely undone by endogenous intergenerational transfers in the opposite direction.

Next consider a rise in W_∞, holding W_t constant. In this thought experiment, intergenerational transfers fall. To see the intuition, if W_∞ increases, holding W_t constant, then one or more future generations in the dynasty must have experienced a rise in wealth. The only way that the current generation can share in the rise in dynastic wealth is by reducing transfers to the future generation, allowing its consumption to rise as indicated by (2.24).

Finally, consider a rise in W_t with no change in the wealth of future generations. In this case, W_∞ rises by the same amount as the rise in W_t. The change in transfers is $\beta^\sigma\left(\frac{n}{R}\right)^{1-\sigma}<1$ times the change in W_t. Thus, part of the rise in the wealth of the current generation is consumed and part is transferred to future generations to allow their consumption to rise.

2.4.2.2 Endogenous Human Capital

Adjusting the *unconstrained* solution above to allow for endogenous human capital is straightforward. Begin by reintroducing (2.17a), the efficiency condition that requires equal rates of return on human and physical assets. Let us assume a specific form for the human capital production function, $H_{t+1} = \Theta x_{t+1}^\theta$, where $\Theta > 0, 0<\theta<1$. Now (2.17a) gives the following explicit solution for x_{t+1}

$$x_{t+1} = \left[\frac{\Theta\theta w}{R}\right]^{\frac{1}{1-\theta}}. \tag{2.26}$$

Notice again that, in the unconstrained case, the solution for human capital investment is simple. It involves equating the returns on the two assets and does not require any knowledge about the generational or dynastic wealth that determines consumption. Higher market wages raise the return to human capital investment, so investment must rise until the rate of return is driven back down to the interest rate. A rise in the interest rate causes a shift away from human capital investment, until its rate of return is driven up to the interest rate.

We complete the unconstrained solution by solving for consumption. Take the solution from (2.26) and define the new variable

$$\hat{w} \equiv w\Theta\left[\frac{\Theta\theta w}{R}\right]^{\frac{\theta}{1-\theta}} - n\left[\frac{\Theta\theta w}{R}\right]^{\frac{1}{1-\theta}}, \tag{2.27}$$

which is the productively efficient lifetime wage income of the current generation minus the investment needed to ensure that the next generation also receives the efficient level of lifetime wages. Next, just substitute $\hat{w}$ for w in the expression for W_∞ in (2.24). This substitution replaces the expression for wages due to exogenous human capital with an expression for wages due to endogenous human capital, net of the expenses of generating human capital across generations. After this substitution, the form of the solution for first-period consumption of the current generation is the same as in the exogenous human capital case. Consumption of subsequent generations then follows from the generational Euler conditions given by (2.17b). Optimal financial transfer behavior will again be given by (2.25).

The *constrained* case is more difficult due to the interaction between household wealth and human capital investment. However, if we specialize a bit more, by assuming $\sigma = 1$, then an explicit solution is still possible. To obtain a solution, we use what is known as a *guess-and-verify* method. First, an educated guess about the form of the solution is made and then the solution is verified to satisfy the Bellman equation. It is similar to a situation where you think you know the answer to an algebraic equation and then you substitute the answer back into the equation to make sure the equation is satisfied.

In order to see the full logic, and the recursive structure of the solution, we will relax the steady-state assumption and allow r_t and w_t to vary across generations. Experience with models assuming logarithmic preferences suggests that a good guess for the value function is

$$V_t(W_t) = E + \left[\frac{1+\beta}{1-\beta\theta}\right] \ln W_t + \beta\left(\Phi_t^R + \left[\frac{1+\beta}{1-\beta\theta}\right]\Phi_t^w\right), \tag{2.28}$$

where E is an undetermined constant, $\Phi_t^R \equiv \sum_{i=1}^{\infty} \beta^{i-1} \ln R_{t+i-1}$ and $\Phi_t^w \equiv \sum_{i=1}^{\infty} \beta^{i-1} \ln w_{t+i}$. Notice that (2.28) bears a family resemblance to the simple indirect utility function, associated with the pure life-cycle model without altruism, given in footnote 6. It is the experience in solving similar problems that form the basis for making guesses in more complicated settings.

To verify that this does indeed represent a solution, go through the steps given in Problem 11. In working out the problem, you will find that the optimal solution for human capital investment is

$$x_{t+1} = \frac{\beta\theta W_t}{n}. \tag{2.29}$$

The constrained solution provides a sharp contrast to the unconstrained solution given by (2.26) for two reasons. First, human capital investment in children now depends on wealth. Second, the relevant wealth concept is once again the wealth of the *current* generation of parents and *not* the wealth of the entire family dynasty. Thus, despite the presence of altruistically motivated investments in children, the family is not connected as completely as in the unconstrained case. The wealth of the current household constrains the investment in its children.

2.4.3 Warm Glow

Another approach to modeling intergenerational transfers is to assume that parents get utility, or a "warm glow," directly from *making* the transfers as opposed to getting utility from the *effects* of those transfers on their children's adult welfare. The warm-glow approach assumes that parents get *direct* satisfaction from taking care of their children and satisfying their sense of duty as good parents, or perhaps from the recognition they get from other adults in doing so. It also allows for the possibility that they enjoy giving one kind of transfer more than another. For example, they may prefer investing in their children's education more than giving them a saving bond, even when the effect on the child's wealth is the same in both cases.

An example of warm-glow preferences is given by the following utility function,

$$U_t = \ln c_{1t} + \beta \ln c_{2t+1} + \psi \ln H_{t+1} + \xi \ln b_{t+1}, \tag{2.30}$$

where ψ and ξ are nonnegative preference parameters. The household values the human capital of children and the financial transfers to children, directly and independently.[7]

Under the warm-glow approach, the household maximizes (2.30) subject to the lifetime budget constraint associated with (2.10) and (2.11), and the human capital production function $H_{t+1} = \Theta x_{t+1}^{\theta}$, to generate the following equations for optimal transfers

$$b_{t+1} = \frac{\xi}{1 + \beta + \theta\psi + \xi} \frac{W_t}{n} \tag{2.31a}$$

$$x_{t+1} = \frac{\theta\psi}{1 + \beta + \theta\psi + \xi} \frac{W_t}{n}. \tag{2.31b}$$

Both transfers are simply fractions of household wealth.

Contrasting (2.31a, b) to the transfer behavior when assuming altruism reveals several important differences. Households always make financial transfers—parents never find it optimal to give no financial transfers to their adult children. In addition, financial transfers are no longer affected by the household wealth of future generations in the family, as they were in (2.25). Under the warm-glow assumption, parents will not attempt to compensate for exogenous changes in their children's wealth.

The presence of financial transfers across generations does not imply that human capital investments are productively efficient as in (2.26). Depending on the wealth of the parents, human capital investments can be less than or *greater than* the efficient level. Some empirical researchers have concluded that marginal educational investments in most primary and secondary school students in the US yield rates of return, in terms of future adult earnings, that are far below the rate of return on financial assets. This observation is inconsistent with the altruistic model, but not

[7] Often, when the focus of the analysis is on intergenerational transfers, the life-cycle feature of the model is dropped. Households are modeled as living only a single period of adulthood in which they consume and make transfers to their children. We will see examples of these models in future chapters.

with the warm-glow model. As indicated, parents may value education for reasons beyond its impact on the wages of its adult children. If household wealth and ψ are sufficiently large, then the optimal human capital investment will exceed the productively efficient level, and the rate of return to educational investment will be below the rate of return on physical assets.

Finally, note that (2.29) and (2.31b) are quite similar. This is an important point. From the perspective of modeling human capital investments in children, assuming warm-glow preferences is similar to assuming altruism when the bequest constraint is binding. A binding bequest constraint is relevant because of the absence of intergenerational loan markets. Thus, warm-glow preferences are a convenient way of capturing the absence of intergenerational loans for human capital investment in children.

2.5 Quantitative Theory

Over the last 30 years, there has been an increasing tendency for macroeconomists to *quantify* their theoretical models. Quantifying a model means determining numerical values for the model's parameters, thereby enabling the model to generate numerical predictions that can be compared to real-world data. This healthy tendency to develop theories that can be quantified has greatly improved the understanding of many different phenomena and has created a progressive scientific paradigm within which to conduct macroeconomic research. Indeed, it is one of the main motivations for writing this book.

In this section, we quantify our simple growth model and compare its predictions to important qualitative patterns we commonly see in the data as economies grow. We are effectively repeating a version of the exercise conducted in the famous article by King and Rebelo (1993). They showed that the standard neoclassical model of physical capital accumulation is not consistent with the pattern of growth rates and interest rates experienced by the USA as it developed.

In most cases, it is not possible to use the traditional econometric approach of parameter estimation (due to a desire to limit the number of variables in the analysis, the nonlinear structure of the model, or the lack of appropriate data). Instead, the model is *calibrated*. That is, parameters are set so as to allow the model to *match* certain *targets*—observations or previously estimated behavioral responses.[8] Once calibrated, the model can generate predictions about the values of

[8] There are differences of opinion about what qualifies as an appropriate target. Some believe that calibration should *not* involve previous econometric estimation. According to this view, all parameters within a model should be set to match particular data points or statistical moments of a data set (sample means, variances, and covariances), but *not* to match econometric estimates found in the literature. Others broaden the targets to include previous statistical estimates of the model's parameters and behavioral responses, *even if the model used in the estimation is not the same as the one used in the calibration*. We are comfortable with either approach. The important point from our perspective is that all quantitative models, *however calibrated*, should be tested by comparing their predictions against observations or statistics *not* used in the calibration process.

variables that were *not* used in the calibration. The predicted values can then be compared against data to assess the model's ability to replicate the real world. Failures to replicate important real-world observations then lead to adjustments in the model, or an entirely new model, that provides a better approximation. The model currently providing the best approximation should be favored to conduct *policy analysis*, where the effects of current and proposed government policies are evaluated. Continually pursuing the best quantitative approximation is the best chance we have of improving our understanding of economies and policies.

Let us make these ideas more concrete by calibrating a simple neoclassical model of physical capital accumulation and then testing its predictions about economic growth. The transition Eq. (2.9) provides the basic model. The equation contains seven exogenous parameters: α, β, δ, σ, d, A, and n. To allow for endogenous growth through increasing physical capital intensity, we will have to start the economy in an initial position that is below its steady state. So, an initial value, k_1, will also have to be determined. Finally, the length of each time period in the model must be chosen. In fact, other parameter values will depend on the time-period choice.

To simplify things at first, let us assume $\sigma = 1$. This assumption yields an explicit transition equation solution for k_t, given k_{t-1} and allows us to compute the economy's growth path with a calculator instead of a computer (although a computer still comes in pretty handy even in this case). The transition equation is simplified to

$$k_t = \left[\frac{\beta}{1+\beta}\right]\frac{(1-\alpha)Ak_{t-1}^{\alpha}}{n(1+d)}. \qquad (2.9')$$

Part of the calibration typically involves matching the steady state of the model to certain observations (for example, the interest rate or return to capital). Since all variables in the neoclassical growth model can be related back to k, we will need the steady-state solution of (2.9′),

$$\bar{k} = \left[\frac{\beta A}{1+\beta}\frac{1-\alpha}{n(1+d)}\right]^{\frac{1}{1-\alpha}}. \qquad (2.32)$$

In our two-period life-cycle model, the first period is designated the "work period" and the second period the "retirement period." In this setting, it is often assumed that each period lasts 30 years. In comparison with the real world, a 30-year period makes the working life too short and the retirement period too long.

(Footnote 8 continued)
The fact that these "tests" or comparisons are not as formal and refined as traditional hypothesis testing in statistics does not particularly concern us. At this stage in the profession's understanding of macroeconomics, models that even roughly approximate reality are difficult to find. Hopefully, as our approximations become more refined, we will need to worry about more formal testing procedure.

The more periods we allow in the life cycle, the more realistic the model becomes. For example, we could instead assume that *three* twenty-year periods represent a lifetime, with two working periods (40 years) and one retirement period (20 years). However, as you add periods, the model becomes more complicated for reasons that we highlight in Appendix B to this chapter. There, we also show that the complication of keeping track of different generations is a clear disadvantage of using an explicit overlapping generations approach rather than the infinitely lived agent simplification. However, advances in computing are lessening the disadvantage over time. For now, we stick with a two-period model.

With the time period selected, we can begin setting other parameter values. Our application will examine the model's ability to explain growth in the USA from the end of the Civil War through the end of the twentieth century. In applying the model, a useful way to proceed is to create a relatively simple *baseline* calibration and then do a *sensitivity analysis* by examining how results change as we deviate from the baseline calibration or model specification.

The annual rate of population growth actually fell over this historical period, from 2.3 % in the late nineteenth century to about 1 % by the end of the twentieth century (Barro 1997). For the baseline calibration, we set the annual rate of population growth to one percent throughout the entire period. Since our time periods last 30 years, the value for population growth in the model is the one percentage point annual rate of growth compounded for 30 years. The value of n is then chosen to satisfy the equation $n = (1.01)^{30} = 1.3478$.

The capital share of output and income has shown no systematic trend in US history or across countries at different stages of development today (Gollin 2002). We set α to a commonly estimated value of 1/3. The annual rate of depreciation on physical capital is estimated to be in a range between 5 and 10 % (e.g., Stokey and Rebelo 1995). We set the annual rate of depreciation to 7 %. To translate the annual depreciation rate into the depreciation rate over 30 years, think about how much capital remains each year after depreciation occurs. In any given year, the physical capital stock at year's end is 93 % of its value at the beginning of the year. If you start with one unit of capital today, then after 30 years, there would be $1 - \delta = (1 - 0.07)^{30} = 0.93^{30} = 0.1134$ units of capital. So, $\delta = 0.8866$.

Note that we can write worker productivity or output per worker as

$$\frac{Y_t}{M_t} = \frac{Ak_t^{\alpha} D_t M_t}{M_t} = Ak_t^{\alpha} D_t. \tag{2.33}$$

So we can write the ratio of worker productivity in 1990 to worker productivity in 1870 as

$$\frac{(Y/M)_{1990}}{(Y/M)_{1870}} = \left(\frac{k_{1990}}{k_{1870}}\right)^{\alpha} \frac{D_{1990}}{D_{1870}}. \tag{2.34}$$

For the baseline case, we arbitrarily set d so that exogenous technical progress explains "half" the economy's growth. The annual rate of growth in labor productivity from 1870 to 1990 was about 1.6 % (Rangazas 2002). If the economy grew at 1.6 % per year over 120 years, then labor productivity was 6.7180 times higher in 1990 than in 1870. In terms of a geometric mean, half of this growth is $6.7180^{1/2} = 2.5919$. The annual rate of technical progress needed to generate this much growth is 0.7968 %. This means that $1 + d = (1.007968)^{30} = 1.2688$, or $d = 0.2688$.

Finally, we set β to match the rate of return to capital. We take the rate of return to capital to be the rate of return on the Standard and Poor's 500 over the twentieth century. The annual real rate of return on this portfolio of stocks averaged 7 % over the twentieth century (Kocherlakota 1996). Due the absence of any trend in the annual rate of return over the twentieth century, we assume that the US economy was close to its steady by the end of the twentieth century. Thus, we have $1 + \bar{r} - \delta = 1.07^{30} = 7.6123$. Using (2.2a) and (2.32), we have

$$\frac{\beta}{1+\beta} = \frac{\alpha}{1-\alpha}\frac{n(1+d)}{\bar{r}}. \tag{2.35}$$

Plugging the calibrated values of the other parameters into (2.35) implies $\beta = 0.1287$.

We still have to set the initial value of k_t. The idea is to set k_1 so that half of the economy's growth is explained by capital accumulation (that portion not explained by technical progress). So, choose k_1 to satisfy

$$\left(\frac{k_5}{k_1}\right)^{\alpha} = 2.5919. \tag{2.36}$$

Since both k values in (2.36) are unknown before the simulation is run, we have to experiment with values for k_1 until we find one that satisfies (2.36).

By assuming that the economy is close to its steady state by 1990, we can get a good guess for k_1 by using (2.36) to write $k_1 = \bar{k}/17.41$. To determine the absolute values of $\bar{k}$ and k_1, we need to set a value for A. This parameter is different than the others because it just scales the level of production. There is no particular reason for us to replicate the *level* of production observed in the real world (even the real-world index numbers for GDP are arbitrary). So, we set A to be one. This implies $\bar{k} = 0.00937$ and, as an initial guess, $k_1 = 0.000538$.

We are now ready to do a historical simulation. Plug the guess for k_1 into (2.9′) and let the model generate values for k_t. Change the guess for k_1 until (2.36) is met. Once finding values for k_t that satisfy (2.36), then compute the predicted interest rates and labor productivity growth rates. The annualized values of predicted interest rates (solid line) and growth rates (dashed line) are displayed in Fig. 2.3.

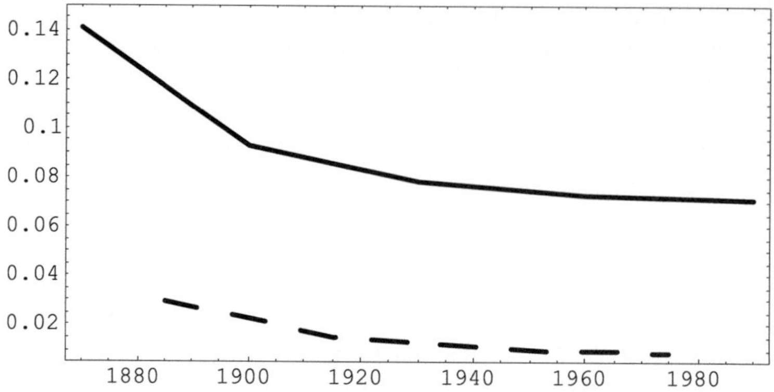

Fig. 2.3 Simulated US interest rates and growth rates: 1870–2000. *Notes* The *solid line* gives the annualized rate of return to capital and the *dashed line* gives the annualized growth rate of labor productivity. The annualized growth rates over 30-year periods were plotted above the midpoint of the intervals between the periods

The model predicts high interest rates (14 %) and growth rates (3 %) for the late nineteenth century and then a decline in both variables over the twentieth century. These predictions miss the mark for a number of reasons.

Returns to capital were probably higher in the late nineteenth century than during the twentieth century. We do not have returns on the Standard and Poor's 500 that go back as far as 1870, but the returns on other assets were 2–6 % points higher in 1870 than in the twentieth century. Wallis (2000, Figure 2), reports that real interest rates on national government debt averaged about 5 % in the first half of the nineteenth century and averaged about 2.5 % during the twentieth century. Barro (1997) reports that real interest rates on commercial paper were 9 % from 1840 to 1880, but averaged about 3 % during the twentieth century. The model predicts initial interest rates out of this range, 7 % points higher than in the twentieth century. Also by 1900, interest rates showed no trend, while the model predicts a downward trend throughout the twentieth century, especially in the first third of the century.

The growth rate predictions are even less accurate. Table 2.1 presents estimates of US labor productivity growth rates for two centuries (Mourmouras and Rangazas 2009). Growth rates showed little trend from 1840 to 2000. In contrast, the model predicts high growth rates in the nineteenth century and then a steady decline.

The fundamental problem with the standard neoclassical growth model is clear. In order to satisfy (2.36), the capital–labor ratio must be set well below its steady-state value in 1870. The relatively low capital–labor ratio produces relatively high returns to capital. The fact that the capital–labor ratio is well below its steady-state value generates high and declining growth rates, as indicated qualitatively by the transition equation diagram in Fig. 2.2.

Table 2.1 Growth rate in output per worker

1820	0.31
1840	1.82
1860	1.32
1880	1.84
1900	1.53
1920	1.40
1940	1.72
1960	2.45
1980	1.58
2000	1.62

Notes The table gives annual growth rates in worker productivity over two centuries of US historical. See Mourmouras and Rangazas (2009) for sources

Sensitivity analysis that allows for minor variations on the theme, such as declining population growth rates or setting $\sigma < 1$, helps a little but not enough to change the basic pattern in Fig. 2.3. These variations help to increase the capital–labor ratio at later stages of development and therefore smooth out growth rates a bit, but we still get a clear declining pattern in growth rates and interest rates (see Problem 13). The fundamental conclusion is that growth due to increased physical capital intensity was not a major cause of growth in the USA over the twentieth century—otherwise, the data would exhibit a clear declining pattern in growth rates and interest rates.

One reaction to this conclusion has been to introduce human capital into growth models. Human capital investments increased dramatically over the twentieth century in the USA and many economists view human capital as an important source of economic growth that is ignored in the standard model. Table 2.2 presents two measures of human capital investment in children: real spending per child in primary and secondary school (x_t) and the fraction of the year spent in school by children ages 0–19 years (e_t). School spending per pupil expanded more than 25-fold since 1870 and time spent in school expanded more than threefold.

The growth implications of increasing human capital investment can be determined by generalizing the human capital production we used in discussing intergenerational transfers. Our previous modeling either treated human capital as an exogenous variable or as an endogenous variable that was a function solely of

Table 2.2 Human capital investments in the USA

Investment	1870	1900	1930	1960	1990
x_{t+1}	1.0	1.8	4.6	9.5	25.2
e_{t+1}	0.09	0.11	0.215	0.29	0.30

Notes School spending is defined as total expenditures per pupil. The first row gives the real spending per pupil for each year divided by the real spending for the 1870 (Rangazas 2002). The time investment data are from Lord and Rangazas (2006)

school spending per pupil. The more general specification given below includes student time as an additional input in the human capital production function. It is defined to include the previous treatments of human capital as special cases. The more general human capital production function is given by

$$H_t = D_t^{1-\theta_1} x_t^{\theta_1} e_t^{\theta_2}, \tag{2.37}$$

where θ_1 and θ_2 are constant parameters that capture the effect of increasing school spending and student time on human capital and wages. We assume the parameters satisfy the restriction $0 \le \theta_1 + \theta_2 \le 1$. Note that the model of exogenous effective labor supply from Sect. 2.3 can be obtained by setting $\theta_1 = \theta_2 = 0$. The simple model of intergenerational transfers from Sect. 2.4 assumed no technical change $(D_t \equiv 1)$ and a full school-time input in every period $(e_t \equiv 1)$.

To carry out a growth simulation, we need to derive the physical capital transition equation with human capital in the model. First, write (2.37) as $H_t = D_t \tilde{x}_t^{\theta_1} e_t^{\theta_2}$, where $\tilde{x}_t \equiv x_t / D_t$. Next, treat H_{t+1} just as D_{t+1} was treated in deriving the transition equation at the end of Sect. 2.3. The adjusted transition equation, with $\sigma = 1$, is

$$k_t = \left[\frac{\beta}{1+\beta}\right] \frac{(1-\alpha)Ak_{t-1}^{\alpha}}{n(1+d)} \left(\frac{\tilde{x}_{t-1}}{\tilde{x}_t}\right)^{\theta_1} \left(\frac{e_{t-1}}{e_t}\right)^{\theta_2}, \tag{2.38}$$

where $k \equiv K/H$.

For this experiment, we will treat school spending and school time as exogenous inputs (government mandated compulsory public schooling).[9] So we will simply take the values from Table 2.1 and plug them into (2.37) and (2.38). In order to proceed, we still need estimates of θ_1 and θ_2. Based on econometric evidence, and consistency with empirical estimates of the rates of return to human capital investments, reasonable settings for these parameters are $\theta_1 = 0.10$ and $\theta_2 = 0.40$ (see a complete discussion in Rangazas 2002).

The experiment is conducted in the same manner as in the model without human capital. The initial value of k is determined by

$$\left(\frac{k_5}{k_1}\right)^{\alpha} \left(\frac{\tilde{x}_5}{\tilde{x}_1}\right)^{\theta_1} \left(\frac{e_5}{e_1}\right)^{\theta_2} = 2.5919 \tag{2.39}$$

.

Notice a few things about (2.39). As was true for Eq. (2.36), this expression accounts for "half" the growth from 1870 to 1990, with the other half accounted for by exogenous technical progress. The fact that (2.39) contains $\tilde{x}$, rather than x,

[9] One can think of the financing of public expenditures as coming from a tax on capital or capital income (similar to the property tax used to finance schooling in the USA). When $\sigma = 1$, a capital tax has no effect on saving and the transition equation.

means that we are giving credit to technical progress for explaining some of the rise in school spending and the resulting effect on economic growth. This is a relatively conservative approach to gauge the *causal* effect of school spending on growth, because it is only school spending increases that exceed technical progress that are given credit for *causing* economic growth. Second, physical capital intensity is now getting help from human capital in explaining half the economy's growth over this period. As a result, k_1 will not have to be as far below k_5 in order to satisfy (2.39) as in our first experiment. This feature should help in eliminating the counterfactual predictions given in Fig. 2.3. Finally, note that while human capital investments rose sharply over the period, both types of investments are subject to diminishing returns because θ_1 and θ_2 are both significantly less than one. Thus, there will be two opposing forces on the economy's growth rates—rising rates of human capital investment versus diminishing returns to those investments.

Figure 2.4 presents the model's historical predictions regarding interest rates and growth rates. Both time series have flattened considerably compared to the series in Fig. 2.3. Growth rates now show no trend over the entire period and interest rates no trend over the twentieth century—making both series more consistent with the data.

The slow growth in human capital inputs caused human capital growth to be slow before 1900. As a result, much of the model economy's growth before 1900 was due to rising physical capital intensity. This is clear from the approximately 2 % age point drop in interest rates from 1870 to 1900—within the range of the decline seen in the historical interest rate data. During the twentieth century, physical capital intensity and interest rates showed no trend—in the model and in the data. The explained growth over this period was due to rising human capital investments. However, growth rates in the model showed no trend during the

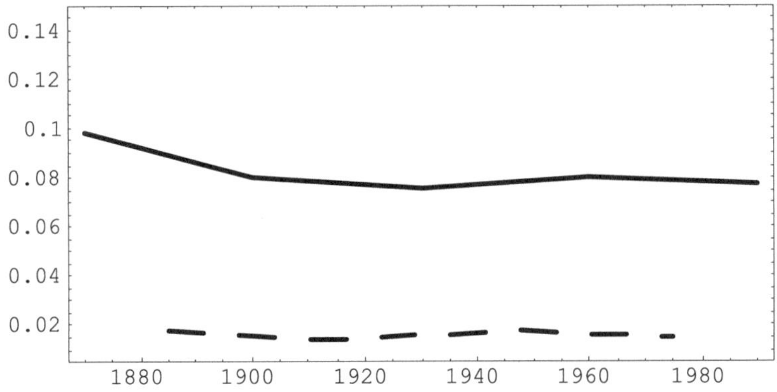

Fig. 2.4 Simulated US interest rates and growth rates: 1870 to 2000—with human capital. *Notes* The *solid line* gives the annualized rate of return to capital, and the *dashed line* gives the annualized growth rate of labor productivity. The annualized growth rates over 30-year periods were plotted above the midpoint of the intervals between the periods

twentieth century, also consistent with the data, because the diminishing returns to human capital investments roughly offset the effect of the rising human capital investments on growth rates.

2.6 Related Literature

The first two-period overlapping generations model with physical capital and production was due to Diamond (1965). It has become one of the two workhorse models of macroeconomics. Unfortunately, most students are not exposed to this model, or any other model built on microeconomic foundations, as undergraduates. If the model does not sound familiar, you may want to read an undergraduate text along side of this book. An excellent intermediate undergraduate textbook treatment of the overlapping generations model is provided by Auerbach and Kotlikoff (1998). Farmer and Schelnast (2013) provide a nice introduction to a graduate treatment of the overlapping generations model, with a special focus on international trade. More advanced and more general treatments of the overlapping generations model can be found in Azariadis (1993) and de la Croix and Michel (2002). These are important books for graduate students who want to concentrate on theoretical work.

The overlapping generation model was extended to include altruistic intergenerational transfers by Barro (1974), Drazen (1978), and Becker (1981, 1988). If the nonnegativity constraint on financial transfers is ignored, altruism provides a justification for infinitely lived agent model, the other workhorse model of macroeconomics. Barro (1997) provides an intermediate undergraduate treatment of macroeconomics using the infinitely lived agent model. A more advanced undergraduate textbook that covers the overlapping generations model, and the extension to include intergenerational transfers is Lord (2001). Graduate treatments of the infinitely lived agent model include Romer (2001) and Acemoglu (2009).

A large empirical literature has developed to test the implications of altruistically motivated transfers. Most econometric tests indicate that either financial transfers are not motivated by altruism alone or altruistic financial transfers are not operative for significant fractions of the population (see, e.g., the papers by Wilhelm (1996) and Altonji et al. (1997). The finding that the intergenerational credit market is imperfect due to binding nonnegativity constraints on financial transfers is consistent with empirical results suggesting that parent's lifetime resources affect the level of investments in their young children (Heckman and Cunha 2007).

There are other reasons, not examined here, for intergenerational transfers. Some transfers are unintended or accidental. Individuals save for their own retirement, but die earlier than expected. The remaining wealth is often left to children. For analysis and applications of models with unintended transfers, start with articles by Davies (1981), Abel (1985), and Hurd (1989). In addition, some transfers may be intentionally made for strategic reasons. In particular, parents might accumulate wealth that is potentially bequeathed to children in order to elicit services from them when they are adults. For more reading on strategic bequests, begin with Bernheim et al. (1985) and Cox (1987).

Calibrated dynamic general equilibrium models were first used in public finance to examine the effects of tax reform (Summers 1981; Auerbach et al. 1983) and in macroeconomics to explain business cycles (Kydland and Prescott 1982). Calibration methods have since been extended to every area of macroeconomics. For a general discussion of the approach, including additional applications, see Kydland and Prescott (1996), followed by a critique from Hansen and Heckman (1996).

The calibration experiment we presented in Sect. 2.5, that uses the model with physical capital to explain economic growth, is based on King and Rebelo (1993). The extension to include human capital is based on Rangazas (2000, 2002). Córdoba and Ripoll (2013) and Manuelli and Seshadri (2014) offer quantitative theories where human capital accumulation is the dominant determinant of an economy's labor productivity. An alternative approach that stresses the connection between TFP and *broad notions* of capital, emphasizing the knowledge embodied in firms rather than individuals, has been developed by Parente and Prescott (2000).

2.7 Exercises

Questions

1. Define the following concepts and give an example of each.
   (a) *technology*
   (b) *capital*
   (c) *physical capital*
   (d) *human capital*
2. Explain the meaning of (2.2a, b). What variables are determined by these two equations?
3. Think of the physical capital stock as fixed, as in the short-run model of the competitive firm from introductory and intermediate microeconomics. Sketch the marginal product of labor as a function of the employment level of an individual firm. Next, add the competitive market wage rate to the diagram. Finally, locate the firm's profit-maximizing employment level. How does the profit-maximizing solution change if there an increase in the firm's capital stock?
4. Explain the differences between *rental rate*, *rate of return on capital*, and *interest rate*.
5. Explain how each of the following affects current consumption, future consumption, and saving: (a) wages, (b) return to capital, and (c) the preference parameter β.
6. Sketch Eq. (2.7) with k on the horizontal axis and r on the vertical axis. Explain what determines the sign of the slope of the sketch. How is the sketch affected by an increase in w? An increase in n? Explain

7. Explain why an increase in this period's capital stock causes an increase in next period's capital stock. Why does the linkage become weaker as the economy accumulates more capital?
8. As the economy moves toward the steady state from below what happens to its growth? What happens to the growth rate if it heads to the steady state from above?
9. Suppose that economy A and economy B have identical structures (production technologies, preferences, and population growth rates), but economy A has a higher capital–labor ratio. Which country is "richer"? Which country grows faster? Your answer explains what is known as *conditional convergence*. Show, by example, that if two countries do *not* have identical structures that *absolute* or *unconditional convergence* is not guaranteed.
10. Explain why a high rate of population growth will make a country poor.
11. How does an increase in exogenous technological change affect capital intensity, interest rates, and labor productivity? In what way is it similar to an increase in population growth and in what way is it different?
12. Give an example of a human capital transfer and a financial transfer. When would a parent's payment of college tuition be equivalent to a financial transfer to the child? Do government guaranteed college loans alleviate the effects of the legal restriction that parents cannot leave debt to their children?
13. If intergenerational transfers are altruistically motivated, explain why human capital investments are productively efficient if financial transfers are positive, but are inefficiently low if financial transfers are zero.
14. Suppose that intergenerational transfers are unconstrained. Intuitively guess what happens to c_{1t} and c_{1t+1} when R_t increases. To make your guess note that (2.17b) has exactly the same form as the expression for the optimal ratio of future to current consumption over the life cycle (see Problem 4 or (14)). Suppose now that households are constrained. Use (2.18b) to guess what happens to c_{1t}, c_{1t+1} and x_{t+1} when w_{t+1} increases.
15. Under special assumptions, Eq. (2.29) gives an explicit solution for constrained human capital investments. Use your answer to question 14 to explain why w_{t+1} does not enter the Eq.
16. Assume that intergenerational transfers are altruistically motivated and that financial transfers are positive. Explain what happens to human capital investments in children and financial transfers if
    (a) W_t increases by one unit and W_∞ is held constant
    (b) W_∞ increases by one unit and W_t is held constant.

Repeat the exercise when (i) financial transfers are zero and then again when (ii) transfers are motivated by warm glow.

17. Explain why (2.29) and (2.31b) are similar despite the fact that they are generated by two different assumptions about intergenerational transfers.
18. Under each of the motives for intergenerational transfers, explain if and when investments in human capital can be greater than the productively efficient level.

19. Explain what it means to calibrate a model. Briefly describe the calibration of the model of physical capital accumulation.
20. Discuss the design and the results of the calibration experiment when the model of physical capital accumulation was used to historically replicate growth in the USA from 1870 to 2000.
21. Discuss the design and the results of the calibration experiment where the model of physical capital accumulation was extended to include human capital.

Problems

1. Show that (2.1) exhibits the neoclassical properties of diminishing marginal productivity and constant returns to scale.
2. Derive Eqs. (2.2a, b) and (2.3a, b). How are they related?
3. What is total income in the model with capital and production? Show that the value of output is equal to the value of income.
4. Derive the optimal life-cycle behavior given by (2.5a, b) and (2.6).
5. Starting from the definition of k^S, derive Eq. (2.7).
6. Starting with the adjusted definition of k^S, derive the transition Eq. (2.9).
7. If $\sigma = 1$, how do we know that the transition equation will be concave in Fig. 2.2? The concavity of the transition function establishes three crucial properties of the steady-state equilibrium: (i) existence (there is a steady state), (ii) uniqueness (there is only one steady state), and (iii) dynamic stability (if you start away from the steady state you will always move toward it). Use the diagram to explain this.
8. Let $\delta = 1$ and $\sigma = \dfrac{2-\alpha}{1-\alpha}$ in (2.9). Derive an explicit transition equation for k_t in terms of k_{t-1}. Sketch the transition equation as accurately as you can.
9. Derive the financial transfer equations under the two motives for intergenerational transfers. In particular, use (2.14b), (2.19a) and (2.24) to derive (2.25). Next, maximize (2.30) subject to the household lifetime budget constraint to get (2.31a).
10. Assuming that (i) intergenerational transfers are altruistically motivated and (ii) the nonnegativity constraint on financial transfers does not bind, derive *aggregate* consumption in period t in terms of the behavior of a "representative agent," whose consumption behavior is a function of the dynasty's wealth. First note that aggregate consumption in period t is $C_t \equiv N_t c_{1t} + N_{t-1} c_{2t} = N_t \left[c_{1t} + \dfrac{c_{2t}}{n} \right]$. Next use (2.14b) and (2.17b) to get $C_t = \kappa N_t c_{1t}$, where $\kappa \equiv 1 + n^{\sigma - 1}$ and c_{1t} are given by (2.24). This shows that aggregate consumption is proportional to the consumption of a single representative agent, the current young adult, of the family dynasty.
11. Take a deep breath and complete the following steps to verify that (2.28) and (2.29) are indeed the solution to the constrained problem with human capital when $\sigma = 1$.

(i) Write (2.28) for generation $t + 1$ instead of generation t.
(ii) Substitute your answer to (i) for $V(W_{t+1})$ in (2.13).
(iii) Use (2.5a, b) to write U_t solely in terms of c_{1t} and then in terms of W_t and x_{t+1} by using the lifetime budget constraint associated with (2.10) and (2.11) (remember that $\sigma = 1$ and $b_{t+1} = 0$)
(iv) Now you have the objective function in (2.13) written solely in terms of the choice variable x_{t+1}. Show the first-order condition for maximizing (2.13) with respect to x_{t+1} yields (2.29).
(v) Finally, substitute (2.29) back into the objective function from (iv) and show that $V(W_t)$ is in fact (2.28). This is done by organizing all the constant terms into a term labeled E and then forming three other expressions that group terms involving W_t, human capital rental rates, and interest rates. Careful, this is probably the most difficult part.

12. Using a calculator or computer, reproduce the historical simulations displayed in Fig. 2.3.
13. Use a computer to generate historical simulations for model of physical capital accumulation when $\sigma = 0.5$. You will need a program that includes a nonlinear equation solver to find a numerical solution for k_t given k_{t-1} in each period.
14. An alternative way of thinking about equilibrium is to focus on the goods market rather than the capital market. In the simple model of physical capital accumulation, with no human capital or technological progress, the goods market clearing condition just says that the supply of goods or output, Y_t, must equal the demand for consumption and investment goods, $C_t + K_{t+1} - (1 - \delta)K_t$, so that

$$C_t + K_{t+1} - (1 - \delta)K_t = Y_t,$$

where, as in Problem 10, you must think of C_t as the total consumption of all generations. We can write this as a transition equation in the capital–labor ratio by dividing by M_t and rearranging a bit to get

$$nk_{t+1} = Ak_t^{\alpha} - (1 - \delta)k_t - \frac{C_t}{M_t}.$$

Show that in the two-period overlapping generation model, this condition is equivalent to the transition Eq. (2.8) that was derived from the capital market equilibrium condition.

Appendix*

A: Derivative of the Value Function

Substituting (2.14a, b) back into U_t gives

$$U_t = \frac{[\Psi_{1t}(W_t - n(x_{t+1} + b_{t+1}))]^{1-1/\sigma}}{1 - 1/\sigma} + \beta \frac{[(\beta R_t)^\sigma \Psi_{1t}(W_t - n(x_{t+1} + b_{t+1}))]^{1-1/\sigma}}{1 - 1/\sigma}$$
$$= \Psi_{1t}^{-1/\sigma} \frac{(W_t - n(x_{t+1} + b_{t+1}))^{1-1/\sigma}}{1 - 1/\sigma}.$$

Next, denote the optimal choices of the intergenerational transfers with an asterisk so that we can write

$$V_t(W_t) = \Psi_{1t}^{-1/\sigma} \frac{(W_t - n(x_{t+1}^* + b_{t+1}^*))^{1-1/\sigma}}{1 - 1/\sigma} + \beta V_{t+1}\left(w_{t+1} H\left(x_{t+1}^*\right) + (1 + r_{t+1}) b_{t+1}^*\right).$$

Note that the optimal intergenerational transfers are in general functions of W_t (in the constrained case, financial transfers are zero and thus do *not* depend on W_t). However, because the derivative of the right-hand side with respect to these choices is zero, then we may ignore these indirect effects of W_t when differentiating V_t with respect to W_t (in the constrained case, the derivative is taken only with respect to human capital investments). Thus, the derivative of the value function with respect to W_t *includes only the direct effect*, working through U_t in the first expression above. This result is a general one and is known as the *envelope theorem*. Equation (2.16) is the envelope theorem applied to $V_{t+1}(W_{t+1})$.

B: Many-Period Models

In models that extend beyond two periods, it is easier to proceed by thinking of the equilibrium or market clearing condition in terms of goods rather than capital. The two ways of thinking about things are actually equivalent, but the exposition is easier if we conduct the discussion in terms of goods (see Problem 14). This is especially true if one wants to contrast the infinitely lived agent approach with the overlapping generations approach. To reduce notation, we will limit the discussion to the simple model of physical capital accumulation with no human capital or technical progress. In addition, the key points can be made for the case with $\sigma = 1$ and $n = 1$.

As shown in Problem 14, using the goods market approach allows the transition equation for the economy to be written as

$$nk_{t+1} = Ak_t^{\alpha} - (1-\delta)k_t - \frac{C_t}{M_t}.$$

In the overlapping generations model with two-period lifetimes, this equation reduces nicely to a first-order difference equation (Problem 14). This is because the right-hand side can be reduced to the consumption behavior of a single generation whose consumption depends only on period t wages and thus only on k_t. The old generation consumes all its income. As a result, their income and their consumption are equal and cancel from the right-hand side of the transition equation.

However, with more periods of life there will be more generations on the right-hand side, whose income is less than their consumption, i.e., who save by purchasing capital. The consumption behavior of these generations will depend on wages earned *before* period t. For example, think of a model with five periods of life—four working periods and one retirement period. The aggregate consumption behavior on the right-hand side sums over five different generations. In general, it is only the generation who is retired that will "cancel out." The saving of other generations will generally not be zero, so all variables that affect their consumption behavior will appear in the transition equation.

Consider the next oldest generation, who is in the last period of its working life. This generation's working life began three periods ago. Their consumption behavior in period t will depend on the wages they earned in each of those periods. Thus, wages as far back at period t-3 will appear in the transition equation. The wages in each period are determined by the capital–labor ratio from that period. This implies that the transition equation will be a *fifth-order* difference equation, including the variables, $k_{t+1}, k_t, k_{t-1}, k_{t-2}, k_{t-3}$. The important point is that the *state variables*, here the capital–labor ratios, characterizing the economy increase as the number of periods of the life-cycle increase. This *curse of dimensionality* raises the computational complexity of the model when the number of periods in the life cycle is large.

In contrast, if one assumes that the generations are linked by intergenerational financial transfers, the transition equation of the economy is a *second-order* difference equation, *no matter how many periods in the life cycle* are included. To see this, first note that as long as financial intergenerational transfers link the generations together, then we can write $C_t = \kappa N_t c_{1t}$ (see Problem 10). As periods in the life cycle are added, only the value of κ changes. For example, $\kappa = 2$, with two periods of life, and $\kappa = 5$, if there are five periods of life.

Next, solve for c_{1t} using the transition equation to get

$$c_{1t} = \frac{M_t}{N_t \kappa}\left[Ak_t^{\alpha} - (1-\delta)k_t - nk_{t+1}\right].$$

Now substitute into (2.17b) to get

$$\left[Ak_{t+1}^{\alpha} - (1-\delta)k_{t+1} - nk_{t+2}\right] = \left[\frac{\beta\left(1 + \alpha Ak_{t+1}^{\alpha-1} - \delta\right)}{n}\right]\left[Ak_{t}^{\alpha} - (1-\delta)k_{t} - nk_{t+1}\right],$$

This is a *second-order* difference equation in k_t that is completely *independent of the number of periods in the life cycle*. Thus, the infinitely lived agent simplification is able to avoid the dreaded curse of dimensionality. A very nifty and useful result.

The lesson is that if you want to do computations, use the infinitely lived agent approach whenever you can get away with it (e.g., business cycle analysis). Unfortunately, the evidence suggests that for the issues we examine in this book, those that directly focus on private intergenerational transfers and government policies that transfer resources across generations, one must stick with the overlapping generations approach.

References

Abel A (1985) Precautionary saving and accidental bequests. Am Econ Rev 75(4):777–791

Acemoglu D (2009) Introduction to modern economic growth. Princeton University Press, Princeton

Altonji J, Hayshi F, Kotlikoff L (1997) Parental altruism and inter vivos transfers: theory and evidence. J Polit Econ 105(6):1121–1166

Auerbach A, Kotlikoff L (1998) Macroeconomics: an integrated approach. MIT Press, Cambridge

Auerbach A, Kotlikoff L, Skinner J (1983) The efficiency gains from dynamic tax reform. International economic review 24(1):81–100

Azariadis C (1993) Intertemporal macroeconomics. Blackwell, Oxford

Barro R (1974) Are government bonds net wealth? J Polit Econ 82(6):1095–1118

Barro R (1997) Macroeconomics. MIT Press, Cambridge

Becker G (1974) A theory of social interactions. J Polit Econ 82(6):1063–1094

Becker G (1981) A treatise on the family. Harvard University Press, Cambridge

Becker G (1988) Family economics and macro behavior. Am Econ Rev 78(1):1–13

Bernheim D, Shleifer A, Summers L (1985) The strategic bequest motive. J Polit Econ 93 (6):1045–1076

Córdoba J, Ripoll M (2013) What explains schooling differences across countries? J Monetary Econ 60(2):184–202

Cox D (1987) Motives for private income transfers. J Polit Econ 95(3):508–546

Davies J (1981) Uncertain lifetime, consumption and dissaving in retirement. J Polit Econ 89 (3):561–577

de la Croix D, Michel P (2002) A theory of economic growth: dynamics and policy in overlapping generations. Cambridge University Press, Cambridge

Diamond P (1965) National debt in a neoclassical growth model. Am Econ Rev 55(5):1126–1150

Drazen A (1978) Government debt, human capital, and bequests in a life-cycle model. J Polit Econ 86(3):505–516

Farmer K, Schelnast M (2013) Growth and international trade: an introduction to the overlapping generations approach. Springer, Berlin

Gollin D (2002) Getting income shares right. J Polit Econ 110(2):458–474

Hansen L, Heckman J (1996) The empirical foundations of calibration. J Econ Perspect 10(1):87–104

Heckman J, Cunha F (2007) The technology of skill formation. Am Econ Rev 97(2):31–47
Hurd M (1989) Mortality risk and bequests. Econometrica 57(4):779–813
King R, Rebelo S (1993) Transitional dynamics and economic growth in the neoclassical growth model. Am Econ Rev 83:908–931
Kocherlakota N (1996) The equity premium: it's still a puzzle. J Econ Lit 34(1):42–71
Kydland F, Prescott E (1982) Time to build and aggregate fluctuations. Econometrica 50(6):1345–1370
Kydland F, Prescott E (1996) The computational experiment: an econometric tool. J Econ Perspect 10(1):69–86
Lord W (2001) Household dynamics, policies, and economic growth. Oxford University Press, New York
Lord W, Rangazas P (2006) Fertility and development: the roles of schooling and family production. J Econ Growth 11(3):229–261
Manuelli R, Seshadri A (2014) Human capital and the wealth of nations. Am Econ Rev 104 (9):2736–2762
Mourmouras A, Rangazas P (2009) Reconciling Kuznets and Habbakuk in a unified growth model. J Econ Growth 14(2):149–181
Parente S, Prescott E (2000) Barriers to riches. MIT Press, Cambridge
Rangazas P (2000) Schooling and economic growth: a King-Rebelo experiment with human capital. J Monetary Econ 46(2):397–416
Rangazas P (2002) The quantity and quality of schooling and U.S. labor productivity growth (1870–2000). Rev Econ Dyn 5(4):932–964
Romer D (2001) Advanced macroeconomics. McGraw-Hill, New York
Stokey N, Lucas R (1989) Recursive methods in economic dynamics. Harvard University Press, Cambridge Mass
Stokey N, Rebelo S (1995) Growth effects of flat-rate taxes. J Polit Econ 103(3):519–550
Summers L (1981) Capital taxation and capital accumulation in a life-cycle growth model. Am Econ Rev 71(4):533–544
Wallis J (2000) American government finance in the long-run: 1790–1990. J Econ Perspect 14 (1):61–82
Wilhelm M (1996) Bequest behavior and the effect of heirs' earnings: testing the altruistic model of bequests. Am Econ Rev 86(4):874–892

Extensions to Neoclassical Growth Theory

3

In this chapter, we extend the basic neoclassical growth model in several ways. In the previous chapter, we learned that human capital is an important source of economic growth. Here, we introduce a simple theory of human capital formation based on parents desire to invest in the "quality" or economic productivity of their children. Parents will also choose the "quantity" of their children, giving us a theory of fertility that makes population growth, another important determinant of economic growth identified in Chap. 2, endogenous. Recall that high population growth makes it difficult to accumulate capital per worker and thus slows the growth in per capita income.

We introduce the government's role in economic growth by including taxation and public capital formation. Modern economic growth is not possible without public infrastructure investments in roads, ports, utilities, and the legal system that protects property rights. We model the government as we do any other economic agent—by specifying its preferences, constraints, and objectives. There is no deep model of the politics that determine how the government is chosen or how their policies are influenced by voters and interest groups. Instead, we take as given the politics of a country that determine the "reduced-form" preference parameters of the government officials. The parameters dictate the government's concern with the welfare of the general population and the welfare of households that make up, or are closely connected to, the government itself.

The new features of the model are combined to study large income differences across rich and poor countries, what is known as *development economics*. At the dawn of the industrial revolution, the differences in per capita income across countries were relatively modest. Per capita income in the richest countries was only 2–4 times greater than per capita income in the poorest countries. Over the course of the last two centuries, per capita income of the rich countries has diverged from that of the poor countries. By the end of the twentieth century, rich countries were 20–40 times richer than poor countries. What could explain such dramatically large gaps in living standards?

As we have seen in Chap. 2, the neoclassical model of physical capital accumulation was unable to explain the relatively modest sevenfold gap in per capita

S. Das et al., *Economic Growth and Development*,
Springer Texts in Business and Economics, DOI 10.1007/978-3-319-14265-4_3

income in US history between 1870 and 1990. It is clear that significant extensions to the neoclassical model are needed to explain the huge long-run income gaps that have evolved across countries in the past two centuries. In this chapter, we explore how far the human capital, fertility, and government policy extensions will take us.

We begin by modeling a representative rich and poor country. One of the reasons that the poor country has low income stems from a *poverty trap* that keeps schooling low and fertility high. The second reason for low income directly relates to its fiscal policy. Many poor countries have relatively high tax rates, relatively high shares of government consumption, and relatively little investment in public infrastructure. We calibrate the preferences of the government based on the fiscal policy outcomes that we observe across rich and poor countries. Our calibration exercises reveal that these extensions go a long way toward explaining large income gaps.

The large income gaps that appeared in the second half of the twentieth century motivated the rich countries of the world to provide various types of aid to poor countries with the hope of accelerating their growth, thereby allowing a convergence of living standards. One of the issues in providing aid is how the policies of the recipient country's government might respond. This is one of the reasons that we extend the model to make fiscal policy endogenous. It allows us to examine the factors that might cause the poor country's government to favor or oppose pro-growth policy reforms. In cases where the government clearly opposes a particular reform, we can also ask what the "aid cost" would be to convince the government to accept the reform.

3.1 A Theory of Income Differences

This section focuses on the sources of poverty. We create a model where a country is poor for two fundamental reasons. First, there is a poverty trap that keeps human capital low and fertility high. Second, the government of the poor country sets relatively high tax rates that are primarily used to finance government consumption rather than infrastructure investment.

3.1.1 Households

Households now live for three periods. The three periods correspond to one period of childhood and two periods of adulthood. This is simply the two-period life-cycle model with childhood now explicitly recognized as a third period. In addition to providing a theory of saving, we now introduce endogenous fertility and schooling decisions.

Households value their consumption over the two periods of adulthood (c_{1t}, c_{2t+1}) and the adult earnings $(w_{t+1}D_{t+1}h_{t+1})$ of all their children (n_{t+1}), similar to the "warm glow" preference for intergenerational transfers from Chap. 2. Earnings are the product of the after-tax market rental rate for skills (w_{t+1}), the productivity index (D_{t+1}), and embodied skills, or human capital (h_{t+1}), of the worker. Formally, preferences are as follows:

$$U_t = \ln c_{1t} + \beta \ln c_{2t+1} + \psi \ln \left(n_{t+1} w_{t+1} D_{t+1} h_{t+1}\right)$$

where $0<\beta<1$ and $\psi > 0$ are preference parameters.[1] Adult human capital of the child is given by $h_{t+1} = e_t^{\theta}$, where e_t is the time the child spends in school and $0<\theta<1$ is a parameter that gauges the effect of schooling on human capital accumulation. For simplicity, we ignore purchased goods and services inputs used in schooling (e.g., tuition) and focus only on student time. Problems 5–7 introduce goods inputs and explore their implications.

Adults inelastically supply one unit of labor when young and zero units when old. Children have an endowment of $T<1$ units of time that they can use to attend school (e_t) or work ($T - e_t$). Children have less than one unit of time to spend productively because early in childhood they are too young to either attend school or to work, and in the middle years, they do not have the mental or physical endurance to learn or work as long as an adult.

While children may work as they become older, providing income to the family, they are also expensive to care for and feed. To raise, each child requires a loss of adult consumption equal to a fixed fraction η of the adult's first-period wages.

We think of the children as being too young to work over the early part of their lives or that a minimum amount of schooling is needed for the child to be productive. Under either interpretation, each child invests at least $\bar{e}$ units of time in learning during the first portion of their childhood. This gives older children $\gamma\bar{h}_t = \gamma\bar{e}^{\theta}$ units of human capital that can be used in production during the later years of childhood, where $0<\gamma<1$ reflects the fact that children lack physical strength or experience in applying knowledge to production compared to an adult. Thus, per hour of work, a person is more productive in adulthood than in childhood because of greater strength and experience ($1 > \gamma$) and additional schooling ($e_t \geq \bar{e}$).

The household maximizes utility subject to the lifetime budget constraint,

$$c_{1t} + \frac{c_{2t+1}}{R_t} + n_{t+1}\eta w_t D_t h_t = w_t D_t h_t + n_{t+1} w_t D_t \bar{h}(T - e_t).$$

The new terms introduced by the extensions are the forgone wages associated with raising children ($n_{t+1}\eta w_t D_t h_t$) and the family income generated by child labor ($n_{t+1} w_t D_t \bar{h}(T - e_t)$). The net cost of raising children is the difference in these two expressions.

[1] Galor and Moav (2002) generalize this specification by allowing for a separate utility weight on the quantity and quality of children. They then go on to develop an evolutionary theory in which households raise the weight they placed on the quality of their children over the course of economic development. Using this more flexible specification would increase the ability of our model to fit the stylized growth facts.

In addition to the standard necessary conditions for optimal life-cycle consumption from Chap. 2, the choices of n_{t+1} and e_t yield the following first-order conditions

$$\frac{\psi\theta}{e_t} \leq \lambda_t n_{t+1} w_t D_t \gamma \bar{h}$$
$$\frac{\psi}{n_{t+1}} = \lambda_t\left[\eta w_t D_t h_t - (T - e_t) w_t D_t \gamma \bar{h}\right],$$

where λ_t is the Lagrange multiplier.

The first equation says the marginal utility of additional child quality, measured by the child's adult human capital, must be equated to the marginal value of consumption lost from allowing children of working age to attend school. The strict inequality holds when the marginal cost of educating children beyond the schooling received in their early years, $\bar{e}$, exceeds the marginal benefit. In this case, parents are content to set $e_t = \bar{e}$, i.e., to have their children begin work as soon as they are able.

The second equation says the marginal utility of additional children must be equated to the marginal value of lost consumption associated with raising a child. Consumption is lost from having an additional child because we assume the cost of children exceeds the earnings that older children bring to the household (otherwise parents would always choose the, biologically determined, maximum number of children).

The first-order conditions are solved for the household's demand functions. The demand functions for children, schooling, and assets used to finance retirement consumption are as follows:

$$n_{t+1} = \frac{w_t D_t h_t}{\eta w_t D_t h_t - w_t D_t (T - e_t)\gamma \bar{h}} = \frac{\psi}{(1 + \beta + \psi)\left(\eta - \gamma(T - e_t)(\bar{e}/e_{t-1})^{\theta}\right)} \tag{3.1a}$$

$$e_t = \max\left[\frac{\theta}{(1-\theta)} \frac{\eta w_t D_t h_t - w_t D_t T \gamma \bar{h}}{w_t D_t \gamma \bar{h}}, \bar{e}\right] = \max\left[\frac{\theta\left(\eta(e_{t-1}/\bar{e})^{\theta} - \gamma T\right)}{\gamma(1-\theta)}, \bar{e}\right] \tag{3.1b}$$

$$s_t = \left[\frac{\beta}{1 + \beta + \psi}\right] w_t D_t h_t. \tag{3.1c}$$

From (3.1a), we see that fertility is positively related to adult income (numerator) and negatively related to the net cost of children (denominator). Equation (3.1b) says schooling is positively related to the minimum net cost of children (the net cost when children work as soon as they can found in the numerator) and negatively related to the forgone earnings associated with schooling (denominator). Schooling is high when children are expensive to raise and forgone earnings are low. However, if children are sufficiently cheap and forgone earnings are high, then fertility is high and parents want only the minimum schooling for each child. Equation (3.1c) gives a saving function similar to that derived in Chap. 2.

Note that for fertility to fall, there must be a rise in schooling. An increase in schooling raises the wages of parents relative to their children, which raises the net cost of children and lowers fertility. From (3.1a, b), we see that the schooling–fertility dynamic is independent of the after-tax rental rates on physical and human capital. A higher rental rate paid to human capital raises the earnings of both parents and children but does not affect *relative* earnings or the net cost of children. Thus, the evolution of schooling and fertility is unaffected by the determinants of human capital rental rates such as fiscal policy, technological change, and physical capital accumulation.

The fact that greater schooling of older children raises the net cost of children and lowers fertility is the reason for the "quantity–quality" trade-off made famous by the Nobel Prize winning economist, Gary Becker (Becker (1960, 1981) and Becker and Lewis (1973)). Less well known is that Becker acknowledged that the interaction between schooling and fertility could be *positive*. "The net cost of children is reduced if they contribute to family income by performing household chores, working in family business, or working in the market place. Then an increase in earning potential of children would increase the demand for children (Becker 1981, p. 96)." Increased schooling of young children, a rise in $\bar{e}$, who do not yet have the capacity to work, clearly increases their earning potential when they are older and able to generate income for the family. This lowers the net cost of children and increases fertility.

It is also important to notice that cross-sectional variation in ψ causes fertility to vary across households with no change in schooling per child. In Problem 9 and in Chap. 5, we find that the same result holds for variation in non-labor income across households. Higher non-labor income leads to greater fertility with no change in schooling per child. This is consistent with empirical findings using cross-sectional data sets that children raised in smaller families receive no more schooling (e.g., Banerjee and Duflo 2011, p. 108). These findings do not reject the quantity–quality tradeoff generated by a causal link from the schooling of older children to fertility. This inverse relationship is clearly present in the time series evidence for historical and currently developing countries (e.g., Lord and Rangazas 2006).

For schooling to begin to rise, the initial generation of parents must have human capital that is sufficiently higher than the human capital of their working-age children. If this condition holds, schooling will rise each period. As schooling rises, the effect of a given increment in schooling has a diminishing effect on human capital formation and wages. The transition equation given by (3.1b) thus will eventually exhibit the standard properties of neoclassical growth as human capital accumulates.

Figure 3.1 sketches the schooling transition equation. The vertical intercept of the graph is at $\bar{e}$ rather than at the origin as with the physical capital transition

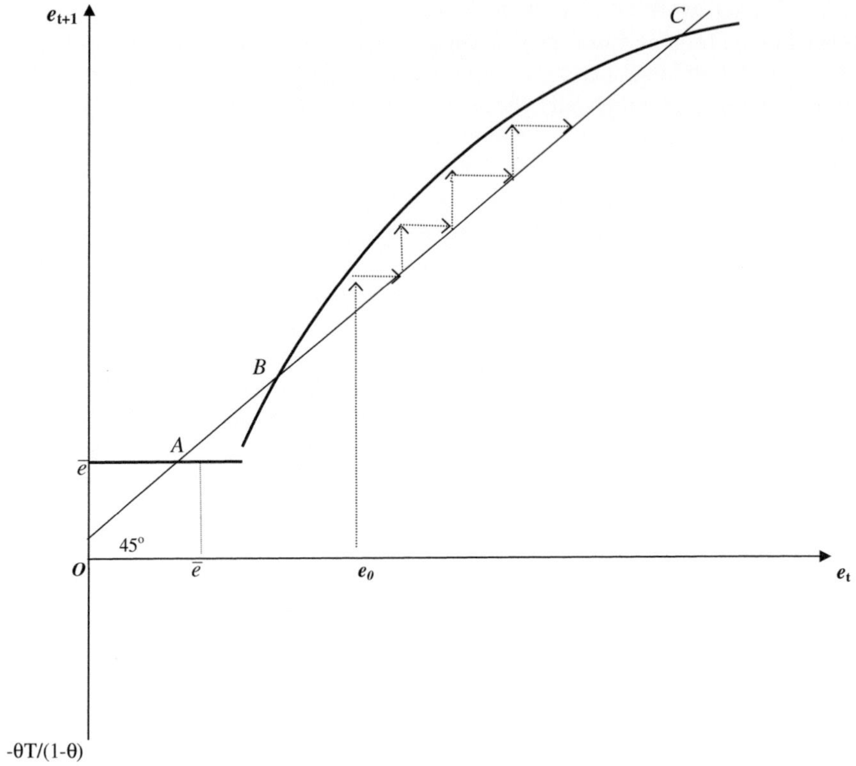

Fig. 3.1 Schooling dynamics

equation from Chap. 2. The position of the vertical intercept implies that the graph intersects the 45° line three times, at points *A, B,* and *C*. The nonconvexity in the transition equation is created by the existence of $\bar{e}$, the minimum level of schooling for young children, drawn here to be less than the schooling level at point *B*. For schooling to increase over time, the schooling level for parents must be to the right of *B* or, more generally, greater than the maximum of the schooling levels associated with point *B* and $\bar{e}$.

Starting to the right of *B* will cause schooling to rise, but in relatively small increments initially. As schooling rises, the increments in schooling across generations become larger, until the economy nears the stable steady state at *C* when the increments once again become smaller and converge to zero. So, *provided that schooling is sufficiently high initially*, the model predicts relatively small increments in schooling at first, an acceleration of schooling in the middle of the transition, and then, a slowdown as the steady state is approached. However, there is no guarantee that the economy has the proper initial conditions to generate growth in human capital. If the economy's initial human capital investments are less than those associated with point B, it will be stuck in a *poverty trap* where schooling remains at $\bar{e}$ indefinitely.

A couple of additional points are worth noting about the poverty trap. First, the rate of return to schooling may be quite high at $\bar{e}$. Parents nevertheless decide that they cannot afford to forgo the family income that would be lost if older children worked less and spent more time in school. If the rate of return to schooling exceeds the market interest rate, then this situation is inefficient because in principle the family could borrow to cover the forgone earnings and then collect more than enough from the enhanced adult earnings of their children to pay back the loan with interest. However, as discussed in Sect. 2.4.1 of Chap. 2 his requires that well-functioning *intergenerational* loan markets exist, where parents assume a debt on behalf of their dependent children, and the lender is able to collect the loan repayment from those same children when there are adults. There are so many difficult incentive and legal issues associated with this type of transaction that intergenerational loan markets do not even exist in developed, let alone developing, countries. Thus, when the rates of returns to schooling are high, some type of policy action that raises schooling is justified in order to improve productive efficiency.

Second, similar poverty traps may exist for physical capital. If there is a significant fixed cost associated with establishing a firm, then borrowing in credit markets becomes important for physical capital accumulation as well. It is generally believed that borrowing to finance physical capital is an easier financial transaction than for human capital, because it does not require an intergenerational loan market and because physical capital may be confiscated if the loan is not repaid. However, at early stages of development, these types of loans may also be quite costly. As a separate matter, the economic environment may be such that physical capital simply cannot compete with land as a productive asset. In Chap. 4, we examine a model where the state of technology must be sufficiently high before production based on physical capital is profitable (even when credit market for physical capital loans exist). In this setting, countries with governments and interest groups that block technological advancement can get stuck in poverty traps where all production takes place using labor and land.

3.1.2 Firms

Production takes place within standard neoclassical firms that combine physical capital and human capital to produce output from a Cobb–Douglas technology

$$Y_t = AK_t^{\alpha}(D_tH_t)^{1-\alpha}. \tag{3.2}$$

The productivity index, D, is now a function of disembodied technology, E, and government capital per adult worker, G, and is given by

$$D_t = E_t^{1-\mu}G_t^{\mu}, \tag{3.3}$$

where $0<\mu<1$ is a constant parameter. This specification captures the idea that public infrastructure raises the productivity of the private sector. We assume that E progresses at the exogenous rate q.

As in Chap. 2, firms operate in perfectly competitive factor and output markets. This implies the profit-maximizing factor mix must satisfy

$$r_t = (1-\tau_t)\alpha A g_t^{\mu(1-\alpha)} k_t^{\alpha-1} \tag{3.4a}$$

$$w_t D_t = (1-\tau_t)(1-\alpha) A E_t g_t^{\mu(1-\alpha)} k_t^{\alpha}, \tag{3.4b}$$

where τ is the income tax rate (net of transfers back to the private sector), and the de-trended, for exogenous technical progress, values of public and private physical capital are defined as $g \equiv G/E$ and $k \equiv K/EH$.

3.1.3 Capital Market Equilibrium

The firm's demands for private physical and human capital are implicitly given by the profit-maximizing conditions in (3.4a, b). The supplies of private physical and human capital from the households are made available for firms to rent in the factor markets and are given by,

$$K_{t+1} = s_t N_t \tag{3.5a}$$

$$H_t = h_t N_t + \gamma \bar{h}_t (T - e_t) N_{t+1} \equiv N_t \hat{h}_t, \tag{3.5b}$$

where the family's total human capital supply, in adult-equivalent units, is defined as $\hat{h}_t \equiv h_t + \gamma \bar{h}_t (T - e_t) n_{t+1}$. Substituting (3.1c), (3.4b), and (3.5b) into (3.5a), gives the equilibrium difference equation for physical capital intensity,

$$k_{t+1} = \left[\frac{\beta}{1+\beta+\psi}\right] \frac{(1-\tau_t)(1-\alpha) A g_t^{\mu(1-\alpha)} k_t^{\alpha} h_t}{(1+q) n_{t+1} \hat{h}_{t+1}}, \tag{3.6}$$

a transition equation that bears a close resemblance to the ones derived in Chap. 2. However, there are four important differences. First, the wages for workers, that provide the basis for household saving, are now affected by the endogenous evolution of public, as well as private, capital. Second, the growth rate of the economy's effective labor supply is now affected by the endogenous accumulation of human capital. Third, income taxation lowers the after-tax wage and lowers saving and private capital accumulation. Finally, the population growth rate is now endogenous because it is determined by the household's fertility choice.

3.1.4 Government

We now introduce a "reduced-form" approach to the formation of fiscal policy. We model the government as we do any other economic agent—by specifying its preferences, constraints, and objectives. There is no deep model of the politics that determine how the government is chosen and how their policies are influenced by voters and interest groups. Instead, we take as given the politics of a country that determine the "reduced-form" preference parameters of the government. The parameters dictate the government's concern about the welfare of the general population of private households and the welfare of households that make up, or are closely connected to, the government itself. The deeper political determinants of these reduced-form parameters are assumed to be given throughout the analysis. Thus, we examine how policies are formed with a given political structure.

We take this approach for several reasons. First, we do not believe that there is a unique mapping from political institutions to the government's preferences over economic policies. Pro-growth policies may be carried out and implemented within a highly democratic political process or by a completely authoritative dictator (think of the dictators that pushed development during the Asian Tiger "Growth Miracles"). Different political institutions can give rise to similar reduced-form preferences of the policy maker. Second, attempting to model the politics of a country is complex and requires that compromises be made in the economic modeling. Jointly modeling political and economic equilibria are particularly difficult in the economic environments that we focus on in this book—the transitional growth of overlapping generation economies.

We assume that the government officials who determine fiscal policy are some fraction, ς, of the population of private households, N_t. Government officials value their own consumption (c_t^g) as well as the welfare of the representative citizen according to a single period utility function, $\ln c_t^g + \phi U_t$, where ϕ is a positive preference parameter that gauges the relative weight the government places on the welfare of private households, U_t. We assume that the current government also cares about the government as an ongoing institution (i.e., they care about the future operations of the government and the welfare of future government officials) and the welfare of the country's future citizens. The preferences of the government are given by [2]

$$\sum_{t=0}^{\infty} \beta^t \left(\ln c_t^g + \phi U_t \right). \tag{3.7}$$

These complicated preferences make explicit that the government's concerns extend indefinitely into the future. This is because there is no natural time horizon

[2] For notational simplicity only, we assume the government's time discount factor is the same as that used by private households. One could allow the discount factor to differ from private households to study how the government's time preference affects policy.

for government planning. Maximizing an objective function such as (7) is somewhat difficult but it turns out that the solutions for the optimal fiscal policy are surprisingly simple.

The government budget constraint is

$$c_t^g \varsigma N_t = \tau_t Y_t - G_{t+1} N_{t+1}. \tag{3.8}$$

The left-hand side gives the government's consumption expenditures. The right-hand side is the difference between government tax revenue, net of transfers, and government expenditures on public capital.[3] Public capital evolves according to the difference equation

$$G_{t+1} = I_t^g + (1 - \delta^g) G_t \tag{3.9}$$

where I_t^g is government investment and δ^g is the rate of depreciation of government capital. We simplify (3.9) by assuming that public capital fully depreciates over what we assume to be 20-year-long periods of the model. So, next period's public capital stock is determined solely by this period's public investment.

To find the optimal fiscal policy, the government chooses sequences of tax rates, government consumption, and government capital to maximize the discounted utility of government officials and private households, given by (3.7), subject to a series of budget constraints and capital accumulation equations given above.[4] In addition, the government takes into account how their policy choices affect all private sector decisions. This only includes private capital accumulation, (3.6), since schooling and fertility, (3.1a, 3.1b), are independent of fiscal policy. Finally, to obtain analytical solutions, we assume $\delta = \delta^g = 1$, so that over our twenty-year periods, both types of capital stocks fully depreciate. The solution to the government's problem is (see the Appendix for a sketch of the derivation)

$$\tau_t = \tau = \frac{(1 - \alpha\beta)(1 + \beta\mu\phi(1 - \alpha)\Gamma)}{1 + (1 - \alpha\beta)\phi\Gamma}, \tag{3.10a}$$

$$g_{t+1} = \frac{\beta\mu(1 - \alpha)}{(1 + q)n_{t+1}} k_t^\alpha g_t^{\mu(1-\alpha)} \hat{h}_t, \tag{3.10b}$$

$$k_{t+1} = \frac{\beta(1 - \tau)(1 - \alpha)}{(1 + \beta + \psi)(1 + q)n_{t+1}} \frac{k_t^\alpha g_t^{\mu(1-\alpha)} h_t}{\hat{h}_{t+1}}, \tag{3.10c}$$

where $\Gamma \equiv 1 + \beta + 1 + (\psi/\beta) + (\beta\alpha(1 + \beta) + \beta(\alpha - 1) + \psi\alpha)/(1 - \alpha\beta)$.

---

[3] We do not study optimal government debt or monetary policy in this setting. These polices are obviously important extensions left for future work.

[4] We assume that the government can commit to its policy choices in advance. For a discussion of commitment issues in regard to the setting of fiscal policy see Lundquist and Sargent (2004, Chap. 22).

Equation (3.10a) tells us the tax rate is constant over time. One can show that the constant tax rate τ is decreasing in ϕ, more concern for private households implies a lower tax rate. Equation (3.10b) gives a transition equation for the public capital stock that is analogous to that for the private capital stock. Here, the government's saving rate out of national income is a constant, $\beta\mu(1-\alpha)$. Combined with (3.10a), this tells us that a more selfish government, with a lower ϕ, will collect more in taxes but invest *a smaller fraction of tax revenue* in public capital—so as to maintain the *same* investment rate out of national income. Equation (3.10c) simply repeats the transition equation for private capital accumulation.

3.1.5 Steady-State Equilibria

It is important to note that the model is recursive, which means that model can be solved in steps rather than all at once. The path for private sector schooling can be determined first using (3.1b). Knowing the schooling path allows one to find a path for fertility using (3.1a). Finally, given the schooling–fertility dynamics, one can then determine the dynamics of government and private capital intensity using the difference equation system given by (3.10b, c).

A country with sufficiently high initial schooling will experience growth and converge to a steady state as determined by (3.1a–c) and (3.10a–c). However, if $e_{t-1} = \bar{e}$, it may be the case that $\frac{\theta(\eta-\gamma T)}{\gamma(1-\theta)} < \bar{e}$. If this is true, then $e_t = \bar{e}$, and the economy is in a poverty trap where neither schooling nor fertility changes over time. For an economy with this initial condition, the only possible dynamics stems from the government and private physical capital accumulation in (10). Thus, different initial conditions may cause economies with identical structures to come to rest at very different steady-state equilibria. One steady state has higher values of h, g, and k, and lower levels of n, than the other.

It is also possible that economies differ in terms of the weight, ϕ, that their governments place on private household welfare in setting fiscal policy. Economies with higher ϕ will have lower tax rates, higher private capital–labor ratios, and higher levels of public capital. Higher ϕ causes higher worker productivity, even if the steady values of e and n are the same.

In summary, worker productivity may differ either because of a poverty trap or because of policy differences. The next question is whether these sources of income differences are quantitatively important.

3.2 Cross-Country Income Differences

To investigate whether the model is able to explain large income difference across countries, we compare the following two steady-state equilibria, where e, n, g, and k are constant but different across countries. Our poor and rich steady states are characterized as follows:

Poor country steady state	(i) a binding poverty trap, $e_t = \bar{e}$ with high fertility, $n = 3.5$
	(ii) a selfish government, $\phi^{\text{poor}} < \phi^{\text{rich}}$ with $\tau = 0.35$
Rich country steady state	(i) $e = T$ (full-time schooling) with low fertility $n = 1$
	(ii) a low-tax government, $\phi^{\text{poor}} < \phi^{\text{rich}}$ with $\tau = 0.15$

To quantify the model's predictions about income differences across these two equilibria, we calibrate the parameters to the rich country steady state. The physical capital income share, α, is set to the standard value of 1/3. The output elasticity for public capital, μ, is set to 0.30. This value is somewhat less than the values estimated by Aschauer (1989) and Clarida (1993). However, the values of α and μ place the product $\mu(1 - \alpha)$ at 0.2, an intermediate value of the estimates surveyed by Glomm and Ravikumar (1997). Based on Lord and Rangazas (2006), we set $\gamma = 0.28$ and $T = 0.50$. This implies potential earnings of a child that are about 14 % of an adult's earnings. The annualized after-tax return to capital is set to 4 %, the after-tax real rate of return to capital in the USA at the end of the twentieth century [Poterba (1997), Table 3.1]. The annualized rate of growth of exogenous technological change, q, is set to 1.0 %. This is intended to reflect a worldwide, transferable, component of exogenous technological change.

The remaining parameters are set to match certain targets. We set ϕ^{rich} to match $\tau = 0.15$, about the ratio of government purchases to GDP in the USA. In the rich equilibrium steady state, we targeted $n = 1$ (one child per household or 2 children per couple), $e = 0.5$ (children spend all their available time in school, similar to the current value in the USA), and a value of k consistent with an annualized after-tax return of 4 %.

In the poor country equilibrium, we targeted $n = 3.5$, which implies 7 children per couple. Despite the fertility decline in Africa since the 1980s, many of its poorest countries have total fertility rates of 7 children per female (Bongaarts 2002). In addition, the parameter settings must to be consistent with an optimal schooling level below $\bar{e}$. The minimal schooling level for young children is set to 0.08. This value implies that children in the rich country spend 6.25 times as much time in school over their childhoods than do children from poor countries. So if poor children spend 2 years in school, then rich children spend 12.5 years in school

Table 3.1 Calibrated parameter values

Parameter		Target
γ	0.2800	Relative child's earning
T	0.5000	Relative child's earnings
η	0.1646	Steady-state fertility (poor)
θ	0.4049	Steady-state schooling (rich)
α	0.3333	Standard value for capital share
μ	0.3000	Intermediate empirical estimate
ψ	0.2956	Steady-state fertility (rich)
β	0.4999	Steady-state return to capital (rich)

Table 3.2 Government size—selected low-income countries (1985)

Country	G/Y	$y^{US}/y^{country}$
Angola	0.36	11
Burkina Faso	0.29	33
Central African Republic	0.44	17
Comoros	0.49	10
Ethiopia	0.28	40
Gambia	0.37	17
Mozambique	0.31	33
Uganda	0.28	33
Average	0.32	24

Source Alan Heston, Robert Summers, and Bettina Aten, Penn World Table Version 6.1, Center for International Comparisons at the University of Pennsylvania, October 2002

(assuming school years of equal length). Finally, we set ϕ^{poor} in the poor country so that $\tau = 0.35$. Table 3.1 summarizes the parameter settings.

Table 3.2 gives examples of poor countries (1/10 of USA worker productivity, denoted by y^{US}, or less) with levels of τ = G/Y that are at least double those of the USA.[5] The comparison is for 1985, a year that generates close to the largest income gaps between the USA and most African countries during the twentieth century. Starting in the 1990s, Africa began growing faster. Most of the countries in Table 3.2 have grown between 4 and 9 % per year since the mid-1990s (World Bank 2008, Table 3.1). The exceptions are the Central African Republic and Comoros, whose growth rates remain low and thus have seen their income gaps expand.

Table 3.3 presents the steady-state worker productivity ratio, across rich and poor countries, generated by the model. The features included in the model cause the rich country to be over 28 times richer than the poor country.[6] The table provides a decomposition of the worker productivity ratio based on the following expression for worker productivity,

[5] There is also the issue of differences in the tax base across rich and poor countries. Poor countries have much larger informal sectors that go untaxed. This causes poor countries to collect a small fraction of output in taxes with the same tax rate. An informal sector is needed to capture this and other important features of poor economies. We discuss this extension in the conclusion.

[6] The large effects on worker productivities are accentuated in a three-period model. With only three periods, the population of households that are saving compared to the future work force is unrealistically small. In addition, the high fertility rate, without a high rate of mortality, will imply a large increase in the size of the future workforce. Both these features cause the capital accumulation financed by the current period's saving to be more thinly spread over the next generation of workers than in a model with many periods of work (and saving) and with the high death rates that mediate population growth in poor countries.

Table 3.3 Steady-state worker productivity differential

Rich to poor ratios	Model prediction
k^{α}	3.68
$g^{\mu(1-\alpha)}$	2.09
$\hat{h}/[1+n(T-s)]$	3.68
y	28.25

$$y_t = \frac{k_t^{\alpha} A E_t g_t^{\mu(1-\alpha)} \hat{h}_t}{1+n_{t+1}(T-e_t)}. \tag{3.11}$$

The numerator gives the various sources of production. The denominator gives the supply of labor per household, the adult worker and the child workers that are beyond school age.

The poverty trap causes the term $\hat{h}_t/(1+n_{t+1}(T-e_t))$, average human capital per worker, to be 3.7 times higher in the rich country for two reasons. First, since $e_t = 0.5$ in the rich equilibrium and $e_t = \bar{e} = 0.08$ in the poor equilibrium, adult human capital differs across countries. This causes output per worker in the rich country relative to that in the poor country to be 2.10, a value similar to that estimated by Hall and Jones (1999) using a much different approach. Second, the high fertilityin the poor country implies that their workforce contains a sizeable fraction of young workers, who are less productive than adult workers due to less strength and experience (captured by $\gamma = 0.28$). This causes worker productivity to be 1.75 times higher in the rich country. The role of worker age in determining low worker productivity is overlooked in most studies.

The poverty trap also causes low values of k and g. High population growth increases the size of next period's workforce relative to the current period's savers. High population growth spreads saving and capital accumulation more thinly across workers in the future, lowering k. Lower values of k and $\hat{h}$ lower the tax base and reduce public investment for any given tax rate.

The relatively low value of ϕ in the poor country raises tax rates and further reduces private saving and private capital formation. Indirectly, this also lowers public capital formation by reducing the level of national income and the tax base. The combination of the poverty trap and the lower ϕ reduces public and private physical capital intensities causing worker productivity to be 7.7 times higher in the rich country. This is over four times as high as the productivity ratio that Hall and Jones (1999) attribute to differences in capital intensity. There are several reasons why the estimate in Table 3.3 is higher.

In Table 3.3, we are assuming that the poor country is a perfectly closed economy. In the next section, we open the economy to international capital flows. An open economy reduces the differences in capital intensity across rich and poor countries, although not completely. The typical poor country is neither perfectly open nor perfectly closed, so our estimates using perfectly closed and perfectly open economies should bound the estimate from Hall and Jones.

However, there are reasons to believe that the Hall and Jones estimates may be too low. Pritchett (2000) estimates that the actual capital stock in poor countries is between 57 and 75 % of the officially measured stock. In poor countries, the level of government consumption is underestimated and the level of investment is overestimated. This fact implies estimates of productivity differences that are based on direct estimates of capital stock differences, as in Hall and Jones, are too small.

The Hall and Jones approach also treats private and public investment as perfect substitutes in production. The estimates of the output elasticity of public capital suggest that this is not the case; the elasticity for public capital is less than two-thirds the elasticity for private capital (Glomm and Ravikumar 1997). Poor countries have relatively more public capital, implying that the perfect substitutes assumption overstates the productivity of the capital stock in poor countries and lowers the estimated role of capital differences in explaining worker productivity differences.

3.3 Poverty Traps: A Closer Look

It has become quite common to explain income differences using poverty traps. Poverty trap theories come in different shapes and sizes and some question whether they provide a convincing empirical foundation for income differences. For this reason, it makes sense to look more closely at the characteristics of the particular poverty trap we use in this chapter.

First, this is not a "multiple equilibria" poverty trap. Multiple equilibria occur when, for given initial conditions, two or more outcomes are possible in a single period. In these types of poverty trap models, a country ends up in a bad equilibrium, with low human capital, just by chance. There is no particular reason why the country could not quickly move to the equilibrium with high human capital. It is a matter of households recognizing that they would all be better off with a different outcome. This is called a coordination problem. In our poverty trap, parents who receive the minimum level of schooling choose the same for their children because it makes them better off than any other outcome. It is a unique solution, and there is no incentive to change.

Second, our poverty trap creates *level* differences in the income of two economies that are both growing. Most poor countries experience positive growth (Kraay and McKenzie 2014). The growth may be too weak to allow convergence to the living standards of rich countries, but there are still absolute gains in productivity and the standard of living. The question is why the growth does not accelerate to allow convergence. Some poverty traps can be eliminated by economic growth. These types of traps cannot explain persistent differences in the level of income across countries. The choice not to educate older children in our model is completely independent of the absolute rental rate on human capital, which could be growing due to technological change or physical capital accumulation. Instead, the poverty trap is driven by the *relative* productivity of children. In environments where the relative productivity of children is high, the poverty trap will persist.

This brings us to the question of why some countries escape the poverty trap and others do not. One reason is culture. Culture, for our purposes, is a collection of non-economic features of society that standard economic models do not directly capture. Culture can certainly have an effect on education. Basic literacy advanced in some countries, but not others, well before the onset of sustained modern growth. Educating the general population could be motivated by social cohesion, enlightenment, religion, or military goals, as well as by economic considerations. Cultural and political differences in the pursuit of these broader goals caused the timing and extent of education to vary across countries before modern economic growth began (Cipolla 1969, pp. 16–22; Galor 2005, pp. 28–34). In some countries, literacy was high at the onset of growth, Germany and Sweden, and in other countries, it was low, England (Lord and Rangazas 2006).

In our model, we can think of Germany and Sweden starting to the right of the poverty trap, which helped accelerate their growth. England, on the other hand, was stuck in a human capital poverty trap in the early stages of its growth. It needed child labor and compulsory schooling legislation during the early nineteenth century to jump-start the schooling of older children (Doepke 2004; Doepke and Zillibotti 2005).

Beyond cultural differences that influence the "initial" level of education and human capital, technological and geographic differences play a role in causing differences in the size of γ. Technological or geographical features that cause γ to be high, increase the likelihood of a trap. In colder northern regions, farming is more physically demanding (hay, wheat, and dairy farming). This makes the relative productivity of children in agriculture low. As the industrial revolution began in England, there was a decline in heavy agriculture and an expansion in the "cottage industry," where textiles were produced at home. This shift in production raised the relative productivity of children significantly (Cunningham 1990; Horrell and Humphries 1995; Hudson and King 2000). The cottage industry was a relatively unique feature of early growth in England, and this may be one reason why the education of older children, whose productivity was relatively high, lagged other countries where it was not.

In southern climates, the farming is less heavy (sugar, cotton, and rice) and the relatively productivity of children is higher. This is one explanation for why education in the southern USA lagged that of the northern USA (Goldin and Sokoloff 1984). Geographic differences that lead to schooling differences are also consistent with the more general econometric findings of Bloom et al. (2003). They regress economic outcomes on geographic characteristics and find evidence for the existence of multiple steady states: A high-income range where income does not vary with geographic characteristics and a low-income range where it does. Warmer climates are associated with lower income among the countries in the low-income range. There are many possible explanations for their finding, but one could be that children have higher relative productivity in the farming of warmer climates and as a result receive less schooling. High levels of schooling, and the resulting economic development, allows countries to become less dependent on their geography. Geography, however, can create poverty traps for developing countries, especially those in warmer climates where the opportunity cost of educating older children is high.

3.4 International Financial Institutions and Foreign Aid

International economic assistance is a prominent feature of the global system since the 1950s. National governments in advanced countries and international organizations jointly owned by governments provide loans and grants to developing nations and other countries in need due to mismanagement, conflict, natural disasters, and other bad luck.

The most prominent of the international financial institutions (IFIs) are the International Monetary Fund (IMF) and the International Bank for Reconstruction and Development (IBRD), which is commonly known as the World Bank. These two US-based financial institutions were created in the 1940s. They have near universal membership of 188 member countries. The IFIs' broad purpose, and of what eventually became the World Trade Organization, is to help underpin a peaceful, market-oriented international economic system and avoid, as the IMF's charter puts it, "policies that are destructive of national and international prosperity." Inefficient policies are sometimes optimal from a narrow national perspective but are zero- or negative-sum games from an international perspective. In the 1930s, for example, tariff wars, competitive devaluations, and other policy mistakes were a natural response of countries trying to shield their employment from foreign competition. But, collectively, these policies resulted in persistently high global unemployment and economic stagnation. This contributed significantly to political instability in major countries, including Germany, and thus helped trigger World War II.

The broad division of labor in the two largest IFIs is as follows: the World Bank supports long-term development through program and project loans and grants, while the IMF focuses on macroeconomics and macro-critical structural reforms in its member countries. These programs are complemented by those of regional development banks (African Development, Asian Development Bank, etc.), as well as bilateral aid provided by national governments directly to countries in need. In the USA, for example, food aid is administered by the US Agency for International Development. Canada and all major advanced countries have ministries or agencies devoted to international development assistance.

International assistance does not stop with the transfer of financial and real resources but is complemented by various specialized technical services. It is recognized that to overcome poverty and underdevelopment requires more than money and resources. For example, countries may not collect enough revenue to be able to pay for badly needed government services, including basic sanitation, health, and education. International technical assistance aims to help countries build their institutions—fix broken tax systems, set up central banks, manage sound money, and otherwise help nurture economic institutions that can help countries run more efficiently.

3.4.1 Conditionality and Ownership

With the exception of humanitarian aid, international assistance often comes with strings attached. *Conditions* aim to help recipient countries improve their policy choices and economize on the donors' or creditors' resources so that the money can be spread to more needy countries and worthy projects. International loans are sometimes backed by collateral, but this is not typically the case for IMF or World Bank loans. Lacking collateral, conditions help assure the international community that these loans will be repaid. Conditions also help give borrowing countries reasonable certainty. They are assured that they will continue receiving international assistance if they meet the conditions specified (this is called uniformity of treatment).

The IMF got involved in structural conditionality in the 1980s for good reasons. Supply side reforms improve the efficiency of the economy and boost exports and growth. They also prevent situations where governments cut the wrong components of spending or follow other inefficient policies. But while well intentioned, the expansion in the scope and complexity of Fund conditionality had unintended consequences. The Fund was spread thin. The content of its programs expanded far beyond macroeconomic and financial stabilization—its traditional areas of expertise. Involvement in complex, multi-stage structural reforms led the IMF away from its core areas in which it possesses a clear comparative advantage and made it lose focus.

Domestic ownership for structural reforms was undermined. Cash-strapped governments sometimes agreed to IMF conditionality mainly to access IMF financing and obtain its seal of approval. Lack of ownership hindered policy implementation and undermined the IMF's credibility and its ability to catalyze reforms. Some politicians learned to treat the Fund as a scapegoat for the tough choices they had to make. Conditionality came to be viewed as an inevitable but much-resented sacrifice of national sovereignty rather than an instrument of international cooperation. Such rhetoric helped galvanize opposition to needed reforms, especially when they were perceived as being imposed from abroad to protect the narrow interests of donors. It became clear that unless the country "owned" the policy reforms, i.e., believed in and supported the implementation of the reforms, there was little chance of success.

The Fund's deepening involvement in structural areas also caused frictions with the World Bank. The roles of the two Bretton Woods institutions converged during the 1980s. The Bank's interest in macroeconomic developments grew after it added structural adjustment lending to its operations following the debt crisis. As the Fund started worrying about structural issues much more in the late 1980s and 1990s, the overlap in the activities of the two institutions increased. Coordinating the activities of the two institutions became a higher priority.

As the Fund and the Bank appreciated the importance of strong ownership for the implementation of structural reforms and for market confidence, they reassessed their approach in low-income countries. In 1999, a transparent, country-driven process was introduced involving tripartite collaboration between the country, the Fund and the Bank. The country draws up its Poverty Reduction Strategy Paper (PRSP), laying out its programs. This is supposed to be done in consultation with the country's own population, the multilaterals and the bilateral donors. This is a partnership between the various groups, but primarily it is the country itself that is expected to draw up the program and take ownership of it.

The IFIs have made important changes in their conditionality in recent years. Following input from policy makers, civil society, and academia, the IMF now aims to have conditions meet five principles: (i) national ownership of programs; (ii) parsimony in conditionality; (iii) tailoring of programs to borrowing country circumstances; (iv) coordination with other multilateral institutions; and (v) clarity in conditionality. Importantly, IFI inclusive processes of transparency, consultation, and persuasion aim to empower members to design and implement programs and make their dialog with the fund authentic. IMF staff members are encouraged to seek at an early stage in negotiations proposals from country authorities and to be flexible in program design. The timing of programs is to become more flexible in order to deal with situations in which time is short or the authorities' capacity is limited.

The Fund aims to help countries build broad support for sound policies, including through public discussion and the adoption of participatory processes (see also Drazen and Isard 2004). IMF staff is encouraged to assist through seminars, meetings with parliamentary committees, trade unions, business groups, and the media. IMF resident representatives are to play a key role in this.

3.4.2 Summary

Left on their own, some countries' economic and political systems generate short-sighted and inefficient policies that harm their national welfare and have systemic effects—meaning regional and global spillovers. The IFIs were created in the 1940s to help countries in need. Their financing and technical support allows countries to discover and adopt policies that are more efficient, more sustainable, and have fewer negative spillovers. Conditions attached to international assistance are simply the way for the international community to ensure that countries it shows solidarity to are directing their efforts in the right direction.

Low country ownership of IFI-supported programs in the 1990s was the result of overreaching of conditionality. Analytical work helped assess the problem by focusing on the incentives of policy makers undertaking reforms, the resistance of interest groups to reforms, and on difficulties in monitoring and implementing reforms. Conditionality must be tailored and targeted to take into account the domestic political economy so as to maximize ownership. In practice, this means taking into account the influence of special interest groups, other domestic divisions, and the state of institutions in countries being assisted. The re-evaluation of conditionality triggered by the difficulties with programs in the 1990s led to important reforms. The focus of conditionality has been sharpened, and the aim is to use it in absolutely critical situations—to tackle first-order problems, not as an opportunity to pass desired but otherwise noncritical reforms.

3.5 Foreign Aid and Policy Experiments

Section 3.2 identified some potentially important sources of income differences across countries. Section 3.4 broadly discusses the attempt to use international aid to increase growth in poor developing countries. Evidence suggests that these attempts have not been generally successful. In this section, we search for policies that can effectively eliminate the sources of poverty and generate growth that would allow the living standards in the poor country to converge to those in the rich country. We begin with a standard form of unconditional aid as our baseline for comparison—government budget support. We then consider four policies: opening the economy to international capital flows, two education policies aimed at eliminating the poverty trap, and a policy reform designed to eliminate the poor country's anti-growth domestic fiscal policy. While there are other policies that might be considered, our model is best suited to analyze these policies. The results of our analysis will reveal many of the issues associated with policy reform and aid in general.

3.5.1 Unconditional Aid—Budget Support

We first analyze *unconditional* aid that takes the form of budget support to the poor country's government. Budget support will serve as a baseline to compare against other aid policies that are *conditional* in the sense that they are tied to specific policy changes.

Radelet et al. (2006) report that current aid flows average about 5 % of the recipient countries' GDP. Our model is calibrated to match poor countries with large governments where government purchases comprise about one-third of GDP. For these countries, the average aid flow is 15 % of the net tax revenue used for government purchases. We consider aid flows equal to 15 % of net tax revenues with varying duration: one, two, and three periods (or 20, 40, and 60 years). The impact of these aid flows on the growth rate in worker productivity is presented in Fig. 3.2.

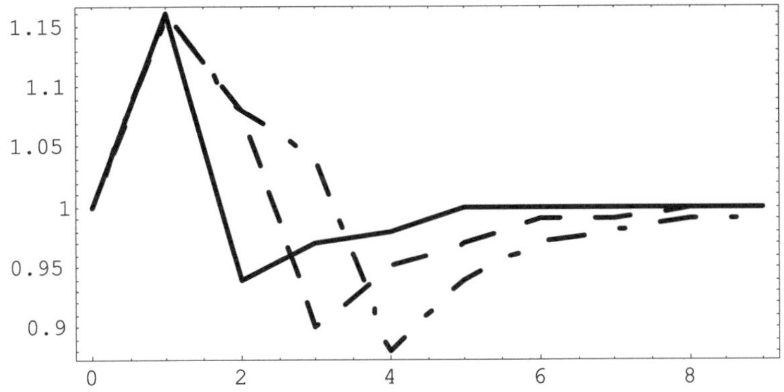

Fig. 3.2 Worker productivity with unconditional aid. *Notes* Fig. 3.2 shows annualized growth rates in worker productivity over time for unconditional aid policies beginning in period 0. The aid provided is 15 % of the government budget. The *solid line* represents the effects of giving aid for a single period; the *dashed line* shows the effects of aid provided for two periods, while the dash dot shows the effects of aid provided for three periods

The initial steady-state growth rate of the economy is 1 %, the exogenous annualized rate of growth due to technological progress. The aid inflows increase growth rates initially, but only by modest amounts. In the initial period, annualized growth rates rise to 1.15 %. The modest initial increase in growth rates results from the fact that the government will save and invest a fraction of the aid causing public capital to increase. Greater public capital raises the marginal product of private inputs and the rental rate on human capital, which raises private saving and private physical capital accumulation.

After the first period, growth rates fall. The economy is unable to sustain even the modest increase in growth rates for two reasons. First, since the aid flow is only temporary, the rise in public saving cannot be sustained. Second, there are diminishing returns to public and private investment that would cause growth rates to decline back to the steady-state level, even if aid inflows were permanent. Growth rates eventually dip below the steady-state level for several periods because the rise in the public and private capital intensity cannot be sustained and the economy must revert back to the initial steady-state capital intensities. In short, unconditional aid temporarily, but not permanently, shifts the economy's transition equations upward. With no permanent structural change in the economy's dynamics, it must return to its original steady state. The empirical analysis of Radelet et al. (2006) shows budget support raises growth rates temporarily. However, our model suggests that there are no long-run income benefits from unconditional budget support.

3.5.2 Opening the Economy

Up until now, we have assumed that the poor country's economy is perfectly closed. As we saw in Sect. 3.4, IFIs encourage countries to open their borders. What happens if the poor economy is opened to trade and international capital flows? What will be the effect on different generations of households in the poor country? Will opening the economy make the poor country's government better off or will it oppose the policy?

To answer these questions, the model must first be resolved under the assumption that the economy is open. In an open economy, private capital flows will equate the poor country's interest rate to the exogenous world interest rate (which we take to be the steady-state interest rate in the rich country). Next, the dynamic path under the open economy assumption is computed as the economy goes through the transition from the initial closed economy steady state to the open economy steady state. Unlike most neoclassical growth models, the "small" poor economy will *not* "jump" to the new steady state in a single period as interest rates are equalized in an open world capital market. This is because, unlike private capital, the government's *public* capital accumulation will adjust *gradually* to the opening of the economy. Public capital (such as roads and public utilities) do not flow across borders in the same way that private capital does. Note from Eq. (3.4a) that interest rates can be equalized due to private capital adjustments alone. Finally, welfare comparisons are made to see who benefits and who loses from opening the economy, and an analysis that includes computing the welfare effect on the poor country's government itself.

After the economy is opened, the poor country's r will converge to the world interest rate, r^w, which we take to be the steady state interest rate of the rich country. The equilibrating force is assumed to be private capital mobility. The poor country's private capital intensity is determined by substituting r^w into (3.4a) and then solving for the new value of k. Note that this does not mean that k is equated across rich and poor countries because g may differ across countries. Smaller values of g lower the marginal product of k, so smaller values of k are needed to drive the return to physical capital down to the world interest rate.

With k determined internationally, the government's optimal fiscal policy will also change. The government now maximizes (3.7) not subject to (3.6), as in the closed economy, but subject to the k determined by international capital markets as described above. The optimal policy in an open economy becomes (see the Appendix for the derivation)

$$\tau = \frac{\beta(1-\alpha)}{\beta + \phi[\psi + \beta(1+\beta)]} \tag{3.12a}$$

$$g_{t+1} = \frac{B\tau}{(1+q)n_{t+1}} \left(\frac{\alpha(1-\tau)}{1+r^w}\right)^{\frac{\alpha}{1-\alpha}} g_t^{\mu} \hat{h}_t \tag{3.12b}$$

where

$$B = \frac{\mu\beta + \phi\mu(\beta(1+\beta) + \psi)}{1 + \phi\mu(\beta(1+\beta) + \psi)}.$$

The coefficient B in the transition Eq. (3.12b) represents the share of the government budget that is invested in public capital. The product $B\ \tau$ is the share of national output that is invested in public capital.

We now compare the poor country's fiscal policy in open and closed economies. Begin by considering the extreme case where $\phi = 0$. Comparing (3.12) to (3.10), we note

$$\begin{aligned} B^{\text{open}} &\equiv \beta\mu > \beta\mu\frac{1-\alpha}{1-\alpha\beta} \equiv B^{\text{closed}}, \\ \tau^{\text{open}} &\equiv 1-\alpha < 1-\alpha\beta \equiv \tau^{\text{closed}}, \\ (B\tau)^{\text{open}} &= \beta\mu(1-\alpha) = (B\tau)^{\text{closed}}, \end{aligned}$$

where all inequalities hold provided that future utility is discounted, i.e., provided that $\beta < 1$. Opening the economy raises the portion of the budget that is invested and lowers the tax rate, but leaves the fraction of national output invested the same.

The fiscal policy differences are due to the *timing* of the impact of fiscal policy on private capital formation in open versus closed economies. In a closed economy, government policy affects private capital formation by affecting the after-tax wage of savers that fund the *next* period's private capital intensity. In an open economy, government policy affects private capital intensity by affecting the marginal product of private investments in the poor country—reducing it with higher tax rates and raising it with higher public capital intensity. International capital flows will anticipate and respond to these changes in private returns to investment, until the after-tax return to investment are equalized across countries. Thus, in an open economy, government policy has a more *immediate* effect on private capital formation—this period's policy affects *this* period's capital intensity rather than this period's saving flow and *next* period's capital intensity (as in a closed economy). With discounting of the future ($\beta < 1$), the cost of high taxes and low public investment, in lowering private capital intensity, is smaller in the closed economy due to the one-period delay in their effect. In this sense, opening the economy makes private capital formation more responsive to policy changes. The government reacts to the new environment by choosing a more "pro-growth" fiscal policy stance.

Table 3.4 gives the fiscal policies in open and closed economies for the calibration in Table 3.2 where, instead of $\phi = 0$, we have $\phi = 0.7461$. The result with $\phi = 0$ extends to positive values of ϕ; taxes are lower and the fraction of the government budget invested is higher in an open economy. However, the share of national output that is invested in public capital is lower in the open economy when

Table 3.4 Fiscal policy in the closed and open economy

Fiscal parameter	Closed economy	Open economy
τ	0.35	0.26
B	0.29	0.31
τB	0.10	0.08

$\phi > 0$, as B rises less than τ falls when the economy is opened. Thus, opening the economy lowers the economy's rate of public investment out of national output.

Figure 3.3 shows the effects on worker productivity of opening the economy to foreign investment. Growth accelerates in the first period as the capital inflow narrows the gap in private capital intensity across rich and poor countries. The capital inflow raises the recipient country's national income and tax base, offsetting the reduction in the rate of investment in public capital. Public capital intensity rises over time to a higher steady-state value. The increase in public capital intensity raises the marginal product of private capital and causes private capital intensity to increase further. The modest additional increases in public and private capital intensities keeps growth in worker productivity above the rate of technological change until period 4, when the economy has approximately converged to its new physical capital intensities.

The growth effects of opening the economy to capital mobility dwarf those of the unconditional aid policy. Moreover, these effects are permanent in nature because the change in the economy is structural. The new steady state is characterized by higher permanent per capita incomes.

The extent to which inflows of private capital narrow productivity differences in the long run is given in Table 3.5; the counterpart to Table 3.3 in a perfectly open economy. Comparing Table 3.5 to Table 3.3, one sees that worker productivity gaps

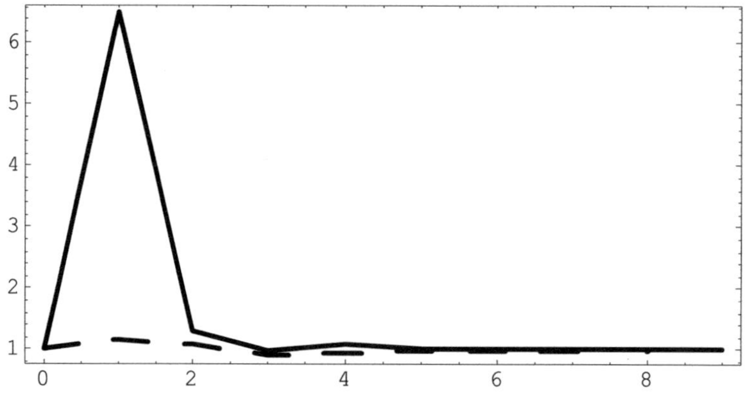

Fig. 3.3 Opening the economy to capital flows. *Note* Fig. 3.3 plots give the annualized growth rates in worker productivity over time from opening the economy compared to a two-period unconditional aid policy. Unconditional aid flows are 15 % of government budgets in each of the two periods. *Solid line*—open economy, *Dashed line*—two periods of unconditional aid

Table 3.5 Steady-state productivity differences—Open Economy

Rich to poor ratios	Model prediction
k^{α}	1.41
$g^{\mu(1-\alpha)}$	1.73
$\hat{h}/[1+n(T-e)]$	3.68
y	8.98

are narrowed by opening the economy. The rich country's advantage in worker productivity is now less than 1/3 of what it was in a close economy setting, although a ninefold difference still remains.

While there are clear gains in worker productivity from opening the economy, not all generations benefit from the opening. The policy affects the welfare of households by affecting factor prices. Households prefer higher current wages for themselves and higher future wages for their children. They also benefit from higher interest rates on their life-cycle saving. Opening the economy will raise wages and lower interest rates as capital flows into the economy. For *most* generations, there is a net gain in utility from these factor price adjustments (the effect of higher wages is greater than the effect of lower interest rates). This is *not* true for the initial generation of young households who are alive at the time the policy is introduced. Their current wages are unaffected by the capital inflows (since the initial capital intensity is fixed) and yet their interest rates are significantly lowered. The sharp drop in interest rates, with no change in current wages, causes their welfare to fall. Thus, welfare falls for the first generation and rises for all others.

The government in the poor country enjoys an increase in public consumption each period—the increase in the tax base from capital inflows offsets the drop in tax rates. The gain in the government consumption, along with the discounted gain in utility to all future generations, is larger than the loss in welfare of the initial generation. Thus, the poor government would want to open the economy, on economic grounds, in our setting.

This finding is obviously sensitive to the particular calibration chosen. If the initial capital intensities were smaller, or if the poor country's government had a higher rate of time preference, then one might see opposition to opening the economy.

3.5.3 Eliminating the Poverty Trap

Schooling is low in the poor country because the value of forgone earnings associated with sending older children to school is a relatively large fraction of parent's income. The value of forgone earnings is high because households have many children and because parental earnings are low. The poverty trap can be removed if parental earnings are increased relative to the earnings of older children. This would make it more costly to have many children (because of the lost work time and forgone consumption of parents associated with child rearing) and it would lower the relative value of children's work in total family income.

Using aid to encourage poor countries to increase the schooling of *younger* children (i.e., to increase $\bar{e}$) will increase earnings but will not remove the poverty trap. This type of policy does not raise the earnings of parents *relative* to those of older children (since they both receive the higher levels of education when they are young children). What is needed is more schooling of *older* children so that when they become parents, their earnings (based on $e_t > \bar{e}$) exceed the earnings of their older children (based only on $\bar{e}$)—thereby making children more costly and relatively less important in generating family income.

One policy that can remove the poverty trap is similar to Mexico's Progresa program.[7] Under this policy, the governments subsidize the forgone earnings of older children who attend school. A sufficiently high subsidy would raise e_t sufficiently above $\bar{e}$, so that transitional dynamics would result, sending the poor country to point C in Fig. 3.1. A potential advantage of identifying and eliminating poverty traps is that aid need not be ongoing. Once sufficient aid has been provided to eliminate the poverty trap, no further aid is necessary.

To begin the analysis of the subsidy policy, introduce the policy parameter v that indicates the fraction of forgone earnings of older children that the government returns to the household. This introduces the expression $vw_t\gamma\bar{h}_t(e_t - \bar{e})n_{t+1}$ on the right-hand side of the household lifetime budget constraint from Sect. 3.1. In the presence of the subsidy, household behavior becomes (see Problem 8)

$$n_{t+1} = \frac{\psi}{(1+\beta+\psi)\left(\eta - \gamma(T - e_t + v(e_t - \bar{e}))(\bar{e}/e_{t-1})^{\theta}\right)} \tag{3.13a}$$

$$e_t = \max\left[\frac{\theta\left(\eta(e_{t-1}/\bar{e})^{\theta} - \gamma T + \gamma\bar{e}v\right)}{\gamma(1-\theta)(1-v)}, \bar{e}\right]. \tag{3.13b}$$

The subsidy increases the optimal schooling level, and if the subsidy is sufficiently high, the optimal schooling level is pushed above $\bar{e}$. For a given level of e_t, fertility is also encouraged by the subsidy. A rise in fertility has the unintended consequence of lowering growth. However, if the subsidy raises e_t enough, then fertility will fall.[8]

---

[7] In 1997 Mexico began *Progresa*, a program designed to increase human capital in poor families by paying families to send their children to school and to visit health care providers. Grants are provided directly by the government to the mothers of children. The school grants cover about 2/3 of what the child would receive in full time work (Krueger 2002).

[8] Our model abstracts from tuition costs (see Problem 5). The government can raise schooling by increasing tuition subsidies. Doepke (2004) and Lord and Rangazas (2006) study the historical impact of government tuition subsidies in England. They find that lower tuition has modest effects on schooling and growth. Lower tuition reduces the cost of all children and, in particular, young children who would have attended school in any case. This raises fertility for several periods and slows the demographic transition. Thus, something like a Progresa program or compulsory schooling is needed to generate a quick demographic transition and rapid economic growth.

Of course, the subsidy must be financed out of tax revenues. In addition, as older children work less in order to attend school, the tax base shrinks. So government revenue is reduced in the first period for two reasons—the subsidy payment and the decline in the tax base. This implies that government consumption and investment will fall initially. As with the possible rise in fertility, reduced government investment may offset the early growth effects of the policy. As the stock of human capital rises and increases the tax base, government consumption and investment will eventually rise.

Table 3.6 and Fig. 3.4 present the effects of the Progresa program with a subsidy, lasting for a single period, that is similar in size to that offered in the Mexican Progresa program ($v = 0.67$). The relatively large one-period subsidy is more than enough to boost the economy out of the poverty trap and in fact creates something close to a "growth miracle." The large rise in schooling is enough to create a fall in fertility. Rising human capital per worker also increases physical and public capital intensities generating growth for a number of periods. As in the case of opening the economy, the growth effects dwarf those of budget support and lead to large permanent increases in income levels.

An advantage of the Progresa program is that no generation is hurt by the policy. Although the positive welfare gain is quite small for the first generation, since parents miss the direct benefit of higher schooling, it is significant from the second generation

Table 3.6 The Progresa program: schooling and fertility effects

Period	1	2	3	4	5	6	7	8	9	10
e	0.29	0.34	0.37	0.41	0.43	0.45	0.47	0.48	0.49	0.49
n	2.5	1.2	1.1	1.0	1.0	1.0	1.0	1.0	1.0	1.0

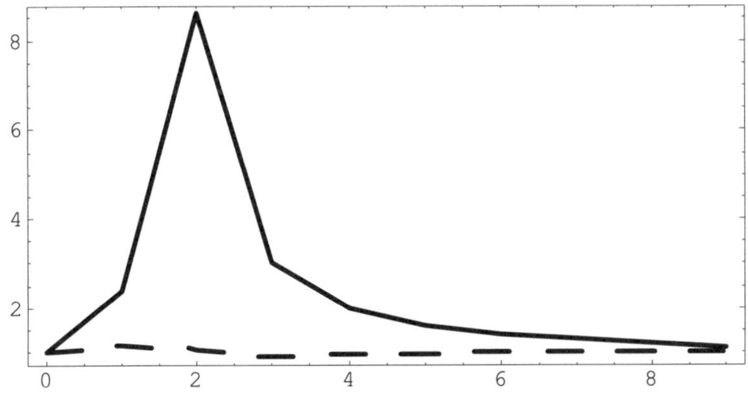

Fig. 3.4 The effects of a Progresa program. *Notes* Fig. 3.4 plots give the annualized growth rates in worker productivity over time from the Progresa program compared to a two-period unconditional aid policy. Unconditional aid flows are 15 % of government budgets in each of the two periods. *Solid line*—Progresa, *Dashed line*—two periods of aid

on. With sizeable welfare gains after the first period, combined with large increases in the tax base, the government's welfare increases due to the policy change.

Other policies designed to increase schooling do not necessarily generate universal private sector benefits. We compare the welfare effects of the Progresa policy to a compulsory schooling policy, frequently seen in practice, that generates the same increase in schooling. This requires that the first generation of students spend 0.29 of their time endowment in school, as under the Progresa policy. After that point, the minimum school requirement of 0.29 is nonbinding and schooling will follow the same path that is displayed in Table 3.6.

The growth effects of compulsory schooling are actually stronger than the Progresa policy. This is because, without the government subsidy, families will choose fewer children relative to the Progresa policy that subsidizes the cost of schooling children. The steeper decline in fertility increases the economy's growth rates marginally above those in Fig. 3.4. However, since the initial family is forced to send their children to school more than what they find optimal, they are made worse off. The government, on the other hand, prefers compulsory schooling. The fact that compulsion eliminates the need for a subsidy and raises growth and tax revenue to a greater degree, more than compensates for decrease in welfare for the initial generation.

3.5.4 Fiscal Policy Reform

Attempting to reform conventional fiscal policy of developing countries is a common target for aid policy. We now consider the effects of imposing a fiscal policy in the poor country that would bring it in line with the fiscal policy of the rich country. In particular, we compute the effects of imposing the τ and B of the rich country, where the optimal values are 0.15 and 0.67, and on the poor country, where the corresponding optimal values in the open economy are 0.26 and 0.31.

The effect of fiscal policy reform on the growth rates of worker productivity are given in Fig. 3.5. The growth effects are relatively modest and short-lived. In part, this is due to the fact that we begin the policy experiment from a perfectly open economy. Opening the economy brings the fiscal policy of the poor government closer to that of the rich government (see Table 3.4). This has the effect of making the differences in tax policy less dramatic, and the returns to accumulating private and public capital smaller (since poor country capital intensities are higher in the open economy than in the closed economy). When the poor economy is relatively close to the rich country's capital intensities to begin with (see Table 3.6), the transition to the new steady state is short.

There is, however, a significant gain in utility of all generations from the fiscal reform. This is because of the growth effects highlighted in Fig. 3.5 and because of the direct benefits of paying lower taxes. Of course, the welfare of the poor country's government falls significantly since they have been moved off their optimal fiscal policy.

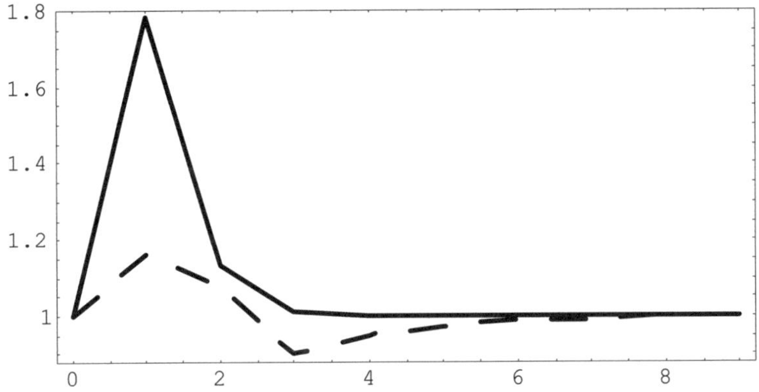

Fig. 3.5 The effects of fiscal reform. *Notes* Fig. 3.5 plots give the annualized growth rates in worker productivity over time from the fiscal reform compared to a two-period unconditional aid policy. Unconditional aid flows are 15 % of government budgets in each of the two periods. *Solid line*—fiscal reform, *Dashed line*—two periods of aid

3.6 The Aid Cost of Reform

We have examined five policies that might be used to promote growth in developing economies. The impact of the policies on growth differed significantly and so do their aid cost. The unconditional aid policy comes at a price and delivers no long-term benefits. Openness and the Progresa-style education subsidy deliver large and sustained increases in income. They also increase the welfare of the poor country's government and thus should be readily accepted. However, openness hurts the initial generation of private households and thus may not increase the government's welfare for all calibrations. At a minimum, the government may use the fact that the current generation is hurt as a "bargaining chip" to induce some aid compensation for opening the economy. Strategic considerations also enter in the case of the Progresa program. The government prefers compulsory schooling, and they may use this as a threat point to induce aid compensation for going forth with the Progresa program.

The domestic fiscal reforms, unlike the other policies, would certainly be opposed by the poor country's government. Aid dollars would have to be used to "purchase" the fiscal reforms from the poor country's government, in compensation for its losses. We can assess the aid cost of fiscal reform by calculating the minimum amount of aid needed to keep the poor country's government indifferent to the reform. We compute the aid cost as a permanent flow of aid, expressed as a fraction of the poor government's budget. The aid flow must be permanent because the government will want to renege and revert back to its optimal fiscal policy as long as it stays in power. Of course, the aid flow will also change the amount that the government invests (while the government consumes most of the aid flow, some is invested), and thus, the growth effects of the fiscal reforms will be larger than those

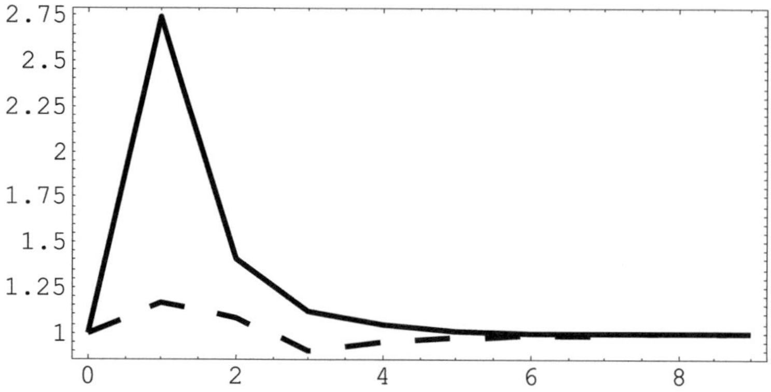

Fig. 3.6 Fiscal reform with required aid. *Notes* Plots give annualized growth rates in worker productivity over time from the fiscal reform versus a two-period unconditional aid policy. The required aid is a permanent flow equal to 87 % of the government budget. Unconditional aid flows are 15 % of government budgets over each of the two periods. *Solid line*—fiscal reform, *Dashed line*—two periods of aid

without aid—an added benefit of the aid that goes beyond purchasing the reforms per se. The growth effects are given in Fig. 3.6.

As mentioned, the growth effects are higher than in Fig. 3.5 because the government chooses to invest some of the aid. However, the amount of aid required to purchase the reform is very high. Aid equal to over 87 % of the poor country's budget is needed. Since the poor country's budget increases as the country grows, the absolute flow of aid must increase over time—long after the growth rate effects of the reforms have been exhausted.

3.7 Aid Failures

It is a discouraging stylized fact about development that no robust correlation between aid and growth has been identified in the econometric literature (e.g., Easterly et al. 2004). There are several possible econometric reasons for the absence of a clear positive relationship, for example, *endogeneity of aid flows* (aid is targeted to slow-growing economies), *specification error* (the relationship between aid and growth is highly nonlinear), and *measurement error* (all aid, including aid not intended to generate growth, is lumped together in a single measure). Attempts to account for these econometric issues have failed to overturn the consensus finding of a zero correlation between aid and growth (see, e.g., Rajan and Subramanian (2005, 2008, 2011). Our analysis is consistent with three possible reasons for the lack of correlation.

3.7.1 Unconditional Aid Is Not Growth-Promoting

Our results suggest that unconditional aid, including aid where conditions are not adequately enforced, will not deliver long-term gains in income. The boost to growth from unconditional aid is short-lived and so modest that it could easily be overshadowed by other developments—e.g., any long-lasting effects of the negative shocks to the economy that initially triggered the scaling up of unconditional aid to begin with.

3.7.2 Domestic Conflict Over Growth Policies

While there are policies that can generate rapid growth and sustained increases in income, there is likely to be domestic conflict over which policy to pursue. The government favors opening the economy and compulsory schooling, but the current generation of private households will oppose both policies. The current generation of private households favors the Progresa program, a program which the government views as clearly inferior to compulsory schooling. These conflicts may undermine attempts to achieve domestic consensus over which growth-promoting and poverty-reducing policies to implement. Such lack of consensus could delay or undermine the negotiation and implementation of conditional aid agreements with donors.

3.7.3 Prohibitive Aid Cost

Fiscal reforms are often part of the conditions for receiving aid. Our analysis suggests that reforms of domestic fiscal policy are likely to be the least successful of the policies that we examined. First, the growth effects of fiscal reform are relatively modest and short-lived. Second, the aid cost of "buying" the reforms from the poor country's government is enormous. Unless the aid keeps flowing to the poor country in sufficient quantity, the domestic government will do what it can to revert back to a high-tax, low-investment regime. In fact, the cost of maintaining effective reforms will increase over time as the government's budget, and the potential to increase government consumption, grows. In practice, aid is likely be far less than what is necessary to keep the government indifferent, and thus, fiscal reforms may be doomed from the beginning.

Even if the aid is carried out in sufficient amounts indefinitely, there will be little correlation between aid and economic growth in the data. The growth effects occur early on, while the aid continues into the future during periods where the growth effects have long since vanished. If aid is reduced or maintained at constant level, rather than increased, there will be a reversion in fiscal policy and growth. Thus, aid could be flowing to a country experiencing negative growth.

3.8 Humanitarian Aid

We have seen that there can be significant difficulties associated with using foreign aid to finance large-scale government investment projects or to induce changes in national policy. When the confidence in the foreign government is low, it is natural to think of bypassing the government in the seemingly less ambitious goal of providing humanitarian aid directly to the country's poor. Unfortunately, even providing food to the poor people of a country is difficult.

In a recent paper, Nunn and Qian (2014) summarize the problems with providing humanitarian aid. Food aid is often diverted to the government or stolen in route by rebel or criminal groups within the country. The problem becomes particularly acute when there is ongoing unrest and conflict in the country. In this type of setting, humanitarian aid is accused of not only being ineffective, but also of promoting conflict.

Nunn and Qian do a careful econometric analysis of the issue. They find that food aid increases the *duration* of civil wars in countries that have a history of internal conflict. They find no evidence that food aid *starts* civil wars or wars with neighboring countries. This suggests that, during civil wars, the combatants are able to divert the food to soldiers and away from the population in general. Thus, just as with other types of aid, the country-specific situation has to be right for aid to have a chance of working in the way the donors intend.

3.9 Conclusion

This chapter introduces three extensions to the standard one-sector neoclassical growth model of physical capital accumulation: endogenous theories of human capital accumulation, fertility, and fiscal policy formation. These extensions are needed to provide a more complete theory of both historical growth within a country and the large income differences across countries. The role of private saving, emphasized in the standard model, is certainly important. However, the majority of economic growth cannot be explained without also considering the effects of investment in schooling and public infrastructure, private sector taxation and government consumption, and population demographics associated with fertility choices.

The extended growth model also allows us to think about the fundamental sources of poverty traps and anti-growth fiscal policy. Identifying these important fundamentals of low income is needed to assess the likely impact of various policy suggestions intended to trigger growth. We saw that the effectiveness of different policies varies dramatically. Political support for different policies from within the recipient country was also shown to vary widely. Even in our simple model, there are clear economic and political reasons why some of the more popular policy recommendations typically made are not likely to generate sustained growth. Difficulties in finding policies that both (i) fundamentally alter the country's long-run growth potential and (ii) receive strong support from the recipient country's government and powerful interest groups explain the disappointing effect of foreign aid on growth in developing countries. In practice, working with recipient countries to identify pro-growth policies with strong political support will make foreign aid more effective.

3.10 Related Literature

Much of the chapter is based on Mourmouras and Rangazas (2007). Several books on economic growth have recently been written with a focus on human capital and fertility. An introduction to human capital and fertility that is appropriate for undergraduates can be found in Lord (2002) and Weil (2009). Two excellent advanced books on the subject are Galor (2011) and de la Croix (2013). The theory in these books is aimed at graduate students and research economists, but there is much material that any serious students of economics could benefit from.

For more on the growth consequences of missing intergenerational markets for human capital loans, including, the connection to poverty traps, see Drazen (1978), Azariadis and Drazen (1990), Becker et al. (1990), Galor and Ziera (1993), Rangazas (2000), Acemoglu (2009, Sect. 21.6), and Córdoba and Ripoll (2013). Azariadis and Stachurski (2004) provide an extensive survey and assessment of poverty traps.

The political economy of policy formation is a growing field in economic theory. A nice nontechnical introduction to the political economy of growth is Acemoglu and Robinson (2012). Galor (2011) and de la Croix (2013) contain political theories of public education based on economic considerations. Advanced texts that provide surveys of political economy more generally include Persson and Tabellini (1990) and Drazen (2000). Grossman and Helpman (2001) focus on the economics of interest group politics in particular.

Popular introductions to the issues associated with foreign aid and growth include Easterly (2001, 2007), Mallaby (2004), and, the slightly more technical, Isard et al. (2006). Most academic work on aid is empirical, but there are advanced journal articles that address various theoretical concerns such as Svensson (2000), Mourmouras and Mayer (2005), Marchesi and Sabani (2007), and Scholl (2009).

3.11 Exercises

Questions

1. Describe in words the key determinants of schooling and fertility.
2. Carefully explain the mechanism behind the trade-off between the "quantity" and the "quality" of children.
3. Use Fig. 3.1 to explain how an economy might experience a "poverty trap," based on its initial conditions.

4. How do the private stocks of physical capital affect the accumulation of public capital?
5. What does it mean to say that a model is recursive? In what sense is our model recursive?
6. How does a more selfish government undermine private capital accumulation?
7. What are the fundamental differences in the economies of the "rich" and the "poor" countries?
8. How are ϕ^{rich} and ϕ^{poor} calibrated?
9. Summarize the results of Table 3.3 where the worker productivity gap between rich and poor countries is estimated and decomposed into its contributing factors.
10. Compare the model's explanation for productivity gaps between rich and poor countries to the explanation of Hall and Jones (1999).
11. Discuss the ways that culture, technology, and geography interact to determine whether a country can be caught in the poverty trap of our model.
12. What is unconditional aid? Explain the effect of unconditional aid on worker productivity growth in the poor country.
13. Explain why opening the economy to international capital flows does not necessarily equate k across countries.
14. Explain why opening the economy to international capital flows alters the economy's fiscal policy? Explain why the new fiscal policy is more pro-growth.
15. What is the worker productivity gap between rich and poor countries after the economy is opened? Explain why the gap is different than in the closed economy case.
16. Do all generations of households benefit from opening the economy to capital flows? Does the government benefit?
17. How can a program such as Progresa eliminate the poverty trap?
18. Compare the effects of the Progresa program to compulsory schooling.
19. Describe the fiscal policy reform experiment? What are the effects on worker productivity?
20. What is the aid cost of reform? For which policies is the aid cost the lowest? The highest?
21. Why does aid often fail to generate economic growth?
22. Can humanitarian aid hurt economic growth? Explain.

Problems

1. Derive (3.1a–c). What is the causal connection between fertility and schooling? What condition must hold for there to be a poverty trap when parent's receive the minimum level of schooling?

2. Derive the transition Eq. (3.6) for private–physical capital intensity. Explain why private–physical capital accumulation is positively affected by public capital and negatively affected by labor taxation.
3. Show that the optimal rate of taxation of output in the model is decreasing in ϕ.
4. Follow the steps in the Appendix to derive (3.10a–c).
5. Suppose that learning of older children requires the family to purchase goods inputs as was discussed in Chap. 2 (continue to assume that learning of young children is only a function of their time). Let the quantity of goods inputs purchased per child be denoted by x_t and the price to the family of purchasing one unit of the goods inputs by p_t. Write the human capital production function as $h_{t+1} = x_t^{\theta_1} e_t^{\theta_2}$. Introduce the schooling expenditures, $p_t\, x_t$, into the family's budget and derive the new expression for the choice of schooling time solely as a function of parent's schooling time and exogenous variables, as in (3.1b). Discuss the new determinants of the poverty trap and how policy can be used to generate a human capital takeoff.
6. Extend your analysis in question 5 to include fertility. Derive the new expression for fertility and discuss how the goods cost of schooling affects the level of fertility.
7. Think more broadly about human capital inputs to include health and nutritional investment in children. Apart from the good inputs used in education, what alternative interpretations can then be given to x_t? Does the relationship between x_t and e_t make sense under the new interpretation? How does the introduction of x_t help to further explain the income gaps across countries?
8. Derive the schooling and fertility demand equations when the government subsidizes the forgone earnings of older children. Explain why the subsidy has an ambiguous effect on fertility.
9. Suppose the government gives parents a lump transfer v that is not tied to the forgone earnings of children. Solve the model for schooling and fertility in the presence of the lump sum transfer. How are schooling and fertility affected by the transfer? Are the effects different than under the subsidy in Problem 8?
10. Formally show that the equalization of the return to capital across countries in an open economy does not generally imply an equalization of private capital intensity.

Appendix*

Optimal Fiscal Policy in a Closed Economy

Domestic fiscal policy is determined by maximizing (3.7) subject to the government budget constraint and the accumulation equations for private and public capital. The private household's indirect utility function may be written as

$$U_t = U_0 + \bar{U}_t + (1+\beta)\ln w_t D_t + \beta \ln(1 + r_{t+1}) + \psi \ln w_{t+1} D_{t+1},$$

where U_0 is a constant, and $\bar{U}_t = (1+\beta)\ln h_t + \psi \ln n_{t+1} + \psi \ln h_{t+1}$ is independent of fiscal policy. For the purpose of setting optimal fiscal policy, the government can then be modeled as choosing tax rates and public capital to maximize,

$$\sum_{t=0}^{\infty} \beta^t \left(\ln c_t^g + \phi\{(1+\beta)\ln w_t D_t + \beta \ln(1+r_{t+1}) + \psi \ln w_{t+1} D_{t+1}\}\right)$$

subject to (3.4a, b), (3.6), (3.8), and (3.9).

Substituting the constraints into the objective function and collecting common terms yield the following equivalent problem

$$\begin{aligned}
&\max_{\{\tau_{t+1}, g_{t+1}, k_{t+1}\}_{t=0}^{\infty}} \sum_{t=0}^{\infty} \beta^t \ln\left[\tau_t k_t^{\alpha} g_t^{\mu(1-\alpha)} \hat{h}_t - g_{t+1}(1+q) n_{t+1}\right] \\
&\quad + \phi \sum_{t=0}^{\infty} \beta^t \{[\beta(\alpha-1) + \psi\alpha + \beta\alpha(1+\beta)] \ln k_{t+1} + \mu(1-\alpha)[(\beta+\psi) + \beta(1+\beta)] \ln g_{t+1} \\
&\quad + [\beta + \psi + \beta(1+\beta)] \ln(1 - \tau_{t+1})\} \\
&\quad + \sum_{t=1}^{\infty} \lambda_t \left\{ \left[\frac{\beta}{1+\beta+\psi}\right] \frac{(1-\tau_{t-1})(1-\alpha) k_{t-1}^{\alpha} g_{t-1}^{\mu(1-\alpha)} h_{t-1}}{(1+q) n_t \hat{h}_t} - k_t \right\},
\end{aligned}$$

where λ is the multiplier associated with the private capital accumulation constraint.

To solve this sequence problem, begin by differentiating to get the first-order conditions for $\tau_t, g_t, k_t, \lambda_t$, for $t \geq 1$. Be careful to differentiate wherever the choice variable appears in the objective function. Next, substitute into the first-order conditions the "guess" $(1+q)n_{t+1}g_{t+1} = B\tau_t k_t^{\alpha} g_t^{\mu(1-\alpha)} \hat{h}_t$, where B is an undetermined coefficient. Finally, solve the first-order conditions for B, τ_t, g_t, and k_t to get (3.10a–c).

A tricky part of the solution given by (3.10a–c) involves the first-order condition for k_t. This equation, along with the first-order condition for λ_t and the guess for the g_t, can be used to solve for the expression $\lambda_t k_t$ by solving the following difference equation, $\lambda_t k_t = \beta^{t-1}\left\{\frac{\alpha\beta}{1-B} + \phi[\beta(\alpha-1) + \alpha\psi + \alpha\beta(1+\beta)]\right\} + \alpha\lambda_{t+1}k_{t+1}$, to get $\lambda_t k_t = \frac{\beta^{t-1}}{1-\alpha\beta}\left\{\frac{\alpha\beta}{1-B} + \phi[\beta(\alpha-1) + \alpha\psi + \alpha\beta(1+\beta)]\right\}$. Use this solution to eliminate $\lambda_{t+1}k_{t+1}$ in the first-order conditions for τ_t and g_t. Using the guess for g_t, these two first-order conditions can be used to solve for τ_t and B to get $\tau_t = \tau = \frac{1-\alpha\beta}{1+(1-\alpha\beta)(1-B)\phi\Gamma}$ and $B = \frac{\frac{\mu\beta(1-\alpha)}{1-\alpha\beta} + \mu\beta(1-\alpha)\phi\Gamma}{1+\mu\beta(1-\alpha)\phi\Gamma}$. Combining these two expressions completes the solution.

Optimal Fiscal Policy in an Open Economy

In an open economy, the government's problem can be written so that it solves

$$\max_{\{\tau_{t+1},g_{t+1}\}_{t=0}^{\infty}} \sum_{t=0}^{\infty} \beta^t \ln\left[\tau_t\left(\frac{(1-\tau_t)\alpha}{1+r^w}\right)^{\frac{\alpha}{1-\alpha}} g_t^{\mu}\hat{h}_t - g_{t+1}(1+q)n_{t+1}\right]$$
$$+\phi[\psi+\beta(1+\beta)]\sum_{t=0}^{\infty}\beta^t\left\{\frac{1}{1-\alpha}\ln(1-\tau_{t+1})+\mu\ln g_{t+1}\right\}$$

This problem differs from the closed economy problem because private capital intensity is now determined by international capital flows rather than domestic saving. In a closed economy, government policy affected private capital formation by affecting the after-tax wage of savers that fund the subsequent period's private capital intensity. Now, government policy affects private capital intensity by affecting the marginal product of private investments in the poor country—reduced by higher tax rates and raised by higher public capital intensity. In an open economy, government policy has a more *immediate* effect on private capital formation—this period's policy affects *this* period's capital intensity rather than this period's saving flow and *next* period's capital intensity.

Differentiating with respect to τ_{t+1} and g_{t+1} generates first-order conditions. As before, guess a solution for g of the form

$$(1+q)n_{t+1}g_{t+1} = B\tau_t\left(\frac{\alpha(1-\tau_t)}{1+r^w}\right)^{\frac{\alpha}{1-\alpha}} g_t^{\mu}\hat{h}_t.$$

Substitute into the first-order conditions and solve for τ_{t+1} and B to get the solution in the text.

References

Acemoglu D (2009) Introduction to modern economic growth. Princeton University Press, Princeton

Acemoglu D, Robinson J (2012) Why nations fail: the origins of power, prosperity, and poverty. Crown Publishers, New York

Aschauer D (1989) Is public expenditure productive? J Monetary Econ 23(2):177–200

Azariadis C, Drazen A (1990) Threshold externalities in economic development. Quart J Econ 105 (2):501–526

Azariadis C, Stachurski J (2004) Poverty traps. In: Aghion P, Durlauf S (eds) Handbook of economic growth. North Holland, Amsterdam

Banerjee A, Duflo E (2011) Poor economics. Public Affairs, New York

Becker GS (1960) An economic analysis of fertility. In: National Bureau of Economic Research, Demographic and economic change in developed countries. Princeton University Press, Princeton

Becker GS (1981) A treatise on the family. Harvard University Press, Cambridge

Becker GS, Lewis HG (1973) On the interaction between the quantity and quality of children. J Polit Econ 81(2):S279–S288
Becker G, Murphy K, Tamura R (1990) Human capital, fertility, and economic growth. J Polit Econ 98(5):S12–S37
Bloom D, Canning D, Sevilla J (2003) Geography and poverty traps. J Econ Growth 8(4):355–378
Bongaarts J (2002) The end of the fertility transition in the developing world. Popul Dev Rev 28 (3):419–443
Cipolla C (1969) Literacy and development in the West. Penguin Books, Middlesex
Clarida RH (1993) International capital mobility, public investment, and economic growth. NBER working paper 4506. National Bureau of Economic Research, Cambridge
Córdoba J, Ripoll M (2013) What explains schooling differences across countries? J Monetary Econ 60(2):184–202
Cunningham H (1990) The employment and unemployment of children in England c. 1680–1851. Past Present 126:115–150
de la Croix D (2013) Fertility, education, growth, and sustainability. Cambridge University Press, Cambridge
Doepke M (2004) Accounting for fertility decline during the transition to growth. J Econ Growth 9 (3):347–383
Doepke M, Zilibotti F (2005) The macroeconomics of child labor regulation. Am Econ Rev 95 (5):1492–1524
Drazen A (1978) Government debt, human capital, and bequests in a life-cycle model. J Polit Econ 86(6):505–516
Drazen A (2000) Political economy in macroeconomics. Princeton University Press, Princeton
Drazen A, Isard P (2004) Can public discussion enhance program ownership? NBER working paper 10927. National Bureau of Economic Research, Cambridge
Easterly W (2001) The elusive quest for growth. MIT Press, Cambridge
Easterly W (2007) The white man's burden. Penguin Press, New York
Easterly W, Levine R, Roodman D (2004) Aid, policies, and growth. Am Econ Rev 94(3):774–780
Galor O (2005) From stagnation to growth: unified growth theory. In: Aghion P, Durlauf S (eds) Handbook of economic growth. North Holland, Amsterdam
Galor O (2011) Unified growth theory. Princeton University Press, Princeton
Galor O, Moav O (2002) Natural selection and the origins of economic growth. Quart J Econ 117 (4):1133–1192
Galor O, Ziera J (1993) Income distribution and macroeconomics. Rev Econ Stud 60(1):35–62
Glomm G, Ravikumar B (1997) Productive government expenditures and long-run growth. J Econ Dyn Control 21(1):183–204
Goldin C, Sokoloff K (1984) The relative productivity hypothesis of industrialization: the American case, 1820–1850. Quart J Econ 99(3):461–490
Grossman G, Helpman E (2001) Special interest politics. MIT Press, Cambridge
Hall R, Jones C (1999) Why do some countries produce so much more output per worker than others? Quart J Econ 114(1):83–116
Horrell S, Humphries J (1995) The exploitation of little children: child labor and the family economy in the industrial revolution. Explor Econ Hist 32(4):485–516
Hudson P, King S (2000) Two textile townships, c. 1660–1820: a comparative demographic analysis. Econ Hist Rev 53(4):706–741
Isard P, Lipschitz L, Mourmouras A, Yontcheva B (2006) High-level seminar on foreign aid and macroeconomic management: overview and synopsis of key lessons. In: Isard P, Lipschitz L, Mourmouras A, Yontcheva B (eds) The macroeconomic management of foreign aid. International Monetary Fund, Washington
Kraay A, McKenzie D (2014) Do poverty traps exist? Assessing the evidence. J Econ Perspect 28 (3):127–145

Krueger A (2002) A model for evaluating the use of development dollars, south of the border. New York Times, May 2

Ljungquist L, Sargent T (2004) Recursive macroeconomic theory. MIT Press, Cambridge

Lord W (2002) Household dynamics, policy, and economics growth. Oxford University Press, Oxford

Lord W, Rangazas P (2006) Fertility and development: the roles of schooling and family production. J Econ Growth 11(3):229–261

Mallaby S (2004) The world's banker. Penguin Press, New York

Marchesi S, Sabani L (2007) IMF concerns for reputation and conditional lending failure: theory and empirics. J Dev Econ 84(2):640–666

Mourmouras A, Mayer W (2005) The political economy of IMF conditionality: a common agency model. Rev Dev Econ 9(4):449–466

Mourmouras A, Rangazas P (2007) Foreign aid policies and sources of poverty: a quantitative framework. IMF Staff Pap 54:59–90

Nunn N, Qian N (2014) US food aid and civil conflict. Am Econ Rev 104(6):1630–1666

Persson T, Tabellini G (1990) Macroeconomic policy, credibility, and politics. Harwood, London

Poterba J (1997) Rate of return to corporate capital and factor shares. NBER working paper 6263. National Bureau of Economic Research, Cambridge

Pritchett L (2000) The tyranny of concepts: CUDIE (cumulated depreciated investment effort) is not capital. J Econ Growth 5(4):361–384

Radelet S, Clemens M Bhavnani R (2006) Aid and growth: the current debate and some new evidence. CGD working paper 133. Center for Global Development, Washington

Rajan R, Subramanian A (2008) Aid and growth: what does the cross-country evidence really show? Rev Econ Stat 90(4):643–665

Rajan R, Subramanian A (2005) What undermines aid's impact on growth? IMF working paper 05/126. http://www.imf.org/external/pubs/ft/wp/2005/wp05126.pdf

Rajan R, Subramanian A (2011) Aid, Dutch disease, and manufacturing. J Dev Econ 94(1):106–118

Rangazas P (2000) Schooling and economic growth: a King-Rebelo experiment with human capital. J Monetary Econ 46(2):397–416

Scholl A (2009) Aid effectiveness and limited enforcement conditionality. Rev Econ Dyn 12 (2):377–391

Svensson J (2000) When is foreign aid policy credible? Aid dependence and conditionality. J Dev Econ 61(1):61–84

Weil D (2009) Economic growth. Addison Wesley, New York

4 Two-sector Growth Models

This section provides an introduction to two-sector growth models. We begin with a model where a single good is produced using traditional means of production. In the *traditional* sector, production is carried out by households using land (natural resources) and labor. There are no firms or factories that rely on heavy plant and equipment and modern production methods to produce goods. This setting can be used to identify the conditions necessary for a *modern* sector to appear that would begin an "industrial revolution," as in Hansen and Prescott (2002).

Next, we examine a two-sector model where two distinct types of goods are produced—agricultural and industrial. The model is first analyzed under the assumption that the economy is perfectly closed to the international trade of goods. An open-economy version is then considered. An important task is determining the circumstances under which opening the economy to the international trade of goods increases growth and welfare in the long run. The answer can be quite different from that obtained in the typical static analysis of international trade, where trade is typically shown to be welfare improving for all countries involved.

Finally, we extend the model to include health benefits from food consumption. The extended model is used to explain several facts about developing economies including the approximate constancy of caloric intake, the rise in body mass and health, and the declining budget share devoted to food. This material is related to the "subsistence constraint," a level of consumption required for survival and a frequent feature of development models. In the literature, the subsistence constraint plays a role in explaining a wide variety of development facts including, rising saving rates, initially rising fertility rates, and falling employment shares in agriculture.

4.1 From Stagnation to Growth

For most of human history, there was virtually no sustained increase in the standard of living of the average person (Clark 2007, Part I; Galor 2011, Chap. 2). Living standards are closely connected with output or income per person—also known as

S. Das et al., *Economic Growth and Development*,
Springer Texts in Business and Economics, DOI 10.1007/978-3-319-14265-4_4

per capita income. Before 1700, per capita income was stagnant across the world (Galor 2005, Fig. 2.1). England began to see some sustained increases in per capita income during the eighteenth century, but the growth rates in per capita income were modest, certainly less than one percent per year (Crafts 1995, Table 1). Before 1800, the growth rate in per capita income in Western Europe as a whole was barely above one-half percent (Galor and Weil 2000, Fig. 1). In the USA, growth rates in per capita income were close to zero before 1800 (Lucas 2002, Table 5.2). The lack of significant sustained growth in any particular region meant that living standards did not differ dramatically *across* regions. In 1820, Western Europe had per capita income that was 1.7 times higher than in Latin America, 2.1 times higher than Asia, and 2.9 times higher than Africa (Galor 2005, Sect. 2.1.1).

After 1800, the nature of economic growth changed. The modest growth in England accelerated and spread throughout Western Europe. Income per capita grew between 1.5 and 2.0 % in Western Europe from 1820 to 1929 (Galor and Weil 2000, Fig. 1). In the USA, growth in income per capita and output per worker exceeded 1.5 % by the middle of the nineteenth century and then remained between 1.5 and 2.5 % throughout the twentieth century (Lucas 2002, Table 5.2 and Mourmouras and Rangazas 2009, Table 4.2).

Not all countries began modern growth in the nineteenth century. As a result, the income gaps between countries began to grow—a phenomenon known as the *Great Divergence*. Over a period of two centuries, Parente and Prescott (2000) compare per capita income across large Eastern countries and Western countries.[1] As mentioned, income gaps were not large at the beginning of the nineteenth century. At this time, per capita income in the West was only 2.1 times higher than in the East. By 1950, the income gap widened considerably, with per capita in the West becoming 7.5 times higher than in the East. More dramatic gaps are found when comparing the richest and poorest countries of the world. A narrower set of Western offshoots, defined by Maddison (1995), comprised of the USA, Canada, Australia, and New Zealand, formed the richest set of countries in the world by the middle of the twentieth century. The per capita income of these countries in 1950 was 15 times higher than those in Africa (Galor 2005). By 2000, rich country per capita income was 18 times higher.

Modeling the sources and timing of the industrialization and the onset of modern growth is important in explaining income differences across countries today. The primary focus of this section is to begin thinking about this issue. To do so, we initially assume that production is highly dependent on land and natural resources and think about the conditions needed for the traditional economy to transform itself into a modern economy where production relies heavily on man-made physical capital.

[1] The East consists of China, Pakistan, India, Bangladesh, Indonesia, Japan, Burma, the Philippines, South Korea, Taiwan, and Thailand. The West consists of Western European countries and their ethnic offshoots: Canada, Mexico, USA, Argentina, Brazil, Chile, Australia, and New Zealand.

4.1.1 A Traditional Economy

During the pre-industrial period, production was carried out by households on "family farms" and other small-scale businesses. To present a sharp contrast to the modern capital–intensive production that provides the basis of standard neoclassical theory, we assume that pre-industrial traditional production uses only land (L) and "farm" labor (F) as inputs. The traditional sector production function is given by

$$O_t = \tilde{A} L_t^{\alpha} \tilde{H}_t^{1-\alpha}, \tag{4.1}$$

where O denotes output produced in the traditional sector, $\tilde{A}$ is TFP in the traditional sector, and $\tilde{H} = \tilde{D}F$ is the effective workforce, indexed by the state of technology, $\tilde{D}$, in the traditional sector.[2]

Throughout this chapter we assume that there are perfectly competitive markets for both labor and land. The extent to which these markets are well-functioning influences the value of $\tilde{A}$. Effective labor can be hired at the competitive wage, $\tilde{w}$, and land can be rented at the competitive rental rate for land, r^L. The conditions for the profit-maximizing use of effective labor and land by traditional sector producers require that marginal products be equated to factor prices,

$$\tilde{w}_t = (1-\alpha)\tilde{A} L_t^{\alpha} \tilde{H}_t^{-\alpha} \tag{4.2a}$$

$$r_t^L = \alpha \tilde{A} L_t^{\alpha-1} \tilde{H}_t^{1-\alpha}. \tag{4.2b}$$

There are N_t young households in each period. Each household lives for two periods. In the first period, each household supplies one unit of labor and earns the wage, $\tilde{w}\tilde{D}$. Part of the wage is consumed, c_1, and part is saved by purchasing land, l, at the competitive land price, p^L. In the second period, households retire and consume goods, c_2, financed by the rent they earn on land and the proceeds from selling their land.

A generation t household chooses consumption and saving to maximize the utility function

$$u_t = \ln c_{1t} + \beta \ln c_{2t+1}$$

subject to the two single period budget constraints

$$c_{1t} + p_t^L l_t = \tilde{w}_t \tilde{D}_t$$

---

[2] Human capital and fertility are treated exogenously in this chapter. We add endogenous schooling and fertility back into the model in Chap. 5.

and

$$c_{2t+1} = \left(r^L_{t+1} + p^L_{t+1}\right)l_t.$$

Combining the two single period budget constraints gives the lifetime budget constraint

$$c_{1t} + \frac{c_{2t+1}}{R^L_t} = \tilde{w}_t\tilde{D}_t,$$

where the return to purchasing one unit of land in period t is $R^L_t \equiv \frac{p^L_{t+1}+r^L_{t+1}}{p^L_t}$. The demand functions that result from solving the maximization problem are as follows:

$$c_{1t} = \frac{\tilde{w}_t\tilde{D}_t}{1+\beta} \tag{4.3a}$$

$$c_{2t+1} = R^L_t\frac{\beta\tilde{w}_t\tilde{D}_t}{1+\beta} \tag{4.3b}$$

$$p^L_t l_t = \frac{\beta\tilde{w}_t\tilde{D}_t}{1+\beta}. \tag{4.3c}$$

These demand functions are similar to those encountered in Chap. 2. Consumption and saving, now in the form of land purchases, are fractions of wages that depend on the household's time preference.

Market clearing in the labor market requires that the demand for labor by traditional producers equals the supply of labor from households, $F_t = N_t$. Market clearing in the land market requires that the households' demand for land as an asset equals the fixed stock of available land, $L_t \equiv N_t l_t = L$. Using the market clearing conditions and assuming exogenous growth factors for technology $(1+\tilde{d})$ and the population (n), the equilibrium price and return to land are given as follows:

$$p^L_t = \frac{\beta\tilde{w}_t\tilde{D}_t}{1+\beta}\frac{N_t}{L} \tag{4.4a}$$

$$R^L_t = \left[1 + \frac{\alpha(1+\beta)}{\beta(1-\alpha)}\right]\left[\left(1+\tilde{d}\right)n\right]^{1-\alpha}. \tag{4.4b}$$

Equation (4.4a) indicates that the price of land rises as the economy grows and the demand for the fixed supply of land increases. Equation (4.4b) tells us that the return to land is constant. This is because the growth rate of land prices is constant and the growth in the marginal product of land, and the rental rate for land, is the same as the growth rate in land prices. The higher is the growth rate in effective labor supply $((1+\tilde{d})n)$, the higher is the return to land.

As indicated in Sect. 4.1, the pre-modern growth period was characterized by very slow, if any, sustained growth in labor productivity and population. For now, we treat both these characteristics as exogenous and for simplicity set $\tilde{d} = 0$, $\tilde{D} = 1$, and $n = 1$. In the pre-modern steady state, we then have

$$\tilde{w} = (1 - \alpha)\tilde{A}\tilde{l}^{\alpha} \tag{4.5a}$$

$$R^L = 1 + \frac{(1+\beta)\alpha}{\beta(1-\alpha)}, \tag{4.5b}$$

where $\tilde{l}$ is land relative to the *effective* work force.

4.1.2 Onset of Modern Growth

Now think of the potential appearance of firms and a modern sector of production. The key issue is under what conditions will modern production be profitable. Firms will have to pay workers at least what they can make in the traditional sector and capital owners at least what they can make by owning land.

As in the one-sector models we have studied, the technology of the modern sector is given by

$$Y_t = AK_t^{\alpha}H_t^{1-\alpha}, \tag{4.6}$$

where $H_t = D_t M_t$. Firms must be able to generate nonnegative economic profit,

$$Y_t - w_t D_t M_t - r_t K_t \geq 0 \tag{4.7}$$

when paying workers what they could earn in the traditional sector, $w_t D_t = \tilde{w}\tilde{D}$, and capital owners what they could earn from owning land, $R_t \equiv 1 + r_t - \delta = R^L$ or $r_t = \delta + \frac{(1+\beta)\alpha}{\beta(1-\alpha)}$.

To uncover the conditions under which (4.7) is satisfied, we need to relate (4.7) to the fundamental features of the economy. Begin by pulling M_t out in (4.7) and write the right-hand-side in terms of K_t/M_t. Using the first-order condition for the profit-maximizing choice of K_t, $\alpha A D_t^{1-\alpha}(K_t/M_t)^{\alpha-1} = r_t$, write K_t/M_t in terms of r_t. Finally, substitute $w_t D_t = \tilde{w}\tilde{D}$ and $r_t = \delta + \frac{(1+\beta)\alpha}{\beta(1-\alpha)}$ into (4.7) and rearrange to get

$$D_t \geq \tilde{A}\tilde{l}^{\alpha}\left(\frac{\delta}{\alpha} + \frac{1+\beta}{\beta(1-\alpha)}\right)^{\frac{\alpha}{1-\alpha}} A^{\frac{-1}{1-\alpha}}. \tag{4.8}$$

The condition in (4.8) gives the threshold value that technological progress in the modern sector must exceed before production becomes profitable at the factor prices paid in the traditional sector. Until technology (D_t) has developed sufficiently, the modern sector will not appear. This raises the question of what caused D_t to grow and eventually reach the threshold in (4.8).

We take technology as exogenous and thus cannot explain why technological progress eventually caused the threshold in (4.8) to be exceeded, opening the way for sustained modern growth. Acemoglu and Robinson (2012), Clark (2007), Galor (2011) provide theories of the early progress in D_t. All the theories argue that technological advances occurred very slowly before 1800. Important determinants of the early progress are believed to be the slow growth in population size (more people, more ideas), institutional change that encouraged property rights and innovation, and genetic transmission of the traits that make humans productive (richer people had bigger families than poorer people).

Even if the state of technology is common knowledge to the world as a whole, the threshold may nevertheless be met in some countries but not in others. Differences in thresholds across countries led to differences in the onset of modern growth, causing standard of livings to diverge beginning around 1800. The technological threshold is higher for countries with plentiful and productive land or natural resources ($\tilde{A}\tilde{l}^{\alpha}$), a type of "natural resource curse."

For example, Habbakuk (1962) argued that United States labor productivity in traditional agriculture was high in the early nineteenth century, due to the abundance of land, and as a result slowed the structural transformation of the economy. The availability of land and natural resources in Africa has often been cited as one reason that its takeoff to a sustained modern growth path has been delayed.

Parente and Prescott (2000) stress the importance of political forces that restrict work practices, use of machinery, and adoption of the available technology, all making A low and increasing the threshold for takeoff. The most famous historical example of such forces were the Luddites, named after one of their leaders (Ned Ludd), nineteenth-century English textile artisans who violently protested against the machinery introduced during the early stages of the Industrial Revolution.

A lack of institutions that support markets, such as property right protection or public infrastructure, lowers TFP in each sector. However, from (4.8), we see that any economy-wide deficiencies that lower A and $\tilde{A}$ proportionally will *disproportionately* harm the modern sector. This is because a lower value of A lowers the demand for physical capital and profits, for given factor prices. A low value of A causes the marginal product of capital to be low, resulting in low capital demand, low production, and low profits in the modern sector. There is no similar indirect effect of TFP in the traditional sector because land is fixed and therefore is not responsive to the level of $\tilde{A}$. Thus, weak support for markets, generally throughout the entire economy, can prevent the onset of modern growth by disproportionately harming the modern sector through its negative effect on capital accumulation.

4.2 The Structural Transformation of a Two-sector Economy

Our focus now turns to the rate of growth of an economy after the threshold condition given by (4.8) is met and a modern sector appears. In other words, we examine what determines the pace of the structural transformation from a traditional economy to a modern economy once both sectors are operating.

As suggested in the previous section, if two different sectors are to operate, they must pay workers the same wage and asset owners the same return,

$$w_t D_t = \tilde{w}_t \tilde{D}_t \tag{4.9a}$$

$$R_t = R_t^L, \tag{4.9b}$$

where we now allow for technological progress in the traditional sector.

Households can work in either sector. Households have the portfolio choice of saving by purchasing physical capital or land, so their budget constraints become

$$c_{1t} + p_t^L l_t + s_t^K = w_t D_t$$

and

$$c_{2t+1} = \left(r_{t+1}^L + p_{t+1}^L\right) l_t + R_t s_t^K,$$

where $p_t^L l_t + s_t^K$ represents total saving and s_t^K is saving through purchases of physical capital. Note that the budget constraints apply to all households, no matter which sector they are employed. This is because the wage is the same in either sector, and any household can purchase land or capital in national markets.

We are after a transition equation for physical capital intensity, so we need to start with an expression for s_t^K. Using (4.9b), the household's optimization problem can be solved to get the following expression for the household's supply of capital

$$s_t^K = \frac{\beta}{1+\beta} w_t D_t - p_t^L l_t \tag{4.10}$$

As in Chap. 2, equilibrium in the capital market requires that the capital demanded by firms for production in period t + 1 be supplied by household purchases of capital in period t, $K_{t+1} = N_t s_t^K$.

We define k to be the capital to effective labor ratio in the modern sector, so $k_{t+1} = K_{t+1}/H_{t+1}$, where $H_{t+1} = M_{t+1} D_{t+1}$. The number of workers in the modern sector is now a fraction π_{t+1} of the entire supply of labor, $M_{t+1} = \pi_{t+1} N_{t+1}$.

Using the same approach as in previous chapters, the capital market equilibrium condition is used to derive the transition equation for k as

$$k_{t+1} = \frac{(1-\alpha)Ak_t^{\alpha}}{\pi_{t+1}n(1+d)}\left[\frac{\beta}{1+\beta} - \frac{p_t^L l_t}{(1-\alpha)Ak_t^{\alpha}D_t}\right]. \quad (4.11)$$

Comparing (4.11) to the transition equation for the basic one-sector model, we see there are two differences. First, the number of workers in the modern sector is now endogenous, even if population growth is exogenous. Migration of workers from the traditional to the modern sector crowds the available capital and lowers k. Second, land holdings offer households an alternative way to save. The larger are the values of land holdings, relative to the household wages, the less saving is devoted to physical capital and the smaller is k. To use (4.11) to solve for capital accumulation, we must close the model by determining the paths of π_t and p_t^L.

4.2.1 Labor Market Equilibrium

The equilibrium allocation of labor across sectors is determined by the condition that the wage is the same in each sector. The flow of labor across sectors forces wages across sectors to equalize. Writing out (4.9a) in terms of the marginal products of labor and using the fact that $\tilde{H}_t = F_t\tilde{D}_t = (1-\pi_t)N_t\tilde{D}_t$ yields the following expression for the fraction of the work force in the traditional sector that equilibrates wages

$$1-\pi_t = \left(\frac{\tilde{A}\tilde{D}_t}{AD_t}\right)^{\frac{1}{\alpha}}\frac{\tilde{l}_t}{k_t}, \quad (4.12)$$

where $\tilde{l} \equiv L/N\tilde{D}$ is now interpreted as the ratio of land to the maximum potential effective labor supply in the traditional sector.

The relative size of the traditional sector's work force is determined by the relative productivity of labor in the traditional sector. The relative productivity of traditional labor is determined by the relative state of efficiency and technology in the traditional sector and by its relative factor endowment. The traditional sector shrinks faster, the faster is the growth in relative technological progress in the modern sector and the faster is physical capital accumulation. Even if (i) technological progress is uniform across sectors and (ii) capital intensity in the modern sector remains constant, the traditional sector will shrink because land becomes scarce relative to the economy's effective labor supply, provided there is positive population growth or positive technological progress.

4.2.2 Land Market Equilibrium

To determine the equilibrium price of land begin with the condition that the return to owning land must equal the return to owning physical capital,

$$\frac{p_{t+1}^L + r_{t+1}^L}{p_t^L} = 1 + r_{t+1} - \delta.$$

Using the profit-maximizing conditions for renting land and capital, along with (4.12), one can derive the following difference equation in p^L,

$$p_{t+1}^L = \left(1 + \alpha A k_{t+1}^{\alpha-1} - \delta\right) p_t^L - \alpha \tilde{A} k_{t+1}^{\alpha-1} \left(\tilde{a} \frac{\tilde{D}_{t+1}}{D_{t+1}}\right)^{\frac{1-\alpha}{\alpha}} \tag{4.13}$$

where $\tilde{a} \equiv \tilde{A}/A$.

The dynamics of the economy is solved by first substituting (4.12), dated for t + 1, into (4.11) to eliminate π_{t+1}. Equations (4.11) and (4.13) then form a system of first-order difference equations in k and p^L. We now have a two-dimensional system rather than the single difference equation that generates the dynamics in a one-sector model. Moreover, there is an important additional difference. We do not have an initial condition that pins down the initial price of land. In this situation, it is possible to have multiple equilibrium paths for the economy, each corresponding to a different initial value for the price of land. It is also possible that there is a unique price of land that is consistent with convergence to the economy's steady state. In this case, a *terminal condition*, convergence to the steady state, replaces an initial condition in determining the initial price of land. Whether or not there is a unique stable equilibrium path depends on the parameter values chosen for the model. We will address the conditions under which there is a unique equilibrium path in the next section. In this section, we sidestep a complete dynamic analysis by focusing only on the steady state of the economy.

4.2.3 Steady-state Equilibrium

With both a traditional and a modern sector producing the *same* goods, it is natural to examine the conditions where the traditional sector gradually disappears and the economy converges to a steady state where the goods are produced in the modern sector only. To begin with, the natural assumptions are that (i) technological progress is faster in the modern sector than in the traditional sector ($d > \tilde{d}$) and (ii) population growth is positive ($n > 1$). Under these assumptions, Eq. (4.12) tells us that if the economy converges to a given value of k, then the fraction of the work force employed in the traditional sector must go to zero. Furthermore, the rental rate on land can be written as follows:

$$r_{t+1}^{L} = \alpha \tilde{A} k_{t+1}^{\alpha-1} \left(\tilde{a} \frac{\tilde{D}_{t+1}}{D_{t+1}} \right)^{\frac{1-\alpha}{\alpha}}.$$

Thus, if the economy converges to a given value of k and $d > \tilde{d}$, then land rents must also go to zero.

Now, with land rents going to zero, one would expect that the price of land would also go to zero. Unfortunately, things are not this simple. It is possible for an asset that has no fundamental value, i.e., an asset that is not productive, to have a positive price. For land to have a positive equilibrium price in the steady state without a traditional sector, the two dynamic equations (4.11) and (4.13) must be satisfied.

For there to be a steady state k that satisfies (4.11) with $\pi = 1$, the term $p_t^L l_t / D_t$ must remain constant. This implies land prices must appreciate at a rate satisfying

$$\frac{p_{t+1}^{L}}{p_t^{L}} = (1+d)n. \tag{4.14}$$

Label the steady-state value of k that solves (4.11), when (4.14) is also satisfied, $\bar{k}$. Next, for (4.13) to be satisfied, with land rents going to zero, land prices must appreciate so that

$$\frac{p_{t+1}^{L}}{p_t^{L}} = 1 + \bar{r} - \delta, \tag{4.15}$$

where $\bar{r}$ is the interest rate associated with $\bar{k}$. Combining (4.14) and (4.15) gives

$$1 + \bar{r} - \delta = (1+d)n. \tag{4.16}$$

There could be a configuration of parameters where the $\bar{k}$ satisfying (4.16) also satisfies (4.11) because there are quite a few parameters in (4.11) that are not in (4.16). If both (4.11) and (4.16) are satisfied at $\bar{k}$, we would have a steady state with a permanent asset "bubble," i.e., land is continually appreciating despite the fact that land has no fundamental value.

To think about the conditions needed to eliminate the possibility of a steady-state bubble, note that if land prices go to zero, the steady state would be characterized by

$$k = \left[\frac{(1-\alpha)A\beta}{n(1+d)(1+\beta)} \right]^{\frac{1}{1-\alpha}} \tag{4.17a}$$

$$r = \left[\frac{\alpha(1+\beta)}{(1-\alpha)\beta} \right] n(1+d). \tag{4.17b}$$

If α is about one-third, as the evidence indicates, and $\beta < 1$ (future utility is discounted relative to current utility), then $r > n(1 + d)$. Next notice from (4.11) that $\bar{k} < k$ and therefore $\bar{r} > r > n(1 + d)$. This means that (4.16) is not satisfied because the return to capital, $1 + \bar{r} - \delta$, is strictly greater than the return to land, $n(1 + d)$, if $\delta \leq 1$. Thus, in this model, for reasonable parameter settings, bubbles are not possible. Eventually, capital dominates land as an asset, and land prices go to zero in the long run. However, it is interesting to note that perfectly competitive models without uncertainty, or special assumptions about speculative behavior, can generate permanent asset bubbles.

4.2.4 Extensions to Human Capital and Fertility

As in the one-sector case, the model can be easily extended to include schooling investments in human capital of children and an endogenous choice of fertility. We do this in Chap. 5, but would like to make one point here. Schooling offers an additional reason why an economy may move from stagnation to growth. Recall the possibility of a poverty trap from Chap. 3. More specifically, the theory of schooling from Chap. 3 is given by

$$e_t = \max\left[\frac{\theta\left(\eta(e_{t-1}/\bar{e})^{\theta} - \gamma T\right)}{\gamma(1-\theta)}, \bar{e}\right]. \tag{4.18}$$

Initially, the relative productivity of children, γ, may be sufficiently high that the optimal choice of schooling is $\bar{e}$. However, the appearance of child labor laws or compulsory schooling laws may reduce the employment opportunities for children and lower their relative productivity. If γ falls sufficiently, there will be a takeoff of human capital accumulation over time. Thus, policies that lower the relative productivity of children can create a takeoff, or at least an acceleration, of growth that compliments the advancement of technology in the modern sector.

Note also that one might give the traditional and modern sectors a geographic interpretation—the traditional sector is rural and the modern sector is urban. Suppose that to work in a given sector, the household must also live in that sector. Now think of an initial division of the population across the two sectors. Households initially born in the traditional sector might start with less schooling than those initially born in the modern sector, $\tilde{e}_t < e_t$ (perhaps because of a limited ability to enforce child labor laws in the traditional sector at some point in history or because of an absence of rural public schools). As indicated by the analysis in Chap. 3, the difference in schooling across sectors would also give rise to a difference in fertility, $n_t < \tilde{n}_t$.

If the underlying theory from Chap. 3 is used, then the differences in schooling and fertility are household-specific and will persist across generations. Thus, regardless of where the households choose to work and live, their past family history will dictate their fertility and schooling investments in their children. In future chapters, we will consider models where the family's locational choice can affect their fertility and human capital investments in children in this and other ways.

4.3 Two Sectors and Two Goods

Suppose now that there are two distinct goods. In the traditional sector, agricultural goods or primary products (O) are produced and in the modern sector, manufactured goods (Y) are produced. To simplify the notation and analysis a bit, assume that the agricultural good is only consumed by young households, and that $n = 1, d = \tilde{d} = 0$, and $D_t = \tilde{D}_t = 1$. These assumptions allow us to focus on the transitional dynamics associated with physical capital accumulation and expansion of the modern sector in a relatively simple setting.

Household preferences are given by $u_t = u_{1t} + \beta u_{2t+1}$, with $u_{1t} = \chi \ln y_{1t} + (1 - \chi) \ln o_{1t}$ and $u_{2t+1} = \ln y_{2t+1}$, and where χ is a preference parameter that weights the relative utility received from manufacturing goods.

The single period budget constraints for the household are $y_{1t} + p_t o_{1t} + p_t^L l_t + s_t^K = w_t$ and $y_{2t+1} = \left(r_{t+1}^L + p_{t+1}^L\right) l_t + R_t s_t^K$, where p is the relative price of the agricultural good. Household demands for goods and assets are then

$$y_{1t} = \left[\frac{\chi}{1+\beta}\right] w_t \tag{4.19a}$$

$$y_{2t+1} = \left[\frac{\beta}{1+\beta}\right] R_t w_t \tag{4.19b}$$

$$o_{1t} = \left[\frac{1-\chi}{1+\beta}\right] \frac{w_t}{p_t} \tag{4.19c}$$

$$s_t^K = \frac{\beta}{1+\beta} w_t - p_t^L l_t. \tag{4.19d}$$

4.3.1 Labor Market Equilibrium

As in Sect. 4.2, the equilibrium allocation of labor across sectors is determined by the condition that wage is the same in each sector. This gives an equilibrium condition that is similar to (4.12),

$$1 - \pi_t = (p_t \tilde{a})^{1/\alpha} \frac{l_t}{k_t}. \tag{4.20}$$

The new feature is that the relative price of agricultural goods affects the allocation of labor. The higher p_t is, the more labor is allocated to the traditional sector, when other things are constant.

4.3.2 Goods Market Equilibrium

The relative price of the agricultural good equilibrates the supply and demand for the agricultural product. The output of the traditional sector is $\tilde{A}L^{\alpha}((1-\pi_t)N)^{1-\alpha}$. Using (4.20), the traditional sector output can be written as $\tilde{A}L(p_t\tilde{a})^{(1-\alpha)/\alpha}k_t^{\alpha-1}$. From (4.19a)–(4.19d), the market demand for traditional sector output is $N\frac{1-\chi}{1+\beta}\frac{(1-\alpha)Ak_t^{\alpha}}{p_t}$. The equilibrium relative price that equates these two expressions is given as follows:

$$p_t = \left[\frac{(1-\chi)(1-\alpha)}{1+\beta}\frac{k_t}{\tilde{a}^{1/\alpha}l}\right]^{\alpha}. \tag{4.21}$$

The relative price of agricultural goods rises with capital accumulation because of rising demand for, and falling supply of, the agricultural good. Capital accumulation causes wages and the demand for agricultural goods to rise. The rise in wages in the modern sector bids workers away from the traditional sector and causes the supply of agricultural goods to fall. Both of these forces result in higher agricultural prices.

Note that substituting (4.21) into (4.20) yields

$$1-\pi_t = \frac{(1-\chi)(1-\alpha)}{1+\beta}. \tag{4.22}$$

Taking into account the effect of capital accumulation on the relative price of the traditional good reveals that the fraction of the work force in the traditional sector is constant. As capital accumulates, it raises the marginal product of labor in the modern sector and wages across the economy, which reduces the demand for labor in the traditional sector. However, capital accumulation also increases the relative price of the agricultural good, which raises the demand for labor in the traditional sector. Under our assumptions, these two effects exactly offset and the fraction of labor employed in the traditional sector remains constant. This is an interesting result because it shows that, in a closed economy, capital accumulation alone does not necessarily generate a structural transformation away from agriculture and toward manufacturing.

4.3.3 Land Market Equilibrium

We now turn to the determination of the rental rate for land and the equilibrium price of land. As in Sect. 4.2, the rental rate for land must equal the value of the marginal product of land in production, $r_t^L = \alpha p_t \tilde{A}(l/(1-\pi_t))^{\alpha-1}$. Using (4.21) and (4.22), the rental rate on land can be written as follows:

$$r_t^L = \frac{\alpha(1-\chi)(1-\alpha)Ak_t^\alpha}{(1+\beta)l}. \tag{4.23}$$

Capital accumulation drives up land rents by increasing wages and the price of agriculture goods. The higher the price of agricultural goods, the higher is the value of the marginal product of land and the higher are land rents.

Next, we move to the price of land as an asset. If both assets are held, the return to owning land must equal the return to owning physical capital,

$$\frac{p_{t+1}^L + r_{t+1}^L}{p_t^L} = 1 + r_{t+1} - \delta.$$

Using the profit-maximizing conditions for renting land and capital gives us the following difference equation in p^L that is similar to (4.13) in the one good case,

$$p_{t+1}^L = \left(1 + \alpha A k_{t+1}^{\alpha-1} - \delta\right)p_t^L - \frac{\alpha(1-\chi)(1-\alpha)A}{(1+\beta)l}k_{t+1}^\alpha. \tag{4.24}$$

Note that an increase in capital intensity lowers the value of the right-hand-side of (4.24), as the return to capital falls and land rents rise. This implies that future land prices must fall relative to current land prices to restore equality. Intuitively, the current price of land rises as demand for land increases due to falling returns to capital and rising land rents. This is different than (4.13) where capital accumulation has an ambiguous effect on land prices because, there, an increase in k *lowers* land rents (as workers are pulled out of the traditional sector as wages rise in the modern sector).

4.3.4 Transition Equation for Capital

The dynamic system is completed by deriving the transition equation for physical capital per worker. Using the same approach to deriving the transition equation as in Sect. 4.2 yields the following:

$$k_{t+1} = \left(\frac{1}{1 - \frac{(1-\chi)(1-\alpha)}{1+\beta}}\right)\left[\frac{\beta A(1-\alpha)}{1+\beta}k_t^\alpha - p_t^L l\right]. \tag{4.25}$$

Similar to (4.11), the introduction of two sectors and land has an ambiguous effect on capital intensity because there are two opposing changes to the one-sector transition equation from Chap. 2. The first expression on the right-hand-side increases capital intensity. This expression appears because only a fraction of the workforce, a fixed fraction under our assumptions, works in the modern sector and uses capital to produce. Since k is defined as capital per worker in the modern sector, the fewer the workers in the modern sector, the higher the capital intensity, when other things are constant. The second change is captured by the second expression in the square brackets on the right-hand-side. This expression captures the fact that land diverts household saving away from capital purchases, causing capital intensity to decrease.

We will examine the transitional dynamics associated with (4.24) and (4.25), a topic for more advanced students, but before doing so we begin by discussing the steady state of the system.

4.3.5 Steady-state Equilibrium

We can further simplify the dynamic analysis by assuming that $\delta = 0$. With no depreciation, the steady-state version of (4.24) gives us the following expression for the steady-state price of land

$$p^L = \frac{(1-\chi)(1-\alpha)}{1+\beta}\frac{k}{l}. \tag{4.26}$$

Using (4.26), the steady-state version of (4.25) can be used to solve for the steady-state capital intensity

$$k = \left[\frac{\beta(1-\alpha)A}{1+\beta}\right]^{\frac{1}{1-\alpha}}. \tag{4.27}$$

Note that (4.27) gives the same steady-state capital intensity as in the one-sector model. Thus, the two new forces in the two-sector setting, that affect capital accumulation in (4.25), exactly offset each other to generate the same steady state k as in the one-sector case.

An important implication of this result is that countries with different quantities of effective land per person ($\tilde{A}^{1/\alpha}l$) have the same long-run values for k and w. In a two-sector model with different goods, w is the purchasing power of wages with respect to manufacturing goods. The purchasing of wages with respect to agricultural goods is w/p. From (4.21), the greater is the quantity of effective land per person, the lower is p and the higher is the purchasing power of the wage in terms of agricultural goods. Thus, there is no lasting "natural resource curse" in this model, once growth is started. Countries with greater natural resources per person will be better off in the long run.

4.3.6 Transitional Dynamics*

We now study the transitional dynamics of the two-sector model. Analysis of the two-sector model is more challenging than in the one-sector model, where plots of the single transition equation are sufficient to determine the model's dynamic properties. One needs a solid background in undergraduate linear algebra to follow the steps. In addition, we also have the problem of the missing initial condition for the price of land that was not present in the one-sector case.

There is a nice mathematical result that allows us to examine the dynamics of the nonlinear system of equations given by (4.24) and (4.25) in the neighborhood of its steady state by studying a linear system of deviations in k and p^L away from their steady-state values. In the neighborhood of the steady state, the nonlinear system and the linear system behave similarly (see, for example, Azariadis 1993, 6.3). While this approach does not tell us about the global dynamics of the system away from the steady state, it does offer clues that may help in a global analysis of the nonlinear system based on numerical methods.

The linear system is formed by taking a linear approximation of the nonlinear system in the neighborhood of the steady state. A linear approximation of a nonlinear equation $f(x) = 0$, where x is a vector of variables and $\bar{x}$ is a vector of particular values of x around which the approximation is constructed, takes the form $f(x) \approx f(\bar{x}) + Df(\bar{x})(x - \bar{x})$. The notation $Df(\bar{x})$ represents a vector of derivatives of the function f with respect to each of its arguments, all evaluated at the point $\bar{x}$. Note that if $f(x) = 0$ is satisfied at $\bar{x}$, then $f(\bar{x}) + Df(\bar{x})(x - \bar{x}) = Df(\bar{x})(x - \bar{x})$.

To take this approach in our setting, begin by writing (4.24) and (4.25) as the following nonlinear system of equations

$$F\left(p_{t+1}^L, p_t^L, k_{t+1}, k_t\right) \equiv k_{t+1} - \left(\frac{1}{1 - \frac{(1-\chi)(1-\alpha)}{1+\beta}}\right)\left[\frac{\beta A(1-\alpha)}{1+\beta}k_t^\alpha - p_t^L l\right] = 0$$

$$G\left(p_{t+1}^L, p_t^L, k_{t+1}, k_t\right) \equiv p_{t+1}^L - \left(1 + \alpha A k_{t+1}^{\alpha-1} - \delta\right)p_t^L - \frac{\alpha(1-\chi)(1-\alpha)A}{(1+\beta)l}k_{t+1}^\alpha = 0.$$

Next, take linear approximations of F and G in the neighborhood of the steady state. Then solve the linear system and simplify to get the following linear system

$$\hat{k}_{t+1} = \left(\frac{\beta(1-\alpha)r}{1+\beta-(1-\chi)(1-\alpha)}\right)\hat{k}_t - \left(\frac{1+\beta}{1+\beta-(1-\chi)(1-\alpha)}\right)\hat{p}_t^L \qquad (4.28a)$$

$$\hat{p}_{t+1}^L = -\left(\frac{(1-\chi)\beta(1-\alpha)^2 r^2}{l(1+\beta)(1+\beta-(1-\chi)(1-\alpha))}\right)\hat{k}_t + \left(1 + \frac{r(1+\beta)}{1+\beta-(1-\chi)(1-\alpha)}\right)\hat{p}_t^L, \qquad (4.28b)$$

where the "^" denotes a deviation of the variable from its steady-state value.

The mathematics of linear difference equations system is well developed. To use the available mathematical results, it is convenient to express (4.28a) and (4.28b) in matrix form as follows:

$$\begin{bmatrix} \hat{k}_{t+1} \\ \hat{p}^L_{t+1} \end{bmatrix} = J \begin{bmatrix} \hat{k}_t \\ \hat{p}^L_t \end{bmatrix}, \tag{4.29}$$

where

$$J \equiv \begin{bmatrix} \frac{\beta(1-\alpha)r}{1+\beta-(1-\chi)(1-\alpha)} & -\frac{(1+\beta)l}{1+\beta-(1-\chi)(1-\alpha)} \\ \left(\frac{(1-\chi)(1-\alpha)}{l(1+\beta)}\right)\left(\frac{\beta(1-\alpha)r}{1+\beta-(1-\chi)(1-\alpha)}\right) & 1+\frac{r(1+\beta)}{1+\beta-(1-\chi)(1-\alpha)} \end{bmatrix}.$$

The solution to (4.29) can be written as

$$\hat{k}_t = C_1\lambda_1^t + C_2\lambda_2^t \tag{4.30a}$$

$$\hat{p}^L_t = C_1 e_{12}\lambda_1^t + C_2 e_{22}\lambda_2^t, \tag{4.30b}$$

where λ_1 and λ_2 are the eigenvalues of J, $\begin{bmatrix} 1 \\ e_{12} \end{bmatrix}$ and $\begin{bmatrix} 1 \\ e_{22} \end{bmatrix}$ are associated eigenvectors, and C_1 and C_2 are undetermined constants (Azariadis 1993, 4.1).[3]

Note that the dynamic properties of the system are determined by the eigenvalues. If the eigenvalues are less than one, then the deviations from the steady-state values will go to zero over time, i.e., the capital–labor ratio and the price of land will converge to their steady-state values. If the eigenvalues are greater than one, then the values of the capital–labor ratio and price of land will diverge away from their steady-state values.

As mentioned previously, the initial condition for the capital–labor ratio can be used to determine one of the unknown constants, but there is no similar initial condition for the initial price of land. One way of determining the second constant is to require that the system converge to the steady state. For this approach to work, the parameter values of the model must be such that one of the eigenvalues is less than one and one of the eigenvalues is greater than one. In this case, convergence to the steady state requires that the undetermined coefficient associated with the unstable eigenvalue be set to zero. In this case, there is a uniquely determined initial value for the price of land that is associated with a stable path to the steady state.

We can investigate further by using additional results from linear algebra that relate the eigenvalues to J. The sum of the eigenvalues is equal to the *trace* of J and the product of the eigenvalues is equal to the *determinant* of J. These results, and

---

[3] To review eigenvalues and eigenvectors consult the technical appendices of Azariadis (1993) or an undergraduate linear algebra textbook.

using the fact that $r = \alpha(1+\beta)/(1-\alpha)\beta$, give us two equations to solve for the eigenvalues

$$\lambda_1 + \lambda_2 = 1 + \kappa[1 + \beta + \beta(1-\alpha)] \tag{4.31a}$$

$$\lambda_1 \lambda_2 = \kappa(1+\alpha), \tag{4.31b}$$

where $\kappa \equiv r/[1+\beta-(1-\chi)(1-\alpha)]$. Using (4.31a) and (4.31b), we can compute the eigenvalues for different parameter settings.

Let us look at the case where $\alpha = 1/3$, $\chi = 2/3$, and $\beta = 1/2$. In this case, we find that $\lambda_1 = 0.6175$ and $\lambda_2 = 2.5346$. So, we have one stable eigenvalue and one unstable eigenvalue. Convergence to the steady state requires that the coefficient associated with the unstable eigenvalue be set to zero, i.e., $C_2 = 0$. Furthermore, the definition of an eigenvector (Azariadiz 1993, pp. 123–127) gives us

$$J\begin{bmatrix}1\\ e_{12}\end{bmatrix} = \lambda_1\begin{bmatrix}1\\ e_{12}\end{bmatrix},$$

which implies $e_{12} = \frac{\lambda_1 - J_{11}}{J_{12}} = \frac{\omega-\lambda_1}{\frac{(1-\chi)(1-\alpha)}{l(1+\beta)}\omega}$, where $\omega \equiv \frac{\beta(1-\alpha)r}{1+\beta-(1-\chi)(1-\alpha)}$. The remaining unknown is the coefficient associated with the stable eigenvector, which is determined by the initial condition for the capital–labor ratio. Applying the initial condition to (4.30a) when $t = 0$ yields $\hat{k}_0 = k_0 - \bar{k} = C_1$.

Our complete solution is then given as follows:

$$k_t = \bar{k} + (k_0 - \bar{k})\lambda_1^t \tag{4.32a}$$

$$p_t^L = \bar{p}^L + (k_0 - \bar{k})\left[\frac{\omega - \lambda_1}{\frac{(1-\chi)(1-\alpha)}{l(1+\beta)}\omega}\right]\lambda_1^t. \tag{4.32b}$$

Note, for the parameters chosen above we have $\omega = 0.3906$, so the expression in the squared bracket of (4.32b) is negative. If we start with a capital–labor ratio below the steady state, the capital–labor ratio rises over time because the negative expression, $(k_0 - \bar{k})\lambda_1^t$, becomes smaller over time. The price of land will start above its steady-state value, because the second expression on the right-hand-side of (4.32b) is positive when $k_0 < \bar{k}$ and falls over time. This was our speculation when we first examined (4.24); capital accumulation will be associated with falling land prices.

Remember that the analysis we just conducted is only valid when the economy is close to its steady state. To conduct a global analysis, numerical methods can be used to compute the dynamic path (e.g., see Hansen and Prescott 2002). If the parameter values are similar to the case we just examined, then it is likely that for an initial value of k there is a unique initial value for p^L that is on the unique convergent path to the steady state. One can guess a value for the initial land price and then use (4.25) to compute next period's capital–labor ratio and (4.24) to compute next period's land price. Iterating in this manner, the entire dynamic path can be solved. If the path is not converging to the steady state, then an alternative initial guess for p^L is tried. Searching over a range of initial values for p^L will eventually identify the convergent equilibrium path.

4.3.7 International Trade

We now examine the dynamics of the economy when there is international trading of goods across countries. We assume that the economy is "small" in the sense that its behavior cannot affect the international or worldwide relative price of agricultural goods, p^w. This means that the relative price of food is no longer determined endogenously by domestic demand and supply, i.e., (4.21) no longer applies. Instead, p^w is taken as an exogenous variable that is determined outside the model by demand and supply conditions in the worldwide market for goods.

The first important implication of opening the economy to trade is that one of the domestic forces that caused the fraction of the work force in the traditional sector to remain constant, as the economy accumulates capital, is now absent. Recall that capital accumulation raises the marginal product of labor and wages in the modern sector, which reduces the demand for labor in the traditional sector. In a closed economy, higher wages increases demand for all goods and services and increases the relative price of the agricultural good. This latter effect raises the demand for labor in the traditional sector. Under our assumptions, these two effects exactly offset and the fraction of labor employed in the traditional sector remains constant. However, the latter effect is now absent because the relative price of agricultural goods is fixed by market conditions at the world level, not the domestic level. An increase in the demand for agricultural goods simply results in fewer exports, or more imports, at the same world price.

In an open economy, the fraction of the workforce in the traditional sector is given by

$$1 - \pi_t = (p^w \tilde{a})^{1/\alpha} \frac{l_t}{k_t}. \tag{4.33}$$

So, capital accumulation serves only to raise the cost of labor in the traditional sector, causing that sector to contract with development.

Furthermore, we see that if the world price for agricultural goods increases, then the traditional sector will expand. This result is related to concerns that if a developing economy begins to trade internationally it may lead to "deindustrialization" (see, for example, Williamson 2011). The idea is that developing countries are likely to have a comparative advantage in producing agricultural goods. This implies that their closed economy relative price of agricultural goods is below the world relative price. When they open to trade, the relative price will rise up to p^w.

The higher the value of p^w, the more labor will be reallocated away from the modern sector and toward the traditional sector.

Many economists believe that there are several connections between the relative size of the modern sector and economic growth in the economy as a whole. We will examine the consequence of "deindustrialization" for growth and welfare in developing countries both here and in the models that we encounter in Chaps. 5 and 6.

With an exogenous price of agricultural goods, the dynamics of the economy change. With international trade of goods, Eqs. (4.24) and (4.25) become

$$p_{t+1}^L = \left(1 + \alpha A k_{t+1}^{\alpha-1}\right) p_t^L - \left(\tilde{a} p^w\right)^{1/\alpha} \alpha A k_{t+1}^{\alpha-1} \tag{4.24′}$$

and

$$k_{t+1} = \left(\frac{1}{1 - \frac{l(\tilde{a}p^w)^{1/\alpha}}{k_{t+1}}}\right) \left[\frac{\beta A(1-\alpha)}{1+\beta} k_t^\alpha - p_t^L l\right]. \tag{4.25′}$$

The steady-state equilibrium is given as follows:

$$p^L = \left(\tilde{a} p^w\right)^{1/\alpha}. \tag{4.26′}$$

$$k = \left[\frac{\beta(1-\alpha)A}{1+\beta}\right]^{\frac{1}{1-\alpha}}. \tag{4.27′}$$

Comparing to the steady state in the closed economy, we see that the price of land will differ but not the capital–labor ratio. This is due to two opposing effects of a higher relative price of agricultural goods on capital accumulation. First, a higher value of p^w raises land prices (see 4.26′). Higher land prices reduce capital accumulation by diverting more saving to land purchases (see 4.25′). Second, a higher value of p^w increases the employment share in the traditional sector (see 4.33). A smaller employment share in the modern sector reduces the crowding of capital and raises the capital–labor ratio. In the current model, these two opposing effects just cancel. So, deindustrialization only applies to the fraction of the workforce in the traditional sector. There is no negative long-run consequence for the capital–labor ratio in the modern sector.

If the long-run capital–labor ratio remains unaffected by opening the economy to trade, then the wage in terms of manufacturing goods will also be unchanged. However, if opening the economy is associated with a higher price of agricultural goods, then the purchasing power of wages with respect to agricultural goods must fall.

The same argument applies to the return to capital. Measured in units of the manufacturing good it remains the same, but it falls in units of agricultural goods. Finally, the long-run rental rate on land, $r^L = \left(\tilde{a} p^w\right)^{1/\alpha} \alpha A k^{\alpha-1}$, is now positive and increasing in the world price of agricultural goods. It is higher both in units of the manufacturing good and in units of the agricultural good (since $1/\alpha > 1$).

The steady-state welfare effects associated with international trade can be determined by writing out the indirect utility function of the steady-state household as $(1+\beta)\ln w + \beta \ln R - (1-\chi)\ln p^w$. In the steady state, w and R are unaffected by opening the economy, while the price of food rises. Thus, the developing country is worse off in the long run. This represents a counterexample to the notion that welfare must rise as a result of trade.

4.3.8 Transitional Dynamics in an Open Economy*

We can study the transitional dynamics of the open economy in the same manner as we did for the closed economy. The linear approximation to the dynamic system in the open economy is

$$\begin{bmatrix} \hat{k}_{t+1} \\ \hat{p}^L_{t+1} \end{bmatrix} = P \begin{bmatrix} \hat{k}_t \\ \hat{p}^L_t \end{bmatrix}, \tag{4.34}$$

where

$$P \equiv \begin{bmatrix} \frac{\alpha}{\pi} & -\frac{(1-\pi)k}{\pi} \\ 0 & 1+r \end{bmatrix}.$$

One can show that there is at most one stable eigenvalue associated with the linear system (see Problem 9). So, if there is a convergent path to the steady state, it is unique. For the same parameter values used in the closed economy setting, there is an array of possibilities for the open economy that depend on the international price of agricultural goods and the corresponding size of the modern sector. The lower the price of agricultural goods, the greater the size of the modern sector. Table 4.1 exhibits some possibilities and the corresponding value of the stable eigenvalue.

Note that the absolute value of the stable eigenvalue can be higher or lower than in the closed economy case. This means that the open economy *may* converge faster to the steady state than in the closed economy. For the parameter values chosen in the closed economy case, the steady-state value of π is a little over 0.85 and $\lambda_1 = 0.6175$. If opening the economy raises the relative price of food, then the value of π would be lower than 0.85. From Table 4.1, we see if the long-run value

Table 4.1 Open-economy dynamics

π	λ_1
0.5	0.6667
0.7	0.4761
0.9	0.3703

of π in the open economy dips close to 0.5, then the stable eigenvalue will be greater than in the closed economy case, and convergence to the steady state will be slower.

4.4 Declining Budget Shares Spent on Food

One feature of development, not yet captured by the model, is the declining share of household budgets devoted to food. Over two centuries of modern growth, from the mid-eighteenth to the mid-twentieth century, the household budget share devoted to food fell from about 60 % to about 30 % (Abdus and Rangazas 2011, Table 5). In contrast, if one interprets the traditional sector good as food, the current version of the model predicts a constant budget share.[4]

One way of generating a declining budget share is to change preferences so that a minimum amount of food consumption is necessary for survival—what is known as a subsistence constraint. We can incorporate a subsistence constraint by writing the utility benefits from food consumption as $(1-\chi)\ln(o_{1t}-\bar{o})$, where $\bar{o}$ is the minimum amount of food consumption needed to survive. With this new specification, the household's first period budget shares become

$$\frac{y_{1t}}{w_t}=\frac{\chi}{1+\beta}\left(1-\frac{p_t\bar{o}}{w_t}\right) \tag{4.35a}$$

$$\frac{p_t o_{1t}}{w_t}=\frac{1-\chi}{1+\beta}+\frac{\beta+\chi}{1+\beta}\frac{p_t\bar{o}}{w_t}. \tag{4.35b}$$

As wages rise relative to food prices, i.e., as the purchasing power of wages in terms of food rises, the share devoted to nonfood rises and the share devoted to food falls.

Fogel (1994, p. 377) points out that the concept of a fixed level of subsistence consumption is potentially misleading. He suggests that there are numerous possible combinations of consumption and health that are consistent with subsistence in a low income setting. Abdus and Rangazas (2011) follow Fogel's lead and provide an alternative approach to subsistence consumption that relates food consumption directly to health. They use the approach to explain why food consumption, measured by caloric in-take, has remained relatively constant over the course of development. This, in turn, explains the falling budget share devoted to food as income rises.

We can change preferences to include health benefits by defining u_{1t} as $u_{1t}=\chi\ln(y_{1t}Q_t)+(1-\chi)(\ln o_{1t}Q_t)$, where the utility benefits of consumption are affected by a health index Q_t. The more healthy the individual, the more he enjoys the activities that give him pleasure. The health index is defined as $Q_t=Q_t^*e^{-\kappa(b_t-b^*)^2/2}$.

[4] This need not be the only interpretation because primary products such as wood and coal might also be included.

The variable Q_t^* is an index of exogenous factors that affect health such as air quality, public sanitation, public health services, and working conditions. The endogenous component of the health index relates health to body weight. Body weight is a well-documented factor in determining health and longevity.

A standard way of recording body weight is the Body Mass Index (BMI), defined as weight in kilograms divided by the square of height in meters. The BMI that maximizes health is in the range of 25–26 (Fogel 1994; Costa 1996). Being too light or too heavy compromises a person's health. In the health index term, the actual BMI is denoted by b_t and the optimal BMI by b_t^*. The parameter κ quantifies the negative health effects of allowing body mass to deviate from its optimal level.

We relate food and work to body weight using the science of energy balance for the human body (Whitney and Cataldo 1983; Fogel 1994). Increased calories consumed as food will raise an individual's body weight unless an equal amount of energy is expended in (i) basal metabolism (the energy cost associated with keeping the body alive at rest), (ii) the thermic effect of food consumption and digestion (about 10 % of the calories consumed) or (iii) physical activity. Calories consumed in excess of calories spent are stored in the body as fat. For each 3,500 kcal taken in excess of expenditures, one pound of body fat is stored.

Scientists have estimated an energy balance relationship that relates daily caloric intake and calories expended in physical activity to the daily change in body weight. We are not interested in daily changes in body weight but rather in the body weight that an individual can maintain in the long term given a regular regiment of daily caloric consumption and physical activity. Toward this end, we use a steady-state version of the energy balance equation for daily changes in body weight. We solve the difference equation that determines the daily change in body weight for the steady state or sustainable body weight associated with different levels of caloric intake and energy expenditure that are maintained over the years. Furthermore, we express the relationship in terms of the body mass index.

The steady-state energy balance equation for an individual who reaches adulthood in period t is given by

$$b_t = \frac{0.9o_{1t} - \bar{b}_1 - \varepsilon_t}{\bar{b}_2 T_t^2} \tag{4.36}$$

where $\bar{b}_1$ and $\bar{b}_2$ are positive parameters that are determined by the physics of energy balance, ε_t measures the required average daily calories expended per unit of work, and T_t is adult height.[5] The parameters $\bar{b}_1$ and $\bar{b}_2$ capture the linear effect of bodyweight on basal metabolism and the energy expended in basic survival activity. The variables ε_t and T_t are both treated as exogenous here, i.e., we do not

[5] For further discussion and application of the energy balance relationship see Abdus (2007).

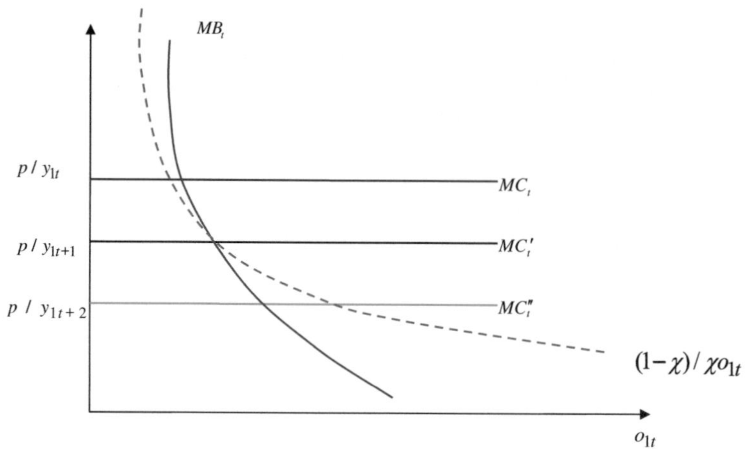

Fig. 4.1 Optimal food consumption

model the choice of occupation and the many factors that cause people to become taller across generations.[6]

The first-order condition associated with choosing the optimal demand for the agricultural good now becomes

$$\frac{1-\chi}{\chi}\frac{1}{o_{1t}}+\frac{(b^{*}-b_{t})0.9}{\bar{b}_{2}T_{t}^{2}}\frac{\kappa}{\chi}=\frac{p_{t}}{y_{1t}}. \tag{4.37}$$

Equation (4.37) equates the marginal benefit of calories consumed (left-hand-side) to the marginal cost of purchasing calories (right-hand-side). If b_t is less than b_t^*, then there are two benefits to consuming calories: the direct pleasure of food consumption (first term) and the increase in body mass that makes the individual healthier (second term).

Sketching the marginal benefit and marginal cost of food (other things constant) produces the optimal food consumption as shown in Fig. 4.1. The dashed curve gives the marginal benefit of food intake when there are no health benefits ($\kappa = 0$). Along the dashed curve, y_{1t} and o_{1t} increase proportionally with wages as the economy grows, for a constant p. A constant budget share devoted to food.

With $\kappa > 0$, the marginal benefit of food exceeds the pleasure of eating when incomes are low, causing food to be a larger fraction of the budget than when

[6] Establishing an endogenous intergenerational connection between child nutrition and adult height is difficult. In the nineteenth century, adult height in England showed no trend, despite a rise in per capita income. This puzzling observation has given rise to a literature that identifies a variety of factors that potentially affect adult height (Kirby 1995; Komles 1998; Voth and Leunig 1996). Modern studies also reveal the complex determination of adult height. For example, food intake is not strongly correlated with height (Graham et al. 1981; Asworth and Millial 1986; Mitchell 1962).

$\kappa = 0$. As income and y_{1t} rise over time, o_{1t} rises less than proportionally along the marginal benefit curve, resulting in a falling fraction of the budget devoted to food.

If the energy requirements of work fall with development and individuals respond by expending less energy, b_t increases for a given level of food consumption. This causes the marginal benefit curve to shift left over time and the optimal food consumption may remain constant or fall even as income grows. The leftward shift gives a second reason for us a declining budget share devoted to food.

Food consumption is most likely to rise when the health effects of food are small, i.e., when b_t is close to b_t^*. In this case, the marginal benefit curve is close to the dashed curve (where y_{1t} and o_{1t} increase proportionally). This helps explain the rise in food consumption in the late twentieth century when body mass was close to optimal.

The subsistence constraint also provides another mechanism that helps to explain the structural transformation. Recall that in the closed economy version of the two-sector model, the share of employment in the traditional sector is constant (see 4.22). With a subsistence constraint, this will not be the case. If there is economic growth that raises the purchasing power of wages across both goods, the fraction of employment in agriculture falls.

To see the reason for this result, let us go back to the simple subsistence constraint specification that does not introduce health benefits directly. With the subsistence constraint assumption, one can use the equilibrium condition in the market for food to write a new version of (4.20)

$$\frac{l}{k_t}(p_t\tilde{a}) = 1 - \pi_t = \frac{1-\chi}{1+\beta}(1-\alpha) + \frac{\beta+\chi}{1+\beta}\frac{\bar{o}}{w_t/p_t}(1-\alpha). \tag{4.38}$$

If $\bar{o} = 0$, then we are back to (4.22), where the labor shares across sectors are fixed. With subsistence consumption, if real wages grow in units of the traditional good, then the traditional sector employment share will shrink.

For example, for a given k_t, a rise in $\tilde{A}$ in our previous analysis caused a proportional decline in p_t, so that the labor shares remained constant. Intuitively, the rise in $\tilde{A}$ caused a proportional increase in the supply *and the demand* for agricultural goods, as the real wage in traditional good units rose, that kept the labor employed in the traditional sector constant. Now, a rise in $\tilde{A}$ will raise supply more than demand because the subsistence component of demand is not a function of real income. The amount of labor needed in the traditional sector to meet demand falls, causing a fall in the traditional sector's labor share. In summary, a higher value of $\tilde{A}$ makes it easier to satisfy the basic subsistence component of food consumption and releases labor to work in the modern sector.[7]

---

[7] In a complete general equilibrium analysis, there would also be a reduction in k as workers move into the modern sector for a given aggregate capital stock. For an analysis of the structural transformation that depends heavily on the demand side effects stemming from subsistence constraints see Herrendorf et al. (2014).

4.5 Conclusion

Sustained modern growth began around 1800. We think of the beginning of modern growth as coinciding with the appearance of factory-based production where man-made physical capital first became an important input. Ideas about what equipment and plants to build, and how to power and operate them using labor, had to evolve until the state of "technology" reached a threshold where these factories became sufficiently productive. The factories had to be productive enough to pay workers what they earned on the farm and capital investors a return at least as high as they could receive by owning land.

Country-specific characteristics caused the threshold level of technology to differ across the world, affecting the timing of the takeoff toward sustained growth. The required threshold level of technology is greater (i) the more abundant and productive is the country's land, (ii) the weaker are the country's institutions in creating the property rights and markets associated with producing and selling at a large and impersonal scale, and (iii) the stronger are the vested interests in the country that block the use of new technologies.

In addition, countries may differ in the fundamentals that determine the takeoff of mass education. Countries that move to prevent child labor and encourage schooling will create sustained gains in human capital and worker productivity that complements the growth in physical capital. A delay in the timing of the modern growth takeoff, by inhibiting the growth in physical and human capital, is one reason that countries fall behind, leading to the large income gaps we see across the world today.

Another source of today's income gaps is the pace of the structural transformation as an economy goes through the lengthy process of shifting it resources away from traditional means of production to modern capital-intensive production. In a two-sector setting, the accumulation of capital is more complicated than is suggested by one-sector models. First, the movement of labor out of the traditional sector crowds the stock of physical capital and lowers the capital–labor ratio (even if there is no population growth). Second, the presence of land provides a substitute asset through which households can save. The accumulation of capital may, in turn, exert a causal feedback effect on the migration of labor and the price of land.

In a closed economy with two distinct goods, agricultural and industrial, we saw that the pace of the migration of labor across sectors is not affected by the accumulation of capital. More capital raises the marginal product of labor and wages in the modern sector, increasing the migration of labor toward the modern sector. However, higher income also raises the price of food, which slows the migration of labor away from the traditional agricultural sector. In our model, these two effects exactly offset and the share of labor in the modern sector is independent of capital accumulation. Thus, capital accumulation alone may not be sufficient to increase the modern sector's labor share. In the same model, we also find that as the capital stock increases, the price of land falls. This helps to accelerate physical capital accumulation because more capital is needed to satisfy households' asset demand as the value of land holding falls.

Opening the economy implies the relative price of agricultural goods is determined outside of the country's domestic economy. This removes the positive effect of capital accumulation on agricultural prices, which speeds the migration of labor out of the traditional sector as the capital stock increases. For this reason, internationally trading goods can speed the transition away from the traditional sector. This result provides a possible counterexample to the deindustrialization hypothesis. The deindustrialization hypothesis argues that opening the economy to the trade of goods slows the structural transformation in countries that experience a rise in the relative price of agricultural goods. Here, we see that a jump in the relative price of agricultural goods does cause a decrease in the modern sector labor share, but it can also prevent further increases in agricultural prices as the economy grows via capital accumulation. This later effect serves to speed the structural transformation. This is just the beginning of our analysis of the effect of trade on growth and the deindustrialization hypothesis. We revisit this topic in Chaps. 5 and 6.

4.6 Exercises

Questions

1. Describe economic growth and cross-country income inequality before and after 1800.
2. Explain the difference between the following concepts.
   (a) price of land
   (b) rental rate for land
   (c) return to owning land
3. In the traditional economy, what happens to the following variables if the economy experiences a one-time unanticipated improvement in TFP ($\tilde{A}$)? A one-time increase in population size (N)?
   (a) wage paid to a worker
   (b) price of land
   (c) rental rate for land
   (d) return to owning land
4. Describe how we established the conditions required for modern growth and industrialization to begin.
5. What are some of the potential causes of the advance of technology in the pre-modern period?
6. Discuss some of the features of an economy that might delay the onset of modern economic growth.
7. Is population growth enough to shrink the relative size of the traditional sector and expand the relative size of the modern sector? Explain.
8. Discuss the major differences between capital accumulation in a two-sector versus a one-sector economy.
9. What is an asset bubble? Is an asset bubble possible in our two-sector model?

10. Explain the role of schooling in initiating or accelerating modern growth.
11. Is there a "natural resources curse" in the two-sector model? In other words, are households in an economy with a higher stock of effective land worse off?
12. Explain why when the economy is open to the trade of goods, the traditional sector shrinks with capital accumulation, whereas in a closed economy, the size of the traditional sector was constant.
13. How might international trade cause "deindustrialization"? Does this lower steady-state welfare in the two-sector model?
14. Do we know that opening the economy to trade lowers the welfare of a developing country in transition to the steady state?
15. Explain why taking account of the health benefits of food helps explain why the budget share devoted to the agricultural good declines with development.
16. Many economists argue that an increase in agricultural productivity shrinks the employment share of the traditional sector. Does this happen in our models?

Problems

1. *Scrimmage for 4.1.* Provide a derivation and an economic interpretation for the following equations: (4.3a)–(4.3c), (4.4a), (4.4b), and (4.8).
2. Sketch the relationship between population size and wages based on (4.5a). How would an increase in $\tilde{A}$ affect wages? Malthus conjectured that an increase in $\tilde{A}$ would NOT have a lasting effect on wages. Why did he did he believe this? (*Hint*: Do a little research and think of a connection between wages and fertility).
3. *Scrimmage for 4.2.* Provide a derivation and an economic interpretation for the following equations: (4.10) and (4.11).
4. Suppose $D_t = \tilde{D}_t$. Use (4.9a), and the marginal product of labor expressions in each sector, to sketch the demand for labor in each sector with the common wage on the vertical axis and the fraction of the work force in the modern sector on the horizontal axis. This is how the static-specific factors model is typically presented. Use the diagram to show how changes in $L, \tilde{A}, A$, and K_t affect w_t and π_t.
5. *Scrimmage for 4.3.* Provide a derivation and an economic interpretation for the following equations: (4.19a–d), (4.25), and (4.28a, b), (4.35a, b).
6. How does the diagram in Question 3 change when you have a closed economy where two distinct goods are traded at the relative price p_t ? Write out the value of the marginal product expressions in units of the manufacturing good in the same manner as in Question 3 and use (4.21) to eliminate the relative price in terms of its closed economy determinants. It will make it more clear that there is a unique equilibrium if the term $\pi_t N_t$ is eliminated from both wage equations before making the sketch. Use the diagram to show how changes in $L, \tilde{A}, A$, and K_t affect w_t and π_t. Next assume that the economy is perfectly open and repeat the exercise. In addition, show how a rise in the international determined relative price affects the labor share.

7. Fun with eigenvalues and dynamics. Check the robustness of a unique and convergent path for the closed economy described by (4.24) and (4.25). Keep the capital share at 1/3 and consider combinations of values for χ and β that are between 0 and 1. Report your findings in a Table
8. Derive the indirect utility function of a household in the open-economy version of the two-sector model. Use the indirect utility function to argue that steady-state welfare falls when developing countries with a comparative advantage in agricultural goods open their economies to trade.
9. Without using numerical values for parameters, argue that there at most one stable eigenvalue to the dynamic system given by (4.34).
10. *Scrimmage for 4.4.* Provide a derivation and an economic interpretation for the following equations: (4.35a), (4.35b), (4.37), and (4.38).
11. Use (4.37) to explain the configuration of Fig. 4.1.

References

Abdus S (2007) Obesity: a dynamic structural model of individuals' body weight choice. Cornell University, Ithaca

Abdus S, Rangazas P (2011) Adult nutrition and growth. Rev Econ Dyn 14(4):636–649

Acemoglu D, Robinson J (2012) Why nations fail: the origins of power, prosperity, and poverty. Crown Publishers, New York

Ashworth A, Millward D (1986) Catch-up growth in children. Nutr Rev 44(5):157–163

Azariadis C (1993) Intertemporal macroeconomics. Blackwell, Oxford

Clark G (2007) A farewell to alms. Princeton University Press, Princeton

Costa D (1996) Health and labor force participation of older men, 1900–1991. J Econ Hist 56 (1):62–89

Crafts N (1995) Exogenous of endogenous growth? The industrial revolution reconsidered. J Econ Hist 55(4):745–772

Fogel R (1994) Economic growth, population theory, and physiology: the bearing of long-term processes on the making of economic policy. Am Econ Rev 84(3):369–395

Galor O (2005) From stagnation to growth: a unified theory. In: Aghion P, Durlauf S (eds) Handbook of economic growth. Elsevier North-Holland, Amsterdam

Galor O (2011) Unified growth theory. Princeton University Press, Princeton

Galor O, Weil D (2000) Population, technology, and growth: from Malthusian stagnation to modern economic growth. Am Econ Rev 90(4):806–828

Graham GG, Creed HM, MacLean WC Jr, Kallman CH, Rabold J, Mellits ED (1981) Determinants of growth among poor children: nutrient intake—achieved growth relationships. Am J clin Nutr 34:539–544

Habbakuk J (1962) American and British technology in the Nineteenth century. Cambridge University Press, Cambridge

Hansen G, Prescott E (2002) Malthus to Solow. Am Econ Rev 92(4):1205–1217

Herrendorf B, Rogerson R, Valentinyi A (2014) Growth and the structural transformation. In: Aghion P, Durlauf S (eds) Handbook of economic growth, vol 2. Elsevier, Amsterdam

Komlos J (1998) Shrinking in a growing economy? The mystery of physical stature during the industrial revolution. J Econ Hist 58(3):779–802

Lucas R (2002) Lecture on economic growth. Harvard University Press, Cambridge

Maddison A (1995) Monitoring the world economy, 1820–1992. Organisation for Economic Co-operation and Development, Paris

Mitchell H (1962) Nutrition in relation to stature. J Am Diet Assoc 40:521–524

Mourmouras A, Rangazas P (2009) Reconciling Kuznets and Habbakuk in a unified growth model. J Econ Growth 14(2):149–181

Parente S, Prescott E (2000) Barriers to riches. MIT Press, Cambridge

Voth H, Leunig T (1996) Did smallpox reduce height? Stature and the standard of living in London, 1770–1873. Econ Hist Rev 49(3):541–566

Whitney E, Cataldo C (1983) Understanding normal and clinical nutrition. West-Wadsworth Publishing Company, Belmont

Williamson J (2011) Trade and poverty: when the third world fell behind. MIT Press, Cambridge

Part II
Dual Economies

Wage and Fertility Gaps in Dual Economies

5

This chapter begins our analysis of two-sector models where markets may be missing. Here, we focus on the fact that wages are lower and fertility is higher in the traditional sector than in the modern sector of economies. This has important consequences for economic growth for two reasons. First, the wage gap suggests that the allocation of labor may be inefficient—the movement of labor from the traditional sector to the modern sector should raise average labor productivity. Second, if fertility falls as households move from the traditional sector to the modern sector, then population growth will decline making it easier to increase physical capital per worker.

Sections 5.1–5.4 lay out the basic theory that explains wage and fertility gaps, based on an updated and revised version of the survey in Mourmouras and Rangazas (2013a). Sections 5.5–5.9 examine the assumptions and interpretation of the theory and provide some new applications.

5.1 Wage and Fertility Gaps

There is substantial evidence documenting the presence of large gaps in worker productivity across agricultural and nonagricultural sectors in the early stages of development (Caselli and Coleman 2001; Gollin 2002, 2004, 2014). To the extent that these productivity gaps reflect gaps in the marginal product of labor, they imply that labor is inefficiently allocated across sectors and that total factor productivity (TFP) and aggregate economic growth increase as labor migrates from the low-productivity traditional agricultural sector to the high-productivity manufacturing sector. Indeed, differences in the allocation of labor across sectors have been shown to explain a significant portion, and in some cases the majority, of TFP differences across countries (Temple and Woessmann 2006; Chanda and Dalgaard 2008; Restuccia et al. 2008; Vollrath 2009a).

S. Das et al., *Economic Growth and Development*,
Springer Texts in Business and Economics, DOI 10.1007/978-3-319-14265-4_5

Table 5.1 Dual economies

% modern	Productivity gap	Total fertility rate	Fertility gap
United States—beginning of the nineteenth century			
20	2–2.5	7	0.67
Sub-Saharan Africa—beginning of the twenty-first century			
29	6	5	0.66

Notes **United States**—*% Modern* is the percentage of labor in nonagriculture in 1800 (David 2005, Table 2.2, column 2), *Productivity Gap* is the ratio of nonfarm to farm productivity in 1840 (David 1967), *Total Fertility Rate* is average fertility rate for the entire economy in 1800 (Haines 2000, Table 4), *Fertility Gap* is urban to rural fertility rate in 1800 (Greenwood and Seshadri 2002). **Sub-Saharan Africa**—*% Modern* is the percentage of labor in non-agriculture in 1996 (Temple 2005, Table 1), *Productivity Gap* is the ratio of nonfarm to farm productivity in 1996 (Temple 2005, Table 1), *Total Fertility Rate* is average fertility rate for the entire economy in 1999 (Galor 2005) and in 2010 (UNESCO-UIS Statistics in Brief), and *Fertility Gap* is the ratio of the urban to rural fertility rate between 1996 and 2003 for 24 African countries (computed from Shapiro and Gebreselassie 2008, Table 1)

There is also evidence that the productivity gaps are more closely connected to differences in production method and institutional arrangements regarding ownership, than to the type of goods produced per se. Even *within urban areas* of developing countries, workers involved in modern firm-based production earn much higher wages than those involved in traditional family-based production (Rosenweig 1988, pp. 756–757; La Porta and Shleifer 2014). For this reason, it may be more accurate to refer to gaps between traditional and modern sectors, rather than between agricultural and nonagricultural sectors. It is primarily because of data limitations that most of the focus is on productivity gaps between farm/rural workers and nonfarm/urban workers.

Table 5.1 gives examples of two dual economies—one from the historical United States and one from contemporary sub-Saharan Africa. Both economies are dominated by traditional agriculture and have large productivity gaps between nonfarm and farm workers. The sixfold productivity gap in Africa today is particularly large, although it is likely an overestimate due to unmeasured output on family and communal farms that is missed by national income accounting (see, for example, Jerven 2013). The available survey data on wages and consumption reveals smaller gaps between nonfarm and farm or between urban and rural workers in Africa (Mourmouras and Rangazas 2007, pp. 38–39; Henderson 2010, Figure 4; and Vollrath 2009a, 2014).[1] Actual gaps in wages and consumption in current developing countries are much closer to the two- to three-fold range witnessed in United States history, but are still larger. For example, Young (2013) finds four-fold consumption gaps for a set of developing countries. We discuss conceptual and measurement issues associated with these gaps in more detail in Sect. 5.7.

[1] The same measurement issue can be raised about the historical gaps in the USA, but Alston and Hatton (1991) make adjustments for noncash payment and cost of living differences and find almost twofold real wage gaps as late as 1940. In fact, Herrendorf and Schoellman (2013) find similar wage gaps in the present day USA.

Fertility is a related determinant of economic growth that differs significantly across sectors. Table 5.1 indicates that in the early stages of development, average fertility is high. Moreover, fertility is much higher in the traditional sector than in the modern sector; 1.5 times higher in both of the dual economies in Table 5.1. This fact suggests that the movement of households from the traditional sector to the modern sector may lower the economy's fertility rate. Reductions in fertility and population growth associated with labor migration to urban areas have the potential to raise labor productivity growth by increasing the accumulation of physical capital per worker and by reducing the fraction of the workforce made up of relatively low-productive children and young adults. Thus, migration of labor from the traditional to the modern sector can increase economic growth directly, due to the gap in labor productivity, and indirectly by reducing fertility.

These observations raise the question of why large gaps in productivity and wages persist for decades. As indicated in Table 5.1, the fraction of the economy's workforce employed in the relatively low-productivity traditional sector is substantial. Why does not labor quickly flow into the more productive and high-paying modern sector to eliminate the wage gaps?

In this chapter, we use a dual economy approach to examine different explanations for how large productivity gaps can persist in equilibrium for long periods of time. We relate the theories of productivity gaps to theories of the fertility gap in order to provide a unified explanation of both gaps and their effect on economic development.

We begin in Sect. 5.2 with a survey of the literature that attempts to explain wage and productivity gaps in models while assuming complete markets for land and labor. The complete markets approach is useful in emphasizing alternative sources of wage gaps (e.g., migration costs and education differences). However, we argue that these sources are not sufficient to explain the persistence of large wage gaps.

In the main part of the chapter, Sects. 5.3 and 5.4, we discuss explanations for productivity and fertility gaps that assume the absence of factor markets in the traditional sector. More specifically, we review models where (i) production in the traditional sector is family/village owned and operated and (ii) there is an absence of formal markets for at least some of the inputs used in production. Thus, we focus on a fundamental source of dualism, the absence of complete markets, as stressed in the older literature (Lewis 1954; Ranis and Fei 1961).

We think of the existence and effectiveness of markets as differing across the two sectors as the markets for inputs used in the modern sector will generally be more developed, supported to a greater degree by formal legal institutions. In the traditional sector, informal family and tribal institutions govern the allocation of land and labor. Under this interpretation of the dual economy, the disappearance of the traditional sector is associated with the spread of formal markets for productive inputs.[2]

[2] One can also go deeper and explore the reasons why the formal institutions and related government infrastructure needed to establish well-functioning markets are not adequately provided to the traditional sector. For some ideas along these lines see, for example, Myint (2001), Galor et al. (2009), Acemoglu and Robinson (2012, pp. 258–271), Mourmouras and Rangazas (2013b).

In addition to Sects. 5.3–5.5 discusses the connection between missing markets and labor mobility.

5.2 Perfectly Competitive Markets in the Traditional Sector

There are several explanations for the wage gap that do not rely on incomplete markets in the traditional sector. Each likely plays some role in explaining the gap, but each also has limitations. More empirical research is needed to determine which of the various explanations, including those that rely on incomplete markets, are the most generally applicable and the most important quantitatively. However, we believe the evidence suggests that the complete market approaches taken thus far cannot fully explain large wage gaps.

5.2.1 Urban Unemployment

One way to explain a relatively low wage in rural areas of developing countries is to assume that labor markets exist and clear in the traditional sector, but that noncompetitive wage setting occurs in modern urban labor markets, say due to powerful unions, resulting in unemployment (Harris-Todaro 1970; Stiglitz 1974; Calvo 1978). The probability of being unemployed must be taken into account by those choosing to locate and work in the urban sector. A worker would only consider seeking employment in the urban sector if the wage there was high enough to compensate for the probability of being unemployment for some period. Thus, a wage gap between the modern and traditional sectors is necessary for equilibrium where workers locate in both sectors.[3]

There are several difficulties with this theory. Unemployment in urban sectors of most poor countries is not particularly high—certainly not high enough to explain large wage gaps (Rosenzweig 1988; Caselli 2005). There is also disguised or unmeasured unemployment in rural sectors (Stiglitz 1988; Mazumdar 1989), suggesting *urban* unemployment is less of a problem when viewed *relative* to unemployment in rural areas.

One way around the absence of high unemployment rates in urban areas, or more precisely the absence of large unemployment rate *differentials* between urban and rural sectors, is to assume that there is an informal or traditional sector located in urban areas. In the informal urban sector, workers are employed but at lower wages than they would receive in traditional agriculture. They are willing to endure this situation temporarily as they wait for high-paying government or union jobs in the formal sector to materialize. In this way, noncompetitive wage setting in the formal labor market of urban areas could still drive an equilibrium wedge between wages

[3] See Temple (2005) and Wang and Piesse (2011) for recent discussions of dual economies that focus on urban unemployment.

in urban and rural areas without the presence of relatively high unemployment rates in the urban sector.

However, there is evidence suggesting that the informal urban sector is not simply a "waiting station" for formal-sector employment. In many cases, the informal sector provides a lifetime employment choice that runs parallel to the possibility of working in the formal sector. As in the rural sector, informal urban workers receive lower wages than those in the formal urban sector. As compensation for the low wages, informal workers expect to eventually find greater rewards in the informal sector through some kind of entrepreneurial activity later in their life when they become owners or managers of informal businesses (Mazumdar 1989; Rosenweig 1988). This situation closely resembles a farm worker waiting to eventually take over the family farm, or otherwise own and operate his own small farm. The close parallel between the urban and rural circumstances of an informal worker provides further reason to focus on a formal–informal wage gap, rather than strictly an urban–rural wage gap.[4]

5.2.2 Human Capital Gaps

The formal sector, which by definition uses relatively advanced technologies and organizational structure, has relatively high payoffs to education (Herrendorf and Schoellman 2014; Vollrath 2014). Caselli and Coleman (2001) explain the declining wage gaps in the USA over the twentieth century by assuming that education only enhances productivity "off the farm." They argue that at the beginning of the twentieth century, high costs of education kept workers from leaving the farm for industry jobs. This caused the supply of qualified workers in industry to be low, creating a large education wage premium, which in their model also doubles as a large nonfarm wage premium. As the cost of education fell over the century, and the relative supply of workers in industry expanded, much of the wage gap was eliminated.

While the payoffs to education might be higher in industry, there is much evidence that they are also significant in agriculture—even in traditional agricultural settings (Schultz 1964; Harris 1972; Feder et al. 1982; Foster and Rosenweig 1996; Goldin and Katz 2000). In addition, some of the empirical literature on the wage gap adjusts for experience and education differences and continues to find that a wage gap exists. Mazumdar (1989, Appendix A) finds that wages increase with firm size (an indirect measure of formal production), for *given* levels of education and experience. Jenkins and Knight (Jenkins and Knight 2002, Table 4.6) find large wage gaps across rural and urban sectors in Zimbabwe for workers with the *same* years of schooling. In Europe and the USA during the nineteenth century, there were relatively small wage gaps *per hour* worked, suggesting that skill levels of

[4] The World Bank (1995) reports that 76 % of workers in sub-Saharan Africa are found in the informal sector—55 % are agricultural workers that own their own farms or work in village farms and 21 % are workers in services and industry.

workers in agriculture and nonagriculture were similar and that the payoffs to skill were not very different across sectors (Mourmouras and Rangazas 2009). However, as we shall see in Chap. 6, wages per worker may nevertheless be large because of differences in annual hours worked per worker across sectors.

Years of schooling for children of households in the modern sector are typically higher than those in the traditional sector (Cordoba and Ripoll 2006; Gollin et al. 2014; Vollrath 2009a, b, 2013). There is some suggestion that the "quality" of schooling is also different across the two sectors, as rural schools in developing countries are less well equipped and have fewer days of attendance over the course of a school year [e.g., Banerjee and Duflo 2011, Chap. 4; World Bank 2013]. The quality differences may explain some of the differences in the rate of return to years of schooling.

We show in Sect. 5.4 that human capital gaps can also create annual wage gaps by influencing fertility and hours worked across sectors. Looking at the direct effect of education differences on productivity per hour worked alone may understate the role of human capital in explaining annual productivity gaps because of the possible connection between schooling and hours worked. On the other hand, the human capital gaps themselves may be due to missing markets and the dual economy structure of poor countries. We will discuss the connection between missing markets and human capital in more depth in Sect. 5.7.

5.2.3 Unmeasured Home Production

At least a portion of the wage gap between nonagriculture and agriculture is due to measurement error and nontraded goods. Workers in rural areas spend a larger portion of their workday producing unmeasured goods that are consumed at home. Mueller (1984) finds that agricultural workers in Botswana devote less than one hour per day to wage labor and the trading, vending, and processing of goods. If these workers are measured as a full unit of labor and their output is measured based only on market transactions, then their measured productivity is much less than their actual productivity.

The measured output of workers in agriculture is likely below the actual output, but it is unclear how large the measurement error is and how much it impacts the productivity gap. As mentioned above, survey data on consumption differences, which would include nonmarket production, nevertheless imply there are large wage gaps left to be explained.

5.2.4 Taxes, Fees, and Migration Costs

Workers migrating to the modern sector are likely to face many costs not found in the rural sector including taxes, discriminatory housing costs, union fees, and the one-time cost of moving to the city. These migration costs imply that there must be a higher gross wage for workers to be willing to choose occupations in the urban sector.

Restuccia et al. (2008) assume that migration costs are the sole reason for the productivity gap between sectors. They focus on the productivity gap between agricultural and nonagricultural workers in currently developing countries. Similar to the estimates reported in Table 5.1, their estimates indicate that nonagricultural workers in poor countries are 6.7 times more productive than workers in agriculture. To explain a 6.7-fold wage gap requires migration costs to be equivalent to an implicit tax on wages in the formal sector of 85 %. The necessary implicit "tax rate" on nonagricultural workers would have to be even higher if one accounts for the fact that (i) marketed agricultural goods are also taxed, (ii) the relevant tax rate should be *net* of any transfers or services generated from the tax revenue, and (iii) shared tenancy arrangements in agriculture carry implicit marginal tax rates. In China, for example, the government's net tax rate on rural households is much *larger* than for urban households (Wang and Piesse 2010). There are certainly migration costs that limit the pace of migration out of traditional agriculture, but these large one-time costs seem much too small to explain large and permanent gaps in wages.

5.2.5 Summary

From our perspective, the literature that assumes complete markets in the traditional sector cannot adequately explain the large wage and productivity gaps that persist in the early stages of development. In Sects. 5.3 and 5.4, we focus on explanations that assume the absence of markets in the traditional sector. A major advantage of this approach is that it offers a single unified explanation of gaps in wages, fertility, and saving rates (see Chapter 6) across sectors.

5.3 Missing Land Markets in the Traditional Sector

This section extends the one-sector neoclassical growth model from Chap. 3 to a dual economy setting, with traditional and modern sectors. The key assumption creating the dual structure is that, in the absence of formal markets for land in the traditional sector, the children of traditional producers inherit the rights to operate a family farm from their parents. As is common in the literature, we assume farm land, or the right to farm the land under a tribal or tenancy agreement, is simply passed from one generation of farmers to the next [e.g., Bertocchi 2006; Doepke 2004; Drazen and Eckstein 1988; Galor et al. 2009; Hayashi and Prescott 2008].

We go one step further and assume the property rights over the farm are passed *only if* the children agree to operate it themselves—this ties the inheritance/management of traditional assets to occupational choice. Without an inheritance that is conditional on the recipient working and then managing the farm, family-based or traditional farming alone cannot explain why wage gaps persist in equilibrium.

To see this last point, suppose that the rights to family or village assets are not inherited. Instead, assume that all land is purchased in land markets by younger households and sold by older households [as in, for example, Chap. 4 and Hansen and Prescott (2002)]. In this case, there is no compensation for low wages in the traditional sector and no reason for workers to accept a wage gap between sectors. In the absence of moving costs and mobility restrictions, migration of labor across sectors would completely eliminate any gap in wages. Alternatively, suppose land markets do not exist but the recipient of the land bequest could own the farm in absentia, without directly working and managing the farm. Here, again there is nothing to prevent migration to the high-wage sector, so wage gaps cannot persist.

An approach based on a bequest that is conditional on the recipient working and managing the land is consistent with the strong tradition of family farming in the USA. The link between the farm and the family in the USA was surprisingly strong well into the twentieth century. At the turn of the century, the farm in the USA was still largely operated individually and organized around the family and most of farm labor was provided within the family. Even by 1930, only 42 % of all farms reported hiring labor outside the family (Ely and Werwein 1940, p. 162). As late as 1978, traditional family farms represented 88 % of all farms, accounting for 63 % of total farm production (Gardner 2002, pp. 56–57).

Intergenerational links to farming seem to be a common feature of developing countries more generally. Hayashi and Prescott (2008) claim that Japan's development was slowed by a social convention of passing the farm across generations within the family. Their paper includes a passage (pp. 605–606), suggested by Andrew Foster, arguing that the social convention may be strong enough to operate even in the presence of a land market. "First, the heir could sell the inherited farmland and live in the city to collect the higher urban income. However, to prevent this, the father could require the son to remain on the farm until he inherits the land. By the time his son inherits the estate, it may be too late for him to start a career in the city." Consistent with Foster's explanation, Collier et al. (1986) find that those individuals who indefinitely migrate away from farms in Tanzania tend to lose their land entitlement. In China, explicit migration rules cause migrants to the city to give up ownership claims to land and small businesses in rural areas (Au and Henderson 2006). Basu (1991, pp. 24, 131–133) discusses the difficulties of establishing property rights over land and the lack of land sales in rural India.

One could also broaden the notion of family inheritance, beyond land, to include inheriting the *skills* to operate a family farm or more generally a small family business (Lord and Rangazas 2006). For example, Hong Kong and Singapore went through the same coincident economic transformations and demographic transitions as other developing countries, without having economies that were based on agriculture to any significant degree. Despite the absence of an agricultural sector, there was nevertheless an economic transformation from informal home-based production to formal firm-based production. In Hong Kong, as late as 1971, 69 % of all manufacturing establishments were located in domestic premises. By 1978, as part of their "Growth Miracle," that share fell to 44 % (Young 1992, p. 19).[5]

5.3.1 Modern Sector

The modeling of the modern sector is taken from the one-sector model in Chap. 3. For the reader's convenience, we provide a quick summary of its main features here.

Producers in the modern sector are neoclassical firms with the standard Cobb–Douglas production function

$$Y_t = K_t^{\alpha} M_t^{1-\alpha}, \tag{5.1}$$

where Y denotes output, K is the physical capital stock, M is the effective labor supply in the modern sector, and α is the capital share parameter. The effective labor supply is endogenously determined by population size, the fraction of the working population in the modern sector, and the schooling received by workers.

The firms operate in perfectly competitive markets for goods and inputs. The standard profit-maximizing factor-price equations for the rental rates on effective labor supply and physical capital are

$$w_t = (1-\alpha)k_t^{\alpha} \tag{5.2a}$$

$$r_t + \delta = \alpha k_t^{\alpha-1}, \tag{5.2b}$$

where r is the net return to capital, δ is the rate of depreciation of physical capital, and $k = K/M$.

Fundamental household characteristics do not differ by sector. All households live for two periods, one period of childhood and one period of adulthood. Households value family consumption (c_t) and the adult human capital (h_{t+1}) of all their children (n_{t+1}). Preferences are given by

$$U_t = \ln c_t + \psi \ln(n_{t+1}h_{t+1}),$$

where $\psi > 0$ is a preference parameter.[6] This preference specification is a simple way of capturing the idea that parents value both the quantity and the quality of children. It has been used extensively in the literature on fertility and growth [e.g.,

[5] Focusing on this interpretation—the inheritance of specific human capital gained from experience and word of mouth—may be a way of explaining wage gaps in the presence of land markets. We explore this possibility in later chapters.

[6] In Chap. 6, we show how one can explicitly model the preference to pass traditional assets to the next generation, with and without land markets. Being explicit about this preference adds notation without altering any qualitative conclusions, so we treat it here as a social convention, that is not explicitly linked to preferences, as has typically been done in the literature [e.g., Drazen and Eckstein 1988; Bertocchi 2006; Hayashi and Prescott 2008; Galor et al. 2009].

Galor and Weil 2000; Greenwood and Seshadri 2002; Hazan and Berdugo 2002; Moav 2005]. For simplicity only, in this chapter, we avoid using a life-cycle assumption with two periods of adulthood or a bequest motive to generate domestic household saving. Instead, we assume a small open economy with perfect capital mobility. All physical capital is owned by foreign households.[7]

Adults inelastically supply one unit of labor. In Sect. 5.4, we relax this assumption and consider differences in work time as a source of the productivity and wage gaps across sectors. Children have an endowment of $T < 1$ units of time that they can use to attend school (e_t) or work ($T - e_t$).[8] Children have less than one unit of time to spend productively because in the very beginning years of childhood, they are too young to work and in older childhood, they do not have the mental or physical endurance to work as long as an adult.

While children may work as they become older, they are also expensive to care for and feed. To raise each child requires a loss of adult consumption equal to a fixed fraction η of the adult's first period wages.

Very young children are not productive but receive some early education. So each child invests at least $\bar{e}$ units of time into learning during the first portion of their childhood. This gives older children $\gamma\bar{h}_t = \gamma\bar{e}^{\theta}$ units of human capital that can be used in production during the later years of childhood, where $0 < \theta < 1$ is a parameter that gauges the effect of schooling on human capital accumulation and $0 < \gamma < 1$ reflects the fact that children lack physical strength or experience in applying knowledge to production compared to an adult. Adult human capital of the same person in the next period is $h_{t+1} = e_t^{\theta}$. Thus, a person is more productive in adulthood than in childhood because of greater strength and experience ($1 > \gamma$) and additional schooling ($e_t \geq \bar{e}$).

The household maximizes utility subject to the budget constraint,

$$c_t + n_{t+1}\eta w_t h_t = w_t h_t + n_{t+1} w_t \gamma \bar{h}(T - e_t).$$

In addition to the standard first-order condition for consumption, the choices of n_{t+1} and e_t yield the following first-order conditions

$$\frac{\psi\theta}{e_t} \leq \lambda_t n_{t+1} w_t \gamma \bar{h} \tag{5.3a}$$

$$\frac{\psi}{n_{t+1}} = \lambda_t[\eta w_t h_t - (T - e_t) w_t \gamma \bar{h}], \tag{5.3b}$$

---

[7] See Chaps. 6 and 7 for the more complicated closed economy case where domestic saving finances physical capital accumulation in a dual economy.

[8] The variable e captures all the time spent in school during childhood and thus is a function of the "quantity" of schooling, years, and also one dimension of the "quality" of schooling, the hours attended within a year, that has been stressed by Banerjee and Duflo (2011), Cordoba and Ripoll (2006), and Rangazas (2000, 2002).

where λ_t is the Lagrange multiplier.

Equation (5.3a) says the marginal utility of additional child quality must be equated to the marginal value of consumption lost from allowing children of working age to attend school. The strict inequality holds when the marginal cost of educating children beyond the schooling received in their early years, $\bar{e}$, exceeds the marginal benefit. In this case, parents are content to set $e_t = \bar{e}$.

Equation (5.3b) says the marginal utility of additional children must be equated to the marginal value of lost consumption. Consumption is lost from having additional children because we assume the cost of children exceeds the earnings that older children bring to the household.

Solving the model gives us the following demand functions for children and schooling:

$$n_{t+1} = \frac{\psi}{(1+\psi)\left(\eta - \gamma(T - e_t)(\bar{e}/e_{t-1})^{\theta}\right)} \tag{5.4a}$$

$$e_t = \max\left[\frac{\theta\left(\eta(e_{t-1}/\bar{e})^{\theta} - \gamma T\right)}{\gamma(1-\theta)}, \bar{e}\right]. \tag{5.4b}$$

Assuming that e_{t-1} is sufficiently high, an assumption that we make throughout, a dynamic interaction results that contributes to economic growth and the demographic transition.[9] Greater schooling raises adult earnings relative to older children's earnings. This raises the net cost of having children, so fertility declines. Reduced fertility and greater consumption lowers both the size and the value of forgone earnings from schooling children, encouraging a further rise in schooling. Thus, the sole factor driving fertility down is the rise in schooling.

5.3.2 Traditional Sector

The traditional sector differs from the modern sector because of differences in the production technology and because the technology and land used in production is inherited and operated by a family—creating lifetime entrepreneurial or residual income to supplement wages. For simplicity, we assume that the same goods are produced in each sector. This is a common assumption in the dual economy approach when the specific focus is not on the relative price of the different goods produced in the two sectors. While the framework is general enough to interpret

[9] In Chap. 3, we focus on the possibility of a poverty trap associated with initial conditions. If parents' education is not sufficiently high, the incentive to educate children beyond their early years is missing. Different initial conditions create schooling differences across sectors that cause productivity gaps. Here, we focus primarily on other sources of the gap.

traditional production as representing any informal business, we refer to traditional firms as "family farms."

Traditional output is produced using the following Cobb–Douglas technology

$$O_t = l_t^{\rho} f_t^{1-\rho}, \tag{5.5}$$

where O output, l is land per farm, f is effective farm labor per household in the traditional sector, and $0<\rho<1$ is a technology parameter. The technology differs from that used in industry because land is an input rather than physical capital. This assumption is meant to capture the idea that production in the traditional sector does not rely heavily on the plant and equipment used in the "factories" of the modern sector. In general, the labor-share parameter may also differ across sectors.[10]

There is no market for the land, either to buy or rent. For now, we will assume that there is a market for farm labor, so that households could hire labor beyond that provided by the family (although in equilibrium, because all households are identical, this will not happen). In Sect. 5.4, we consider how things change if there is no labor market in the traditional sector. We assume that the young household inherits the skills and land needed to operate a farm from their parents.

The presence of residual income from the inherited family farm and the fact that the rental rate on effective labor earned working on family farms ($\tilde{w}$) will in general differ from that earned working for firms (w) are two important differences between farming and working in the modern sector. Although not our main focus, we can also consider a third difference. Schooling in the traditional sector may lag behind schooling in the industrial sector. This could be because schooling became available in urban areas of the modern sector before the rural areas of the traditional sector or because it was generally harder to enforce child labor/mandatory schooling laws in the traditional sector. If initial schooling is lower in the traditional sector then schooling in the traditional sector will lag behind, via the dynamics of (5.4b), for every subsequent generation. These three potential differences will in general cause all farm choice variables to differ from those chosen in the modern sector.

The lifetime budget constraint for a household choosing to follow their parents and work in the traditional sector is

$$\tilde{c}_t + \tilde{n}_{t+1}\eta\tilde{w}_t\tilde{h}_t = \tilde{w}_t\tilde{h}_t + \tilde{n}_{t+1}\tilde{w}_t\gamma\bar{h}(T - \tilde{e}_t) + (O_t - \tilde{w}_t f_t), \tag{5.6}$$

where $O_t - \tilde{w}_t f_t$ is the residual income from farming. Maximizing utility subject to (5.5) and (5.6) yields the following demands for children, schooling, and farm labor

$$\tilde{n}_{t+1} = \left(\frac{\psi}{1+\psi}\right)\frac{1 + (\rho/(1-\rho))\left(f_t/\tilde{h}_t\right)}{\eta - \gamma(T - \tilde{e}_t)(\bar{e}/\tilde{e}_{t-1})^{\theta}} \tag{5.7a}$$

[10] We could also introduce TFP and labor-augmenting technology and allow each to differ across sectors, but this would not affect our major points.

$$\tilde{e}_t = \max\left[\frac{\theta\left(\eta(\tilde{e}_{t-1}/\bar{e})^{\theta} - \gamma T\right)}{\gamma(1-\theta)}, \bar{e}\right] \tag{5.7b}$$

$$f_t = \left[\frac{1-\rho}{\tilde{w}_t}\right]^{\frac{1}{\rho}} l_t \tag{5.7c}$$

Contrasting (5.7a) to (5.4a) reveals that production on the family farm introduces a new term in the fertility demand function, $\rho f_t/(1-\rho)\tilde{h}_t$, that raises fertility (other things constant). The numerator of this term is residual farm income, which can be shown to be proportional to the labor employed at the farm. The denominator is the potential "full" wage that can be earned as a worker, which determines the opportunity cost of having children. The more important family production is, relative to the opportunity cost of children, the stronger the demand for children. This is not a pure wealth effect, but rather is an effect that arises when one form of wealth, residual income from the ownership of family production that does *not* affect the net cost of children, increases relative to another form of wealth, adult earnings from work effort, that *does* affect the net cost of children. A shift in the composition of family wealth away from family production and toward adult wages causes the net cost of children to rise, for a given level of total family wealth, and the demand of children falls.

The demand for schooling takes the same form as in (5.4b), although there may be different initial conditions for households living in the traditional sector. There is no effect of family production on schooling because of two offsetting effects. To see these effects, first note that fertility raises the cost of schooling children (more children means greater forgone consumption of parents as schooling rises and child labor income falls). Second, note that the level of parental consumption determines the marginal *value* of forgone consumption associated with greater schooling (a higher parental consumption level means parents can better "afford" the lost consumption associated with more schooling). Family production raises *both* fertility and parental consumption, other things constant. As just mentioned, higher fertility lowers the incentive to school children, but a higher consumption level raises the incentive to school children. With our functional forms for preferences and human capital production, these two effects always exactly offset.

The demand for labor in (5.7c) results from the farm owner hiring labor to equate the marginal product of effective labor to the agricultural rental rate on human capital, perfectly analogous to the demand for labor by neoclassical firms in competitive factor markets. Note that we allow the demand for labor at an individual farm to be lesser or greater than the supply of labor coming from the household owning the farm. From the perspective of individual farms, some of the household labor may have to be supplied to neighboring farms or, alternatively, farm "hands" may have to be hired to supplement family labor supply.

5.3.3 Equilibrium

In a small open economy, the interest rate and rate of return to physical capital must equal the exogenous international interest rate, r. Equating r_{t+1} to r in (5.2b) allows one to solve for the equilibrium value k. Equation (5.2a) can then be used to solve for the equilibrium w_t.

A household born into the traditional sector has the option of staying there (receiving land and then farming it) or of working for a firm in the modern sector. Those who were born in families that work in the modern sector must stay there because they have no possibility of obtaining land. As discussed, fertility is higher in the traditional sector, so there must be some movement of the population from traditional to the modern sector, otherwise the fraction of workers in the modern sector would *fall* over time (contradicting the economic transformation associated with development). For there to be some movement, but not a *complete* shift of the population to the modern sector, the human capital rental rate gap between the two sectors must be such that a worker born into the traditional sector is indifferent about staying there.

Calculating the indirect utility function of the household under each option and then equating them gives an expression for the equilibrium human capital rental rate gap that makes traditional households indifferent about their locational/occupational choice

$$\frac{w_t}{\tilde{w}_t} = \left[1 + \frac{\rho f_t}{(1-\rho)\tilde{h}_t}\right]^{1+\psi}. \tag{5.8}$$

The term in the square bracket on the right-hand side exceeds one due to the residual income received from operating a family farm. Rental rates in modern sector must exceed those in the traditional sector to compensate for giving up the farm and its additional source of income.

The equilibrium rental rate gap is further widened by the fact that the exponent on the term in square bracket exceeds one. With endogenous fertility, being indifferent about working in the two sectors requires more than the equality of lifetime resources. The higher wages in the modern sector increase the opportunity cost of time spent away from work. Thus, working in the modern sector raises the cost of having and raising children relative to working in the traditional sector. This results in fewer children for nonfarm households. Given that parents like children ($\psi > 0$), they must receive a wage premium in the modern sector that compensates them for the fewer children they will have.

Finally, we must ensure that the labor market in the traditional sector clears. Let $\tilde{N}_t$ denote the number of households choosing the traditional sector. The aggregate demand for farm labor is $\tilde{N}_t f_t$. Each household supplies their own labor and that of their children to the market for farm labor. The aggregate supply of effective labor to the traditional sector is $\tilde{N}_t \tilde{h}_t \left[1 + \tilde{n}_{t+1} \gamma_{\frac{\bar{h}}{\tilde{h}_t}} (T - \tilde{e}_t)\right]$. All households that remain in the traditional sector are identical, thus in equilibrium, each household must demand enough labor to absorb the quantity of labor they supply,

$$f_t = \tilde{h}_t\left[1 + \tilde{n}_{t+1}\gamma\frac{\bar{h}}{\tilde{h}_t}(T - \tilde{e}_t)\right]. \quad (5.9)$$

The aggregate quantity of raw land is fixed at L. The quantity of land per farmer is then $l_t = L/\tilde{N}_t$. Thus, l_t falls over time as long as the population of farming households increases over time.

Equations (5.7a–c)–(5.9) determine the equilibrium paths of $\tilde{e}_t, \tilde{n}_{t+1}, \tilde{w}_t, f_t$, and $\tilde{N}_t$. In particular, using (5.7c), the number of farmers is given by

$$\tilde{N}_t = \frac{L[(1-\rho)]^{\frac{1}{\rho}}}{f_t\tilde{w}_t^{1/\rho}}.$$

The number of farmers is decreasing in both $\tilde{w}$ (the cost of farm labor) and the effective supply of farm labor from a farm family (to absorb a larger effective supply of family workers, more land per farmer is needed to generate a rise in labor productivity and a greater demand for labor).

The supply of *potential* farmers in period t includes the entire population of children of the previous generation of farmers, $\tilde{n}_t\tilde{N}_{t-1}$. In equilibrium, we must have $\tilde{N}_t \leq \tilde{n}_t\tilde{N}_{t-1}$. Along a transitional growth path, we will have $\tilde{N}_t < \tilde{n}_t\tilde{N}_{t-1}$, so that a fraction of the potential farmers leave for the modern sector each period. This implies that there are actually three types of households: (i) the original dynastic line of modern sector households, (ii) modern sector households that have migrated from the traditional sector, and (iii) households remaining in the traditional sector.

In general, the initial schooling of types (i) and (ii) will differ, causing the schooling of *all* households in each of their dynastic lines to differ during the transition. The schooling difference causes fertility of the migrant households to be different from a household whose dynastic line originated in the modern sector area. The migrant household's fertility is given by

$$\hat{n}_{t+1} = \frac{\psi}{(1+\psi)\left(\eta - \gamma(T - \tilde{e}_t)(\bar{e}/\tilde{e}_{t-1})^{\theta}\right)}. \quad (5.10)$$

Although the migrant's schooling is the same as workers that remain in the traditional sector, their fertility is lower because of the absence of residual income from operating the family farm. Thus, the modern sector will contain two distinct types—both of which differ from the household remaining in the traditional sector, along at least one dimension.

Both sources of the wage gap, rents from inherited land and schooling differences, help explain higher fertility in the traditional sector. Average fertility in the economy falls as schooling rises in both sectors and as households migrate from the traditional to the modern sector. The fraction of the population in the traditional sector shrinks as the effective labor supply grows while increasing wages lowers the demand for labor in the traditional sector.

Note that because fertility is higher in the traditional sector than it is for migrants, consumption for traditional households must be lower than for migrants in order for utility of the two households to be equal. If urban natives have greater schooling and human capital than the migrants, then they will have higher potential income. Since consumption is a normal good, this implies that they will also have higher consumption than migrants. Thus consumption will be highest for urban natives, lowest for traditional households, with consumption of migrant households in the middle.

During the structural transformation and demographic transition of the economy, the wage gap due to differences in human capital rental rates shrinks. To see this, substitute (5.9) into (5.8) to write the rental rate gap as

$$\frac{w_t}{\tilde{w}_t} = \left[1 + \frac{\rho\left(1 + \tilde{n}_t \frac{\gamma\bar{h}}{\tilde{h}_t}(T - \tilde{e}_t)\right)}{1 - \rho}\right]^{1+\psi}. \quad (5.11)$$

As the relative importance of child labor falls, due to lower fertility and rising schooling, the relative value of land rents falls, and the rental rate gap shrinks. Wage gaps due to human capital differences also shrink over time, assuming schooling is greater than $\bar{e}$ in both sectors. There is "neoclassical growth" given by (5.4b) and (5.7b), with schooling in the traditional sector converging to the schooling in the modern sector.

5.3.4 Summary

With an absence of land markets in the traditional sector, there is a greater tendency for land and family farms to be passed from one generation to the next. Historical and cross-country observations suggest that an important condition for receiving an inheritance of this type is that children remain in the traditional sector to gain the experience needed to operate the farm and "keep it in the family." This institutional arrangement ties occupational choice and geographic location to landownership in the traditional sector. In equilibrium, traditional workers are willing to take lower wages than those offered in the modern sector because they are compensated by rental income on the land they eventually own and by their larger families.

5.4 Missing Labor Markets in the Traditional Sector*

Chapter 6 documents that in the historical development of Europe and the USA, most of the measured annual wage gap between agriculture and nonagriculture was due to lower annual hours worked in agriculture rather than lower productivity per hour worked. In many developing countries today, differences in hours worked explain a significant portion of the annual gaps in worker productivity (Gollin et al. 2014; Vollrath 2013). In Chap. 6, we show how one can adjust the analysis of this Chapter to reinterpret the wage gap as a gap in hours worked. Our approach is to think of hours worked in the traditional sector as being *constrained* by the seasonality and the physical demands of traditional agriculture, and by the time spent securing property rights. Similar to Sect. 5.3, the loss in hours worked in the traditional sector is compensated in equilibrium by rents from inherited land and from a larger family.

Vollrath (2009b) takes a different approach and explains the shortfall in agricultural hours as a *choice* made by traditional farmers to work less than workers in the modern sector. This section follows Vollrath's lead and allows for an endogenous choice of work effort. An important assumption, needed to generate lower work effort as a *choice* of farmers, is the absence of labor markets in the traditional sector. We begin with a simple case where work effort is the only choice variable and then extend the analysis to include fertility and schooling.

5.4.1 Endogenous Work

In the modern sector, we continue to assume perfectly competitive markets exist for labor and capital as in Sect. 5.3. We also continue to assume that the international market for capital determines the return to capital, r, that the small open economy takes as given. The competitive wage rate is $w_t = (1-\alpha)k^{\alpha}$, where k is the physical capital intensity that satisfies (5.2b) when $r_t = r$.

As before, each household is endowed with one unit of time, but now, they can choose either to work, z_t, or to consume leisure (or engage in home production), $1 - z_t$. The modern sector household chooses z_t to maximize $\ln c_t + \zeta \ln(v + 1 - z_t)$, where ζ and v are preference parameters, subject to the budget constraint $c_t = w_t z_t$. The solution is $z_t = \frac{1+v}{1+\zeta}$. We set $\zeta = v$, so that the modern household chooses to work the full unit of time, as was assumed in Sect. 5.3.

Households in the traditional sector have preferences and skills identical to those in the modern sector. As in Sect. 5.3, assume that there is no market for the buying and selling of land and each traditional household inherits l_t from their parents (or is granted the property rights to farm a portion of village landholdings).[11] In addition, unlike Sect. 5.3, we now assume that there is no labor market in the traditional sector. The farm household is the only supplier of labor to the farm. The budget

[11] The key assumption needed to generate the shortfall of work effort in the traditional sector is the absence of a labor market. Vollrath (2009b) shows the result holds in the presence of a *rental* market for land provided the farmers themselves own the land and rent it to each other rather than from absentee landlords. The situation where farmers are the predominant owners of land is more likely where there is no *asset* market for land and the ownership of land is passed down from one generation of farmers to the next.

constraint of the traditional household is then $\tilde{c}_t = l_t^{\rho}(\tilde{z}_t)^{1-\rho}$, where $\tilde{z}$ is the labor supply choice of the individual farmer.

The solution to the traditional household's problem is $\tilde{z}_t = (1-\rho)/\left(1-\frac{\rho}{1+v}\right) < 1$, where $\zeta \equiv v > 0$. As in Vollrath (2009b), the traditional household chooses less work effort than the modern sector household because the diminishing marginal product of labor on the family farm lowers the marginal benefit of work relative to the situation where the marginal reward to work is determined by a perfectly competitive wage rate that is independent of the household's work choice.

The fact that the traditional household works less and enjoys more leisure implies that in equilibrium, in order to be indifferent about locational choice, the traditional household must generate less income and consumption. Thus, modern sector households have greater income, (annual) labor productivity, and consumption, all of which are compensation for taking less leisure.

5.4.2 Schooling and Fertility

We now show that the argument above extends to the situation where the quantity and quality of children are also household choice variables. The extended choice problem creates an interaction between schooling, fertility, and work effort that increases the wage gaps across sectors.

Now let total time be allocated across work, leisure/home production, and rearing children, so that leisure time is $1 - z_t - \eta n_{t+1}$. The modern sector household chooses z_t, e_t, and n_{t+1} to maximize $\ln c_t + \zeta \ln(v + 1 - z_t - \eta n_{t+1}) + \psi \ln h_{t+1} n_{t+1}$, subject to $c_t = w_t h_t z_t + n_{t+1} w_t \gamma \bar{h}(T - e_t)$. The solution is

$$e_t = \max\left[\frac{\theta\left(\eta(e_{t-1}/\bar{e})^{\theta} - \gamma T\right)}{\gamma(1-\theta)}, \bar{e}\right] \tag{5.12a}$$

$$n_{t+1} = \frac{\psi(1-\theta)(1+v)}{\eta(1+\psi+\zeta)} \frac{1}{\left(1 - (\gamma T/\eta)(\bar{e}/e_{t-1})^{\theta}\right)} \tag{5.12b}$$

$$z_t = \frac{(1+v)}{1 + \frac{\psi(1-\theta)}{1+\theta\psi-(1+\psi)(\gamma T/\eta)(\bar{e}/e_{t-1})^{\theta}}\left(1 + \frac{\zeta}{\psi(1-\theta)}\left(1 - (\gamma T/\eta)(\bar{e}/e_{t-1})^{\theta}\right)\right)}. \tag{5.12c}$$

The schooling equation is identical to that derived in Sect. 5.3. Although the form of the fertility equation is somewhat different, fertility is declining in schooling as before. The main new wrinkle is that now there is a connection between education, fertility, and work. One can show that as e_{t-1} increases, and adult human capital rises, the optimal level of work effort in (5.12c) also rises.

In most settings with log preferences, the rise in the reward to work has offsetting income and substitution effects that leave work effort unchanged. Here, as human capital rises and fertility falls, time available for leisure increases. The freed leisure time causes a decline in the marginal value of time and lowers the cost of market work. Thus, fewer children allows more time for both leisure/home production and market work.

The traditional household has the same preferences as the modern sector household and chooses $\tilde{z}_t$, $\tilde{e}_t$, and $\tilde{n}_{t+1}$ to maximize $\ln \tilde{c}_t + \zeta \ln(v + 1 - \tilde{z}_t - \eta \tilde{n}_{t+1}) + \psi \ln \tilde{h}_{t+1} \tilde{n}_{t+1}$, subject to $\tilde{c}_t = l_t^{\rho} \left(\left(\tilde{h}_t \tilde{z}_t + \tilde{n}_{t+1} \gamma \bar{h}(T - \tilde{e}_t) \right) \right)^{1-\rho}$, where family farm labor now includes the work time of the household's older children. The solution to the traditional household's problem is

$$\tilde{e}_t = \max \left[\frac{\theta \left(\eta (\tilde{e}_{t-1}/\bar{e})^{\theta} - \gamma T \right)}{\gamma (1-\theta)}, \bar{e} \right] \tag{5.13a}$$

$$\tilde{n}_{t+1} = \frac{\tilde{\psi}(1-\theta)(1+v)}{\eta(1+\tilde{\psi}+\tilde{\zeta})} \frac{1}{\left(1 - (\gamma T/\eta)(\bar{e}/e_{t-1})^{\theta}\right)} \tag{5.13b}$$

$$\tilde{z}_t = \frac{(1+v)}{1 + \frac{\tilde{\psi}(1-\theta)}{1+\theta\tilde{\psi} - (1+\tilde{\psi})(\gamma T/\eta)(\bar{e}/\tilde{e}_{t-1})^{\theta}} \left(1 + \frac{\tilde{\zeta}}{\tilde{\psi}(1-\theta)} \left(1 - (\gamma T/\eta)(\bar{e}/\tilde{e}_{t-1})^{\theta} \right) \right)}, \tag{5.13c}$$

where $\tilde{\psi} \equiv \psi/(1-\rho)$ and $\tilde{\zeta} \equiv \zeta/(1-\rho)$.

The form of (5.13a–c) is the same as (5.12a–c), except that $\tilde{\psi} > \psi$ and $\tilde{\zeta} > \zeta$. The presence of diminishing marginal productivity to family labor $(1-\rho<1)$ has an effect on behavior that is equivalent to raising the relative value of fertility and leisure time. One can show that this implies $\tilde{z}_t < z_t$ and $\tilde{n}_{t+1} > n_{t+1}$, so traditional households work less and have more children than modern sector households. This is true even if there is no difference in schooling across sectors. In equilibrium, this implies consumption, and income of traditional households is lower than in modern households.

As discussed in the case of the modern sector household we know, when e_{t-1} increases, and adult human capital rises, the optimal level of work effort also rises. The same dynamic is true of traditional households. Thus, any differences in schooling across sectors not only increases the productivity gap directly but also does so indirectly by creating a larger gap in market work effort. Just as schooling is one of the fundamental causes of fertility differences across sectors, schooling is also one of the causal factors in explaining differences in market hours.

5.4.3 Summary

The absence of a labor market in the traditional sector causes family producers to rely on family labor. The diminishing returns to work on the family farm lower the reward to work relative to a market setting where the competitive market wage is independent of an individual's labor supply choice. The absence of a labor market therefore leads to less work in the traditional sector creating an annual wage gap due to differences in hours worked.

A difference in schooling across sectors widens the difference in hours worked. More schooling lowers fertility and frees time for leisure and work. Thus, greater schooling and lower fertility in the modern sector lead to greater hours of market work per adult worker and a larger annual wage gap. This particular effect applies even when there are complete markets in both sectors.

5.5 The Forces that Bind Us: Missing Markets and Labor Mobility

In this section, we present additional discussion of the ways missing markets restrict labor mobility, using examples from historical and current development.

5.5.1 Missing Land Markets in Historical Development

Alan Macfarlane wrote an influential work on the early history of the English economy called the *Origins of English Individualism* (1978a). The study sought to determine the importance of the traditional sector, or what Macfarlane called the peasant economy, in English history. In a summary of his work, Macfarlane (1978b, p. 256) characterized the peasant economy as being centered around the family, in the same way we are thinking about the traditional sector in our dual economy model.

> For our purposes, the central feature is that ownership is not individualized. It was not the single individual who exclusively owned the productive resources, but rather the household. Thus, the heirs have as much right to the resources as the present "owners." The present occupants of the land are managers of an estate; they cannot disinherit their heirs, and the father is merely the leader of a production team. This is an ideal-type situation, but something like it has been documented for many parts of the world up to this century, for instance in Eastern Europe, India, and China. In this situation, farm labor is family labor. Hired labor is almost totally absent. Production is mainly for use, rather than for exchange in a market. Cash is only occasionally used within the local community. Land is not viewed as a commodity which can be easily bought and sold. There is a strong emotional identification with a particular geographic area. Consequently, there is rather little geographic mobility: Any movement to the towns is one-way, with few people returning to the countryside.

Macfarlane argued that while the traditional economy was important in most of Europe through the nineteenth century, it had almost disappeared in England centuries earlier. Even before the sixteenth century in England, he argues (1978b, p. 257)

> These again gave no hint that on any of the criteria elaborated above, England faintly resembled a peasant society. Land is a marketable commodity, geographic and social mobility is widespread, property is held by the individual rather than the family.

He cites visitors to England from Europe that noted this feature of the economy with surprise and concluded that "individualism" was unique to England. He also suggested that this helps explain why the industrial revolution started there, rather than in other countries of Europe.

Research motivated by Macfarlane's work has generally confirmed that land markets existed in England early on. There was clearly the legal right to disinherit and to buy and sell land freely. The question is the extent to which the legal rights were actually used. In a review of the recent evidence on the matter, French and Hoyle (2003, p. 261) conclude that while land markets and legal rights to buy and sell existed, they were not used frequently.

> No one would deny that the English had the right to buy and sell land without reference to their kin (although they might give them the first option). However, we now have some indication of how often they sold their land and the answer is not often.

Thus, in traditional settings, even when land markets exist, most households behave as if they do not. This is evidently due to some preference to keep the land within the family. Assuming that land markets do not exist can be viewed as a modeling shortcut that includes situations where there literally are no markets, which certainly is the case in many settings, and where there are markets that are rarely utilized.

In Chap. 6, we show how one can model the preference to keep land or the farm in the family. In Chap. 7, we argue that it is not just the land or assets that bind the family together in traditional settings. In addition to possible physical inheritance, children gain specific human capital, local business knowledge, and community relationships when they work in the family business of the traditional sector. In short, they inherit the traditional sector technology.

5.5.2 Missing Land Markets in Cities of Currently Developing Countries

As we mentioned in the introduction to this chapter, the traditional sector extends beyond rural areas. Many cities of developing countries have large informal sectors that share many of the characteristics of the rural traditional sector. One of the most important common characteristics is the absence of formal land markets. Field (2007) examines the effect of missing land markets on the labor supply of urban households.

The lack of formal property rights on landholdings forces urban households in the informal sector to expend resources guarding their property. Protecting their landholdings diverts labor time from the market and production. Field estimates the magnitude of the effect on labor supply using data from a nationwide program in Peru that issued formal property titles to more than 1.2 million urban households between 1995 and 2003—the first major titling effort in the developing world. Her objective was to assess whether security improvements associated with titling increased hours worked in the formal labor market.

Field finds that households with no legal claim to property spend 13 h a week maintaining security. They are also 40 % more likely to work at home rather than in the market. Overall, household labor supply was 16 h a week greater for households with titled property. Another consequence of titling was a reduction in child labor. Evidently, child labor is used to compensate for the lost market work of adults who spend time securing their untitled property.

5.5.3 Missing Credit and Insurance Markets in Current Development

Munshi and Rosenzweig (2009) provide a different example of how missing markets can lower labor mobility. They begin by acknowledging that the mechanisms we have been stressing generally serve to restrict labor mobility in developing countries (p. 1).

> Increased mobility is the hallmark of a developing economy. Although individuals might be tied to the land they were born on and the occupations that they inherit from their parents in a traditional economy, the emergence of markets allows individuals to seek jobs and locations that are best suited to their talents and abilities.

However, their main goal was to explain the unusually weak labor mobility in India. Their explanation is based on missing credit and insurance markets, rather than missing land markets.

India's labor mobility significantly lags that of other developing countries of similar size and state of development. In 1975, China, Indonesia, India, and Nigeria all had adult populations that were between 17 and 24 % urbanized. In 2000, the urbanization rate was between 35 and 45 % for China, Indonesia, and Nigeria, but was only about 27 % for India. Generally, India's urbanization rate is about 15 % points lower than that of other developing countries with comparable per capita income. The permanent migration rate of Indian men out of their original village is less than 10 %.

Munshi and Rosenzweig provide evidence that workers in India have low mobility because they are bound to their villages by the services provided by rural *jati*-based communities. In the absence of formal credit and insurance markets, *Jatis* (tribes or clans) have been active in smoothing household consumption for centuries. The *Jati* social network is effective in providing loans and insurance because of its ability to monitor, and potentially punish, behavior of local villagers. While households could instead obtain informal credit from moneylenders and employers, the cost tends to be much higher.

Thus, similar to missing land markets, missing credit and insurance markets can restrict the movement of labor out of the traditional sector. Relatively low-cost financial services in the village cause households to ignore better work opportunities in the modern sector.

5.6 Asian Growth Miracles

We can talk more explicitly about the connection between the structural transformation and growth by writing out the model's expression for worker productivity. Worker productivity is the total output of modern sector firms and traditional sector producers, divided by the total population of workers. The population of workers includes the older children who do not attend school. For simplicity, in writing out the average productivity expression, we assume the labor share and schooling are equal across sectors. Worker productivity is then

$$\frac{Y_t + \tilde{N}_t O_t}{N_t^* + N_{t+1}^*(T - e_t) + \tilde{N}_t + \tilde{N}_{t+1}(T - e_t)},$$

where N_t^* denotes the number of modern sector households.

Begin by noting that the first-order conditions related to the production decisions in each sector imply labor shares are a constant fraction of output. This allows us to write output in terms of total wages in each sector,

$$\frac{\frac{w_t M_t}{1-\alpha} + \tilde{N}_t \frac{\tilde{w}_t f_t}{1-\alpha}}{N_t^* + N_{t+1}^*(T - e_t) + \tilde{N}_t + \tilde{N}_{t+1}(T - e_t)}.$$

Next, note that the effective labor supply of modern sector households, in adult equivalent units, can be written as $h_t(1 - \eta n_{t+1}) + n_{t+1}\gamma \bar{h}(T - e_t) = h_t \frac{1}{1+\psi}$. Thus, the net effect of bearing children, even when taking into account child labor, is to reduce the family's adult equivalent work hours from 1 to $\frac{1}{1+\psi}$. The analogous expression for a traditional sector household is $\frac{1}{1+\psi} - \frac{\psi}{(1+\psi)(1-\alpha)} \frac{\alpha f_t}{h_t}$. The effective labor supply from traditional households is smaller because they have more children as a result of the presence of nonlabor income later in life. Using this result, and noting that $M_t = N_t h_t/(1 + \psi)$, allows us to write worker productivity as

$$\frac{w_t h_t}{1-\alpha} \frac{\pi_t \frac{1}{1+\psi} + (1 - \pi_t)\frac{\tilde{w}_t}{w_t}\left(\frac{1}{1+\psi} - \frac{\psi}{(1+\psi)(1-\alpha)} \frac{\alpha f_t}{h_t}\right)}{1 + (T - e_t)(\pi_t n_{t+1} + (1 - \pi_t)\tilde{n}_{t+1})}. \tag{5.14}$$

Now it is easy to see that as π increases, other things constant, output per worker will rise for three reasons. First, workers are more productive per unit of labor supply in the modern sector (as reflected in the wage gap). Second, households in the modern sector have a higher effective labor supply (since they have fewer children). Third, there are fewer child workers, lowering the supply of labor for a given level of output. This analysis ignores any changes in human capital accumulation and any effects of the structural transformation on saving and physical capital accumulation (to be discussed in Chaps. 6 and 7).

In a famous paper, Young (1995) conducts a careful growth accounting for the four Asian Tiger's "Growth Miracles." Hong Kong, Singapore, South Korea, and Taiwan experienced annual growth in labor productivity between 4 and 6 % for more than a quarter century. Hong Kong and Singapore are city-states without agricultural sectors and thus did not experience structural transformations in the usual sense. South Korea and Taiwan did see large reallocations of labor away from agriculture and toward manufacturing. Young estimates that the reallocation of labor raised annual growth rates in worker productivity by 0.7 % points in South Korea and 0.6 % points in Taiwan.

Although increasing growth rates between ½ and 1 % point per year is a large effect, it is an underestimate of the impact of the structural transformation. His measurement approach does not link the structural transformation to human and physical capital accumulation through fertility effects. For example, he carefully accounts for many determinants of human capital including a worker's age. The reduction in fertility associated with the structural transformation reduces the fraction of the workforce that is very young and raises human capital per worker. As suggested above, there are also links between the structural transformation and saving, as we will see in Chaps. 6 and 7, that raise physical capital per worker.

China has internal restrictions that inhibit the movement of labor from rural to urban areas to a greater degree than in South Korea and Taiwan, as we will discuss in more detail in Chap. 8. These restrictions on labor mobility add to the wage gaps across agriculture and manufacturing sectors that are created by the family farming mechanism highlighted in this chapter. As China has grown, more labor has been allowed to migrate to the manufacturing sector to ease labor shortages. The large gaps in labor productivity across sectors imply a large potential output gain from labor reallocation. Bosworth and Collins (2008) estimate that the reallocation of labor in China raised growth rates in worker productivity by 1.7 % points from 1978 to 1993 and by 1.2 % points from 1993 to 2004.

5.6.1 Asia and Africa

If several Asian countries have experienced Growth Miracles, why haven't more African countries? This is made more puzzling by the fact that one of the most impressive Growth Miracles belongs to Botswana, whose per capita income grew 7.7 % per year from 1965 to 1998.[12] Botswana's Growth Miracle arose from some very unfavorable initial conditions: The country is landlocked (bad for trade), has a tropical climate (bad for health), abundant diamonds (a natural resource curse in

[12] In the last couple of decades, Africa as a whole has experienced above-average growth that has led to some convergence to the living standards of richer countries (Miguel 2009; Young 2012). However, there are concerns over whether the growth can be sustained because it is heavily dependent on international commodity prices and because progress in the political institutions of many Africa countries is uncertain. In fact, optimism about African convergence has waned in recent years [see, for example, The Economist (2014)].

other African countries), and who, after gaining independence from Britain in 1966, had little public infrastructure and only two secondary schools in the entire country (Acemoglu et al. 2003). If Botswana can experience a Growth Miracle, why can't other African countries?

McMillan and Rodrik (2011) provide a clue. They document large productivity gaps, between two- and four-fold, across traditional and modern sectors of developing countries. Due to these productivity gaps, they view the flow of labor across sectors as an important driver of a country's economic growth. In particular, they find that the labor flows associated with the structural transformation can explain much of the difference in economic growth between Asian and African countries from 1990 to 2005. While Asian countries have generally experienced a flow of labor away from traditional agriculture and informal urban production, enhancing their economic growth due to the labor productivity gap, African labor flows have gone in the opposite direction, lowering their economic growth. From 1990 to 2005, per capita income in Asian countries grew 3 % points higher than in Africa. McMillan and Rodrik estimate that labor flows over this period increased Asian growth by 0.54 % per year and reduced African growth by 1.3 % per year. Thus, 1.84 % points of the 3 % point difference in growth can be attributed to differences in labor flows.

McMillan and Rodrik explain the different experiences of Asian and Africa based on different responses to increased openness of their economies. In labor-abundant Asia, international trade created an expansion in the low-skilled manufacturing sector. In resource-abundant Africa, openness created an expansion in the commodity and agricultural sectors. In effect, opening their economies to trade has caused Africa to "deindustrialize" causing labor to flow from high to low productivity uses. We first encountered the "deindustrialization" hypothesis in Chap. 4 and will explore it further in Chap. 6. The McMillan and Rodrik study shows that trade can have negative effects on growth by slowing or reversing the structural transformation.

5.7 Productivity Gaps: Measurement and Interpretation

Measuring worker productivity is a difficult task, especially in the traditional sector of developing countries. It is even more difficult to measure the *marginal* product of labor, which is not directly observable. The marginal product of labor is the concept of ultimate interest because gaps in the marginal product tell us about the efficiency of labor allocations. This section discusses these important measurement issues in more detail.

Let us begin with the following expression for the gap in annual worker productivity across sectors,

$$\frac{\text{APL}}{\tilde{\text{APL}}} = \frac{\text{APH}}{\tilde{\text{APH}}} \times \frac{h}{\tilde{h}} \times \frac{\text{hours}}{\tilde{\text{hours}}}, \tag{5.15}$$

where APL denotes the average annual product of labor or worker productivity, APH is the average product of a unit of human capital supplied per hour worked, and *hours* refers to the average annual hours worked per worker. In principle, one can use this equation to decompose the sources of the worker productivity gap. The average product of labor, hours worked, and human capital are *relatively* easy to measure. With these measures, the equation can then be used to complete the accounting decomposition by solving for the residual productivity gap that satisfies (5.15), which is interpreted as a gap in the productivity per unit of human capital across sectors.

There are conditions under which the gap in average productivity can be interpreted as a gap in marginal productivity. The size of this gap can then be interpreted as a measure of inefficiency in the labor market, as an efficient allocation of labor should equate the marginal product of a unit of human capital across sectors. However, before discussing the conditions that imply an equality between average and marginal productivity gaps, we need to recognize that obtaining good estimates of the average product of labor, hours worked, and human capital is a nontrivial task.

5.7.1 Average Product of Labor

To estimate the average product of labor, one needs to measure output and the number of workers in each sector. Both are difficult to measure in developing countries because most of the economic activity takes place away from formal markets. In the poorest developing economies, the vast majority of production is consumed at home and not traded. In addition, most workers are family members and sole proprietors, rather than formally paid employees.

The situation is not hopeless because accounting practices have been developed to deal with this problem by focusing on measurements of crop yields rather than on market transactions. In addition, the number of workers, their occupation, and even their hours of work, are collected from household surveys. Gollin et al. (2014) discuss recent measures of production and hours worked in a large data set of 151 countries. They find for the poorest 25 % of their sample that the nonagricultural/agricultural productivity gaps average 5.6, with a median value of 4.3. Their measures are roughly consistent with urban/rural consumption gaps, which also rely on household surveys, in developing countries measured by Young (2013). He finds average consumption gaps of around 4.

There is a fair amount of agreement that developing countries are characterized by large gaps in worker productivity in the four- to six-fold range. Agreeing on the decomposition and interpretation of these large gaps has proven to be more difficult.

5.7.2 Hours Gap

The proximate causes of the large measured gaps in annual worker productivity can be identified using the accounting decomposition in (5.15). Of the three right-hand side determinants, hours is the easiest to measure as they are also collected from household surveys. Gollin et al. (2014) measure an annual hours gap of 1.3 for the poorest 25 % of countries in their sample. For some of the poorer countries, the hours gap is quite large. For example, the hours gap in Uganda is over 2. Their average estimate is in the ballpark of the hours gap measured for the historical USA of 1.4–1.5 that we discuss in Chap. 6.

There is not much disagreement over the estimates of the hours gap. Differences in hours worked explain a significant portion, but not the majority, of the worker productivity gap in developing countries.

5.7.3 Human Capital Gap

Human capital is a more abstract concept than production and hours of work. It must be measured indirectly using methods that have limitations and are open to criticism. Estimates of human capital start by first measuring years of schooling. The years of schooling are translated into a human capital measure by using regression estimates that correlate years of schooling with wages. This common approach to measurement should be viewed as a starting point because the "quality" of a given year of schooling depends on student and teacher attendance throughout the year, teacher qualifications, class size and composition, and other inputs such as books and computers. In addition, it ignores investment in health and skills obtained from experience on the job.

Using the simplest approach to measuring human capital, based on years of schooling alone, Gollin et al. (2014) find that there is a human capital gap of 1.4 across sectors in the poorest 25 % of their sample. Using their measure of human capital, the combined hours and human capital gaps explain a 1.82 worker productivity gap, leaving an estimated gap in the average product of human capital for these countries of 3 and a median gap of 2.4.

The residual worker productivity gap can be further reduced by attempting to measure the other types of human capital investments mentioned above, which likely differ across sectors as well. One way to begin accounting for the omitted investments is to allow for sector-specific returns to years of schooling. There is evidence that the return to a given year of schooling is lower in agriculture than in nonagricultural. After adjusting for the different rate of return to schooling across sectors, Vollrath (2014) finds little remaining residual gap in a small sample of developing countries. Herrendorf and Schoellman (2014) obtain the same result for the U.S. in current times.

In summary, the residual productivity gap estimated by Gollin, Lagakos, and Waugh of 2–3 is quite large. At least some of this gap can be accounted for by adjusting for the different rates of return to schooling across sectors and for other differences in human capital investments that may not be reflected in rates of return to years of schooling (i.e., some of the human capital investments may have a constant or "intercept-effect" that does not alter the estimated return to a marginal year of schooling). It is important to resolve any disagreement over the correct way to measure human capital across sectors because the implied residual estimate of $\mathrm{APH}/\tilde{\mathrm{APH}}$ from (5.15) is often interpreted as the gap in the *marginal* product of a unit of human capital across sectors, a measure of labor market efficiency. We now turn to assumptions needed to justify this interpretation.

5.7.4 Average and Marginal Products of Human Capital

In the theory we use in this book, the connection between, wages, marginal products, and average products is made clear by the following equalities

$$\frac{w_t}{\tilde{w}_t} = \frac{(1-\alpha)k_t^{\alpha}}{(1-\rho)(l_t/f_t)^{\rho}} = \frac{\mathrm{APL}}{\tilde{\mathrm{APL}}}.$$

The first equality says that the rental rate on human capital is equal to the marginal product of human capital in each sector. So, for a given level of human capital, wage ratios equal marginal productivity ratios. However, this is only true under perfectly competitive markets. For example, suppose there was a national market for human capital that forces human capital rental rates to be equated across the two sectors. Suppose further that the two sectors produce different goods and that the modern sector is dominated by a monopolist. In the modern sector, human capital would then *not* be hired until the marginal product was equated to the common rental rate. Profit maximization for a monopolist causes production and employment to fall short of the levels needed to equate the marginal product to the rental rate. This would cause a gap in the marginal products across sectors even when there is no gap in rental rates (or in wages for a given level of human capital). Thus, imperfect competition can cause the first equality to fail.

Next, the exact form of the marginal product expression results from our assumption of Cobb–Douglas technologies. With Cobb–Douglas technologies, the marginal product of human capital is equal to the sector labor share times the average product of human capital. If the labor shares are equal across sectors, then the ratio of the marginal products equals the ratio of the average products, the second equality above. However, the equality of the labor shares across sectors is at least somewhat controversial. Vollrath (2009a) and Gollin et al. (2014) argue for equality and Herrendorf and Schoellman (2013) claim the labor shares differ across sectors. To go from the average product estimates directly to the marginal product estimates, one needs the equality.

We assume throughout that the ratios of rental rates, marginal products, and average products are always equal. This is a reasonable and common approach, but not without controversy because markets may not always be sufficiently competitive and labor shares may differ across sectors.

5.7.5 The Structural Transformation, Growth, and Economic Efficiency

As discussed in Sect. 5.6, the structural transformation can increase growth in worker productivity by increasing average hours worked, increasing the average age and experience of the workforce, and, if the marginal product of human capital is higher in the modern sector, by increasing the productivity of an experience-adjusted hour of work. It is also possible that the structural transformation increases education and human capital. The lower years of schooling observed in the traditional sector may be due to a binding poverty trap that does not exist in the modern sector. This can happen because the relative productivity of children may be lower in the modern sector, either due to more effectively enforced child labor and compulsory schooling laws or because the relative productivity parameter of children (γ) is fundamentally lower in the modern sector due to differences in technologies or types of goods produced. Schooling may also be lower because the price of purchased school inputs, such as quality-adjusted teacher time and school materials, is lower in the modern sector (see the extension of the human capital modeling to include purchased inputs in the problems from Chap. 3).

Even if growth in worker productivity rises due to the structural transformation, it may cause no significant improvement in economic efficiency. Suppose, for example, the marginal product of a unit of human capital supplied is roughly equal across sectors, as indicated by the estimates of Vollrath (2014) and Herrendorf and Schoellman (2014). In this case, labor markets are interpreted as efficiently allocating human capital across agriculture and manufacturing. However, it is important to note that efficiency considerations in dual economies should not be restricted to the allocation of human capital alone.

We saw in Sect. 5.5 that the lack of efficiently operating land and insurance markets can bind workers to the traditional sector. This can cause workers to supply less labor hours than they optimally prefer over the year. Also, because intergenerational loan markets are incomplete (see Chaps. 2 and 3), the education of children is dependent on the wages of parents and thus can be lower than is productively efficient (the marginal return to investment in human capital can be greater than the market interest rate). If parental incomes are lower, compulsory schooling laws are less effective, the relative productivity of children is higher, or purchased school inputs are more expensive in the traditional sector, the underinvestment in years of schooling can be more severe there than in the modern sector. Furthermore, the fact that the marginal returns to schooling, for a given number of years attended, is higher in the modern sector may be due to under investment in the health of mothers and young children in the traditional sector, causing the "ability" of traditional sector students to be lower than students in the modern sector. This is a legitimate concern because, generally, public health measures and health outcomes are worse in rural areas than in cities (World Bank 2013).

For all these reasons, the structural transformation can reduce inefficiencies in hours worked and human capital investments, even if the economy is allocating a given stock of human capital reasonably well. As rising wages pull workers into the modern sector, fewer workers are dependent on land inheritance, and as a result, they can freely supply the optimal amount of work effort. Children will be raised by parents with higher wage incomes in environments that lead to more investment in their health and education, reducing the gap between the returns on these investments and the market rate of return on physical assets.

5.8 Rising Fertility in Early Development

Our focushas been on explaining why fertility falls with development. However, fertility actually rises in the early stages of development before it begins to fall (Galor and Weil 2000; Jones 2001). For example, in the early stages of the industrial revolution in England, fertility first rose modestly from a TFR of about 4.5 in 1750 to a TFR of about 5.5 in 1820 (Woods 2000). Fertility began to fall after 1820, reaching a low of a little over 2 by 1940.

One possible explanation for the rise in fertility is a rise in the relative productivity of children as economies shift from agricultural production to informal manufacturing production in the traditional sector and early factories in the modern sector (as we first discussed in Chap. 3). The share of employment in England's agricultural sector fell during the eighteenth century, but it was largely offset by increases in family production outside of agriculture, as well as some expansion in early factory employment. As noted by Sokoloff and Dollar (1997, p. 289),

> Cottage manufacture (or putting-out), where workers labored at home as individuals or in family groups for piece rates, was common in England into the late nineteenth century. It was rare in the United States, however, where the overwhelming share of manufactures intended for sale came instead from centralized plants, which operated as manufactories or so-called nonmechanized factories. This mode of manufacturing organization, where workers routinely left home each day to labor together in a structure intended for that purpose, was also used in England but appears to have been much less prevalent.

Thus, from 1740 to 1820, there was a decline in agriculture, but an expansion in another aspect of the traditional sector, the "cottage industry." This caused a decline in employment opportunities for children in agriculture, but an expansion in both the cottage industry and in early factories of the modern sector (Cunningham 1990; Horrell and Humphries 1995; Hudson and King 2000). The earnings of children relative to adults were significantly higher in the factories, and especially the cottage industry, than in agriculture (Horrell and Humphries 1995, Table 5). Thus, as the employment of children shifted from agriculture to domestic and formal industry, the relative productivity of children rose. In our model, this would be captured by a general rise in γ from 1740 to 1820. A rise in γ lowers the cost of children and increases fertility. Fertility began to fall when γ fell back after the cottage industry declined and the employment opportunities for children in factories and mines were curtailed by child labor laws.

Another possible explanation for the early rise in fertility is related to the subsistence constraint (Galor and Weil 2000). We have shown that introducing the health benefits of food, as in Sect. 4.4, leads to a fertility equation of the form

$$n_t = \frac{\psi(y_{1t}/wh_t)}{\left(\eta - \gamma(T - e_t)(\bar{e}/e_{t-1})^{\theta}\right)},$$

where recall that y_{1t} represents nonfood consumption. In the early stages of growth, before mandatory schooling and child labor laws, schooling may not rise above the education of young children. In this case we have $e_t = \bar{e}$ and the fertility equation reduces to $n_t = \psi(y_{1t}/wh_t)/(\eta - \gamma(T - \bar{e}))$. The only source of variation in fertility is then y_{1t}/wh_t. In a standard version of the model, with no health effects, the nonfood consumption share of potential income is constant, implying that fertility is also constant. However, with health benefits from food, we showed that y_{1t}/wh_t will tend to rise with income. This lowers the value of forgone income associated with having and raising children, and increases fertility via an income effect. Thus, exogenous technological change that raises income will cause fertility to rise in the early stages of growth before schooling begins to increase.

5.9 One-Child Policy

Countries have long understood the negative effects of population growth on living standards and have attempted to encourage a reduction in fertility in various ways. In the late 1970s, China went beyond encouragement by enacting a law prohibiting families, except in special circumstances, from having more than one child. At this time, the fertility rate had already been falling dramatically, but it was still high, just below three children per woman. Thus, the policy clearly imposed a binding constraint on household behavior. The purpose of the policy was to reduce unemployment and the demand for natural resources. Recently, China has relaxed its policy to allow two children per household.

In this section, we think about how an exogenously imposed reduction in fertility would affect the equilibrium in our model. Obviously, constraining household choice in any manner will reduce welfare for the initial generation of households in both sectors. However, there are some less obvious impacts.

One possible benefit to the one-child policy is to increase schooling. We find that this is the case in our model. To begin, combine the first-order conditions for schooling and consumption in the modern sector to get the following expression:

$$e_t = \frac{\psi \theta c_t}{n_{t+1} w_t \gamma \bar{h}}.$$

The numerator captures any wealth effect on schooling that is associated with a rise in consumption. The denominator is the marginal cost of schooling measured in terms of the forgone wages that children could earn working. In the unconstrained model, when fertility is a choice variable, changes in family resources affect consumption and fertility choices proportionately, leaving schooling independent of fertility, as you see in (5.7b). In our model, schooling affects fertility with no reverse causation. Larger families, due to higher income or stronger preferences for children, are not associated with lower schooling per child. The quantity–quality trade-off in our model is driven by rising schooling that causes the cost of children to increase and fertility to fall.

Now suppose fertility is *exogenously* determined. In this case, one can show that higher fertility both reduces family resources and raises the cost of schooling, causing a decline in schooling (see Problem 6). Thus, an exogenous decline in fertility increases schooling in the modern sector.

The analysis is more difficult in the traditional sector. The two effects of an exogenous change in fertility that we discussed for modern sector households are also present in the traditional sector. However, in the traditional sector, there is a third effect. Lowering fertility reduces child labor and the total supply of labor in the traditional sector. The fall in labor supply reduces rental income from land, family resources, and schooling. One can show that this last effect does not dominate the two effects that increase schooling in the modern sector, so schooling also increases in the traditional sector as fertility is exogenously reduced. Thus, fertility restrictions have the benefit of increasing schooling and economic growth, which could lead to welfare gains for future generations.

Using data from China, recent empirical studies have attempted to estimate the effect of the one-child policy on schooling. The evidence thus far is mixed. For example, Rosenzweig and Zhang (2009) provide estimates supporting the idea that restricting the number of children *increases* schooling per child. On the other hand, Qian (2013) finds that restricting the birth of a second child, for families with only one child, actually causes the schooling of the first child to *fall* (although she finds the effect of restricting further children, in families with more than one child, increases schooling per child).

There is another effect of interest that will influence the welfare of the initial generation in the traditional sector. With exogenous fertility, the wage gap can be written as

$$\frac{w_t}{\tilde{w}_t} = \left[1 + \frac{\rho}{1-\rho}\frac{1 + n_{t+1}\gamma(\bar{h}/\tilde{h}_t)(T - \tilde{e}_t)}{1 - (\eta - \gamma(\bar{h}/\tilde{h}_t)T)n_{t+1}}\right]^{1+\psi\theta}.$$

An exogenous reduction in n_{t+1} lowers land rents relative to labor sources of family income. This implies that the wage gap must shrink. Modern sector wages are fixed by the initial capital–labor ratio, so this implies a rise in traditional sector wages. The rise in the traditional wage provides a benefit of the policy that helps to offset the negative welfare effects on the initial generation of traditional sector households.

5.10 Conclusion

Persistent wage and productivity gaps across sectors are common features of developing countries. Attempts to explain these gaps while assuming complete markets in the low-productivity traditional sector are not entirely convincing. Institutional arrangements in traditional agricultural and other informal production structures are not well captured by assumptions that markets are complete. One way to distinguish between the two sectors is by the absence of fully developed markets for land and labor in the traditional sector. Regarding land ownership, for example, the evidence suggests that arrangements are made that keep land in the family over many generations. The absence of these factor markets helps to explain the wage gap in two ways.

First, an absence of land markets in the traditional sector fosters the tradition of passing land and farms from one generation of the family to the next. An important condition for receiving an inheritance of this type is that children must remain in the traditional sector to gain the experience needed to operate the farm and "keep it in the family." This institutional arrangement ties occupational choice and geographic location to land ownership in the traditional sector. In equilibrium, traditional workers are willing to take lower wages than those offered in the modern sector because they are compensated by rental income on the land they eventually own and by bigger families.

Second, if the labor market in the traditional sector is also thin, family farms must rely predominantly on family labor. The diminishing returns to work on the family farm lower the reward to work relative to a market setting where the competitive market wage is independent of an individual's labor supply choice. The lower reward to work results in less hours worked throughout the year and a larger annual gap in productivity and wages.

In summary, missing markets for land and labor both contribute to large gaps in wages and fertility that can persist for many decades. As a result, the movement of households away from the traditional sector and toward the modern sector increases productive efficiency, reduces population growth, and raises worker productivity.

5.11 Exercises

Questions

1. What are wage and fertility gaps? How large are they? What is their connection to economic growth?
2. Summarize the explanations for wage gaps that do not rely on missing markets. Discuss the weaknesses of each explanation?
3. Offer some reasons why land and labor markets might not exist in the traditional sector. What evidence suggests the absence of land and labor markets in developing countries?

4. Explain why inheritance of the family farm raises fertility. Why does the inheritance have no effect on schooling?
5. Explain how each of the following affect the wage gap.
   (a) traditional sector fertility
   (b) traditional sector schooling
   (c) the relative productivity of child labor
   (d) the strength of parent's preferences for children
6. Explain the ordering of household consumption across native households in the modern sector, traditional sector migrants to the modern sector, households who remain in the traditional sector. What is the ordering of utility for these household types?
7. Use the model to explain how each of the following change over the course of economic development.
   (a) average fertility in both sectors
   (b) the wage gap across sectors
   (c) child labor in both sectors
   (d) human capital rental rate in the traditional sector
8. There is an annual wage gap across traditional and modern sectors. Is this due to differences in productivity per hour or differences in hours worked over the course of a year?
9. When would traditional households choose to work less than modern households? What is the intuition for this result?
10. Consider the situation when adult work and the quantity and quality of children are all household choice variables. How do schooling, fertility, and work effort interact to determine the wage gap across sectors in this setting?
11. Explain why inefficient or missing markets can reduce labor mobility?
12. Explain how the structural transformation directly raises average worker productivity. How important was the structural transformation in determining the growth rates of the Asian Tiger countries during their Growth Miracle?
13. Discuss the difference in the growth experiences of Asia and Africa and relate the difference to the structural transformation?
14. In many cases, as during the industrial revolution in England, fertility rises in the early stages of development. How can this be explained using the models you have seen?
15. Discuss how an *exogenous* reduction in fertility, such as those under the One-Child policy in China, affects schooling per child. Explain why *endogenous* variations in family size, due to variation in parental income or preferences for children, have no effect on schooling per child. What then creates the quantity-quality trade-off?

Problems

1. Derive the following equations and offer an economic explanation for each: (5.7a–c), (5.8), and (5.11).
2. Use Vollrath's approach to carefully prove, showing all work, that if there is an absence of labor markets in the traditional sector, then traditional households will choose to work less than modern households.
3. Show that when households choose work, fertility, and schooling of their children, that $\tilde{z}_t < z_t$ and $\tilde{n}_{t+1} > n_{t+1}$, i.e., that traditional households work less and have more children than modern sector households.
4. Show that greater adult human capital raises work effort in (5.12c).
5. *Worker Productivity*. Derive the expression that relates the structural transformation to worker productivity by carrying out the following steps. First, show that output can be written in terms of labor income in both modern and traditional sectors. Next, write out expressions showing that the total effective labor supply from modern sector households exceed that from traditional households. Finally, write out worker productivity in terms of the wage gap, the household supply of effective labor from each sector, and the fraction of the households in the modern sector, as in (5.14).
6. Suppose that a fertility limit is imposed by the government across the economy. Derive the schooling equation in the modern and the traditional sector, as well as the equation for the wage gap in this case. Show that a reduction in fertility increases schooling in both sectors and lowers the wage gap.

References

Acemoglu D, Robinson J (2012) Why nations fail. The origins of power, prosperity, and poverty. Crown Publishers, New York

Acemoglu D, Johnson S, Robinson J (2003) An African success story: Botswana. In: Rodrik D (ed) In search of prosperity. Princeton University Press, Princeton

Alston L, Hatton T (1991) The earnings gap between agricultural and manufacturing laborers, 1925–1941. J Econ Hist 51(1):83–99

Au C, Henderson J (2006) How migration restrictions limit agglomeration production in China. J Dev Econ 80(2):350–388

Banerjee A, Duflo E (2011) Poor economics. Public Affairs, New York

Basu K (1991) Agrarian structure and economic underdevelopment. Harwood Academic Publishers, New York

Bertocchi G (2006) The law of primogeniture and the transition from landed aristocracy to industrial democracy. J Econ Growth 11(1): 43–70

Bosworth B, Collins S (2008) Accounting for growth: comparing China and India. J Econ Perspect 22(1):45–66

Calvo G (1978) Urban unemployment and wage determination in LDCs: trade unions in the Harris-Todaro model. Int Econ Rev 19(1):65–81

Caselli F (2005) Accounting for cross-country income differences. In: Aghion D, Durlauf S (eds) Handbook of economic growth. Elsevier, Amsterdam, pp 679–741

Caselli F, Coleman W (2001) The US structural transformation and regional convergence: a reinterpretation. J Polit Econ 109(3):584–616

Chanda A, Dalgaard CJ (2008) Dual economies and international total factor productivity differences: channeling the impact from institutions, trade, and geography. Economica 75 (300):629–661
Collier P, Radwan S, Wangwe S (1986) Labour and poverty in rural Tanzania: Ujameen and rural development in the United Republic of Tanzania. Oxford University Press, New York
Cordoba J, Ripoll M (2006) Agriculture, aggregation, wage caps, and cross-country income differences. Working paper 246, University of Pittsburgh, Department of Economics
Cunningham H (1990) The employment and unemployment of children in England c. 1680–1851. Past Present 126:115–150
David P (1967) The growth of real product in the United States before 1840: new evidence, controlled conjectures. J Econ Hist 27(2):151–197
David P (2005) Real income and economic welfare growth in the early republic. Stanford University Department of Economics working paper 06–001
Doepke M (2004) Accounting for the fertility decline during the transition to growth. J Econ Growth 9(3):347–383
Drazen A, Eckstein Z (1988) On the organization of rural markets and the process of development. Am Econ Rev 78(3):431–443
Ely R, Wehrwein G (1940) Land economics. Macmillan Co., New York
Feder G, Just D, Zilberman D (1982) Adoption of agricultural innovation in developing countries: a survey. World Bank staff working paper 542. World Bank, Washington, DC
Field E (2007) Entitled to work: urban property rights and labor supply in Peru. Quart J Econ 122 (4):1561–1602
Foster A, Rosenzweig M (1996) Technical change and human capital returns and investments: evidence from the green revolution. Am Econ Rev 86(4):931–953
French H, Hoyle R (2003) English individualism refuted and asserted: the land market of Earls Coline (Essex), 1550–1750. Econ Hist Rev 56(4):595–622
Galor O (2005) From stagnation to growth: a unified growth theory. In: Aghion P, Durlauf S (eds) Handbook of economic growth. North Holland, Amsterdam
Galor O, Weil DN (2000) Population, technology, and growth: from Malthusian stagnation to the demographic transition and beyond. Am Econ Rev 90(4):806–828
Galor O, Moav O, Vollrath D (2009) Inequality in land ownership, the emergence of human capital promoting institutions, and the great divergence. Rev Econ Stud 76(1):143–179
Gardner B (2002) American agriculture in the twentieth century. Harvard University Press, Cambridge
Gollin D (2002) Getting income shares right. J Polit Econ 110(2): 458–474
Goldin C, Katz L (2000) Education and income in the early 20th century: evidence from the prairies. J Econ Hist 60(3):782–818
Gollin D, Lagakos D, Waugh M (2014) The agricultural productivity gap. Quart J Econ 129 (2):939–993
Gollin D, Parente S, Rogerson R (2004) Farmwork, homework, and international income differences. Rev Econ Dyn 7(4):827–850
Greenwood J, Seshadri A (2002) The US demographic transition. Am Econ Rev 92(2):153–159
Haines M (2000) The population of the United States 1790–1920. In: Engerman S, Gallman R (eds) The Cambridge economic history of the United States. Cambridge University Press, New York
Hansen G, Prescott E (2002) Malthus to solow. Am Econ Rev 92(4):1205–1218
Harris B (1972) Innovation adoption in Indian agriculture: the high-yielding variety programs. Mod Asian Stud 6:71–98
Harris J, Todaro M (1970) Migration, unemployment, and development: a two-sector analysis. Am Econ Rev 60(1):126–142
Hayashi F, Prescott E (2008) The depressing effect of agricultural institutions on the prewar Japanese economy. J Polit Econ 116(4):573–632
Hazan M, Berdugo B (2002) Child labor, fertility, and economic growth. Econ J 112(482):810–878

Henderson V (2010) Cities and development. J Reg Sci 50(1):515–540
Herrendorf B, Schoellman T (2013) Why is measured productivity so low in agriculture? Arizona State University working paper. http://www.public.asu.edu/~tschoell/papers/AgricultureSubmissionNovember2013.pdf
Herrendorf B, Schoellman T (2014) Wages, human capital, and the allocation of labor across sectors. Arizona State University Working Paper. In: Society for Economic Dynamics 364, 2014 Meeting Papers. https://www.economicdynamics.org/meetpapers/2014/paper_364.pdf
Horrell S, Humphries J (1995) The exploitation of little children: child labor and the family economy in the industrial revolution. Explor Econ Hist 32(4):485–516
Hudson P, King S (2000) Two textile townships, c. 1660–1820: a comparative demographic analysis. Econ Hist Rev 53(4):706–741
Jenkins C, Knight J (2002) The economic decline of Zimbabwe. Palgrave Press, New York
Jerven M (2013) Poor numbers. Cornell University Press, Ithaca
Jones C (2001) Was an industrial revolution inevitable? Economic growth over the very long run. B.E. J Macroecon 1(2):1–45
La Porta R, Shleifer A (2014) Informality and development. J Econ Perspect 28(3):109–126
Lewis W (1954) Economic development with unlimited supplies of labor. Manchester Sch 22(2): 139–191
Lord W, Rangazas P (2006) Fertility and development: the roles of schooling and family production. J Econ Growth 11(3):229–261
Macfarlane A (1978a) The origins of English individualism: the family, property, and social transition. Oxford University Press, Oxford
Macfarlane A (1978b) The origins of English individualism: some surprises. Theor Soc 6(2):255–277
Mazumdar D (1989) Microeconomic issues of labor markets in developing countries: analysis and policy implications. EDI Seminar Paper No. 40. World Bank, Washington DC
McMillan M, Rodrik D (2011) Globalization, structural change, and productivity growth. In: Bacchetta M, Jansen M (eds) Making globalization sustainable. International Labour Organization and World Trade Organization, Geneva
Miguel E (2009) Africa's turn? MIT Press, Boston
Moav O (2005) Cheap children and the persistence of poverty. Econ J 115(500):88–110
Mourmouras A, Rangazas P (2007) Wage gaps and development: lessons from U.S. history. IMF working paper 07/105. International Monetary Fund, Washington, DC
Mourmouras A, Rangazas P (2009) Reconciling Kuznets and Habbakuk in a unified growth model. J Econ Growth 14(2):149–181
Mourmouras A, Rangazas P (2013a) Efficient urban bias. J Econ Geogr 13(3):451–471
Mourmouras A, Rangazas P (2013b) Wage and fertility gaps in dual economies. Eurasian Econ Rev 3(1):59–83
Mueller E (1984) The value and allocation of time in rural Botswana. J Dev Econ 15(3) 329–360
Munshi K, Rosenweig M (2009) Why is labor mobility in India so low? Social insurance, inequality, and growth. NBER working paper 14850. National Bureau of Economic Research, Cambridge
Myint A (2001) International trade and domestic institutional framework. In: Meier G, Stiglitz J (eds) Frontiers of development economics. Oxford University Press, New York
Qian N (2013) Quantity-quality and the one child policy: the only-child disadvantage in school enrollment in rural China. Yale University Working Paper
Rangazas P (2000) Schooling and growth: a King-Rebelo experiment with human capital. J Monetary Econ 46(2):397–416
Rangazas P (2002) The quantity and quality of schooling and U.S. labor productivity growth (1870–2000). Rev Econ Dyn 5(4):932–964
Ranis G, Fei J (1961) A theory of economic development. Am Econ Rev 51(4):533–565
Restuccia D, Yang D, Zhu X (2008) Agriculture and aggregate productivity: a quantitative cross-country analysis. J Monetary Econ 55(2):234–250

Rosenzweig M (1988) Labor markets in low-income countries. In: Chenery HB, Srinivasan TN (eds) Handbook of development economics, vol 6. Elsevier, Amsterdam
Rosenzweig M, Zhang J (2009) Do population control policies induce more human capital investment? Twins, birth weight and China's one-child policy. Rev Econ Stud 76 (3):1149–1174
Schultz T (1964) Transforming traditional agriculture. Yale University Press, New Haven
Shapiro D, Gebreselassie T (2008) Fertility transitions in sub-Saharan Africa: falling and stalling. Afr Population Stud 23(1):3–23
Sokoloff K, Dollar D (1997) Agricultural seasonality and the organization of manufacturing in early industrial economics: the contrast between England and the United States. J Econ Hist 57 (2):288–321
Stiglitz J (1974) Wage determination and unemployment in LDCs. Quart J Econ 88(2):194–227
Stiglitz J (1988) Economic organization, information, and development. In: Chenery HB, Srinivasan TN (eds) Handbook of development economics, vol 6. Elsevier, Amsterdam
Temple J (2005) Dual economy models: a primer for growth economists. Manchester Sch 73:435–478
Temple J, Woessmann E (2006) Dualism and cross-country growth regressions. J Econ Growth 11 (3):187–228
The Economist (2014) Economic convergence: the headwinds return. Sept 14
Vollrath D (2009a) How important are dual economy effects for aggregate productivity? J Dev Econ 88(2):325–334
Vollrath D (2009b) The dual economy in long-run development. J Econ Growth 14(4):287–312
Vollrath D (2013) Measuring aggregate agricultural labor effort in dual economies. Eurasian Econ Rev 3(1):39–58
Vollrath D (2014) The efficiency of human capital allocations in developing countries. University of Houston working paper 201307956
Wang X, Piesse J (2010) Inequality and the urban-rural divide in China: effects of regressive taxation. China World Econ 18(6):36–55
Wang X, Piesse J (2011) The micro-foundations of dual economy models. Manchester Sch 81:80–101
Woods R (2000) The demography of victorian England and Wales. Cambridge University Press, Cambridge
World Bank (2013) Global monitoring report 2013: rural-urban dynamics and the millennium development goals. World Bank, Washington
Young A (1992) A tale of two cities: Factor accumulation and technical change in Hong Kong and Singapore. In: Blanchard O, Fisher S (eds) NBER macroeconomic annual. MIT Press for the National Bureau of Economic Research, Cambridge
Young A (1995) The tyranny of numbers: confronting the statistical reality of the east Asian growth experience. Quart J Econ 110(3):641–680
Young A (2012) The African growth miracle. J Polit Econ 120(4):696–739
Young A (2013) Inequality, the urban-rural gap, and migration. Quart J Econ 128(4):1727–1785

Physical Capital in Dual Economies

6

In this chapter, we shift attention to industrialization and economic growth in dual economies. We focus again on the consequence of missing land markets, a common characteristic of developing economies that was documented in the previous chapter. Here, we examine the connections between land ownership, saving, and physical capital formation.

We consider two common situations that are associated with nonexistent or thin land markets. The first situation is one where households that farm the land either own the land or have informal property rights over the income generated from the land. In the case of the USA, land policy was intentionally designed to transfer ownership of public land holdings across the entire rural population (Libecap 2007). In other cases, the ownership of land remained communal but was effectively divided across local community farmers who were given autonomy in making decisions about land use and had clear claims to income from agricultural production. This occurred in the early stages of development in the Netherlands (de Vries and van de Woulde 1999, Chap. 5), a country where there was no strong feudal legacy, and in African villages (Collier et al. 1986).

The second situation is one where land ownership is highly concentrated in the hands of a relatively few landlords. The landlords do not farm but instead hire landless workers as farm hands. This situation was common in the historical development of Latin America (Deninger and Squire 1997) and Mexico (Acemoglu and Robinson 2012, pp. 35–38). In both of these situations, we assume that with thin land markets, the dominant way that land is transferred is through an intergenerational bequest designed to keep land within the family or village.

The inheritance of land during an individual's later years substitutes for saving as a way of financing consumption during old age. This common feature of traditional agriculture undermines the incentive to save when young. Workers that move away from family production to work in factories often lose the claims to family or tribal lands. The loss of a land bequest implies that workers must save more of their wages to finance retirement consumption. Thus, the structural transformation of the economy away from traditional agriculture and toward modern manufacturing causes an increase in the aggregate saving rate.

S. Das et al., *Economic Growth and Development*,
Springer Texts in Business and Economics, DOI 10.1007/978-3-319-14265-4_6

When land ownership is concentrated, as in our second scenario, landowners are often able to exert political pressure to change policy in ways that raise land rents. Policies that increase land rents are ones that lower capital accumulation, reduce the opportunities of workers in the modern sector, and keep wages low. Underlying forces that generate a structural transformation, such as technological progress, help pull workers out of the traditional sector despite anti-growth policies. This weakens the power of land owners and leads to more pro-growth policies, which serves to increase capital accumulation and accelerate the structural transformation.

There are other explanations for the rise in capital accumulation over the course of development. Recall from Chap. 1 that Lewis (1954) also thought that a dual economy approach was needed to explain rising saving rates. He conjectured that the income of capital owners in the modern sector would increase relative to incomes of workers and land owners as "surplus" labor from the traditional sector is pulled into the modern sector with little upward pressure on wages. Lewis believed that the relative expansion of capital income was important for growth because capital owners saved a larger fraction of their income than land owners and workers. In contrast to Lewis, our explanation is consistent with rising wages, a constant share of capital income, and an endogenous saving rate that does not depend on the source of income. See Gollin (2014) for a discussion and critique of the classic Lewis model.

Another theory of capital accumulation is based on freeing the entrepreneurial activity of small informal businesses in the traditional sector. The argument is that these entrepreneurs have access to potentially profitable technologies, but their investment is held back by credit market imperfections, costly regulations, and high taxes on capital income. While this is likely true in some cases, the evidence suggests that capital accumulation arising out of small informal businesses is small (Banerjee and Duflo 2011, Chap. 9; La Porta and Shleifer 2014). During development, the vast majority of small informal businesses simply die out as the larger and already established firms operating in the modern sector expand. In our model, technological progress, as well as human capital accumulation (see Chap. 7), drives up the productivity of workers in the modern sector causing wages to rise relative to the value of rents from traditional or informal production. The exit of workers from the traditional sector causes informal production to die out and also raises the savings rate, in the manner described above, helping to finance the expansion of capital in the modern sector.

While the absence of markets for land helps motivate the models of this chapter, we assume that there is a competitive labor market, as in the first part of Chap. 5. Labor markets seem to operate more consistently than land markets at early stages of development. After the demise of the European feudal system in the fourteenth century, labor markets quickly formed (Acemoglu and Robinson 2012, Chap. 4). In fact, Clark (2007, Chap. 3) provides evidence of market wages for building and farm laborers that stretch back into the thirteenth century. At least by the nineteenth century, labor markets were working well enough in the USA and Europe to virtually eliminate hourly wage gaps across sectors (Mourmouras and Rangazas 2009a, pp. 154–156). Vollrath (2014) argues that labor markets perform well in currently developing countries. He finds only small sector gaps in wages per unit of human capital supplied. However, Gollin et al. (2014) find that large wage gaps still exist after controlling for hours worked and education. While Chap. 5 discusses several explanations for these wage gaps that are consistent with well-functioning labor markets, their findings suggest that one cannot rule out labor market imperfections at the early stages of development altogether. The approach we take in this chapter is best interpreted as a simplification that allows us to focus solely on the lack of land markets.

Sections 6.1–6.3 offer three historical applications where the absence of complete land markets was important. The three applications are self-contained and focus on different topics, so readers can pick and choose among the applications based on their interests.

In two of the applications, land was owned predominately by small farmers. In Sect. 6.1, we use land inheritance to explain the persistence of large wage gaps in US history. As mentioned above, as well as in Chap. 5, the US wages gaps were not due to differences in hourly wages but rather were caused by differences in the annual hours worked per worker. Annual work hours were much higher in the nonfarm sector, leading to higher annual productivity per worker. Section 6.2 reintroduces the deindustrialization hypothesis from Chap. 4. We focus on the Ottoman Empire in the nineteenth century because it experienced an unusually large increase in the relative price of its agricultural goods as it expanded its trade with Europe. We examine the effects of trade on economic growth and the distribution of income across the population.

Unlike Sects. 6.1 and 6.2, in Sect. 6.3, we assume that landownership is highly concentrated among a few large landowners. As mentioned, concentrated landownership is interesting, in part, because it tends to coincide with political power. We look at the incentives of large landowners to influence fiscal policy in ways that slow the structural transformation. The version of the two-sector model we use in this section also explains a possible connection between the structural transformation and the growth of government.

6.1 Farmer-owned Land I—Wages Gap in US History

We maintain the same two-sector structure as in Chap. 5, where we have a modern sector of landless households and a traditional sector of landed households, with different production technologies used in each sector. However, now we use the two-period overlapping generations model to allow for saving behavior. Also, to focus attention on physical capital formation, we ignore human capital and assume that fertility is exogenous. Human capital and endogenous fertility will be reintroduced in Chap. 7. Finally, unlike in Chap. 5, we now make explicit the preference to bequeath land to children working on the family farm.[1]

---

[1] Explicitly introducing the preferences that underlie the desire to bequeath land to children who continue the "farming" tradition does not affect the analysis qualitatively. It is worth showing that

6.1.1 Modern Sector

Producers in the modern sector are neoclassical firms that use the standard Cobb–Douglas production function

$$Y_t = K_t^{\alpha} M_t^{1-\alpha}, \tag{6.1}$$

where Y denotes output, K is the physical capital stock, M is the effective labor supply in the modern sector, and α is the capital share parameter.

The firms operate in perfectly competitive markets for goods and inputs. The standard profit-maximizing factor price equations for the rental rates on effective labor supply and physical capital are

$$w_t = (1 - \alpha) k_t^{\alpha} \tag{6.2a}$$

$$r_t = \alpha k_t^{\alpha - 1} \tag{6.2b}$$

where r is the net return to capital and $k = K/M$.

6.1.2 Traditional Sector

The traditional sector differs from the modern sector because of differences in the production technology and because the technology and land used in production is inherited and operated by a family—creating lifetime rental income to supplement wages. For simplicity, we continue to assume that the same goods are produced in each sector. This is a common assumption in the dual economy approach when the specific focus is not on the relative price of the different goods produced in the two sectors. Section 6.2 provides an application where it is important to think of the two sectors as producing distinct goods with a relative price that generally differs from one.

Traditional output is produced using the following Cobb–Douglas technology

$$O_t = l_t^{\rho} f_t^{1-\rho}, \tag{6.3}$$

where O is the output, l is land per farm, f is effective farm labor per household in the traditional sector, and $0 < \rho < 1$ is a technology parameter. This technology differs from that used in industry because land is an input rather than physical capital. This assumption is meant to capture the idea that production in the traditional sector does not rely heavily on the plant and equipment used in the

(Footnote 1 continued)
it can be done to complete the analysis and ensure that it is logically consistent. After Sect. 6.1, we return to the simpler approach that does not explicitly model the desire to keep land within the family.

"factories" of the modern sector. While in general ρ and α may differ, we assume that $\alpha = \rho$. This assumption implies the labor share of income is independent of the stage of development, a stylized fact about economic growth (see, for example, Gollin 2002).

There is no market for the land, either to buy or rent. We assume that there is a market for farm labor, so that households could hire labor beyond that provided by the family.

6.1.3 Households

There are two types of households, landed and landless. The landed households inherit the traditional technology/land from their parents. Parents are only willing to pass the land on to those children who remain in the traditional sector full time in order to learn the traditional technology and tend to the farm. The paid labor supply of landed households is constrained by the length of the work year and by the physical demands of work in the traditional sector. Landless households are free to work in either sector and can freely choose their work time.

All households live for three periods, one period of childhood and two periods of adulthood. In the first period of adulthood, households are endowed with one unit of time. Preferences are identical across households, regardless of occupational choice or residence. All households value their consumption over the two periods of adulthood (c_{1t}, c_{2t+1}), the time spent taking leisure $(1 - z_t)$ and the transfer of land to children who continue the tradition of family farming (if land is owned). Preferences are given by

$$U_t = \ln c_{1t} + \beta \ln c_{2t+1} + \xi \ln(\kappa + \varphi_{t+1} n b_{t+2}) + \zeta \ln(v + 1 - z_t), \qquad (6.4)$$

where the preference parameters $\beta, \xi, \kappa, \zeta$, and v are nonnegative, φ gives the fraction of the household's children that work in the traditional sector, and b is the bequest of land passed to each member of the next generation of traditional households. In the absence of a land market, the land inherited by a generation t household, in the second period of their life, satisfies the condition $b_{t+1} = l_{t+1} = \varphi_{t+1} n b_{t+2}$, i.e., all land that is inherited is ultimately bequeathed to the next generation.[2]

The preference specification includes a term that involves the bequest of land made to the children who continue the tradition of family farming. However, while households value land bequests, it is not essential if $\kappa > 0$. This means that traditional households may be willing to give up their claim to family land to move to the modern sector under the right conditions. In similar fashion, leisure is valued but is not essential—it may be optimal for households to take no leisure.

[2] We assume that the land is passed at death, rather than inter vivos, because this binds the children expecting to receive land to work on the family farm in their first period of adulthood.

1. *Landless Households*

Landless households choose the fraction (z_t) of time they devote to work. The landless household maximizes utility subject to the lifetime budget constraint,

$$c_{1t} + \frac{c_{2t+1}}{R_t} = w_t z_t$$

where the return on the ownership of physical capital, purchased in period t and rented to producers in period $t + 1$, is $R_t \equiv r_{t+1} + 1 - \delta$. To simplify some of the expressions, we assume $\delta = 1$, so that $R_t = r_{t+1}$.

In addition to the standard first-order conditions for life cycle consumption, the choice of z_t yields

$$\frac{\zeta}{v + 1 - z_t} = \lambda_t w_t \tag{6.5}$$

where λ_t is the Lagrange multiplier. Equation (6.5) says that the marginal value of taking more leisure must equal the marginal value of the forgone consumption associated with working less.

Solving the model gives us the following saving and work behavior

$$s_t = \left[\frac{\beta}{1 + \beta}\right] w_t z_t \tag{6.6a}$$

$$z_t = \frac{(v + 1)(1 + \beta)}{1 + \beta + \zeta} \tag{6.6b}$$

As is clear from (6.6b), the optimal time devoted to work is constant. To simplify notation and reduce the number of parameters, we set $z_t = 1$ by setting $\zeta = v(1 + \beta)$. This means that landless households provide one unit of labor when young, as has been assumed throughout.

2. *Landed Households*

In the case of landed households, we assume that the skills and land needed to operate a traditional technology are inherited from parents, but only if children remain in the traditional sector when young. Time spent producing in the traditional sector is exogenously constrained so that $\tilde{z} < 1$. Thus, households that reside in the traditional sector are only able to work for a fraction $\tilde{z}$ of the time that modern sector households do.

The motivation for this assumption is that traditional production involving land is constrained by the weather and the length of day, both of which vary with the seasons. In addition, some types of traditional sector work are too physically strenuous for women and younger children, limiting their labor input relative to that of women and children in the modern sector.[3] In equilibrium, it will be the case that the constraint on the work of traditional workers is compensated for by the land rents they receive from inheriting land and the traditional technology.[4]

Operating the traditional technology generates land rents for the household during the second period of adulthood. The lifetime budget constraint for households choosing to follow their parents and work in the traditional sector is then

$$\tilde{c}_{1t} + \frac{\tilde{c}_{2t+1}}{R_t} = w_t \tilde{z} + \frac{O_{t+1} - w_{t+1} f_{t+1}}{R_t}. \tag{6.7}$$

The timing of the land bequest, and the fact that residual income accrues in the second period of adulthood, captures the idea that the family farm provides a source of retirement income that substitutes for retirement saving. The presence of land as a source of retirement income is a potentially important factor in slowing physical capital accumulation during the early stages of development (see Carter et al. 2003).

Also note that traditional workers are paid the same per hour as modern sector workers. Remember that landless workers can work in either sector. If the traditional sector employs some landless workers, then the wages in each sector must be the same. Landed workers will therefore make the same *hourly* wage as landless workers but make a lower *annual* wage because they work fewer hours over the course of the year.

Maximizing (6.4) subject to (6.7) yields the following equations for traditional household saving and for the farm labor demanded by a traditional producer

$$\tilde{s}_t = \left[\beta - \frac{\rho O_{t+1}}{R_t w_t \tilde{z}}\right] \frac{w_t \tilde{z}}{1+\beta} \tag{6.8a}$$

$$f_{t+1} = \left[\frac{1-\alpha}{w_{t+1}}\right]^{\frac{1}{\alpha}} l_{t+1}. \tag{6.8b}$$

The savings function in (6.8a) exhibits the effect of family farming suggested by Carter et al. (2003). The presence of second-period income from operating the traditional technology discourages retirement saving. The fraction of current period wages that is saved is smaller as a result. Thus, saving per household is lower in the traditional sector for two reasons: wages are lower, because of the shorter paid work year, and there is a smaller fraction of wages that is saved.

---

[3] The physical demands of farming help explain why the onset of the cottage industries and early factories increased the employment of women and children in the early stages of the industrial revolution, especially in regions dominated by the more strenuous northern farming—hay, wheat, and dairy farming. For evidence in England, see Cunningham (1990), Horrell and Humphries (1995). For the USA, see Goldin and Sokoloff (1984).

[4] Note that because preferences are identical, households in the traditional sector would prefer to work as much as those in the modern sector.

6.1.4 Equilibrium

We now determine equilibrium in the factor markets for labor and physical capital. Given k_t and l_t, the market clearing values of the factor prices and the labor demand chosen by a traditional sector producer are given by (6.2a), (6.2b), and the period t version of (6.8b). This leaves only the equilibrium values of k_t and l_t to be determined.

1. *Equilibrium* l_t

Determining the equilibrium quantity of land per traditional producer is equivalent to finding the number of equilibrium traditional sector producers (since total land is fixed). For a household to remain in the traditional sector and inherit land from their parents, the lifetime utility of doing so must be at least as great as the utility associated with forgoing the inheritance and becoming unrestricted in the choice of occupation.

We assume throughout that land is sufficiently scarce to cause some children born in the traditional sector to choose work in the modern sector. In other words, if all children born in the traditional sector remained in the traditional sector as adults, the quantity of land per producer would be too small to generate sufficient land rents to compensate for the constraint on paid work, causing the lifetime utility of traditional sector households to fall below that of landless households. The "competition" for land among traditional sector siblings must be strong enough to create an equilibrium exit from the traditional sector that equates the lifetime utility of the landed and landless households in each generation. This scenario matches what we see in history, a gradual structural transformation away from traditional production to modern production.

The fact that the lifetime utility of the landed and landless households must be equated gives an equilibrium condition for determining, along with (6.2a, b), the number of traditional sector producers in each period. Equating the indirect utility functions for landed and landless household implies that land rents must satisfy

$$\frac{\alpha O_{t+1}}{R_t w_t \tilde{z}} = \Omega_{t+1} \tag{6.9}$$

where $\Omega_{t+1} \equiv \left(\frac{1}{\tilde{z}}\right)\left(\frac{\nu}{\nu+1-\tilde{z}}\right)^{\nu}\left(\frac{\kappa}{\kappa+l_{t+1}}\right)^{\frac{\xi}{1+\beta}} - 1.$

Equation (6.9) states that the equilibrium ratio of the present value of land rents to potential wages in the traditional sector is affected by the extent of the labor supply constraint in the traditional sector. One can show that the more severe the constraint, i.e., the lower is $\tilde{z}$, the higher is the required land rent ratio. Actual land rents per household vary inversely with the number of traditional sector households.

Thus, the more severe the constraint, the smaller is the total number of households that are able to produce in the traditional sector in order to generate sufficient land rents for those that stay.

The size of land holding per household, and their value as a bequest, also affects the equilibrium land rent ratio. The larger are land holdings, and the more bequests to children are valued, the lower is the equilibrium land ratio. Intuitively, the more direct utility that is generated from owning and bequeathing land, the less income compensation is needed to offset the labor supply constraint.

2. *A National Labor Market*

Before solving for the equilibrium capital intensity, we need to establish how much effective labor will be allocated to each sector.

We know that the total effective labor supply for the entire economy in period t is $\pi_t N_t + (1 - \pi_t)N_t\tilde{z}$, where π denotes the fraction of young households that reside in the modern sector, as in Chap. 4.[5] The labor allocated to the traditional sector in period t must equal the traditional producer's demand for farm labor multiplied times the number of farm owners. Farm owners in period t are the older households that remained in the traditional sector to live and work in period $t - 1$. The total number of older traditional households that own farms in period t is therefore $(1 - \pi_{t-1})N_{t-1}$. The total demand for labor in the traditional sector is then $f_t(1 - \pi_{t-1})N_{t-1}$. This implies that the effective labor supply in the modern sector is simply the remainder of the workforce,

$$M_t = \pi_t N_t + (1 - \pi_t)N_t\tilde{z} - f_t(1 - \pi_{t-1})N_{t-1}. \tag{6.10}$$

An additional equilibrium condition is needed to ensure that the traditional sector is not constrained in the labor it uses, i.e., the demand for labor from the traditional sector must be greater than or equal to the supply of labor coming from landed households. If this were not the case, then there would be a "dual" labor market that could give rise to different wages per hour across sectors and across household types. Some hiring of part-time labor from landless households, "farm hands," is necessary to integrate the labor markets. Thus, an integrated labor market must satisfy

$$f_t(1 - \pi_{t-1})N_{t-1} \geq (1 - \pi_t)N_t\tilde{z}, \tag{6.11}$$

[5] It is trickier to keep track of households in this chapter than in Chap. 4. In Chap. 4, it did not actually matter where we thought of workers residing because all households could work in either sector. Here, landless households can work in either sector, but landed households must reside and work in the traditional sector.

the total demand for labor by traditional sector landowners must exceed the labor that is collectively provided by their children that decide to work and remain in the traditional sector.

3. *Equilibrium* k_t

Physical capital intensity is determined by the equilibrium condition that equates the physical capital demanded for production in the modern sector to the supply of capital that results from retirement savings of the households one period before,

$$K_{t+1} = \pi_t N_t s_t + (1 - \pi_t) N_t \tilde{s}_t. \tag{6.12}$$

Dividing both sides of (6.12) by M_{t+1}, defining $k_{t+1} \equiv K_{t+1}/M_{t+1}$, then using (6.9) and (6.10) allows us to write the transition equation for capital intensity as

$$k_{t+1} = \frac{[\pi_t \beta + (1 - \pi_t)(\beta - \Omega_{t+1})\tilde{z}](1 - \alpha)k_t^{\alpha} + (1 + \beta)(L/N_t)}{(1 + \beta)n(\pi_{t+1} + (1 - \pi_{t+1})\tilde{z})}. \tag{6.13}$$

We can now discuss the avenues through which the structural transformation from traditional to modern production affects physical capital intensity. First, the movement of households out of the traditional sector increases saving because it increases wage income ($\tilde{z} < 1$) and because it increases the rate of saving ($\beta - \Omega_{t+1} < \beta$).

The positive effect on saving is countered by a negative effect that occurs as the supply of workers that must be absorbed by the modern sector rises, causing the effective workforce that must be supplied with capital to rise, thereby lowering physical capital intensity. Equation (6.10), applied to period $t + 1$, and (6.8b) can be used to write out the labor that must be absorbed by the modern sector as $\left[\pi_{t+1} + (1 - \pi_{t+1})\tilde{z} - \frac{1}{k_{t+1}} \frac{L}{nN_t}\right] N_{t+1}$. More households living in the modern sector (higher π_{t+1}) and a weaker demand for farm labor because of less land available per old household (lower L/N_t), both cause the labor that must be supplied with capital to rise and k_{t+1} to fall. This explains the appearance of $\pi_{t+1} + (1 - \pi_{t+1})\tilde{z}$ in the denominator and L/N_t in the numerator of the solution for k_{t+1}.

In summary, the overall effect of the structural transformation on physical capital intensity is ambiguous. The positive effects stemming from an increased saving rate must be weighed against the negative effect of needing to provide capital to a growing modern sector workforce. Qualitatively, the transition equation, and the economic forces at work, is similar to the transition equation from Chap. 4, where we assumed perfectly competitive land markets (see Eq. (4.11) from Chap. 4). In Chap. 4, the relative size of land holdings, as an alternative mode of saving, and the fraction of the workforce in the modern sector both served to slow the growth in capital intensity. The same forces are at work here. The relative size of land holdings lowers saving and capital intensity via Ω_{t+1}, the equilibrium ratio of land rents relative to wages.

The main difference for capital accumulation is that *without* a land market, the traditional households that inherit land are the ones who save less in the form of physical capital (and may even borrow). *With* land markets, the saving of *all* households is equally diverted away from physical capital when land is purchased. The relatively low saving of traditional sector households creates a positive effect on capital accumulation associated with the structural transformation that was not present when there were perfectly competitive land markets in Chap. 4. Now, the saving rate of the economy will rise as households move from the traditional to the modern sector because of the different saving behavior of the households in the two sectors.

6.1.5 Labor Productivity

To examine how the structural transformation affects economic growth, we need to examine the behavior of two different measures of worker productivity. To begin, total output of the economy, $Y_t + O_t(1 - \pi_{t-1})N_{t-1}$, can be written in terms of k_t and π_t as

$$k_t^{\alpha}[\pi_t + (1 - \pi_t)\tilde{z}]N_t. \tag{6.14}$$

To compute labor productivity, it is common to divide total output by either the number of *hours worked* ($[\pi_t + (1 - \pi_t)\tilde{z}]N_t$) or the number of *workers* (N_t). Labor productivity per hour worked is simply k_t^{α}, while labor productivity per worker is $k_t^{\alpha}[\pi_t + (1 - \pi_t)\tilde{z}]$. The structural transformation can only affect labor productivity per hour indirectly by altering the economy's capital intensity. However, the structural transformation has a direct effect on labor productivity per worker because as labor moves from the traditional to the modern sector, hours worked increase. This distinction can be quite important, as in the case of US economic growth in the nineteenth century.

Table 6.1, taken from Mourmouras and Rangazas (2009a), presents both the relative annual output per worker and the annual wage in nonfarm occupations relative to those in farming. While not as large as those observed in some developing countries today, the wage and productivity gaps in US history were substantial.

Table 6.1 Ratio of nonfarm to farm productivity/wages in the USA

Time period	Output per worker	Annual nominal wages	Annual real wages
1840	2.0–2.5*		
1880	2.7⁺	5.0⁺	2.7⁺⁺⁺
1940	2.5⁺	2.9⁺; 3.3⁺⁺	1.8⁺⁺

Notes Values are the ratio of annual value for the nonfarm sector to the annual value to the farm sector

*David (1967). ⁺Caselli and Coleman (2001). ⁺⁺Alston and Hatton (1991). ⁺⁺⁺Ratio assuming same correction as Alston and Hatton for 1940

Note that the nominal annual wage ratios measured by Caselli and Coleman (2001) are much larger than the productivity ratios. There are at least two reasons for this. First, the wage ratios do not include noncash compensation, a relatively large portion of the compensation paid to farm workers. Second, there is no adjustment for the fact that farm workers lived in rural areas where the cost of living was lower. Alston and Hatton (1991) show that accounting for these two factors is important. They find that in 1940, monthly cash earnings in manufacturing were 3.3 times those in agriculture, even greater than the Caselli and Coleman estimate of a 2.9-fold wage gap for that year. However, after adjusting for noncash payments and cost-of-living differences, Alston and Hatton find that the gap shrinks to a 1.8-fold difference. If we apply the same proportional adjustment to the nominal wage in 1880, we get a real wage ratio of 2.7. Thus, after adjustment, the real wage and productivity gaps are roughly consistent and are in the twofold to threefold range during the nineteenth and early twentieth centuries.

The gaps in annual wages and productivity per worker could be due to differences in hours worked per worker or differences in productivity per hour. The evidence suggests that the vast majority of the gap is due to differences in hours worked per year. Table 6.2 documents the fact that hours worked by full-time employees were higher in the nonfarm sector. David (1967) uses data from Kendrick (1961) to argue that the hours gap was larger than is indicated by the difference in hours worked by full-time employees because more of the labor in agriculture is part-time (including family members). David estimates that, over the course of a year, the average agricultural laborer worked about half the hours of the average laborer in industry in 1840. Thus, the difference in hours worked alone could explain a twofold gap in annual productivity.

The literature attempting to measure the historical gaps in wages earned per hour is consistent with David's estimate. The main finding in this literature is that the gaps in wages per hour across industry and agriculture were very small. Margo (2000) estimates very small wage gaps of 10–15 % for the USA in the nineteenth century. Hatton and Williamson (1992) find relatively small wage gaps in the USA from 1890 to 1920, ranging from 5 to 30 %. They find larger gaps from 1920 to 1940 which are mostly explained by the high urban unemployment rates during the great depression.

In summary, the data above indicate that there were twofold to threefold gaps in the annual productivity and annual wages across nonfarm and farm sectors in the USA during the nineteenth and early twentieth centuries. The data also suggest that the wage gap was primarily due to the greater number of hours worked per worker

Table 6.2 Hours worked (full-time equivalents)

Time Period	Nonfarm	Farm
1840*	67.8	
1880**	62.7	45.5
1940**	42.2	44.9

Notes *Margo (2000)
** Kendrick (1961. Table A–IX)

in the nonfarm sector. This assessment of the productivity/wage gaps implies there should be a significant difference between the growth in labor productivity per *worker* and per *hour worked* during the structural transformation.

When there are significant differences in worker productivity per *hour worked*, then as workers move from agriculture to industry, there should be a significant increase in the average productivity of an hour worked in the economy as a whole. On the other hand, if the sector productivity gap is largely due to differences in hours spent producing measured output, then as labor migrates to industry, the growth in productivity per hour worked would not show much rise. However, measured productivity *per worker* would rise significantly due to an increase in hours worked per worker.

Table 6.3 presents the US economy's growth rate in output per worker and the growth rate in output per hour worked. During the nineteenth century, there were large differences in the two growth rates. The annualized growth rate for output per worker was 1.36 % over the nineteenth century compared to 0.65 % for output per hour worked. An average growth rate in output per worker that was double that of output per hour worked supports the claim that the main cause for lower output per worker in agriculture was fewer hours worked. As farm workers migrated to industry over the century, output per worker expanded significantly due to an increase in hours worked per worker. Output per hour worked did not increase as much because farm workers hourly productivity was not much different from that of nonfarm labor.

For output per hour worked to grow only weakly in the early stages of growth, there cannot be large changes in physical capital intensity. This means the conflicting effects of the structural transformation on *k* discussed earlier in this section must approximately offset. Mourmouras and Rangazas (2009a) show that this was the case in the USA during the nineteenth century. Throughout most of the nineteenth century, growth in productivity per hour worked was due to technological change and not private capital accumulation per worker.

By the end of the nineteenth century and early twentieth century, the growth rates equalized. The change in the relationship between the two growth rates is likely explained by two common features of development. First, the end of the structural transformation saw the size of the agricultural sector decline to a very small and stable fraction of the labor force, thereby ending the movement of labor from a low to a high productivity sector and slowing the growth rate of output per worker relative to output per hour worked. Second, the secular decline in hours

Table 6.3 Growth rates in US history

Time period	Per hour worked	Per worker
1820	0.39	0.31
1840	0.39	1.82
1860	0.56	1.32
1880	1.06	1.84
1900	1.53	1.53

worked off the farm further slowed the growth in output per worker relative to output per hour worked. In the USA, the decline in average hours worked off the farm was significant, as indicated in Table 6.2.

6.2 Farmer-owned Land II—Deindustrialization in the Ottoman Empire*

From Chap. 4, we know that one explanation for the beginning of the great divergence focuses on international trade between the rapidly industrializing countries of Western Europe, particularly Great Britain, and a "periphery" of slowly industrializing countries (see, for example, Williamson 2011). Countries in the periphery had a comparative advantage in making primary products. Expanding international trade in the nineteenth century caused the relative price of primary products to increase in the periphery and decrease in Western Europe. As trade expanded, the change in relative prices caused deindustrialization in the periphery and accelerated industrialization in Western Europe. According to the theory, deindustrialization slowed economic growth in the periphery and sped economic growth in Western Europe, thus contributing to the great divergence.

We examine the deindustrialization hypothesis as it applies to the nineteenth century Ottoman Empire. The Empire experienced an unusually large increase in its relative price. The relative price of primary products rose twofold to 2.5-fold in the middle of the century (Pamuck and Williamson 2011). What impact did the dramatic rise in relative prices have on industrialization and growth? Would the standard of living have been higher in the early Turkish Republic of the nineteenth century had the rulers of the Ottoman Empire not opened trade with Western Europe at the beginning of the nineteenth century and avoided this rise in the relative price of primary products?

We answer these questions by constructing a dynamic version of the specific factors model that captures some of the key features and stylized facts of the Ottoman Empire.[6] The purpose of the exercise is to imagine what the Ottoman Empire might have looked like if there had not been a dramatic rise in the international price of primary commodities in the middle of the century. In other words, we examine the quantitative significance of deindustrialization hypothesis for the Empire.

There are two sectors of production, agriculture and manufacturing. The economy is open, and the relative price of agricultural goods is determined in international markets. In the agricultural sector, land and labor are used to produce food and primary products. Older generations of farmers have informal ownership claims on the land. The adult children of the farmers, along with migrant workers, provide the farm labor. There is no active market for land. The right to farm the land is passed from the older generation to the younger generation of farmers as a bequest.

[6] Static versions of the specific factors model date back to Jones (1971) and Samuelson (1971). A dynamic version of the model was first presented by Eaton (1987).

In the manufacturing sector, skilled craftsmen work in informal shops. They rent physical capital and hire unskilled migrant workers to assist them in production. The relative size of the rural and urban population is determined by where the migrant workers are employed. In summary, the model is essentially a dynamic version of the specific factors model that is used to study international trade in developing economies. Here, the specific factors are land in agriculture, and capital and skilled craftsmen in manufacturing.

We calibrate the model to be consistent with the following stylized facts related to the Ottoman economy in the period from 1820 to 1920.[7]

1. Weakly positive growth in per capita real income (less than 1 %)
2. Positive population growth (approximately 1 %)
3. Increasing real wage in manufacturing units, but falling real wages in agricultural units during mid-century.
4. Modest urbanization (from 17 to 22 %)
5. Dramatic increase in the relative price of primary products in mid-century (a twofold to 2.5-fold rise)
6. High interest rates throughout the century (between 10 and 30 % annually)

We then compare aggregate growth and the welfare of different groups within the economy had there been *no* increase in the international price of primary products.

6.2.1 The Model

The model is an extension of the standard two-period overlapping generations model of physical capital accumulation. Young households provide an exogenous unit of labor to production during the first or working period of their life. The wages they earn are used for consumption and savings in the form of physical capital purchases. In the second period, all households retire. They finance retirement consumption from the physical capital they own and rent to manufacturing firms in exchange for a rental fee. Farmers have a second source of income for retirement consumption in the form of land rents.

The preferences of all households are identical. Lifetime utility for a household of generation t takes the form

$$u_t = u_{1t} + \beta u_{2t+1}$$

where β is the time discount factor that values utility from future consumption relative to current consumption. The single-period utility flows result from the consumption of both manufacturing and agricultural goods,

---

[7] For more details see Mourmouras and Rangazas (2014).

$$u_{it} = \chi \ln y_{it} + (1 - \chi) \ln o_{it}$$

where y is the manufacturing good and o is the agricultural good, and χ is a preference parameter that weighs the utility from consuming the two different goods.

Within each age cohort, there are three different household types: unskilled migrant workers that can be used to produce both goods, skilled craftsmen that produce manufacturing goods, and farmer/landowners that produce agricultural goods.

6.2.2 Migrants

Migrant workers are mobile across sectors. They provide unskilled labor that is used in the production of both types of goods, so there is an aggregate labor market for their services. They are free to work and reside in either the rural area, where they work as farm hands, or the urban areas, where they work in the shops assisting craftsman in making manufacturing goods. They receive the same competitive market wage in either location.

The two single-period budget constraints of migrant workers take the form,

$$y_{1t} + p_t o_{1t} + s_t = w_t D_t \quad (6.15a)$$

$$y_{2t+1} + p_{t+1} o_{2t+1} = R_t s_t, \quad (6.15b)$$

where p is the internationally determined relative price of agricultural goods, s is saving via the purchases of physical capital, w is the competitive wage per unit of effective labor supply in units of the manufacturing goods, D is the exogenous labor productivity index that determines the effective labor supply associated with one unit of labor time, and $R_t \equiv 1 + r_{t+1} - \delta$ is the total return to one unit of physical capital. For simplicity, we assume that capital fully depreciates when used in production, so the rate of depreciation (δ) equals one. This implies the return to capital is completely determined by the competitive rental rate paid to use capital in manufacturing production (r).

Note, we assume that the same labor productivity index applies regardless of where the worker is employed. If the productivity index increases, it is due to *balanced* technological change across the sectors. The technological progress could be occurring for different reasons in the two sectors (e.g., expanding cultivation of raw land in agriculture and new types of physical capital used in manufacturing), but there is no systematic difference in the resulting exogenous growth in worker productivity across sectors. The economy-wide growth rate in D is denoted by d.

The optimal behavior of the migrant workers is given by the following functions: $y_{1t} = \frac{\chi}{1+\beta} w_t D_t$, $p_t o_{1t} = \frac{1-\chi}{1+\beta} w_t D_t$, $y_{2t+1} = \frac{\chi}{1+\beta} \beta R_t w_t D_t$, $p_{t+1} o_{2t+1} = \frac{1-\chi}{1+\beta} \beta R_t w_t D_t$, and $s_t = \frac{\beta}{1+\beta} w_t D_t$. These demand functions simply say that present value of expenditures on goods and assets is a function of wages in manufacturing units.

6.2.3 Craftsmen

Craftsmen individually operate a small manufacturing firm or "shop." One can interpret the craftsman as being truly skilled in the sense that they are uniquely able to operate the shop technology. Alternatively, they may be interpreted as being no different than the unskilled labor and are simply the lucky recipients of government licenses that allow them to operate local monopolies in the urban area. They supply one unit of untraded labor for which they are compensated with a residual rent that can be interpreted either as an implicit skilled wage or as monopoly profit. In addition, the craftsman rent physical capital (k) and hire unskilled migrant labor (m) in competitive factor markets. The craftsman's production technology is given by a Cobb–Douglas production function in capital, unskilled labor, and skilled labor.

$$y_t = k_t^{\alpha}(D_t m_t)^{\bar{\alpha}} D_t^{1-\bar{\alpha}-\alpha}, \tag{6.16}$$

where $\bar{\alpha}$ is the output share of the unskilled migrant labor and $1 - \bar{\alpha} - \alpha$ is the output share of the skilled craftsman. Labor-augmenting technological progress increases the productivity of both skilled and unskilled labor.

The craftsman chooses k and m to maximize profit, resulting in the following first-order conditions that equate the marginal products of these inputs to their competitive factor prices,

$$\alpha \hat{k}_t^{\alpha-1} m_t^{\bar{\alpha}} = r_t \tag{6.17a}$$

$$\bar{\alpha} \hat{k}_t^{\alpha} m_t^{\bar{\alpha}-1} = w_t, \tag{6.17b}$$

where $\hat{k}$ is k/D, the "de-trended" capital stock. This measure of capital intensity is per craftsman or per urban shop. It differs from the measure of capital intensity in Sect. 6.1, which is per modern sector worker. It is not natural to define capital intensity per modern sector worker here because $1 - \alpha \neq \bar{\alpha}$ and the factor price equations do not simplify in the usual manner by combining k and m. Note also that we can write the profit, or income paid to the skilled craftsman, as $D_t w_t^* = D_t(1 - \alpha - \bar{\alpha})\hat{k}_t^{\alpha} m_t^{\bar{\alpha}}$, so that the skill premium is

$$\frac{w_t^*}{w_t} = \frac{1 - \alpha - \bar{\alpha}}{\bar{\alpha}} m_t. \tag{6.17c}$$

Except for the difference in wages, the demand functions of the craftsman are perfectly analogous to those of the unskilled laborer: $y_{1t}^* = \frac{\chi}{1+\beta} w_t^* D_t$, $p_t o_{1t}^* = \frac{1-\chi}{1+\beta} w_t^* D_t$, $y_{2t+1}^* = \frac{\chi}{1+\beta} \beta R_t w_t^* D_t$, $p_{t+1} o_{2t+1}^* = \frac{1-\chi}{1+\beta} \beta R_t w_t^* D_t$, and $s_t^* = \frac{\beta}{1+\beta} w_t^* D_t$.

6.2.4 Farmers

The farm technology used to produce agricultural goods is

$$O_t = l_t^{\alpha}(D_t f_t)^{1-\alpha}, \tag{6.18}$$

where l is the land holdings of an individual farm and f is farm labor. Farm labor in period t is unskilled and consists of the young, generation t, members of the farm family that have informal claims to the use of land, as well as migrant workers that are landless and hired as farm hands. Both types of labor are paid the unskilled wage, $w_t D_t$.

The rights to farm the land are passed down to generation t members of the farm family when they become old in period $t + 1$. The old members of the farm family manage the farm and generate residual income, $p_{t+1}O_{t+1} - w_{t+1}D_{t+1}f_{t+1}$, to help finance retirement consumption. Note that if there is positive population growth, the *individual* farm managed by each of the old households becomes smaller than those managed by the previous generation, because the land holdings are split across all old family members. This is one reason why there is migration to the city.

To maximize residual income, or land rents, the amount of farm labor hired satisfies

$$p_{t+1}(1-\alpha)(D_{t+1}f_{t+1})^{-\alpha} l_{t+1}^{\alpha} = w_{t+1}. \tag{6.19}$$

Using (6.19), we can define rental income from farming as $\text{rent}_{t+1} \equiv \alpha p_{t+1}O_{t+1} = \frac{\alpha}{1-\alpha} w_{t+1}D_{t+1}f_{t+1} = \alpha p_{t+1}^{1/\alpha}\left(\frac{1-\alpha}{w_{t+1}}\right)^{\frac{1-\alpha}{\alpha}} l_{t+1}$. The present value of the lifetime income of a farm household can then be written as $w_t D_t[1 + \frac{\text{rent}_{t+1}}{w_t D_t R_t}]$. The demand functions for a farm household are $\tilde{y}_{1t} = \frac{\chi}{1+\beta} w_t D_t[1 + \frac{\text{rent}_{t+1}}{w_t D_t R_t}]$, $p_t \tilde{o}_{1t} = \frac{1-\chi}{1+\beta} w_t D_t[1 + \frac{\text{rent}_{t+1}}{w_t D_t R_t}]$, $\tilde{y}_{2t+1} = \frac{\chi}{1+\beta}\beta R_t w_t D_t[1 + \frac{\text{rent}_{t+1}}{w_t D_t R_t}]$, $p_{t+1}\tilde{o}_{1t+1} = \frac{1-\chi}{1+\beta}\beta R_t w_t D_t[1 + \frac{\text{rent}_{t+1}}{w_t D_t R_t}]$, and $\tilde{s}_t = w_t D_t\left[\frac{\beta}{1+\beta} - \frac{1}{1+\beta}\frac{\alpha}{1-\alpha}\frac{\text{rent}_{t+1}}{w_t D_t R_t}\right]$. Note especially that land rent substitutes for retirement income from capital and thus reduces saving.

6.2.5 Labor Market Equilibrium

The number of young households of our three types is denoted as $\bar{N}_t$ (migrant workers), N_t^* (craftsmen), and $\tilde{N}_t$ (farmers). Labor market equilibrium requires that the demand for workers by craftsmen and farmers (net of young members of the farm households) must equal the supply of migrant workers looking for work,

$$N_t^* m_t + \tilde{N}_{t-1} f_t - \tilde{N}_t = \bar{N}_t. \tag{6.20}$$

Using the fact that $l_t = L/\tilde{N}_{t-1}$, where L is the total amount of raw land available for farming, and (6.17b) and (6.19) to solve for the demand for labor by craftsmen and farmers, allows us to rewrite (6.20) as

$$N_t^* \left(\frac{\bar{\alpha}}{w_t}\hat{k}_t^{\alpha}\right)^{\frac{1}{1-\bar{\alpha}}} + \left(\frac{(1-\alpha)p_t}{w_t}\right)^{\frac{1}{\alpha}} \left(\frac{L}{D_t}\right) = \bar{N}_t + \tilde{N}_t. \tag{6.21}$$

Note that technological progress reduces the demand for labor by farmers because, with greater productivity per worker, fewer farm hands are needed to work the available land. This inverse relationship between technological progress and the demand for labor does not necessarily hold for craftsmen because, unlike land, the de-trended capital stock can increase independently from the pace of technological progress. If the capital stock at least keeps pace with technological change, the demand for labor in manufacturing will not decrease for a given wage.

Also note that a higher relative price of agricultural goods increases the demand for farm hands, raising the wage in manufacturing units, and lowers the demand for labor by the craftsmen. This is one of the ways that higher agricultural prices cause deindustrialization—it reduces the fraction of the workforce in the manufacturing sector.

6.2.6 Capital Market Equilibrium

The supply of capital, acquired for retirement saving by the three household types, must equal the demand for capital by craftsmen in the next period,

$$\bar{N}_t s_t + N_t^* s_t^* + \tilde{N}_t \tilde{s}_t = N_{t+1}^* k_{t+1}. \tag{6.22}$$

We assume that the population of each type increases at the same rate. The common population growth factor is n. Using the saving equations for each type, the demand for labor expressions, and the labor market equilibrium condition, we can derive the following transition equation for the de-trended capital stock,

$$\hat{k}_{t+1} = \frac{\beta w_t}{(1+\beta)(1+d)n}\left[\frac{\bar{N}_t}{N_t^*} + \frac{w_t^*}{w_t} + \frac{\tilde{N}_t}{N_t^*}\left(1 - \frac{\alpha}{(1+\beta)(1-\alpha)}\frac{\text{rent}_{t+1}}{w_t D_t R_t}\right)\right]. \tag{6.23}$$

The transition equation is similar to the standard ones derived in simpler one sector overlapping generations models. Next period's capital stock per craftsman is determined by the saving of this period's young households, whose savings are fractions of their first-period income. Growth in the effective labor supply of craftsman (determined by d and n) makes it more difficult to raise the capital intensity at any one shop. These familiar mechanisms are captured by the term outside of the squared bracket.

The terms inside the squared brackets appear because there are three different household types in the model. The first term accounts for the different population sizes of migrant workers and craftsmen. The second term adjusts for the wage premium received by craftsmen. The final term results from the lower saving rate of farmers relative to the other two household types.

An increase in the relative price of agricultural products increases land rents and reduces the capital stock, other things constant. This is the second type of deindustrialization effect from higher agricultural prices—it reduces saving and lowers the capital stock. From (6.21), lowering the capital stock also serves to reduce the fraction of the workforce employed in the manufacturing sector.

The solution of the model involves solving simultaneously for $\hat{k}_{t+1}$ and w_{t+1} using (6.21) and (6.23). The Appendix discusses this solution in more detail.

6.2.7 The Urban/Manufacturing Share and Aggregate Output

We will need to keep track of the urban share and the growth in total output in determining our calibration of the model to the Ottoman economic history. We define the urban share as the craftsmen plus the workers they hire divided by the total population,

$$\text{urbanshare}_t \equiv \frac{N_t^* + N_t^*\left(\frac{\bar{\alpha}}{w_t}\hat{k}_t^{\alpha}\right)^{\frac{1}{1-\bar{\alpha}}}}{N_t^* + \bar{N}_t + \tilde{N}_t}. \tag{6.24}$$

Total output is the sum of the manufacturing goods produced by craftsmen and agricultural goods produced by farmers,

$$N_t^* y_t + \tilde{N}_t p_t O_t = N_t^* D_t \hat{k}_t^{\alpha}\left(\frac{\bar{\alpha}\hat{k}_t^{\alpha}}{w_t}\right)^{\frac{\bar{\alpha}}{1-\bar{\alpha}}} + \left(\frac{1-\alpha}{w_t}\right)^{\frac{1-\alpha}{\alpha}} p_t^{1/\alpha} L. \tag{6.25}$$

Notice in (6.25) that technological change only increases output in the manufacturing sector. Why is this the case, given that we assume balanced technological change throughout the economy?

Going back to (6.21), we see that technological progress reduces the demand for labor in the agricultural sector proportionally. Other things constant, farmers need to employ a certain quantity of *effective* labor to profitably produce agricultural goods. A higher level of technology increases the productivity of a worker and reduces the number of workers needed. Thus, technological change frees labor from agriculture but does not directly increase output.

In the manufacturing sector, technological progress does not necessarily reduce employment because the demand for labor is also determined by the de-trended capital stock which, unlike land, can be increased with sufficient saving. So, while technological progress is balanced throughout the economy, the larger is the manufacturing sector, the stronger is the effect of technological progress on total output. What is "special" about the manufacturing sector is that it relies more heavily on man-made physical capital. This means that technological progress in manufacturing does not just reduce labor cost, but may also increase output. Thus, there is mechanism through which deindustrialization, in the sense of a lower manufacturing share or a lower capital stock, can reduce economic growth.

6.2.8 Calibration

Each period in the model lasts 20 years, and we think of the initial period as 1820. We set the capital share to the commonly chosen value of 1/3. We set the exogenous population growth rate to 1 % annually based on the estimate from Issawi (1980). Also from Issawi, we target urban population shares equal to 17 % in 1820 and 22 % in 1920. We assume that a constant 10 % share of the population is comprised of craftsmen. This means that the percent of the population that are migrant workers living and working for the craftsmen in the city begins at 7 % and then grows to 12 % by 1920. We targeted an initial interest rate at the beginning of the century of 20 % to capture the lack of advancement in financial intermediation and the very high interest rates in the Empire over the century. Given the absence of data, we somewhat arbitrarily target an initial craftsman skill premium of 1.5. The four targets, initial and end of century urbanization, initial interest rate, and initial skill premium, determine $\beta = 0.065$, $\bar{\alpha} = 0.21$, and the initial values for the de-trended stocks of land and physical capital.

The exogenous rate of technological progress is set to keep the annual growth in per capita income between 0.5 and 1 % over the century, based on the estimates from Pamuk (2006). The exogenous rate of technological change was set to 0.3 % annually. The initial value for the international relative price of agriculture goods is one. In 1840 the price rise to 1.5 and then to 2.0 in 1860, after which it is kept constant.[8]

Table 6.4 gives the result of the calibrated development of the nineteenth century Ottoman Empire. The associated annual growth rate in per capita income was 0.78 %. The reported wage rate is w, i.e., the wage de-trended for technological progress.

Clearly, the jump in agricultural prices in the middle of the century slowed the structural transformation. The urban share and the skill premium both declined,

---

[8] We could have chosen a greater rise in the relative price but did not for the following reasons. As stressed by Quataert (1993), the rural sector, as is typically the case in developing economies, actually engaged in some informal manufacturing production. This means that the relative price of rural production did not rise as much as the relative price of food and primary commodities. We found that, with greater increases in the relative price of rural production, it was difficult to match the 1920 urbanization target without also assuming greater growth than was consistent with Pamuk's findings (growth in per capita of less than one percent). A better way of addressing these points would be to allow the farmers to produce all types of goods, but we leave this for future work.

Table 6.4 Nineteenth-century Ottoman Empire

Time period	Wage (manufacturing units)	Interest rate (%)	Urban share (%)	Skill premium	Farmer's land rent (manufacturing units)
1820	0.025	20.2	17	1.50	0.64
1840	0.035	15.0	19	1.82	0.92
1860	0.043	14.0	17	1.56	1.21
1880	0.039	12.9	19	2.04	1.16
1900	0.036	12.9	21	2.32	1.11
1920	0.034	12.9	22	2.55	1.07

before rising again later in the century. We will not actually know the full extent of the slowdown until we compute the counterfactual simulation where we assume there is no rise in the international price of agricultural goods. Land rents rose and then fell as agricultural prices stabilized at their higher value and the land per farm fell. The rise in land rents increased the demand for labor, driving up the wage in manufacturing units. As we shall see below, the higher wage is the main reason for the slow growth in urban employment as a share of the population.

6.2.9 Counterfactual Simulation

Now we compute the counterfactual development path, assuming the relative price of agricultural goods remains constant at one throughout the century. The results are given in Table 6.5. The effect on urbanization is dramatic; instead of 22 %, the urban share hits 38 % in 1920. The annual growth rate in per capita income increases modestly to 0.91 % from 0.78 % per year. The higher growth rate is due to a rise in capital intensity and a shift of the labor to the modern production, both of which raise the impact of exogenous technological progress. The qualitative predictions of the deindustrialization hypothesis clearly hold.

However, there are distributional effects that make it unclear whether the majority of the population was in fact hurt by the rise in agricultural prices. There is

Table 6.5 Counterfactual Ottoman Empire (constant *p*)

Time period	Wage (manufacturing units)	Interest rate (%)	Urban share (%)	Skill premium	Land rent (per farmer)
1820	0.025	20.2	17	1.50	0.64
1840	0.024	13.9	27	3.64	0.57
1860	0.023	13.4	30	4.35	0.54
1880	0.021	13.3	33	4.86	0.51
1900	0.02	13.4	35	5.37	0.49
1920	0.018	13.5	38	5.92	0.46

a dramatic rise in the skill premium in the counterfactual simulation, indicating that the craftsmen would have been much better off if the price rise had not occurred. Farmers/landowners would have seen a decline in land rents rather than the rising rents that they actually experienced. In addition, migrant workers would have seen a decline in their real wage in manufacturing units rather than the significant rise we see in Table 6.4. On the other hand, migrant workers would not have confronted the higher price of agricultural goods. To draw clear conclusions, we need a more complete metric for the overall welfare effects.

To compare the welfare effects associated with the growth paths from Tables 6.4 and 6.5, we compute the value function for each household type.

Migrants

$$V_t^M = \Gamma_t + (1+\beta)\ln w_t + \beta \ln R_t - (1-\chi)(\ln p_t + \beta \ln p_{t+1})$$

Craftsmen

$$V_t^C = \Gamma_t + (1+\beta)\ln w_t^* + \beta \ln R_t - (1-\chi)(\ln p_t + \beta \ln p_{t+1})$$

Farmers

$$V_t^F = \Gamma_t + (1+\beta)\ln w_t + \beta \ln R_t - (1-\chi)(\ln p_t + \beta \ln p_{t+1}) + (1+\beta)\ln\left(1 + \frac{\text{rent}_{t+1}}{w_t D_t R_t}\right).$$

The expression Γ_t is comprised of parameters and exogenous variables that are independent of the endogenous variables along the growth path. The welfare effects are obviously going to depend on the fraction of budget spent on food, $1-\chi$. In a developing economy, the food share will be high. We compute the welfare difference between the counterfactual case and the historical simulation for $1-\chi$ set to 3/4.

Table 6.6 reports the lifetime welfare effects for each generation of our three household types. There are small differences in the return to capital across the historical and counterfactual simulations, so the small resulting differences in welfare due to changes in the return to capital will be ignored in our discussion.

For the initial generation of migrants and craftsmen, eliminating the price rise makes them better off. The price increase did not begin until 1840 and so did not

Table 6.6 Welfare effects from counterfactually eliminating the rise in p

Time period	Migrants	Craftsmen	Farmers/ landowners
1820	0.0073	0.0073	−0.0422
1840	−0.0587	0.6794	−0.119
1860	−0.1191	0.973	−0.1616
1880	−0.1157	0.8088	−0.1616
1900	−0.1066	0.7918	−0.1595

affect the wages of the young workers in 1820. However, the higher price of food lowers purchasing power for these households when they are old and lowers their lifetime welfare. The older farmers received more than enough additional land rents in 1840 to cover the higher price of food, so they would be worse off had the price rise been eliminated. Not surprisingly, all generations of craftsmen are made better off, and all generations of farmers worse off, when eliminating the relative price increase.

Starting in 1840, eliminating the rise in prices also affects wages. Wages would have been lower if the strong demand for labor by the agricultural sector was eliminated. The main result from Table 6.6 is that, starting in 1840, migrant workers would have been worse off had the international price of food not risen. The rise in their wages was enough to offset the rise in the price of food, even when assuming that 75 % of their expenditures were on food. This is because without the rise in p, the de-trended wage in manufacturing units would have fallen by 29 % instead of rising by 33 %. By century's end, wages were 86 % higher with the rise in p than without it. This is more than enough to compensate for the rise in p.

After 1840, only craftsman would have benefited, had the Empire not been exposed to the price rise in international markets. Skilled wages, or monopoly rents, would have been much higher had the relative price not turned so dramatically against the goods that craftsmen produced. Thus, while economic growth would have been somewhat higher had the relative price rise not occurred, only a very small fraction of the society would have benefited.

This conclusion ignores the negative effects of an increase in the volatility of relative prices, "terms of trade," due to opening the economy. Blattman et al. (2007) find that opening the economy increased volatility for developing economies in the nineteenth and early twentieth centuries. They also estimate that an increase in terms-of-trade volatility is associated with slower growth in per capita income. Increased volatility can also reduce welfare directly. A more complete analysis of opening the economy should include the potentially important effects of increased volatility in the terms of trade.

6.3 Other Theories of Trade and Growth

In Sect. 6.2, we have seen that international trade may lower growth in developing countries that have a comparative in traditional agricultural production. In this section, we discuss some other arguments suggesting that trade may lower growth.

6.3.1 Reduced Incentives for Human Capital Investment

A closely complimentary theory about how trade may lower growth in developing countries is offered by Galor and Mountford (2006, 2008). They argue that higher relative prices in the traditional sector will lower the demand for skilled labor and reduce human capital accumulation. In our formal models, primarily for simplicity, the evolution of human capital is independent of the structural transformation. This is because we have exclusively emphasized how the reliance of families on child labor affects their willingness to educate children (see Chaps. 3 and 5).

A second consideration involved in the decision to educate children is the relative wage paid to skilled labor versus unskilled labor. To analyze this situation, skilled and unskilled labor must be treated as distinct inputs in production. In our model, units of human capital are perfect substitutes, known as "efficiency units,"—it simply takes more units of unskilled labor to do what a skilled worker can do. Alternatively, skilled labor could be an important input in the modern sector, while unskilled labor suffices for traditional sector production. If this is true, then an increase in the relative price of traditional sector goods lowers the relative demand for skilled labor and lowers the incentive to attend school. This argument is overly strong because there is evidence that schooling increases farmers' productivity even in traditional settings. However, the relative return to schooling may nevertheless be higher in the modern sector and the argument will go through more generally.

6.3.2 Efficiency Advantages and External Effects from Urbanization

It is often assumed that there is a productivity advantage of producing manufacturing goods in urban locations rather than producing primary commodities in rural locations. (e.g., Williamson 2011, p. 49). The ideas underlying this assumption include the possibility that (1) technological change occurs more rapidly in manufacturing than in agriculture, (2) greater manufacturing production generates economies of scale, and (3) urbanization creates economic externalities and spillovers.

It is quite difficult to directly detect a productivity advantage simply by looking at data across sectors. In the USA and Europe, the productivity advantage of urban manufacturing certainly did not show up as large differences in hourly labor productivity of agricultural and nonagricultural workers during the nineteenth century. Measures of productivity and wage gaps per hour worked were quite small, less than 25 %, even without adjusting for differences in education per worker. As discussed in Chap. 5, some researchers also find small hourly productivity gaps in current developing countries, adjusted for human capital differences.

Of course, sector–wage differences will motivate labor flows that limit the size of the wage gaps. Small gaps in productivity and wages may be consistent with large advantages of urban manufacturing that cause labor to consistently flow toward cities. Thus, the productivity advantages of producing manufacturing goods in an urban setting may not show up as large or rising wage gaps, but rather as increasing labor shares.

In most countries, there is a steady increase in the fraction of the workforce in urban manufacturing as economic growth takes place. However, this observation alone also fails to imply the presence of urban manufacturing productivity advantages like the ones mentioned above. If the rural population is increasing, a movement of labor to the city is necessary to offset a declining marginal productivity of rural labor as the labor–land ratio grows. This force for urbanization simply results from the fact that man-made physical capital can be more easily expanded to accommodate a larger workforce than can land.

Others point to the time series correlation between average worker productivity and urbanization as a country grows, but again the causation is far from clear. Henderson (2003) finds "little support for the idea that urbanization per se drives growth." Rather he argues that "urbanization is a "by-product" of the move out of agriculture and the effective development of a modern manufacturing sector, as economic development proceeds, rather than a growth stimulus." In other words, there are fundamental changes that cause *both* manufacturing and growth to increase, such as *balanced* technological change across all sectors or increased capital formation, that do not imply any causal feedback effect from urbanization to aggregate growth. In fact, we saw this in Sect. 6.2. Uniquely rapid growth in manufacturing technologies, or endogenous external effects from urbanization, is not necessary to explain the time series correlation between growth and urbanization. We discuss the link between urbanization and growth further in Chap. 8.

6.3.3 Power of Anti-growth Landowners

There is a political economy argument that links urbanization to growth. The idea is that in the early stages of development, large landowners are often politically influential. Their objective is to maximize land rents from traditional agricultural production. Land rents are high when the supply of labor is plentiful and cheap. Landowners are against policies that increase the demand for labor in other sectors and wages throughout the economy. Thus, landowners will oppose policies that promote physical and human capital formation that impact worker productivity more in manufacturing than in traditional agriculture. The greater is the relative size of the urban population, the more interest there is in promoting capital formation and the more likely the interest of the large landowners can be defeated, setting the stage for more pro-growth policies. We provide an example of how the influence of landowners can affect policy in Sect. 6.4.

6.3.4 Volatility and Growth

There is a literature relating short-run volatility to long-run average growth rates. The studies consistently show greater volatility is associated with lower average growth rates [see the review in Cavalcanti et al. (2012)]. As mentioned in Sect. 6.2, one important source of volatility is the variation in a country's terms of trade.

Blattman et al. (2007) provide evidence that terms-of-trade volatility was associated with lower growth rates in the 1870–1939 period.

In addition to terms-of-trade volatility, openness can increase output volatility. A recent study by Haddard et al. (2012) finds that modern day developing economies that are more open experience more volatility in total production. Much of the increased volatility is generated by increased export concentration. They find that openness and export concentration interact to create greater volatility in production. So, export concentration has a larger impact on aggregate volatility, the larger is the country's trade share (export plus imports divided by GDP).

6.4 Large Landowners—Growth and Endogenous Fiscal Policy

Now we suppose that there are two rather different private sector household types—workers and large landowners. The workers might farm land, but they do not own the land. The main motivation for this setup is that large landowners are viewed as having an important impact on the political economy of many developing countries, as mentioned in Sect. 6.3. Landowners derive their income from land rents and thus seek to establish and maintain conditions where land rents are high. This motivation comes in conflict with economic progress that raises wages and the cost of labor, so large land owners tend to support policies that stifle economic growth. In this section, we focus on landowner support for fiscal policies that serve their interest.

The dual economy approach also allows us to examine the connection between development and the size of government. Several studies have found a strong negative correlation between the relative size of the agricultural sector and the relative size of government, other things constant (Burgess and Stern 1993; Peltzman 1980; Stotsky and WoldeMarian 1997; Tanzi 1991). In fact, the studies find that the relative size of the agricultural sector is more closely correlated with the relative size of government than are other indicators of development, such as income per capita. One reason for this negative correlation is that the traditional sector generates unrecorded sales and income that are relatively difficult to tax.

The political influence of large landowners is one factor that keeps both the modern sector and the size of government small. There is a growing literature suggesting that land inequality may hamper growth. The survey by Erickson and Vollrath (2004) mentions general mechanisms for the negative effects of land inequality that work through institutions, influence over agricultural policy, credit market development, and support for public schooling. A common feature of the mechanisms is the attempt by politically powerful landowners to maintain a low-cost workforce in agriculture by limiting the options of workers outside of agriculture (see Burgess and Stern 1993 for some specific examples from Latin America).

We argue that an additional way that landowners might maintain a low-cost workforce is to support high tax rates on labor and capital. If incomes are easier to identify and tax in urban manufacturing, then a high tax rate environment will favor the agricultural sector. As workers avoid high tax rates by supplying labor to agriculture, the wage rates in agriculture will be driven down to the benefit of landowners. Thus, landowner support for high tax rates will reduce the modern sector, the tax base, and the size of government.

6.4.1 Households

We continue to assume that all households have the same preferences,

$$U_t = \ln c_{1t} + \beta \ln c_{2t+1}. \tag{6.26}$$

Households supply one total unit of labor with no explicit labor/leisure choice. There is no land market, and landowners pass their land holdings to their children but derive no explicit utility from doing so.

All working households are now landless and derive their income from supplying labor to both the modern and traditional sectors during the first period of their lives, so they can freely move across sections to work. They retire in the second period. Their only source of lifetime income is, ω_t, after-tax wage income. For simplicity, we assume the government is completely unable to tax wages earned in the traditional sector. All results go through with a partial ability to tax the traditional sector. After-tax wage income is the sum of after-tax wages earned by workers in each sector, $\omega_t = \pi_t(1-\tau_t)w_t + (1-\pi_t)\tilde{w}_t$, where π is the fraction of work effort supplied to the modern sector.

If both sectors are to operate, workers must be indifferent about where they work. This means that after-tax wages must be equalized across sectors, $(1-\tau_t)w_t = \tilde{w}_t$. Thus, we have a wage gap in *before-tax* wages, resulting from taxation in the modern sector only.

Landowners have the same preferences as workers. In this section, we assume the landowners derive *first*-period income from the residual income generated by traditional production. This income may be interpreted as a combination of land rents and compensation for the landowner's work time. Land is then passed to the next generation inter vivos at the end of the first period. This timing of the land transfers allows us to bypass the effect of inheritance on the landowners saving rate because it is no longer a source of retirement income.

The landowners' lifetime income is then $O_t - \tilde{w}_t f_t$. The first-order condition for the labor demand that maximizes residual income allows us to write landowner lifetime income as

$$\rho O_t = \frac{\rho \tilde{w}_t f_t}{1-\rho}. \tag{6.27}$$

The demand for labor is given by a new version of (6.8b),

$$f_t = \left[\frac{(1-\rho)}{(1-\tau_t)w_t}\right]^{\frac{1}{\rho}} l_t. \tag{6.28}$$

Note that, if we define the number of landowners as $\tilde{N}_t$, then $\tilde{N}_t f_t = (1 - \pi_t)N_t$. So, $\pi_t = 1 - \frac{L}{N_t}\left[\frac{1-\rho}{(1-\tau_t)w_t}\right]^{\frac{1}{\rho}}$.

6.4.2 Open Economy

For simplicity, as in the later portion of Chap. 3, we assume that the economy is open to international capital flows. This assumption forces the domestic rate of return to capital to equal the exogenous world interest rate. The capital–labor ratio in the modern sector is therefore also fixed (see 6.2b) at a value we call k^*, causing the before-tax wage in the modern sector to be fixed at w^* (see 6.2a). This means the welfare of all households is completely driven by the wage tax. In addition, the total capital stock of the country will vary with the size of the modern sector as defined by π_t because $K_t = k^* \pi_t N_t$. Policies that reduce labor in the modern sector will cause the economy to lose physical capital or deindustrialize.[9]

6.4.3 Government Policy

We take the same "reduced-form" approach to the formation of policy that was introduced in Chap. 3. We model the government as any other economic agent—by specifying its preferences, constraints, and objectives. There is no deep model of the politics that determine how the government is chosen and how its policies are influenced by voters and interest groups. Instead, we take as given the politics of a country which determine the "reduced-form" preference parameters that dictate the government's concern with the welfare of the general population, of different household types, and of the households that make up the government itself.

Government officials have preferences defined over their own consumption and the welfare of the two private sector household types, based on their political influence.

[9] Taxing the return to capital, in addition, to wages would not alter the results much. In an open economy, the after-tax return to capital must remain equal to the after-tax world interest rate. Thus, country-specific taxes cannot alter the after-tax return. However, higher taxes on capital in a given country will reduce that country's capital–labor ratio. Thus, taxing capital in an open economy will be entirely shifted to labor by lowering before-tax wages. The primary difference between an income tax and a wage tax is that the economy reduces its capital–labor ratio as well as its total capital stock. See Problem 6.12.

The government officials retire in the second period just as the private agents. Their first-period wages are financed by taxes on the wages of the private sector workers. The single-period government budget constraint is $w_t^g N_t^g = \tau_t w_t \pi_t N_t$, where all government consumption is in the form of wages paid to the officials and where N_t^g is the number of government officials. The number of government officials is an exogenous fraction of the total population.

The preferences that determine government policy are given by the function, $\phi^g V_t^g + \phi V_t + \tilde{\phi}\tilde{V}_t$, where ϕ^g, ϕ, and $\tilde{\phi}$ are constant preference parameters that are determined by the political power of the three agents and the V functions are the indirect utility functions of each type. We think of the government's preference parameters as functions of exogenous political institutions and the de facto political power of the private sector households. Countries with less democratic institutions, and fewer "constraints on the executive," will tend to have governments that place less weight on the welfare of the private sectors households as a whole (low values for both ϕ and $\tilde{\phi}$), or perhaps that give disproportionate influence to wealthy landowners (a high value for $\tilde{\phi}$ and a low value for ϕ).

The indirect utility functions of the households can be written out as

$$V_t = E + (1+\beta)\ln(1-\tau_t) \tag{6.29a}$$

$$\tilde{V}_t = \tilde{E} - (1+\beta)\frac{1-\rho}{\rho}\ln(1-\tau_t) \tag{6.29b}$$

$$V_t^g = E^g + (1+\beta)(\ln\tau_t + \ln\pi_t), \tag{6.29c}$$

where the uppercase E expressions on the right-hand side of each equation contain exogenous constants that will not affect the policy choice. The tax rate lowers the welfare of workers by lowering the after-tax wage in the modern sector and the before-tax wage in the traditional sector. Landowners prefer a high wage tax because it lowers the cost of labor and increases total land rents. The government officials also benefit from a high tax, although they must consider that a higher tax rate lowers the tax base—i.e., the total wage bill in the modern sector.

Using (6.28) and the equilibrium condition for the labor share, the first-order condition for the optimal tax rate is

$$\frac{\phi^g}{\tau_t} = \frac{1}{(1-\tau_t)}\left\{\phi^g\left(\frac{1-\pi_t}{\rho\pi_t}\right) + \phi - \frac{1-\rho}{\rho}\tilde{\phi}\right\}, \tag{6.30}$$

which is sketched in Fig. 6.1.

The left-hand side of (6.30) is the decreasing marginal benefit of taxation that stems from the marginal utility of consumption by government officials whose salaries are financed by the tax revenue. The right-hand side of (6.30) is the increasing marginal cost of taxation, comprised of three distinct terms. The first term captures the effect of raising the tax rate on the tax base. A higher tax rate

Fig. 6.1 Optimal tax rate

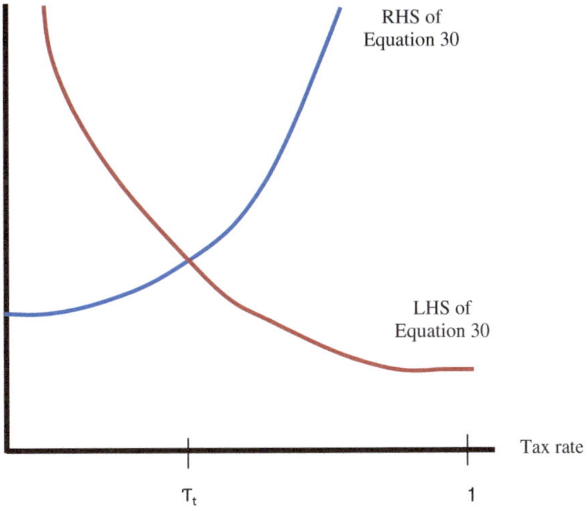

shrinks the taxable wage bill in the modern sector as workers move to the traditional sector to avoid taxation. If there was no weight placed on the welfare of private sector households ($\phi = \tilde{\phi} = 0$), the government would maximize the tax revenue collected by equating the left-hand side to the first term on the right-hand side

The second term on the right-hand side captures the marginal cost of taxation to working households resulting from a reduction in their after-tax wage. The third term reduces the marginal cost of taxation, because it represents the gain to landowners from the fall in traditional sector wages when the tax rate is increased. If the sum of these last two terms is positive, the optimal tax will be less than the tax rate that maximizes tax revenue because of the net welfare loss that taxes inflict on the private sector. However, with sufficiently powerful landowners, the net welfare effect of taxation on the private sector could be positive. In this case, the tax rate would exceed the revenue maximizing level.

There are two important general points demonstrated by (6.30). First, the greater the political influence of landowners (higher $\tilde{\phi}$), the higher is the tax rate. A higher tax rate lowers wages, the size of the modern sector, and the economy's capital stock. Powerful landowners prevent industrialization of the economy at the expense of working households.[10]

Second, exogenous factors that cause the size of the modern sector to grow, i.e., that cause π_t to increase for a given tax rate, lower the marginal cost of taxation and cause the optimal tax rate to increase. The intuition is that the *marginal* loss in the tax base, as the tax rate rises, is smaller and less valuable, the larger is the *total* tax base. Thus, tax rates will tend to increase, other things constant, as economies grow and modernize. This result helps explain Wagner's Law, the observation that the

[10] Galor et al. (2009) provide a theory and supporting evidence that larger landowners have acted to slow the accumulation of human capital for similar reasons.

Table 6.7 Government in developed and developing countries

	Government purchases (% of GDP)	Capital income tax rate (maximum statutory rate)	Personal income tax rate (maximum statutory rate)
Developed countries (1990s)	18.9	29.6	42.8
Developing countries (1990s)	14.2	26.7	34.7
Developing countries (1870)	4.6	n.a.	n.a

Sources Government purchase share for 1990 from Jha (2007, Table 9). Government purchase share for 1870 from Tanzi and Schuknecht (2000, Table II. 1). Tax rates for 1996–2001 are from Gordon and Ii (2005)

relative size of government increases with development.[11] Some evidence for Wagner's Law is provided in Table 6.7.

The rise in the relative size of the government over the course of development is associated with constant or rising economic growth rates. We have seen that taxation can reduce private capital accumulation. So, what explains this apparent paradox? The answer is that the government uses some fraction of rising tax revenue to invest in public education, public health, and infrastructure, as we saw in Chap. 3. As the structural transformation generates a relatively larger government, there need not be a drag on growth if the government uses a sufficiently high fraction of the tax revenue on investment. Mourmouras and Rangazas (2009b) discussed these points in detail.

6.5 Conclusion

In this chapter, we see that the structural transformation expands hours worked per worker because workers are constrained to work significantly fewer hours per year in the traditional agricultural sector. Agricultural workers are willing to accept this constraint because they are compensated by the rents they receive from the land they inherit from their parents. The structural transformation has ambiguous effects on physical capital per worker. Migration out of the traditional sector has two opposing effects on capital intensity; saving rates rise, but the number of workers that must be supplied with capital in the modern sector also rises.

[11] Our analysis ignores the growth in the size of government due to the growth in social transfers. This reason for the growth in government tends to occur in later stages of development as countries become more democratic. See Lindert (2004) for a thorough discussion of the connection between democracy and government size.

In the USA, we find the structural transformation in the nineteenth century did not have a significant impact on capital intensity but did significantly expand hours worked per worker. This resulted in a much larger increase in output per worker than in output per hour worked.

We also examined the extent to which international trade "deindustrialized" the Ottomon Empire in the nineteenth century. We find that the sharp rise in the relative price of agricultural products did significantly slow the migration of labor into the urban manufacturing sector. There was also a small negative impact on labor productivity per hour worked. As in the case of the USA, the pace of structural transformation was not closely related to the growth in capital intensity. Deindustrialization did not cause significant changes in capital intensity. In addition, we showed that it is possible for the vast majority of the population to have benefited from the rise in the relative price of agricultural goods. Incorporation of the effect of greater volatility in the term of trade is needed to provide a more conclusive assessment.

While the results from this chapter suggest a weak connection between private capital accumulation and the structural transformation, there is an important connection to public capital accumulation. Factors that reduce the size of the traditional sector increase the government ability to raise tax revenue. The rise in tax revenue increases the funding for expanding public investment projects in countries with pro-growth governments.

6.6 Exercises

Questions

1. Explain how landed and landless households might differ in terms of (a) preferences, (b) constraints, and (c) behavior.
2. How does the structural transformation affect physical capital accumulation when many smaller farmers own land? Compare the theory of capital formation in Sect. 6.1 to that in Chap. 4 where land markets are assumed to be perfectly competitive.
3. Explain why the structural transformation affects labor productivity growth differently depending on whether it is measured per hour or per worker. How does US economic growth indicate that this distinction is important?
4. Describe the three types of households in Sect. 6.2. What is the motivation for introducing these particular household types?
5. In the model in Sect. 6.2, explain why it is possible to interpret the income of the craftsmen as either the "skilled worker's wage" or as "monopoly profit." Under what condition is the craftsman's income greater than the wage of the migrant worker?

6. Explain two ways in which international trade might "deindustrialize" an economy. Based on the analysis in Sect. 6.2, did international trade "deindustrialize" the Ottoman Empire in the nineteenth century?
7. *Thinking about Table* 6.4. (a) Use (6.21) to explain why wages in manufacturing units rise and then fall (b) Use (6.17a) to explain why the decline in interest rates implies the de-trended capital stock per craftsman must rise (c) Use (6.17c) to explain the time path of the skill premium (d) Why does a farmer's land rent rise and then fall?
8. Based on the analysis in Sect. 6.2, how did international trade alter growth and economic welfare in the Ottoman Empire over the nineteenth century?
9. Discuss alternative theories of how international trade affects economic growth. Do these theories compliment or compete with the theory in this chapter?
10. Is encouraging developing economies to open their economies a good idea? Base your answer on the analysis from this chapter and Chap. 3.
11. How are each of the three households in 6.3 affected by wage taxation?
12. Explain how powerful landowners can slow the structural transformation through their influence on tax policy.
13. Give two explanations for Wagner's Law.
14. Use Fig. 6.1 to explain your answers to questions 12 and 13.
15. How does an increase in the political power of the government officials affect tax policy? Careful—this is a bit harder than it appears.

Problems

1. Derive and interpret the saving function of a young household that eventually inherits the family farm as in (6.8a).
2. Derive the indirect utility functions of landed and landless households and use them to derive (6.9). Show that Ω_{t+1} is decreasing in $\tilde{z}$.
3. Show that (6.9) can be written as a function of π_t. So given k_t and N_t, one can use (6.9) to solve for the split of the population across sectors.
4. Derive the transition equation for physical capital intensity in 6.1. Carefully explain how one could simulate the transition path of the economy during the structural transformation.
5. Derive the labor market equilibrium condition from Sect. 6.2. How does technological change affect the demand for labor, other things constant?
6. Derive the expression for total output from Sect. 6.2. Why does the impact of technological change on output depend on the fraction of the workforce in the modern sector?
7. In the Appendix, we claim that an increase in the supply of unskilled labor $\left(\bar{N}_{t+1} + \tilde{N}_{t+1}\right)$ lowers the present value of land rents relative to wages and raises saving. To see this first show that $\text{rent}_{t+1}/w_t D_t R_t = \frac{\alpha}{1-\alpha}\frac{(1+d)f_{t+1}}{w_t}\frac{w_{t+1}}{R_t}$. Next use (6.17a, b, and c) and (6.20) to show $\frac{w_{t+1}}{R_t} = \frac{w_{t+1}}{r_{t+1}} = \frac{\bar{\alpha}}{\alpha}\frac{N^*_{t+1}}{(\tilde{N}_{t+1}+\bar{N}_{t+1})-\tilde{N}_t f_{t+1}}$.

8. Use the information in Tables 6.4 and 6.5 to compute the value of χ that would make each generation of migrant workers indifferent about the rise in the relative price of the agricultural good. Why is it valid to use the *same* values computed in Tables 6.4 and 6.5, when considering *different* values of χ?
9. Derive the indirect utility function for each household in 6.3.
10. Show that $\frac{d\pi_t}{d\tau_t} = \frac{-1}{\rho}\frac{1-\pi_t}{1-\tau_t}$. So the *marginal* decline in the modern sector tax base is smaller, the larger is the tax base.
11. Derive the equation determining the optimal wage tax rate in Sect. 6.3.
12. Suppose that instead of a wage tax, the government imposes an income tax that taxes both wages and the return to capital, r_t. Redo the analysis in Sect. 6.3 under the income tax.

Appendix*

Here are a few notes about solving for the dynamic path of the model from Sect. 6.2. The transition equation given by (6.23) can be written out in terms of wages and capital intensity,

$$\hat{k}_{t+1} = \frac{\beta w_t}{(1+\beta)(1+d)n}\left[\frac{\frac{\bar{N}_t+\tilde{N}_t}{N_t^*}+\frac{1-\bar{\alpha}-\alpha}{\bar{\alpha}}\left(\frac{\bar{\alpha}\hat{k}_t^{\alpha}}{w_t}\right)^{\frac{1}{1-\bar{\alpha}}}}{1+\frac{1}{1+\beta}\frac{\bar{\alpha}}{1-\alpha}\frac{\left(\frac{(1-\alpha)p_{t+1}}{w_{t+1}}\right)^{1/\alpha}(L/D_{t+1})}{\bar{N}_{t+1}+\tilde{N}_{t+1}-\left(\frac{(1-\alpha)p_{t+1}}{w_{t+1}}\right)^{1/\alpha}(L/D_{t+1})}}\right]. \tag{6.23}$$

Given an initial value for $\hat{k}_t$, one can use (6.21) to solve for w_t. Next, given the values for $\hat{k}_t$ and w_t, use (6.21), updated one period, and (6.23) to solve simultaneously for $\hat{k}_{t+1}$ and w_{t+1}.

It is important to note from (6.21) and (6.23) that the split of the population across migrant workers and farmers does not affect the equilibrium determination of the capital stock or wages ($\bar{N}_t$ and $\tilde{N}_t$ only appear together as a sum). In the numerator of (6.23), the farmers and migrants can be aggregated because they receive the same wage. In the denominator, the supply of farmers and migrants minus the farm demand for labor determines the equilibrium employment of unskilled labor in the urban sector (see 6.21). More unskilled labor in the urban sector lowers the capital to unskilled labor ratio and the wage interest rate ratio (see 6.17a, b, and c). A lower wage to interest rate ratio lowers the present value of land rents relative to wages, thereby increasing the saving of farmers and capital formation (see Problem 7 for more details).

The fact that $\bar{N}_t$ and $\tilde{N}_t$ only appear together as a sum is important because ownership claims on land in the early stages of development are unclear and it is difficult to determine what fraction of the population were migrant workers and what fraction earned some land rent. In addition, note that the capital stock and factor prices can be determined independently of the composition of output between manufacturing and agricultural goods (i.e., (6.21)–(6.23) are independent of χ).

References

Acemoglu D, Robinson J (2012) Why nations fail. The origins of power, prosperity, and poverty. Crown Publishers, New York

Alston L, Hatton T (1991) The earnings gap between agricultural and manufacturing laborers, 1925–1941. J Econ Hist 51(1):83–99

Banerjee A, Duflo E (2011) Poor economics. Public Affairs, New York

Burgess R, Stern N (1993) Taxation and development. J Econ lit 31(2):762–830

Blattman C, Hwang J, Williamson J (2007) The impact of terms of trade on economic development in the periphery, 1870–1939: volatility and secular change. J Dev Econ 82(1):156–179

Carter S, Ransom R, Sutch R (2003) Family matters: the life-cycle transition and the unparalleled fertility decline in antebellum America. In: Guinnane T, Sundstrom W, Whately W (eds) History matters: essays on economic growth, technology, and demographic change. Stanford University Press, Stanford, California

Caselli F, Coleman W (2001) The US structural transformation and regional convergence: a reinterpretation. J Polit Econ 109(3):584–616

Cavalcanti T, Mohaddes K, Raissi M (2012) Commodity price volatility and the sources of growth. IMF working paper 12/12. International Monetary Fund, Washington DC

Clark G (2007) A farewell to alms. Princeton University Press, Princeton, New Jersey

Collier P, Radwan S, Wangwe S (1986) Labour and poverty in rural Tanzania: Ujameen and rural development in the United Republic of Tanzania. Oxford University Press, New York

Cunningham H (1990) The employment and unemployment of children in England c. 1680–1851. Past Present 126:115–150

David P (1967) The growth of real product in the United States before 1840: new evidence, controlled conjectures. J Econ Hist 27(2):151–197

Deninger K, Squire L (1997) Explaining agricultural and agrarian policies in developing countries. J Econ Lit 35(4):1958–2005

de Vries J, van de Woude A (1999) The first modern economy. Cambridge University Press, Cambridge

Eaton J (1987) A dynamic specific factors model of international trade. Review of Economic Studies 54:325–338

Erickson, L Vollrath D (2004) Dimensions of land inequality and economic development. IMF working paper 158. International Monetary Fund, Washington DC

Galor O, Mountford A (2006) Trade and the great divergence: the family connection. Am Econ Rev 96(2):299–303

Galor O, Mountford A (2008) Trading population for productivity: theory and evidence. Rev Econ Stud 75(4):1143–1179

Galor O, Moav O, Vollrath D (2009) Inequality in landownership, the emergence of human capital promoting institutions, and the great divergence. Rev Econ Stud 76(1):143–179

Goldin C, Sokoloff K (1984) The relative productivity hypothesis of industrialization: the American case 1820–1850. Quart J Econ 99(3):461–490

Gollin D (2002) Getting income shares right. J Polit Econ 110(2):458–474

Gollin D (2014) The Lewis model: a sixty year retrospective. J Econ perspect 28(3):71–88

Gollin D, Lagakos D, Waugh M (2014) The agricultural productivity gap. Quart J Econ 129 (2):939–993
Gordon R, We L (2005) Tax structure in developing countries: many puzzles and a possible explanation. NBER working paper 11267. National Bureau of economic research, Cambridge
Haddard M, Lim J, Pancaro C, Saborowski C (2012) Trade openness and growth volatility. ECB working paper 1491. European Central Bank, Frankfurt
Hatton T, Williamson J (1992) What explains wages between the farm and city? Exploring the Todaro model with American evidence, 1890–1941. Econ Dev Cult Change 40:267–294
Henderson V (2003) The urbanization process and economic growth: the so-what question. J Econ Growth 8(1):47–71
Horrell S, Humphries J (1995) The exploitation of little children: child labor and the family in the industrial revolution. Explor Econ Hist 32(4):485–516
Issawi C (1980) The economic history of Turkey 1800–1914. Chicago University Press, Chicago
Jha R (2007) Fiscal policy in developing countries: a synoptic view. Australia South Asia Research Centre working paper 2007/01
Jones R (1971) A three-factor model in theory, trade, and history. In: Bhagwati J et al (eds) Trade, balance of payments, and growth. North-Holland, Amsterdam
Kendrick J (1961) Productivity trends in the United States. Princeton University Press, Princeton, New Jersey
La Porta R, Shleifer A (2014) Informality and development. Journal of Economic Perspectives 28(3):109–126
Lewis W (1954) Economic development with unlimited supplies of labor. Manchester School 22(2):139–191
Libecap G (2007) Property rights and federal land policy. In: Fishback P (ed) Government and the American economy. University of Chicago Press, Chicago
Lindert P (2004) Growing public. Cambridge University Press, Cambridge
Margo R (2000) Wages and labor markets in the United States 1820–1860. University of Chicago Press, Chicago
Mourmouras A, Rangazas P (2009a) Reconciling Kuznets and Habbakuk in a unified growth model. J Econ Growth 14(2):149–181
Mourmouras A, Rangazas P (2009b) Fiscal policy and economic development. Macroecon Dyn 13(4):450–476
Pamuk S (2006) Estimating economic growth in the Middle East since 1820. J Econ Hist 66(1):809–828
Pamuk S, Williamson J (2011) Ottoman de-industrialization, 1800–1913: assessing the magnitude, impact, and response. Econ Hist Rev 64:159–184
Peltzman S (1980) The growth of government. J Law Econ 23(2):209–287
Samuelson P (1971) Ohlin was right. Swedish Journal of Economics 73:365–384
Stotsky JG, Asegedech W (1997) Tax effects in sub-Saharan Africa. IMF working paper 97/107. International Monetary Fund, Washington DC
Tanzi V (1991) Structural factors and tax revenue in developing countries: a decade of evidence. International Monetary Fund, Washington DC
Tanzi V, Schuknecht L (2000) Public spending in the twentieth century. Cambridge University Press, New York
Quataert D (1993) Ottoman manufacturing in the age of the industrial revolution. Cambridge University Press, Cambridge
Vollrath D (2014) The efficiency of human capital allocations in developing countries. University of Houston working paper 201307956
Williamson J (2011) Trade and poverty: when the third world fell behind. MIT Press, Cambridge

A Complete Dual Economy

7

In this chapter we combine the main features introduced in previous chapters into a complete dual economy model. The model includes physical and human capital, fertility, wage gaps, and technological change. We then examine the ability of the model to replicate key features of the economic growth observed in real-world economies.

In order to include all the features together in one model, we introduce one simplification. In several of the applications of the two-sector model from Chaps. 4 and 6, we interpreted the traditional sector as specializing in agricultural production and the modern sector as specializing in manufacturing production. This interpretation seems quite natural and useful for some purposes, but in this chapter we argue for use of the one-good interpretation of the dual economy. We continue to assume that sectors are distinct because the traditional sector's production is dependent on land, while the modern sector's production is capital intensive. In addition, traditional production is conducted by families in a localized and specialized manner, while modern sector production is carried out in factories using general methods.

The family, and not the firm, was the predominant center for production in the USA during the nineteenth century (Ruggles 2001; Carter et al. 2003). The family was a multigenerational producer with assets and management provided by older generations and labor provided by younger generations. Goods were produced not only for home consumption but also to sell and trade in the market as well. Moreover, family production was not limited to agricultural products; manufacturing goods (leather products, flour, furniture, tools) and services (retail sales) were also prominent.[1]

The quantitative importance of the multigenerational family producer was striking. Ruggles (2001) provides data from the middle of the nineteenth century,

---

[1] Across today's developing countries, high percentages of the poor operate small businesses: 50 % for urban poor and 25–98 % for rural poor (Banerjee and Duflo 2011, p. 135). La Porta and Schleifer (2014) estimate the informal sector accounts for 30–40 % of economic activity in poor countries and an even higher share of employment.

S. Das et al., *Economic Growth and Development*,
Springer Texts in Business and Economics, DOI 10.1007/978-3-319-14265-4_7

showing that 80 % of the elderly lived with their adult children. He further demonstrates that the property was owned by the elderly and that the children remained at home to provide the labor needed to operate the family farm. Family-based production was so prevalent that only about 45 % of prime-aged white males were employed in wage and salary jobs.

Land inheritance was certainly an important consideration binding young workers to family production but it was not the only consideration. Young workers also inherited specific skills, local knowledge of productive factors, and business relations based on trust and familiarity with the family. In short, children inherited not only land, but also an entire family production technology that was passed down from working with their parents. The following quote from Ruggles (2005, p. 11), again regarding the USA in the nineteenth century, attests to historical relevance of this mechanism, even outside of agriculture.

> In the nineteenth century, the bulk of men in the high-status occupations were proprietors of one sort or another. Many of these people inherited their businesses from their fathers. To a lesser extent, that was true in mid-status jobs as well; among the common titles in that category were bakers, brickmasons, cabinet-makers, carpenters, and shoemakers, who typically had their own shops in that period. Many craftsmen inherited their occupations from their fathers, and a son who lived with his parents was no doubt more likely to inherit. Sales clerks had especially high rates of coresidence in the nineteenth century; many of them probably worked in their fathers' stores with the expectation of eventual inheritance.

Similar views on the nature of traditional production are common. Quataert (1993, p. 2), in his detailed study of rural manufacturing in the nineteenth century Ottoman Empire, makes a strong case for the idea that traditional production generally involved a mix of production activities.

> We now know from studies of the American, British, German, Chinese, and other economies that manufacturing often is an integral, variously important, part of agrarian life. Agrarian economies commonly were mixed and rural families engaged in both agriculture and manufacturing, both for subsistence and commercial purposes.

Ranis and Fei (1961, p. 534), among the original founders of the dual economy approach, used the two-good interpretation in their work. However, they recognized it was not entirely accurate.

> We wish to underscore the absence of any necessary one-to-one relationship between the subsistence sector and agriculture, or between the capitalistic sector and industry in most less-developed economies. The existence of substantial islands of commercialized production in the primary sector and of sizable subsistence enclaves in the small-scale and service industries does not, however, bar Lewis, or us, from using this short-hand terminology.

La Porta and Schleifer (2014) find evidence of an informal sector in the production of *most* goods. They argue that the informal sector in developing countries today is best interpreted as the traditional sector in dual economy models. They document large wage gaps between the informal sector and the more capital-intensive formal sector. An expansion in the formal sector, due to physical and human capital accumulation, gradually pulls labor out of the informal sector over time. This is the same mechanism we focus on in this chapter.

With the broader interpretation of the dual economy, the assumption that land markets do not exist is no longer as critical to the analysis because specific skills, along with local knowledge and business relationships, are sufficient to bind children to the traditional technology. This makes it easier to understand why informal agreements are made to include intergenerational transfers of land and other assets, *even in the presence of land markets*. Land is more valuable if kept within the family because its productivity is tied to the other features of the specific traditional technology that children learn while working for their parents.

We ignore land and use the one-good model to study the sources and patterns of long-run growth, as well as the connection of growth with other features of the economy. Section 7.1 presents the model. Section 7.2 calibrates the model and then simulates long-run transitional growth paths. Section 7.3 compares the general features of the growth simulations to historical and more recent data from developing countries. Section 7.4 presents a case study of the South Korean Growth Miracle. Section 7.5 discusses ways that the modeling of human capital can be expanded to explain more of a developing economy's transitional growth. Section 7.6 reports the empirical evidence regarding convergence of poor to rich countries. Section 7.7 adds to our ongoing discussion of the interaction between politics and the dual economy. Section 7.8 provides a conclusion.

7.1 The Dual Economy

The model in this chapter shares elements from all previous chapters. As in Chap. 3, households choose how many children to have and how much time the children spend in school rather than work. As in Chap. 4, there are two sectors with two different technologies. As in Chaps. 5 and 6, there are features that distinguish the traditional and modern sectors that go beyond the technologies used. First, by working for the family in the traditional sector, assets are inherited (the family technology or specific human capital) that allows one to manage family production in the second or "retirement" period of adult life. Second, when young, working in the traditional sector constrains work opportunities. Specifically, there are limits to how many hours one can work over the course of the year because of physical demands of the work, seasonal constraints of the weather, or because of the lack of modern features of the technology used such as electricity. As in Chaps. 2 and 6, we include physical capital accumulation and, in particular, how it is influenced by the structural transformation.

7.1.1 Production Technologies and Factor Prices

Producers in the modern sector are neoclassical firms that use the standard Cobb–Douglas production function

$$Y_t = AK_t^{\alpha}(D_tM_t)^{1-\alpha}, \tag{7.1}$$

where Y denotes output, K is the physical capital stock, M is the human capital employed in the modern sector, D is the index of exogenous labor-augmenting technology in the modern sector, and α is the capital share parameter.

The firms operate in perfectly competitive markets for goods and inputs. The standard profit-maximizing factor-price equations for the rental rates on human capital and physical capital are as follows:

$$w_t = (1-\alpha)Ak_t^{\alpha} \tag{7.2a}$$

$$r_t = \alpha Ak_t^{\alpha-1}, \tag{7.2b}$$

where r is the return to capital and $k = K/(DM)$.

Traditional output is produced by a family business that we will continue to refer to as a "farm," to make a clear contrast between informal production and formal production by firms. The traditional technology used on the farm is given as

$$O_t = \tilde{A}\left(\tilde{D}_t f_t\right)^{1-\alpha}, \tag{7.3}$$

where O output, f is effective demand for labor per farm in the traditional sector, and $\tilde{D}_t$ is the index of exogenous labor-augmenting technology in the traditional sector. Note, for simplicity only, we ignore land. As before, we assume there is a market for farm labor. Households can hire labor beyond that provided by the family.

7.1.2 Household Behavior

Preferences are the same for all households and are represented by the utility function used in past chapters, $u_t = \ln c_{1t} + \beta \ln c_{2t+1} + \psi \ln(n_{t+1}h_{t+1})$, and the human capital production function is once again $h_{t+1} = e_t^{\theta}$.

The single-period budget constraints for the modern sector households are given as

$$c_{1t} + s_t + n_{t+1}\eta w_t D_t h_t = w_t D_t h_t + n_{t+1} w_t D_t \gamma \bar{h}(T - e_t) \tag{7.4a}$$

and

$$c_{2t+1} = R_t s_t, \tag{7.4b}$$

where, as before, $R_t \equiv 1 + r_t - \delta$. As in previous chapters, we assume that the rate of depreciation is one, for simplicity. The modern household's demand for goods, assets, children, and schooling are given as

$$c_{1t} = \left[\frac{1}{1+\beta+\psi}\right] w_t D_t h_t \tag{7.5a}$$

$$c_{2t+1} = \left[\frac{\beta}{1+\beta+\psi}\right] R_t w_t D_t h_t \tag{7.5b}$$

$$s_t = \frac{\beta}{1+\beta+\psi} w_t D_t h_t \tag{7.5c}$$

$$n_{t+1} = \frac{\psi}{(1+\beta+\psi)\left(\eta - \gamma(T-e_t)(\bar{e}/e_{t-1})^{\theta}\right)} \tag{7.5d}$$

$$e_t = \max\left[\frac{\theta\left(\eta(e_{t-1}/\bar{e})^{\theta} - \gamma T\right)}{\gamma(1-\theta)}, \bar{e}\right]. \tag{7.5e}$$

Note that modern sector households are free to work in either the modern or traditional sectors. They can spend part of the year working in the modern sector and part of the year in the traditional sector, and thus they have much more mobility than we assume for the worker that lives in the traditional sector.

There are two fundamental differences between the budget constraints of traditional and modern sector households. First, instead of a full unit of labor, workers who live in the traditional sector must remain on the farm all year and are constrained to work $\tilde{z} < 1$ units of labor time. During downtime in production, the workers stay in the traditional sector to maintain and to protect the farm. Second, traditional sector households have residual income from operating the farm in the second period of life, $O_{t+1} - \tilde{w}_{t+1}\tilde{D}_{t+1} f_{t+1}$. The farm technology is jointly operated by all siblings that remain in the traditional sector during the second period of life. The number of siblings from generation t that operate the farm is some fraction, $\varphi_t \leq 1$, of all siblings ($\tilde{n}_t$). Each of the siblings then passes down knowledge of how to operate a farm to the children who remain in the traditional sector. The children of each parent jointly manage the farm and share in the residual income, as in the previous generation.

The two single-period budget constraints for the traditional households are given as

$$\tilde{c}_{1t} + \tilde{s}_t + \tilde{n}_{t+1}\eta\tilde{w}_t\tilde{D}_t\tilde{z}\tilde{h}_t = \tilde{w}_t\tilde{D}_t\tilde{z}\tilde{h}_t + \tilde{n}_{t+1}\tilde{w}_t\tilde{D}_t\gamma\tilde{z}\bar{h}(T-\tilde{e}_t) \tag{7.6a}$$

and

$$\tilde{c}_{2t+1} = R_t\tilde{s}_t + \left(O_{t+1} - \tilde{w}_{t+1}\tilde{D}_{t+1}f_{t+1}\right)/\varphi_t\tilde{n}_t. \tag{7.6b}$$

Traditional household behavior is given by

$$\tilde{c}_{1t} = \left[\frac{1}{1+\beta+\psi}\right]\tilde{w}_t\tilde{D}_t\tilde{z}\tilde{h}_t\left[1+\frac{O_{t+1}-\tilde{w}_{t+1}\tilde{D}_{t+1}f_{t+1}}{R_t\tilde{w}_t\tilde{D}_t\tilde{z}\tilde{h}_t\varphi_t\tilde{n}_t}\right] \tag{7.7a}$$

$$\tilde{c}_{2t+1} = \left[\frac{\beta}{1+\beta+\psi}\right]R_t\tilde{w}_t\tilde{D}_t\tilde{z}\tilde{h}_t\left[1+\frac{O_{t+1}-\tilde{w}_{t+1}\tilde{D}_{t+1}f_{t+1}}{R_t\tilde{w}_t\tilde{D}_t\tilde{z}\tilde{h}_t\varphi_t\tilde{n}_t}\right] \tag{7.7b}$$

$$s_t = \frac{\tilde{w}_t\tilde{D}_t\tilde{z}\tilde{h}_t}{1+\beta+\psi}\left[\beta-(1+\psi)\left(\frac{O_{t+1}-\tilde{w}_{t+1}\tilde{D}_{t+1}f_{t+1}}{R_t\tilde{w}_t\tilde{D}_t\tilde{z}\tilde{h}_t\varphi_t\tilde{n}_t}\right)\right] \tag{7.7c}$$

$$\tilde{n}_{t+1} = \frac{\psi}{(1+\beta+\psi)\left(\eta-\gamma(T-\tilde{e}_t)(\bar{e}/\tilde{e}_{t-1})^{\theta}\right)}\left[1+\frac{O_{t+1}-\tilde{w}_{t+1}\tilde{D}_{t+1}f_{t+1}}{R_t\tilde{w}_t\tilde{D}_t\tilde{z}\tilde{h}_t\varphi_t\tilde{n}_t}\right] \tag{7.7d}$$

$$\tilde{e}_t = \max\left[\frac{\theta\left(\eta(\tilde{e}_{t-1}/\bar{e})^{\theta}-\gamma T\right)}{\gamma(1-\theta)}, \bar{e}\right] \tag{7.7e}$$

$$f_{t+1} = \left[\frac{(1-\alpha)\tilde{A}}{\tilde{w}_{t+1}}\right]^{\frac{1}{\alpha}}\frac{1}{\tilde{D}_{t+1}}. \tag{7.7f}$$

As in Chap. 5, the nonwage income from operating the family business raises fertility (7.7d). Traditional schooling is only different from the schooling in the modern sector if there are differences in initial conditions across the two sectors (7.7e). As in Chap. 6, the family farm provides income during retirement, a substitute for retirement saving when young (7.7c). Traditional households have lower wage income because of the constraints on their hours worked. Saving from a traditional household will be relatively low because both their earnings and their saving rate are lower than households in the model sector. Thus, the traditional household will tend to have lower wage income and saving, and higher fertility, than households in the modern sector.

7.1.3 Labor Market Equilibrium and Locational Choice

We assume a national labor market so that the wages paid to a unit of human capital must be equalized across sectors, $\tilde{w}_t\tilde{D}_t = w_tD_t$. All productivity differences are "annual," based on differences in hours worked, and not due to differences in productivity per "hour." A national labor market requires that the total demand for labor from the traditional sector in each period t, $\frac{\tilde{N}_{t-1}}{\varphi_{t-1}\tilde{n}_{t-1}}f_t$, must exceed the supply of labor coming from younger members of traditional households in period t, $\tilde{N}_t\tilde{h}_t\tilde{z}(1-\eta\tilde{n}_{t+1})+\tilde{N}_{t+1}\gamma\bar{h}\tilde{z}(T-\tilde{e}_t)$. Remember that each of the grandparents pass along the family technology to their children that remain in the traditional sector to share in their second period of life. So, if the population of older parents in the traditional sector is $\tilde{N}_{t-1}$, then the number of distinct farms is $\frac{\tilde{N}_{t-1}}{\varphi_{t-1}\tilde{n}_{t-1}}$, each of which demand f_t units of human capital from the younger generation of workers.

For some households to stay in the traditional sector and other households to leave the traditional sector, households must be indifferent about their locational choice. Equating the indirect utility functions for the traditional households under each option yields the following condition that determines the relative importance of income from the farm in equilibrium

$$\frac{O_{t+1}-w_{t+1}\tilde{D}_{t+1}f_{t+1}}{R_t w_t \tilde{D}_t \tilde{z}\tilde{h}_t \varphi_t \tilde{n}_t}=\Omega\equiv\left(\frac{1}{\tilde{z}}\right)^{\frac{1+\beta}{1+\beta+\psi}}-1. \tag{7.8}$$

The condition indicates that *actual* relative income from the farm (the left-hand-side) must achieve a *required* value (the right-hand-side) in order to compensate traditional households for the hours constraint on their work time when young. The lower is $\tilde{z}$, the greater must be the relative income from inheriting the farm. The degree to which residual income must compensate for the hours constraint is lessened by the exponent on the right-hand side, which is less than one. The exponent reflects the fact that, with endogenous fertility, being indifferent about working in the two sectors requires more than the equality of lifetime resources. Staying in the traditional sector to operate the farm also means having more children (higher wages when young raises the cost of children, while higher residual income when old does not). Given that parents like children ($\psi > 0$), the wealth compensation that is necessary for accepting less work hours when young is not as great when families are larger, as was first discussed in Chap. 5.

Condition (7.8) is important for all relationships in the model that involve the behavior and allocation of households across sectors. Condition (7.8) can be substituted back into (7.7a)–(7.7d) to simplify the demand functions for traditional households.

The differences in saving behavior, fertility, and work effort across the households in the two sectors are all affected by Ω. Due to the presence of Ω, the saving rate out of wages is lower for traditional sector households, $(\beta-(1+\psi)\Omega)/(1+\beta+\psi)<\beta/(1+\beta+\psi)$.

Comparing (7.7d) to (7.5d) shows fertility that is higher in the traditional sector, even if schooling is the same across sectors. The ratio of traditional fertility to modern fertility is $1+\Omega$.

Beyond the labor supply constraint that limits work for a traditional household relative to a modern household, the higher fertility of the traditional household will further reduce the adult-equivalent units of labor supply (combining the labor of parents and children) relative to the modern household. This is because the increase in child labor does not fully offset the lost labor time associated with raising the child. The adult-equivalent units of labor supply for a modern household can be shown to be $1 - n_{t+1}(\eta - \gamma \frac{\bar{h}}{h_t}(T - e_t)) = (1 + \beta)/(1 + \beta + \psi)$, while the supply from a traditional household is $(1 + \beta - \psi\Omega)/(1 + \beta + \psi)$, a lower value due to the presence of Ω.

Condition (7.8) can also be used to solve for the number of young households that must remain in the traditional sector. Using the first-order conditions for labor demand in each sector, (7.8), and $\tilde{w}_t\tilde{D}_t = w_t D_t$, yields the following expression for the fraction of young households in period t that remain in the traditional sector,

$$\varphi_t = \frac{\left(\tilde{a}\frac{\tilde{D}_{t+1}}{D_{t+1}}\right)^{1/\alpha}(1 + d)}{\Omega \tilde{n}_t (1 - \alpha) A k_t^{\alpha} \tilde{z} \tilde{h}_t} \left(\frac{1}{\tilde{D}_{t+1}}\right), \tag{7.9}$$

where $\tilde{a} \equiv \tilde{A}/A$ is the relative TFP in the traditional sector. Migration out of the traditional sector is greater the lower is the relative TFP value in the traditional sector and the higher is wage income. Migration is also affected by Ω because the higher is the required residual income ratio, the more siblings must exit the traditional sector.

Equation (7.9) determines the value of φ_t and the number of households in each sector. The sector-specific demographics are given by

$$\tilde{N}_t = \varphi_t \tilde{n}_t \tilde{N}_{t-1} \tag{7.10a}$$

$$N_t^* = n_t N_{t-1}^* + (1 - \varphi_t)\tilde{n}_t \tilde{N}_{t-1}. \tag{7.10b}$$

Using (7.10a) and (7.10b), the fraction of households living in the modern sector can be defined by the following difference equation

$$\pi_t = \frac{n_t \pi_{t-1} + (1 - \varphi_t)\tilde{n}_t (1 - \pi_{t-1})}{n_t \pi_{t-1} + \tilde{n}_t (1 - \pi_{t-1})}. \tag{7.10c}$$

Note that π is no longer equivalent to the labor share in the modern sector, as it was in previous chapters. Here, π represents the fraction of young households that live in the modern sector. The labor share is now a more complicated concept and will be defined later. Note also that π will rise as φ_t falls, reflecting a smaller fraction of the children born in the traditional sector that remain there as adults. As indicated by (7.9), for φ_t to fall over time requires growth in wages from physical and human capital accumulation and technological progress.

7.1.4 Capital Market Equilibrium

The capital supplied per unit of human capital employed in the modern sector is given by

$$k_{t+1} = \frac{s_t N_t + \tilde{s}_t \tilde{N}_t}{D_{t+1} M_{t+1}}, \tag{7.11}$$

where M is the total supply of human capital in the economy as a whole minus the human capital demanded to work in the traditional sector (remember that modern sector households can temporarily migrate to work in the traditional sector). Using the other equations of the model, (7.11) can be written out as the following transition equation for k,

$$k_{t+1} = \left[\bar{\beta}_t + \Omega\tilde{z}(\tilde{h}_t/h_t)(1-\pi_t)\right]\frac{(1-\alpha)Ak_t^{\alpha}}{1+g_t^{\text{eff}}} \tag{7.12}$$

where,

$$\bar{\beta}_t \equiv \frac{\beta\pi_t + (\beta-(1+\psi)\Omega)\tilde{z}(\tilde{h}_t/h_t)(1-\pi_t)}{1+\beta+\psi},$$

and

$$1+g_{t+1}^{\text{eff}} \equiv (n_{t+1}\pi_t + \tilde{n}_{t+1}(1-\pi_t))((1+d)h_{t+1}/h_t)$$
$$\left[\frac{1+\beta}{1+\beta+\psi}\pi_{t+1} + \frac{1+\beta-\psi\Omega}{1+\beta+\psi}(\tilde{z}\tilde{h}_{t+1}/h_{t+1})(1-\pi_{t+1})\right].$$

The transition equation for physical capital intensity takes the same basic form as other we have encountered. Next period's physical capital intensity is determined by the average saving rate ($\bar{\beta}_t$) out of the current rental rate on human capital ($(1-\alpha)Ak_t^{\alpha}$) and by the growth rate of the effective labor supply (g_{t+1}^{eff}) that uses next period's capital stock.

The extension to a two-sector dual economy creates two new influences on physical capital intensity. First, the structural transformation releases labor from the traditional sector and increases the growth in the modern sector's working population. The size of the migration flow depends on how fast the traditional labor supply is growing relative to the traditional sector demand for labor. Faster growth in labor supply lowers capital intensity in the modern sector. This effect is captured by the expression in the denominator that describes the average work effort across sectors, $\frac{1+\beta}{1+\beta+\psi}\pi_{t+1} + \frac{1+\beta-\psi\Omega}{1+\beta+\psi}(\tilde{z}\tilde{h}_{t+1}/h_{t+1})(1-\pi_{t+1})$. An increase in π increases the effective supply of labor because of an expansion in hours supplied and, possibly, an expansion in human capital per hour. For a given supply of labor, a decline in the traditional sector demand for labor also releases labor that must be absorbed in the modern sector. The demand for traditional labor is captured by the second term in the numerator (see problem 2), $\Omega(1-\alpha)Ak_t^{\alpha}\tilde{z}(\tilde{h}_{t+1}/h_{t+1})(1-\pi_t)$. As the traditional sector becomes smaller, this expression shrinks and the modern sector capital intensity falls.

The negative migration effect of the structural transformation on capital intensity is countered by a second effect, working through $\bar{\beta}_t$, that serves to increase capital intensity. Traditional sector households save at lower rates than modern sector households. As households migrate to the modern sector, the economy's average saving rate increases and capital intensity rises. Overall, the structural transformation then has an ambiguous effect on physical capital intensity, just as we saw in Chap. 6.

7.2 Transitional Growth in the Long Run

In this section we use the model to simulate growth paths. The simulations will reveal two characteristics that are not associated with standard one-sector neoclassical models of physical capital accumulation. First, transitional growth goes on for some time—even for centuries. Second, the growth rates first rise and then stabilize for many decades before falling. As we shall discuss, these predictions of the model are consistent with the data. In contrast, the neoclassical model of physical capital accumulation predicts declining growth rates and a relatively quick convergence to the steady state. The predictions of the standard model have caused many to doubt the relevance of neoclassical growth, leading to the creation of *endogenous growth theory* that attempts to explain technological change or steady state growth. Our goal is to demonstrate that the transitional growth of an extended neoclassical theory can contribute significantly to our understanding of real-world growth and development.

To begin, we further simplify the model in two ways. We assume that human capital is equal across the two sectors, i.e., the fundamental initial conditions for human capital are the same in both sectors. We also assume that exogenous technological change is balanced, so that the exogenous index of labor productivity grows at the same rate in each sector. We set $D_t = \tilde{D}_t$ because any level difference in the productivity differences can be captured by $\tilde{a} \equiv \tilde{A}/A$. These assumptions allow us to trace the dynamics of the economy using (7.5d), (7.5e), and the following three equations

$$\varphi_t = \frac{\tilde{a}^{1/\alpha}}{\Omega(1+\Omega)n_t(1-\alpha)Ak_t^{\alpha}\tilde{z}h_t}\left(\frac{1}{D_t}\right) \tag{7.13a}$$

$$\pi_t = \frac{\pi_{t-1} + (1-\varphi_t)(1+\Omega)(1-\pi_{t-1})}{\pi_{t-1} + (1+\Omega)(1-\pi_{t-1})} \tag{7.13b}$$

$$k_{t+1} = \frac{\beta(1-\alpha)Ak_t^{\alpha}[\pi_t + (1+\Omega)\tilde{z}(1-\pi_t)]}{n_{t+1}(\pi_t + (1+\Omega)(1-\pi_t))((1+d)h_{t+1}/h_t)[(1+\beta)\pi_{t+1} + (1+\beta-\psi\Omega)\tilde{z}(1-\pi_{t+1})]} \tag{7.13c}$$

Note that in (7.13c) that the right-hand side depends on k_{t+1} via π_{t+1}. This makes the computation a bit tricky because (7.13c) has to be solved implicitly for k_{t+1}.

In addition to (7.13a)–(7.13c), we will need to compute the average productivity per worker (prod) and the labor share in the traditional sector (shr)

$$\text{prod}_t = Ak_t^{\alpha}D_t h_t \frac{\frac{1+\beta}{1+\beta+\psi}\pi_t + \frac{1+\beta-\psi\Omega\tilde{z}}{1+\beta+\psi}(1-\pi_t)}{(1+n_t(T-\mathrm{e}_t))\pi_t + (1+n_t(1+\Omega)(T-\tilde{e}_t))(1-\pi_t)} \tag{7.13d}$$

$$\text{shr}_t = \frac{(1-\pi_{t-1})\Omega(1-\alpha)Ak_{t-1}^{\alpha}h_{t-1}\tilde{z}}{(1+d)n_t(\pi_{t-1} + (1+\Omega)(1-\pi_{t-1}))h_t k_t\left(\frac{1+\beta}{1+\beta+\psi}\pi_t + \frac{1+\beta-\psi\Omega\tilde{z}}{1+\beta+\psi}(1-\pi_t)\right)}. \tag{7.13e}$$

Equation (7.13d) gives worker productivity as measured by total output divided by the number of workers (young adults and their working-age children). Worker productivity grows as a result of the accumulation of physical and human capital as well as by an increase in the adult-equivalent labor supply per worker.

The contribution of the effective labor supply to worker productivity is captured by the last term which gives the adult-equivalent labor supply divided by the number of workers. A decrease in the fraction of traditional sector households will cause worker productivity to rise because it increases work hours and lowers the number of workers. Also a decline in fertility clearly raises labor supply per worker because it does not change the total labor supply coming from the family (reduced child labor is offset by higher adult labor one-for-one) but does reduce the number of family workers by lowering child labor.

Equation (7.13e) gives the share of labor in the traditional sector. It is the demand for human capital by the traditional sector divided by the total supply of human capital in the economy (see Problem 5).

7.2.1 Calibration and Numerical Analysis

We now analyze the model numerically. Many of the parameters are set using the calibration from the extended one-sector model in Chap. 3. The differences in calibration are based on the fact that it is no longer necessary to generate high fertility simply based on a low cost of children. We now have two household-types, one of which will have high fertility because of the residual income from family production. As a consequence, we set the parameter η, that determines the time cost of raising children, to a somewhat higher value than in Chap. 3 (0.18 rather than 0. 165). This causes us to recalibrate some of the closely related parameters to

Table 7.1 Calibrated parameters

$\beta = 0.5000$
$\alpha = 0.3333$
$\gamma = 0.276$
$\eta = 0.1800$
$\theta = 0.4000$
$\psi = 0.3290$
$\tilde{z} = 0.6667$
$\Omega = 0.3940$
$\pi_0 = 0.3333$
$r_0^a = 0.070$
$A = 1$
$D_0 = 1, d^a = 0.01$

maintain two other targets: a fertility rate of 1 and fulltime schooling in the steady state. The new parameters values are $\psi = 0.329$ and $\bar{e} = 0.10$.

Note also that there is a poverty trap under the calibration when $\gamma = 0.28$ (the value from Chap. 3). We assume that the economy overcomes this trap by invoking marginal increase in compulsory schooling or child labor legislation that lowers the work opportunity for children and γ. We first reduce γ just below 0.28 to initiate a relatively slow rise in schooling that we observe in countries that began modern growth around 1800. Later, we consider more aggressive attempts to increase in schooling that are similar to what happen in the Asian Tiger Growth Miracle countries.[2]

As in Chap. 6, Table 2, we set $\tilde{z} = 2/3$ in order to match data on differences in annual hours worked across agriculture and manufacturing in the USA during the nineteenth century. This value implies that $\Omega = 0.394$, or that households in the traditional sector have about 40 % more children than those in the modern sector. This number seems reasonable given that urban households had about 50 % more children than rural households in the USA during the nineteenth century and that at least some of the fertility difference was likely due to small differences in schooling across rural and urban households (which we do not allow in the model).

We set A and the initial value of D both equal to 1. The annualized growth rate of d is set to 1 %, as in Chap. 3. We set the initial k to generate an initial annualized interest rate of 7 %. Given the initial value of k, $\tilde{a}$ is set to target an initial value of φ of 0.90, using (7.13a), so that most traditional households remain in the traditional sector in the initial period. Finally, we choose initial values of $\pi = 1/3$ and shr = 0.80. Table 7.1 summarizes the parameter values of the calibration.

Before looking at the transition paths for the economy, first consider the consequences of the calibration for some of the individual components of (7.13c). The

[2] In more realistic models of human capital accumulation the schooling takeoff can be generated in ways other than through compulsory schooling or child labor laws. See Chap. 3 for discussions of how schooling could be increased using subsidies, including tuition subsidies.

saving rate of traditional households is slightly negative, $\beta - (1 + \psi)\Omega = -0.0236$. So, traditional households not only save less than modern households, they are actually borrowers. An increase in π clearly raises the saving rate. However, recall that an increase in π also lowers physical capital intensity because it implies a reduction in the demand for labor in the traditional sector, which causes migration to the modern sector. The sign of the total effect that combines the saving effect with the demand for labor effect is given by $1 - (1 + \Omega)\tilde{z} = 0.0704$. The saving effect slightly dominates the demand for labor effect, meaning the numerator of (7.13c) rises with π.

Now move to the denominator of (7.13c), where we can compute the expansion in the total labor supply associated with an increase in π. This effect is given by $\frac{\beta}{1+\beta+\psi}\left(1 - (1 - \frac{\psi\Omega}{1+\beta})\tilde{z}\right) = 0.2734(0.9424) = 0.2576$. An increase in π increases the adult-equivalent labor supply by more than one quarter of a full unit. Thus, the movement of households out of the traditional sector increases saving to fund investment but also creates a significant increase in the modern sector labor supply that must be supplied with physical capital.

Another effect on capital intensity comes through the effect of the structural transformation on the demographic transition. Migration of households out of the traditional sector will reduce the growth in the total population of young households and labor supply because households in the rural sector have 40 % more children than households in the modern sector. The reduction in the population growth will make it easier for the economy to increase physical capital intensity. The question is whether the reduction in population growth will offset the release of labor, for a given population, when the traditional sector shrinks.

Table 7.2 gives the transitional growth over 10 periods (two centuries). Growth rates in output per worker rise over much of the first century, level off, and fall during the second century. There is no clear trend in growth rates over the two centuries. Interest rates also exhibit no clear downward trend until late in the second century. Conventional wisdom explains trendless growth rates and interest rates over long periods of time by an economy being close to its steady state. Indeed, the common observation of long-run trendless growth caused the profession to de-emphasize transitional growth in favor of developing *endogenous growth theory* that attempts to explain steady state growth.

Table 7.2 Transitional growth and development

Period	0	1	2	3	4	5	6	7	8	9	10
% Δ prod (annual)		1.06	1.65	1.92	1.99	1.95	1.86	1.79	1.74	1.68	1.60
shr	0.80	0.69	0.63	0.49	0.33	0.19	0.10	0.04	0.01	0.00	0.00
r—δ (annual)	0.070	0.078	0.081	0.082	0.081	0.078	0.073	0.067	0.061	0.055	0.050
n (per woman)	6.6	6.4	6.0	5.6	5.0	4.6	4.0	3.6	3.2	2.8	2.6
e	0.100	0.101	0.104	0.108	0.115	0.127	0.145	0.172	0.206	0.248	0.291

The problem with this conventional perspective is that in many respects real-world economies do not appear to be in a steady state. Despite trendless growth rates, the share of labor in manufacturing rises, fertility falls, and time investments in schooling increase—just as we see in Table 7.2. Lucas (2002, p. 80), one of the founders of the endogenous growth approach, noted this inconsistency but decided to take an alternative approach in his analysis.

> One is left with two choices: first, we can identify increases in average schooling levels with net human capital investment. Since schooling levels are increasing in virtually all societies today, this is a possibility worth developing, but it cannot be pursued in a steady state framework. This is an important and neglected respect in which neither advanced nor most backward economies can be viewed as moving along balanced growth paths. Alternatively, we can think of a balanced path on which the time spent in schooling is constant but the quality of schooling is improving as a result of increases in general knowledge.

In this chapter we make the first choice from the Lucas quote by demonstrating that trendless growth can be generated for long periods of time while an economy is in transition to a steady state.

The rising growth rates during the first century in Table 7.2 have little to do with capital accumulation. Interest rates are modestly increasing, indicating a drop in k, and schooling time rises only modestly. The rise in growth rates is primarily the result of the structural transformation and the associated rise in adult-equivalent labor supply, as workers work longer hours in the modern sector where they are unconstrained and where they have fewer children. At the end of the first century and beginning of the second century, physical and human capital accumulation takes over and keeps growth going, until diminishing returns begins to offset the rise in investment rates later in the century.

Rodrik (2013) sees similar growth patterns in the development of countries after WWII. He points out that the structural transformation can often generate fast growth during the early stages of development. This is particularly true when the structural transformation is from traditional agriculture to modern manufacturing, However, the growth associated with moving labor from low to high productivity sectors will reach a limit. Additional growth must then result from the slow process of capital accumulation and technological progress across sectors.

Table 7.3 indicates that the most single important source of transitional growth after 200 years is an increase in the adult-equivalent labor supply. The increase in the adult-equivalent labor supply results from the migration of workers to the modern sector as well as the within-sector decline in fertility that occurs as schooling increases. More work in the modern sector and less child labor increase

Table 7.3 Transitional growth

Growth due to	200 years of growth
k	1.21
h	1.53
Labor supply	3.62
Total growth	6.70

Table 7.4 Rapid transitional growth

Period	0	1	2	3	4	5
% Δ prod (annual)		3.0	3.2	3.1	2.8	2.3
shr	0.80	0.70	0.56	0.37	0.21	0.09
r—δ (annual)	10.0	8.6	7.5	6.5	5.4	4.6
n (per woman)	6.6	5.2	4.0	3.0	2.6	2.2
e	0.10	0.13	0.18	0.25	0.33	0.41

hours worked per worker. The endogenous transitional growth causes a 6.70-fold increase in worker productivity, slightly less than the growth due to exogenous technological change. After 200 years, technological change of 1 % annually raises output per worker 7.32-fold. As we discuss later in this chapter, it is clear that we have formed a conservative estimate of the contribution from transitional growth. It is likely that the contribution of transitional growth significantly exceeds the technological progress that can be sustained in the long run.

Growth can be increased more dramatically when a less-developed country takes a more aggressive approach to increasing schooling, as in the Asian Tiger countries. In Table 7.4, we consider a country that (i) has less capital intensity, an initial annual interest rate of 10 %, and (ii) pushes schooling more aggressively (reducing γ to 0.26). As a consequence, the growth rates are much higher. However, the pattern of growth is the same; rising growth rates that level off before declining.

7.3 Great Waves of Growth

Gordon (1999) refers to US growth as one "Big Wave." This is his way of describing the pattern where growth rates rise, level off for several decades or more, and then decline. Table 7.5 presents two measures of US growth, GDP per capita and GDP per worker, for two centuries. Growth rates rose through much of the nineteenth century, leveled off for most of the twentieth century, and then declined in the last quarter of the century. Similar patterns can be observed in countries that began modern growth

Table 7.5 The great wave: US growth 1800–2000

1800–1840	1840–1880	1880–1920	1920–1980	1980–1990	1990–2000	2000–2010
Average annual growth rate in GDP per capita						
0.58	1.44	1.78	2.18	2.28	2.16	0.62
Average annual growth rate in GDP per worker						
1.07	1.58	1.47	1.92	1.58	1.62	

Notes Average growth in GDP per capita is based on Farmer and Schelnast (2013, Table 5.1). Average growth in GDP per capita is from Chap. 2, Table 7.1

two centuries ago [see, for example, Farmer and Schelnast (2013, Fig. 5.3)]. This growth rate pattern is similar to the growth pattern we simulated in Table 7.2.

One difference, between the simulation and the US historical growth, is the absence of a steady rise in the actual growth rate of worker productivity from the middle of the nineteenth century to the early decades of the twentieth century. As discussed in Chap. 6, hours worked per manufacturing worker fell during the nineteenth and early twentieth centuries, settling close to the now standard 40 h work-week before WWII. This pattern of hours worked is not captured in the model. The decline in hours worked over this period slowed the growth in output per worker in the data. Failing to capture the decline in hours worked also means that the model overstates the contribution of increased labor supply to growth in worker productivity over the entire transition.

On the other hand, the model assumes no difference in worker productivity *per hour* worked across sectors. Accounting for some gap in productivity per hour worked, i.e., an hourly wage gap, would increase the contribution of the structural transformation to growth. This may not be a large omission for US history or European history, but could be in other settings where labor markets are less efficient. As documented by Gollin et al. (2014), after adjusting for differences in hours worked and education, the poorest developing countries today continue to exhibit large wage and productivity gaps. This is one of the reasons that McMillan and Rodrik (2011) find the structural transformation is so important in explaining the growth rate differences between Asia and Africa (see Chap. 5). In applying the model to the poorest currently developing countries, one would want to allow for a general wage gap that includes all sources of the difference in productivity across sector, similar to the approach we took in the first part of Chap. 5.

Table 7.6 reports the growth in GDP per capita in the Asian Tiger Growth Miracle countries. The more rapid and compressed growth we simulated in Table 7.4 is similar, although not nearly as rapid, as we see in the Asian Tigers. We discuss some of the reasons for the very rapid growth in these Growth Miracle countries in Sect. 7.4.

Overall, the general wave pattern is common to countries experiencing moderate growth for centuries and in countries experiencing more dramatic "Growth Miracles." Our model explains this growth pattern as follows. The diminishing returns associated with capital accumulation are initially more than overcome by the gains in productivity associated with the structural transformation and by rising investment rates. These two features of development cause growth rates to rise initially.

Table 7.6 Great waves: Asian tigers 1950–2010

Average annual growth rate in GDP per capita				
	1950–1965	1965–1980	1980–2000	2000–2010
Hong Kong	6.2	6.7	3.9	3.5
South Korea	3.4	7.5	7	3.8
Singapore	2.6	8.9	4.9	3.3
Taiwan	5.2	7.3	5.8	3.5

Notes Average growth in GDP per capita is based on Farmer and Schelnast (2013, Table 5.1)

However, there are ultimately growth slowdowns as investment rates level off and the structural transformation becomes complete.

The wave-like growth pattern offers a pessimistic forecast for growth in the twenty-first century. One can become even more pessimistic if there are reasons to believe that technological progress cannot continue indefinitely at the same rate we observed in the twentieth century. Jones (2002) extends the analysis of this chapter by relating technological progress to the growth in researchers (scientists and engineers engaged in research and development). In the twentieth century, the growth in researchers was based on population growth and on growth in research intensity (the fraction of the available work force devoted to research). Jones points out that the only growth that is sustainable comes from population growth (as with all investment rates, the fraction of the work force devoted to research is bounded). Assuming that population growth remains similar to that of the second half of the twentieth century, long-run growth is expected to be less than ½ %.

The issue of twenty-first century growth was recently made popular by an article appearing in the *Economist* (January 12, 2013), entitled "Innovation Pessimism." The article offers another reason to be pessimistic about growth. Academic research suggests that there may also be diminishing returns to research and development efforts (which Jones does not assume). For example, Vijg (2011) argues that the pace of technological progress will slow, and in fact has already begun to, particularly in the important areas of energy, transportation and medicine. This pessimism is contested by those who argue that the growth impact of innovations in computing, biotechnology, and personal communications has not yet been fully realized. Brynjolfsson and McAfee (2014) claim that we are just on the cusp of a second machine-age built around the computer. To maintain growth rates similar to the twentieth century, given the past importance of physical and human capital accumulation, it would not be enough to argue that technological progress will continue, it will have to accelerate. Given what we currently know, this seems unlikely.

7.4 South Korea: A Development Success Story

> The Korean experience suggests that mismanagement and not original position is more often the cause of *continuing* underdevelopment, combined on occasion with social and cultural attitudes—and not necessarily those associated with traditional values—held by authorities hostile toward the entrepreneurial and pragmatic spirit required for development.
>
> L.L. Wade and B.S. Kim, *Economic Development of South Korea* (p. vii).

At the end of the Korean conflict in 1953, the Korean peninsula was a war-ravaged, resource-scarce, and over-populated backwater that was poorer than many countries in Africa or Latin America. The ceasefire provided a convenient natural experiment into the nature and causes of the wealth of nations. Korea was divided into a totalitarian, one-party communist state in the north, the Democratic People's Republic of Korea (current population about 25 million). North Korea has languished in terms of economic attainment to the extent that it has required the mobilization of international food aid at times to avoid mass starvation of its citizens. In the south, the United Nations and USA helped establish and nourish the Republic of Korea, which has thrived. South Korea (current population 50 million) is the thirteenth most prosperous country in the world, with a per capita income higher than the European Union average. Today's Korea, centered on its vibrant capital Seoul, is a highly successful and innovative industrial country that organized a summer Olympics and is a member of the Organization of Economic Cooperation and Development (OEDC), the club of 34 advanced industrial economies based in Paris, France.

At independence, the overwhelming majority of Korea's resources and industry were located in the north. South Korea had been devastated by the war, and its refugee-swelled population had to depend on basic agriculture and US food aid for survival. Yet, while its initial industrial and resource bases were thin, South Korea was able during the following 60 years to register an impressive economic record, including economic growth that averages over 7 % per annum in real terms (see charts). South Koreans invested heavily in human and physical capital and also adopted an economic model that combines an outward-oriented development strategy with state direction of the financial system and the real economy. Hard work, innovation, trade openness, and the promotion of exports through trade-friendly policies, such as realistic exchange rates and reduction of tariffs and nontariff trade barriers, have made South Korea a global economic power house.

7.4.1 The Onset of Growth

Several preconditions necessary for the subsequent growth takeoff were established during the 1950s. First, a land reform was enacted in 1949, distributing to peasants lands that became available following the end of Japanese rule in 1945. This was instrumental in establishing property rights and in pacifying rural areas. It also weakened the political power of large landlords that tends to inhibit pro-growth policy. Second, grass root demand for education exploded, reflecting Korean family and societal values and repression of the Korean culture during the long foreign dominations. The education drive laid the foundation for later achievements as it provided younger generations with the skills they would later need in the subsequent industrialization drive. Despite these early achievements, however, population growth in the 1950s was such that per capita incomes did not rise, a coherent long-term economic development strategy was lacking, and growth in part reflected temporary US relief and reconstruction assistance.

7.4.2 Growth Acceleration

South Korea's growth surge began in earnest in 1963. Elections that year were preceded by political unrest and a military intervention in 1961. In the years that followed, the political system was stable and the government was able to formulate effective investment plans without political interference, which succeeded in fostering economic development and helped it gain greater political legitimacy. South Korea's rate of economic growth between 1965 and 1972 was truly impressive, over 8 % per annum, second only to Singapore's and Japan's. During this period an impressive shift occurred in the composition of GDP away from agriculture toward industry. The share of agriculture declined from about 40 % to about 25 %, while that of manufacturing rose from the high teens to about 30 %. Also rising were the shares in GDP accounted for by construction, industry-related services, finance (banking and insurance), and education. Regarding the size of government employment, whose swelling in developing countries is often cited as a factor inhibiting development, Korea offers an interesting lesson: during this period, there was a decline in the size of Korea's government (including public administration and defense).

The expansion of Korea's manufacturing sector was broad-based, including the production of transportation equipment (cars, ship building), electrical machinery, and chemicals and petroleum products. This broad-based industrial development effort was made possible by a high saving rate, which fostered physical capital accumulation, and also by Korean families' legendary drive for educational attainment, as human capital investments led to the improved workforce skills. Abundance of physical and human capital went hand in hand with investments in research and development (R&D), which facilitated imitation and innovation—the adoption of existing technologies and the creation of new ones. Korea also imported large amounts of capital from abroad, which embodied newer technologies and enabled South Korean conglomerates to export their manufactures abroad.

Successful Korean firms (Samsung, Hyundai) have become familiar global brands that earn and invest in R&D billions of dollars every year. They are the most visible of a number of diversified conglomerates called *chaebol*, which facilitated Korea's industrial prowess. Controlled by powerful families, these conglomerates' success lies in a combination of visionary management, special advantages enjoyed in the domestic market place, and also adherence to market discipline. Among the advantages, preferential access of the chaebol to affordable finance from Korea's banking system was crucial for their expansion and competitive advantage internationally. This is a form of "industrial policy," where government policy favors certain industries. However, the market discipline for the chaebol was provided by their export orientation: Firms able to survive in the international market place were promoted, which helped steer the economy to internationally profitable sectors.

7.4.3 Lessons

What are some of the lessons behind South Korea's remarkable transformation from a poor, resource-scarce, over-populated backwater to an advanced country in the span of 60 years (two generations)? One takeaway concerns the role of national will and determination in overcoming obstacles to development—recall the discussion of the role of ownership in Chap. 3. In 1950, Korea was a poor but classless society. One of the early lessons all Koreans internalized was that foreign aid was transitory and that their future depended on their actions. Government and private sector joined forces on a path to capital accumulation (broadly construed to include human and physical capital).

There were important sources of growth not captured by the model from Sect. 7.2. These omissions explain why our model could not generate the very high growth associated with the Asian economic miracles. First, the South Korean government invested heavily in public infrastructure, which was modeled in Chap. 3, but omitted for simplicity in Chap. 7. Second, the government used an industrial policy that subsidized private capital formation. Industrial policy in promoting private capital formation is a common but controversial feature of the Asian Tigers approach to growth. Finally, the Korean economy was opened to international trade and capital flows. We saw in Chap. 3 that opening developing economies to international capital flows have the potential to accelerate growth. International trade can also increase growth by increasing the pace of the structural transformation for countries with a comparative advantage in manufacturing, as we have discussed in Chaps. 4–6. Furthermore, the international competition associated with an open economy helped discipline Korean industries supported by the government. The government subsidized those industries that performed best in the open economy.

Korea's exciting economic story has been accompanied by an equally impressive political evolution. Since the 1980s, it has evolved into an open, free, and thriving democracy. While growth can be initiated by pro-growth dictatorships, the rise of democratic institutions helps limit the rise of government corruption and mismanagement that could derail growth.

7.4.4 Challenges

While Korea's broad-based success and remarkable decline in poverty have helped maintain social cohesion, challenges remain. One important challenge is to address widening income inequality. Like other countries, there are two labor market tracks in Korea: Many workers have regular, stable jobs that pay decent wages and benefits, while others (about a third of the total) are only able to get temporary or part time employment. To address such *labor market duality* and make labor markets more inclusive, it is important to expand training and facilitate access to job opportunities of certain groups.

The participation of young Koreans in the labor force is lower than the OECD average, reflecting in part high enrollments in tertiary education, but also lack of skills demanded by firms, which could be addressed by expanding training. The participation of women in the labor force is much less than that of men, which offers a big opportunity going forward: As Korea ages—it will be one of the oldest societies in the world by the middle of the century—more women holding paid jobs could help raise Korea's growth.

There is also room to improve the productivity of firms in non-traded goods sectors, including many services, where firms are small and wages are lower than in the export-oriented sectors. Another challenge comes from the power of Korea's chaebol and other corporate groups and the challenge they pose for regulators. Longer-term challenges, as already alluded to, also arise from Korea's rapidly aging population. Finally, Korea faces the prospect of reunification and absorbing into its thriving economy the 25 million Koreans living in impoverished North Korea.

Korea: Employment, Growth, and PPP Per Capita GDP

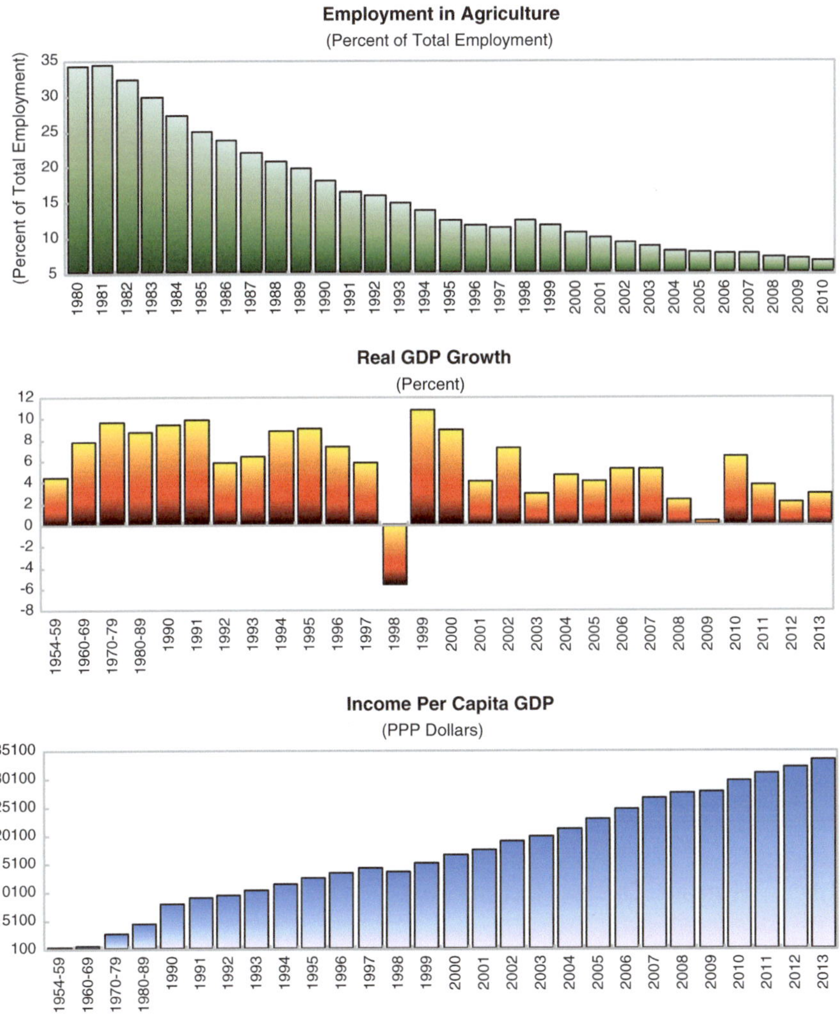

Sources: World Economic Outlook; World Development Indicators.

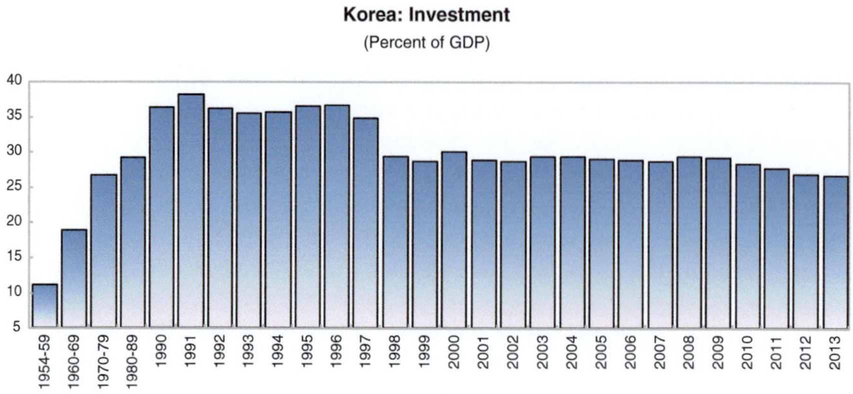

Sources: World Economic Outlook; World Development Indicators

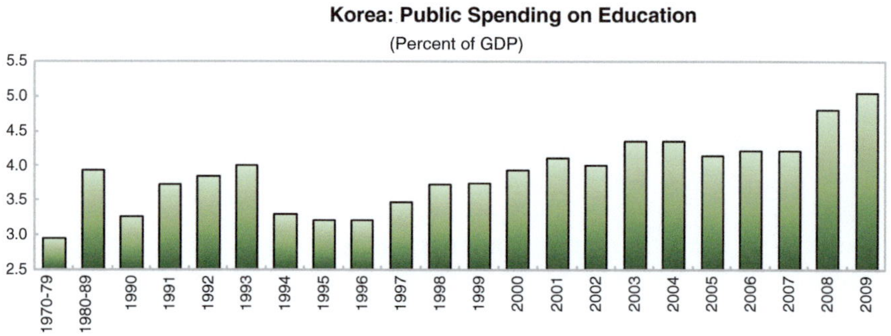

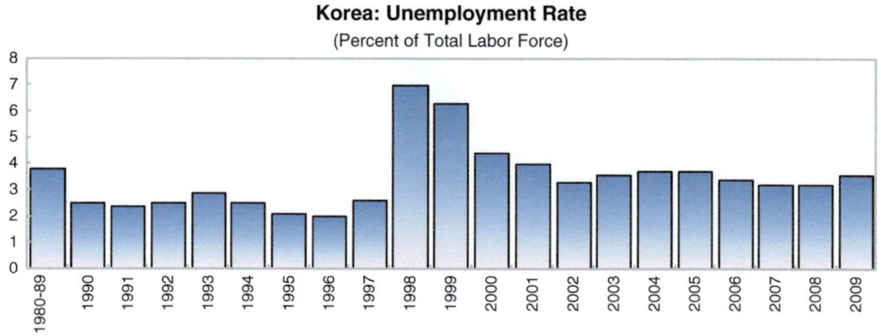

Sources: World Economic Outlook; World Development Indicators

7.5 Human Capital Extensions

There are various ways that one can extend the human capital production function in order to explain more of the growth in worker productivity. In our simple model, we include only student time spent in school. Other inputs are also important, including goods and service inputs (e.g., tuition costs that include teachers, books, and other classroom materials), the human capital of people in the community (including parents, relatives, and teachers), and health inputs that improve student learning and worker productivity directly.

7.5.1 Goods Inputs

We mentioned in Chaps. 2 and 3 that purchased goods and services associated with schooling are needed to develop human capital. Some argue that variations in goods inputs have little effect on human capital and therefore can be reasonably omitted. However, this is far from clear as the evidence on the effect of "school quality" on human capital formation is mixed.

For example, Krueger (2002) estimates that an increase in school quality measures (such as class size) not only increases human capital, but also they do so at a reasonably high 6 % rate of return. Even if *marginal* changes in school quality have small effects, at *current levels of school quality in developed countries*, this does not imply that improvements in school quality are unimportant when the level of overall quality is very low, as in developing countries. In fact, there are several reasons to expect that marginal changes in quality could have high payoffs at low levels while having low payoffs at high levels.

First, there are surely diminishing returns to reducing class size and increasing the availability of textbooks and other school inputs. Second, there are likely to be compositional differences in school expenditures in poor and rich countries. In rich countries, increases in school expenditures could reflect a variety of factors, some of which are likely not closely related to learning. In poor countries, increased expenditures are more likely to reflect increases in fundamental inputs such as teachers and textbooks. Third, school expenditures in poor countries are more concentrated on young children, since few older children are in school. Evidence suggests that the returns to education investments of all types are highest for young children (Heckman 1999; Carneiro and Heckman 2003).

7.5.2 Community Externalities

There is little evidence of significant human capital externalities at the state, national, or international levels (Aghion and Howitt 1998, Chap. 11; Heckman and Klenow 1998; Acemoglu and Angrist 1999; Krueger and Lindahl 2001; Ciccone and Peri 2006). However, Borjas (1992, 1995) finds important intergenerational human capital spillovers at the community level in US data. This is impressive since, as with school quality, one would expect there to be diminishing returns to human capital externalities (Heckman 1999). When education levels are generally low, there might be a much greater impact on children's learning from increasing the average education level of teachers, parents, and role models in the community than when the education levels are high. This makes it harder to identify external effects from data collected in countries where the population is relatively well educated. To this point, there is consistent evidence of community-level externalities in developing countries (Shavit and Pierce 1991; La Ferrara 2003; Cox and Fafchamps 2007; Angelucci et al. 2010 and Wantchekon et al. 2013).

Extending the human capital production function to include goods inputs and community externalities could take the form, $h_{t+1} = x_t^{\theta_1} e_t^{\theta_2} h_t^{\theta_3}$, where x is the goods input and where the community externality is captured by the human capital of the previous generation. As long as the three exponents still sum to be less than one, we have diminishing returns and can explain growth rate slowdowns. Adding goods inputs and community externalities will increase the contribution of human capital to explaining transitional growth. In addition, transitional growth will extend, at higher rates, over longer period before the slowdown begins. Rangazas (2002, 2005) does a quantitative analysis of growth with similar human capital production functions and shows significant increases in the duration of transitional growth.

7.5.3 Health Investments

We should at least mention the growing literature on how health interacts with learning and worker productivity. First, there is evidence that nutrition directly affects worker productivity in currently developing countries (Strauss and Thomas 1998) and in historical settings (Fogel 1997). Second, early (Bharadwaj et al. 2013) and contemporaneous (Miguel and Kremer 2004; Bleakley 2007) health interventions in children improve educational outcomes. Finally, there is at least some evidence that increases in longevity encourages individuals to invest in more schooling because the expected payoff period increases (Oster et al. 2013).

7.6 Convergence Revisited

The neoclassical growth models we have used predict that if the fundamentals of countries are similar then, regardless of when modern growth begins, all countries should eventually converge to similar long run per capita income levels and living standards. Fundamentals refer to the preferences, technology, and policies of the country. The convergence prediction means countries that begin modern growth later must grow *faster* than countries that began modern growth earlier, in order to "catch-up."

In the standard neoclassical growth model of Chap. 2, economic growth rates uniformly fall with the level of income as countries develop, making the prediction of convergence obvious and potentially rapid. However, the growth model of this chapter suggests that convergence may be a very slow process. From Table 7.2, we see that growth rates first rise and then exhibit little trend for many periods. In this model, a country that begins modern growth later will typically first grow *slower than*, and then grow at a rate *similar to*, the leaders in per capita income. There could easily be no sign of convergence for two centuries after growth first begins in the lagging country. This may be true even if the fundamentals of the leading and lagging economies have become similar.

We noted in Table 7.5 that the pattern of rising and then moderate and trendless growth rates over long periods of time was evident in US history. The same was true for the history of all currently high-income countries, with the exception of a relatively small number of Growth Miracle countries. Now consider the currently developing countries, whose growth takeoff lagged that of the current leaders. Since World War II, most countries of the world have begun sustained economic growth. The standard neoclassical growth model from Chap. 2 would predict that many of these countries, those that have established decent fundamentals, would grow faster than the leaders. However, the average growth rates of countries at every stage of development have been similar to that of the income leaders [see, for example, Jones and Vollrath (2013, Fig. 3.6), Kraay and McKenzie (2014, Table 1)]. This means that, on average, we have not seen countries converge. The lack of convergence for many decades, while not consistent with the standard neoclassical model, is quite consistent with extended neoclassical model from this chapter.

A recent study by Im and Rosenblatt (2013) looked at the lack of convergence in detail. The main question was whether developing countries have grown faster (in per capita terms) than the rich countries, the requirement for convergence. The study used the average Post-WWII growth rates of high-income countries as the benchmark. Over the last 50 years, 1961–2011, high-income countries have grown about 2 % per year. If one looks at the average per capita growth rates for 141 developing countries over this period, the average growth rate was also about 2 %. Thus, on average, developing countries are not converging. More precisely, 80 of the developing countries grew by at least 1.5 %—of which, 64 grew by at least 2 %. While these 64 countries are, in fact, converging, this is painfully slow convergence. Thirty-one countries grew by 3 % or more, while only 9 reached 5 % growth. So, convergence is only taking place in a minority of developing countries. It is even fewer developing countries that have experienced Growth Miracles and rapid convergence.

There has been some concern that the Growth Miracles countries have recently experienced a decrease in growth rates that is slowing their convergence. Evidence of this can be seen in Table 7.6. As we have discussed, our model predicts that the high growth rates of countries that generate unusually high levels of investment in physical and human capital, coupled with unusually rapid structural transformations, will naturally experience growth slowdowns, as exhibited in Table 7.4. It is not clear that special theories of "middle-income traps" are needed to explain these slowdowns (see, for example, Agenor and Canuto 2012; Aiyar et al. 2013). The middle-income trap theories focus on the possibility that TFP growth may slowdown in countries that are not able to compete in the production of human-capital-intensive goods associated with a fast pace of innovation. However, TFP growth will slow for more basic reasons such as slowdowns in the efficiency gains associated with the structural transformation or in the quality dimensions of schooling that are not typically measured (e.g., length of the school year, teacher inputs, and the average ability of students attending school). Nor should there be major concerns about most Growth Miracle countries since, even at their slower growth rates, they are converging quite rapidly to the income leaders of the world.

The same World Bank study mentioned above looked for evidence of "middle-income traps" in the form of a general tendency of middle-income countries to experience abrupt slowdowns or other unusual growth patterns. They found that the pattern of growth was no different for middle-income countries than for countries at other income levels. Middle-income countries that have experienced Growth Miracles, or even above average growth, are naturally going to experience more dramatic growth slowdowns than those in moderately growing economies. However, this does not seem to be the result of a special trap that afflicts all middle-income countries. The average middle-income country is experiencing similar growth rates, and the associated very slow convergence, that the average country at all levels of income is experiencing in the Post-WWII period.

We discussed in Chap. 5 that the growth experience of African countries has been particularly disappointing. In recent years, there has been some renewed hope that Africa is finally beginning to convergence. From 2000 to 2011, per capita income in Africa grew 4.7 % annually (Devarajan and Fengler 2012). The increase in growth rates is attributed to several factors including improved macroeconomic policies and the early stages of a demographic transition. Poor macroeconomic policies have been shown to create economic disasters that have long-term negative consequences for growth (such as hyper-inflations). The elimination of bad macroeconomic policies gives growth a chance (Easterly 2005). Africa is also benefiting from a demographic dividend associated with falling fertility. The most rapidly growing demographic group in Africa is now working-age adults (Devarajan and Fengler 2012, pp. 13–14). The number of adult workers is increasing rapidly relative to the number of children, causing rising worker productivity for many of the reasons we have stressed in the book.

Despite the recent success, there are doubts about whether Africa's growth can be sustained (Rodrik 2011; Devarajan and Fengler 2012). The concerns center around the weak structural transformation in Africa. Most workers are still employed in traditional agriculture and small informal family businesses. For example, 70 % of the work force in Uganda is employed in agriculture and informal family businesses.

As mentioned in Chap. 5, much of Africa's recent success has been caused by a boom in international commodity prices that while benefiting some groups in the economy also creates a deindustrialization that slows the structural transformation and sends labor generally into less productive occupations. This has caused some economists to support industrial policies, similar to those that sped the structural transformation in Asia, that serve to raise employment in the formal manufacturing sector where labor productivity is higher (see Sect. 7.4, for example).

There are domestic sources of the weak structural transformation in Africa as well. The continent is lacking in public infrastructure. Many of the services associated with the public infrastructure that does exist are poorly provided. Ports are inefficiently run, creating long delays in the shipping and distribution of products. Utilities are unevenly distributed according to political patronage. The trucking industry in many African countries is protected and operates with very high profit margins, driving up transportation costs. Regulatory costs associated with starting and running businesses are the highest in the world. The quality of schools is very poor due to poorly educated and frequently absent teachers. All of these features drive business costs up and labor productivity down in the formal manufacturing sector.

7.7 Politics and Growth

We have seen that the Great Divergence is a byproduct of the timing and nature of modern growth. Once growth begins, there is no strong force that slows growth down, making it difficult for lagging countries to catch up to leading countries. The slow pace of the structural transformation and the rising investment rates in physical and human capital per worker keep growth rates from falling over a lengthy transition marked by relatively trendless growth rates. For a lagging country to converge, it requires government to take unusual actions that accelerate the structural transformation and the rise in investment rates beyond the historical norm of the leaders. Only a few countries have been able to do this to the extent that it allows for a rapid convergence to the leaders' standard of living.

All of this means that the timing of the initial takeoff of sustained modern growth is generally the key to explaining the differences in the standard of living across countries today. The takeoff of the modern sector means conditions favor production that is intensive in physical and general human capital over traditional methods of production that rely heavily on land, raw labor, and the specific human capital that is passed down over many generations of family-based production. This raises the question of what prevents the conditions needed for the modern sector to begin to dominate over traditional production (see Chap. 4).

Acemoglu and Robinson (2012) offer an explanation of why the take off of modern growth is delayed in many countries. They argue for a type of poverty trap that becomes engrained in the political institutions of the country. When a country is undeveloped, it is nevertheless possible for a small fraction of the population to become rich by exploiting the country's available resources and labor. The rich elite are naturally also those that have seized political power. The political power allows the elite to create policies and laws that maintain the status quo and prevent economic competition from anyone outside the small fraction of the population that rules the country. Monarchies, dictators, one-party rulers, and overly influential landowners and traditional craftsmen maintain control by creating monopolies, blocking innovation, and arbitrarily seizing land and taxing income. For our purposes, one can think of this situation as one where the traditional sector of the economy being protected from competition because most of the generated income there is flowing to a small group in power and its supporters.

To break this type of poverty trap requires a major change in political institutions. Changing political institutions under an autocratic regime requires conflict. For example, sustained modern growth is generally believed to have started with the Industrial Revolution in England. Acemoglu and Robinson argue that the Industrial Revolution never would have occurred without a long political struggle, involving much unrest and even civil war, culminating in the Glorious Revolution. The political struggle shifted power from the autocratic monarchy to the more democratic Parliament. The Parliament, representing a broad coalition of interest throughout the country, ended the creation of monopolies, the selective granting of patents, and the arbitrary taxation and seizures of property that were the hallmarks of the monarchy's reign. In addition, the government became more focused on the general infrastructure of the economy; roads, banks, and education for the masses. The country became ruled by more even-handed laws and policies and not by a ruling elite that intended to maintain its power and wealth. The dramatic change from an exclusive and extractive political rule to a inclusive one leveled the playing field and set the stage for the Industrial Revolution.

7.7.1 Natural Resources and the Politics Trap

In Chaps. 4 and 6, we discussed how natural resources can potentially slow growth by creating comparative advantages in the traditional agriculture and commodity sector. In particular in open economies, a comparative advantage in the traditional sector slows the structural transformation and adds volatility to the economy that slows growth. The natural resources of a country also play a role in the political poverty trap by weakening democracies and inducing the creation of autocratic regimes that are looking to get rich quick by gaining control of the income flows from the traditional sector (Collier 2007, Chaps. 2 and 3).

Ironically, autocratic regimes can also create Growth Miracles (Glaeser et al. 2004). After WWII, the Asian Tigers began as dictatorships. However, they were pro-growth dictatorships, imposing policies that forced and encouraged public and private investments of various types on their poor populations. In democratic regimes, with limited central government power, high levels of saving and investment are not going to be the preferred choice of an impoverished electorate. So, when do autocratic governments work for growth and when don't they?

Autocracies are clearly risky for the growth; they can lead to Growth Miracles or Growth Disasters. It appears that autocracies are particularly detrimental for growth when the country's population is ethnically diverse (Collier 2007, Chap. 3). In this case, the tendency of those in power is to control resources for its own ethnic group at the expense of the country as a whole. A particularly bad mix for a developing country is to have an autocratic regime, with an ethnically diverse population, and rich natural resources. Unfortunately, this toxic mix is quite common in developing countries, particularly in Africa and the Middle East. The relatively low current standard of living in these underdeveloped regions is largely the result of a legacy of extractive regimes that have been generated by the combination of autocratic government, ethnic diversity, and natural resources.

7.8 Conclusion

In this chapter we use a complete dual economy model to conduct a quantitative study of transitional growth over long periods of time. Unlike the standard neoclassical growth model, that predicts declining growth rates and rapid convergence to a steady state, the dual economy generates rising growth rates that eventually level off for several decades before finally begin to decline after a long transition.

The analysis shows that the early stages of growth are dominated by the structural transformation. The migration of labor from the traditional sector to the modern sector expands work hours and reduces the number of child workers, resulting in a rise in productivity per worker. Later in the growth process, we see rising investment rates in physical and human capital cause high growth rates for many decades. Finally, as the rise in investment rates stabilize, diminishing returns dominates, and growth rates begin to fall.

We left out several factors that would increase the ability to explain growth and extend the duration of the transition with relatively constant growth rates. These factors include broader investments in human capital, human capital externalities, and investments in R&D. Eventually, all of these sources of growth will weaken and growth rates will decline. This suggests that growth in the twenty-first century will likely be weaker than in the twentieth century.

7.9 Exercises

Questions

1. Explain why young households may choose to remain in the traditional sector even if they do not inherit land from their parents or village.
2. In the model used in this chapter, how do traditional and modern households differ in their behavior and why?
3. What does it mean for there to be a "national" labor market? Does it imply that annual wages are the same for modern and traditional workers? What condition must be satisfied for the labor market to be national?
4. What is the "required" residual income from operating a family business? What would make the required income increase? How does an increase in required income affect
   (a) the saving rate of traditional households
   (b) fertility of a traditional household
   (c) family labor supply of a traditional household in adult-equivalent units
   (d) fraction of households that live in the traditional sector.

5. How does the structural transformation affect the capital–labor ratio in the modern sector? The rental rate on human capital throughout the economy?
6. List all the ways that the structural transformation may affect economic growth.
7. What features of economic growth do the simulations reported in Tables 7.2, 7.3 and 7.4 capture well and what features do they miss?
8. Based on Table 7.3, what is the most important quantitative connection between the structural transformation and growth in worker productivity? Explain the connection in detail.
9. Why can the model of this chapter be viewed as generating a conservative estimate of the role of endogenous transitional growth in explaining real-world growth?
10. What are the implications for twenty-first century growth that are suggested by the research discussed in this chapter?
11. Discuss the events that initiated the South Korean Growth Miracle.
12. Why does the standard growth model from Chap. 2 have trouble explaining the lack of convergence across economies of the world? How does the extended model of this chapter help explain the lack of convergence?
13. What has slowed the structural transformation in Africa?
14. Explain the political poverty trap.

Problems

1. Use the first-order conditions for labor demand in each sector, Eq. (7.8), and $\tilde{w}_t\tilde{D}_t = w_t D_t$, to derive (7.9), the fraction of young households in period t that remain in the traditional sector.
2. Show that the total demand for labor from the traditional sector can be written as $\tilde{N}_t \frac{\Omega(1-\alpha)Ak_t^\alpha \tilde{z}\tilde{h}_t}{(1+d)k_{t+1}}$.
3. Show how (7.12) simplifies to become (7.13c). Explain how the structural transformation affects physical capital intensity.
4. Carefully explain why one cannot explicitly solve (7.13c) for k_{t+1}.
5. Derive (7.13e). Explain the different ways that the structural transformation affects the traditional labor share.

References

Acemoglu D, Angrist J (1999) How large are the social returns to education? Evidence from compulsory schooling laws. NBER working paper 7444. National Bureau of Economic Research, Cambridge

Acemoglu D, Robinson J (2012) Why nations fail. In: The origins of power, prosperity, and poverty. Crown Publishers, New York

Agenor P, Canuto O (2012) Middle-income growth traps. World Bank policy research working paper 6210. World Bank, Washington

Aghion P, Howitt P (1998) Endogenous growth theory. MIT Press, Cambridge

Aiyar S, Duval R, Puy D, Wu Y, Zhang L (2013) Growth slowdowns and the middle-income trap. IMF working paper 13/71. International Monetary Fund, Washington
Angelucci M, De Giorgi G, Rangel M, Rasul I (2010) Family networks and school enrollment: evidence from a randomized social experiment. J Public Econ 94(3–4):197–221
Banerjee A, Duflo E (2011) Poor economics. Public Affairs, New York
Bharadwaj P, Loken K, Neilson C (2013) Early life interventions and academic achievement. Am Econ Rev 103(5):1862–1891
Bleakly H (2007) Disease and development: evidence from hookworm eradication in the American South. Q J Econ 122(1):73–117
Borjas GJ (1992) Ethnic capital and intergenerational mobility. Q J Econ 107(1):123–150
Borjas GJ (1995) Ethnicity, neighborhoods, and human-capital externalities. Am Econ Rev 85 (3):365–390
Brynjolfsson E, McAfee A (2014) The second-machine age. Norton, New York
Carneiro P, Heckman J (2003) Human capital policy. In: Heckman J, Krueger A, Friedman B (eds) Inequality in America: what role for human capital policies?. MIT Press, Cambridge
Carter SB, Ransom RL, Sutch R (2003) Family matters: the life-cycle transition and the unparalleled fertility decline in antebellum America. In: Guinnane TW, Sundstrom WA, Whately W (eds) History matters: essays on economic growth, technology, and demographic change. Stanford University Press, Stanford, California
Ciccone A, Peri G (2006) Identifying human capital externalities: theory with applications. Rev Econ Stud 73(2):381–412
Collier P (2007) The bottom billion. Oxford University Press, Oxford
Cox D, Fafchamps M (2007) Extended family and kinship networks: economic insights and evolutionary directions. In: Schultz P, Strauss JA (eds) Handbook of development economics, vol 4. Elsevier, Amsterdam, pp 3711–3784
Devarjan S, Fengler W (2012) Is Africa's recent economic growth sustainable?. Institut Francais des Relations Internationals, Paris and Brussels
Easterly W (2005) National policies and economic growth: a reappraisal. In: Agion P, Durlauf S (eds) Handbook of economic growth, vol 1A. Elsevier, Amsterdam
Farmer K, Schelnast M (2013) Growth and international trade: an introduction to the overlapping generations approach. Spring, Berlin
Fogel R (1997) New finding on secular trends in nutrition and mortality: some implications for population theory. In: Rosenzweig M, Stark O (eds) Handbook of population and family economics. North Holland, Amsterdam, pp 433–481
Glaeser E, La Porta R, Lopez-de-Salines F, Shleifer A (2004) Do institutions cause growth? J Econ Growth 9(3):271–303
Gollin D, Lagakos D, Waugh M (2014) The agricultural productivity gap. Q J Econ 129 (2):939–993
Gordon R (1999) U.S. economic growth since 1870: One big wave? Am Econ Rev 89(2):123–128
Heckman J (1999) Policies to foster human capital. NBER working paper 7288. National Bureau of Economic Research, Cambridge
Heckman J, Klenow P (1998) Human capital policy. In: Boskin M (ed) Policies to promote capital formation. Hoover Institute, Washington
Im F, Rosenblatt D (2013) Middle-income traps: a conceptual and empirical survey. Policy research working paper 6594. World Bank, Washington
Jones C (2002) Sources of U.S. growth in a world of ideas. Am Econ Rev 92(1): 220–239
Jones C, Vollrath D (2013) Introduction to economic growth. W.W. Norton, New York
Kraay A, McKenzie D (2014) Do poverty traps exist? assessing the evidence. J Econ Perspect 28 (3):127–145
Krueger A (2002) Economic considerations and class size. NBER working paper 8875. National Bureau of Economic Research, Cambridge, Massachusetts
Krueger A, Lindahl M (2001) Education for growth: why and for whom? J Econ Lit 39 (4):1101–1136

La Ferrara E (2003) Model of credit transactions in Ghana. Am Econ Rev 93(5):1730–1751
La Porta R, Shleifer A (2014) Informality and development. J Econ Perspect 28(3):109–126
Lucas R (2002) Lecture on economic growth. Harvard University Press, Cambridge
McMillan M, Rodrik D (2011) Globalization, structural change, and productivity growth. In: Bacchetta M, Jansen M (eds) Making globalization sustainable. International Labour Organization and World Trade Organization, Geneva
Miguel E, Kremer M (2004) Worms: identifying impacts on education and health in the presence of treatment externalities. Econometrica 72(1):159–217
Oster E, Shoulson I, Dorsey E (2013) Limited life expectancy, human capital, and health investments. Am Econ Rev 103(5):1977–2002
Quataert D (1993) Ottoman manufacturing in the age of the industrial revolution. Cambridge University Press, Cambridge
Rangazas P (2002) The quantity and quality of schooling and U.S. labor productivity growth (1870–2000). Rev Econ Dyn 5(4):932–964
Rangazas P (2005) Human capital growth: an alternative accounting. J Macroecon 5(1):1–43
Ranis G, Fei J (1961) A theory of economic development. Am Econ Rev 51(4):533–565
Rodrik D (2011) The future of economic convergence. NBER working paper 17400. National Bureau of Economic Research, Cambridge
Rodrik D (2013) Structural change, fundamentals, and growth: an overview. Institute for Advanced Studies, Princeton
Ruggles S (2001) Living arrangements and the well-being of older persons in the past population. Bull Unit Nations 42(43):111–161
Ruggles S (2005) Intergenerational coresidence and economic opportunity of the younger generation in the United States, 1850–2000. Minnesota Population Center Working Paper
Shavit Y, Pierce J (1991) Sibling size and educational attainment in nuclear and extended families: Arabs and Jews in Israel. Am Sociol Rev 56(3):321–330
Strauss J, Thomas D (1998) Health, nutrition, and development. J Econ Lit 34(2):766–817
Vijg J (2011) The American technological challenge. Algora Press, New York
Wantchekon L, Novta N, Klasnja M (2013) Education and human capital externalities: evidence from colonial Benin. Department of Politics, Princeton University, Princeton

Urbanization

8

In this chapter, we study migration to the city and its effects on *urbanization*. In previous chapters, we studied how the structural transformation affects economic growth and, in particular, how migration to the modern sector may alter private sector behavior. Here, we focus on the question of the best pace of urbanization as it relates to the allocation of rural and urban government services. Our motivation comes from the fact that the vast majority of governments around the developing world are concerned about the adequacy of public goods provision and the crowding associated with rapid urbanization (Bloom and Khanna 2007).[1] In this sense, the structural transformation, which generally raises economic growth, can occur too quickly. A second important issue we address is the role politics plays in exacerbating rural–urban inequalities. As first stressed by Lipton (1977), the disproportionate political power of urban interests (the "urban elite") in some developing countries' economic policies may distort the allocation of government services, exacerbate rural–urban inequalities, and intensify migration beyond efficient levels.[2]

To investigate the issues surrounding regional migration and the allocation of government services, we use our dual economy framework by interpreting the traditional sector as rural and the modern sector as urban. The rural technology is traditional in the sense that land and labor are used as inputs. The urban technology is modern in the sense that physical capital and labor are used as inputs. Thus,

[1] The concern is so significant that 73 % of the governments surveyed have designed policies with the goal of slowing urbanization. A major concern over urbanization is the ability to finance the necessary public infrastructure associated with a growing urban population. According to some estimates, trillions of dollars of investment will be needed to extend the urban infrastructure due to the high urbanization rates in Asia.

[2] In addition to providing a voting-based theory of urban bias, Majumdar et al. (2004) empirically document the extent to which public services in urban areas exceed those in rural areas. McCormick and Wahba (2003) examine the effects of an urban bias in the allocation of public sector jobs. Bezemer and Headey (2008) discuss continuing concerns over the presence of an urban bias in domestic and international development policy. Bates (1981) focuses on how urban bias affects the pricing of agriculture products.

S. Das et al., *Economic Growth and Development*,
Springer Texts in Business and Economics, DOI 10.1007/978-3-319-14265-4_8

similar to Chap. 7, the rural and urban sectors are distinguished by the different technologies used to produce a common good.[3]

The main contribution of this chapter is to introduce fiscal policy into the dual economy framework. To abstract from the effects of the structural transformation on private capital intensity, a major focus of Chaps. 6 and 7, we study a government operating in a small open economy. We also simplify the analysis by abstracting from explicitly modeling human capital and endogenous fertility in order to concentrate on endogenous fiscal policy. The policy maker's problem is how to allocate a given budget for productive services across the rural and urban sectors. The government inputs are interpreted as any service that raises productivity either through human capital development (e.g., training, education, or public health programs), physical infrastructure (e.g., roads, bridges, or public utilities), or property protection (e.g., policing or fire protection services). As is commonly alleged, we assume that the policy maker "favors" urban households over rural households.

In our setting, if the government also has the ability to directly allocate labor across sectors, then the first-best, productively efficient outcome would require no urban bias in the allocation of productive government services. If both sectors operate, an equal allocation of productive services is first-best, equating the marginal productivity of both labor and government services across the two sectors. Thus, the requirement of an urban bias is tied to the fact that the government cannot directly allocate laboracross sectors when maximizing total output.

When households choose their location, they compare the relative wage opportunities in the rural and urban sectors. There is a wage gap in this chapter because it is costly to migrate from the traditional to the modern sector. If the wage gap across sectors is sufficiently high, then some households in the low-wage rural sector incur the cost of moving to the high-wage urban sector. We focus on the commonly observed historical pattern in developing countries where low-wage rural households migrate to the high-wage urban sector over long periods of time.

In the presence of endogenous rural–urban migration based on household choice, we find that the second-best allocation of government services across rural and urban sectors is independent of the weight the policy maker places on rural households; politics plays no role in the allocation. Nevertheless, we find that the second-best efficient allocation of government services is "biased" toward the urban sector.

The efficient urban bias—more government services per capita are available in the city than in the country—is driven by two key features of the economy. First, because of unrestricted migration across sectors, there is a close link between rural and urban wages. An increase in the quantity of government services in the city

---

[3] For the purpose of the issue that we address, the apparent policy bias against the poorer and less developed rural sector during the development process, distinguishing the sectors by differences in traditional and modern technologies seems reasonable. There are certainly other differences between the rural and urban sectors that we ignore. Also by focusing on an "urban sector", we do not address the expansion of cities across geographic areas or heterogeneity in city types. For an analysis of systems of cities, where cities specialize in the production of different goods see Henderson (1974), Black and Henderson (1999), Duranton and Puga (2004), and Henderson and Wang (2005).

raises the productivity and wages of urban workers. A higher urban wage increases rural-to-urban migration and thereby raises rural wages as well. Second, migration to the city does not directly alter the urban wage. Migration to the city, where the modern technology is operated, raises the marginal product of private capital. In an open economy, the higher marginal product of capital causes an inflow of foreign capital that maintains the interest rate and the urban wage rate. Therefore, migration to the city only affects wages through a crowding of urban government services per capita. Taken together, these two features suggest that to maximize wages across the economy, the government must choose the allocation of productive services to generate a migration flow that maximizes *urban* government services per capita.

The fact that rural government services have an effect on migration suggests that it is not efficient—even for a government dominated by urban households—to spend the entire government budget on urban services. Such a policy would intensify migration, placing a strain on the government budget that reduces government service per capita in the city and wages in both sectors. Instead, the efficient policy—the one that maximizes urban government service provision per capita and wages in both sectors—is to provide some government services in the rural area in order to limit migration.

Given the urban biasdoes not depend on the weight the government places on rural household welfare, then how is redistribution effected if, as Lipton argued, politics of developing countries are often dominated by urban elites? In our model, a "redistributive" urban bias designed to increase urban welfare must take the form of restricting migration to the city. To redistribute income, the government needs to reduce migration by imposing direct administrative measures, such as migration quotas and other restrictions that raise the cost of migration.[4] We show that an increase in migration restrictions, even allowing for a policy response in the allocation of government services, will raise urban wages and lower rural wages. This result suggests that political debates are more likely to center on migration restrictions rather than on the allocation of government goods.

Section 8.1 presents a simple baseline model that generates an unambiguous urban bias in government service provision on efficiency grounds. Section 8.2 analyzes the effects of economic growth, stemming from both balanced and unbalanced technological change, on migration and the rural–urban wage gap. Section 8.3 discusses several extensions of the basic model. Section 8.4 considers the possibility of an optimal city size. Section 8.5 discusses the recurrent problem of slums that form in the cities of developing economies. Section 8.6 describes China's system of internal migration restrictions. Section 8.7 notes that urbanization can be reversed, using important examples of de-urbanization. Section 8.8 ends with some concluding remarks.

---

[4] Clear examples of where such policies have been carried out include the former Soviet Union and China. See also Sect. 8.6.

8.1 Urban Bias

Our baseline economy is small and perfectly open to both the trade of goods and the flow of physical capital across borders.[5] There are two sectors of production that produce the same good, urban and rural, of fixed geographic size. Production in each sector is carried out by perfectly competitive firms. Households can only work in the sector in which they reside, but they choose to locate in the rural or urban sector. Locational choices are made by young households before work begins. We focus on the typical pattern seen over the course of development, where young households from the rural sector migrate to the urban sector over relatively long periods of time in response to wage gaps between sectors.

The fundamental difference between sectors is the technology used in production. The technology used in the rural sector is traditional in that land is combined with labor to produce output, while a modern technology is used in the urban sector where physical capital and labor are combined to produce output. It is important to note that because the same good is produced in each sector, one sector may be viewed as being redundant. In particular, the policy makers favoring the urban sector may choose to ignore the rural sector altogether by failing to provide government services there. Feler and Henderson (2011) discuss how some governments enact regulations that withhold public services from low-income households to slow migration to the city.

8.1.1 Production

Urban Sector

The urban sector technology for producing goods is given by

$$Y_t = K_t^{\alpha}(D_t M_t)^{1-\alpha} \tag{8.1}$$

where Y is output, K is the capital stock, M is the number of workers employed, D is a labor productivity index, and α is the constant capital share parameter. Similar to Chap. 3, the productivity index is a function of effective productive government services per worker, G_t/M_t, and an exogenous technology index, E,

$$D_t = \left(\frac{G_t}{M_t}\right)^{\mu} E_t^{1-\mu} \tag{8.2}$$

where μ is a constant parameter. The technology index, E, grows at a constant rate q.

[5] The next three sections are based on Mourmouras and Rangazas (2013). In an unpublished appendix, we consider the closed economy case. The appendix can be found as supplement to the article on the *Journal of Economic Geography's* Web site.

Profit maximization and competition generate the standard equations relating factor prices to the marginal productivity of the factors

$$r = (1 - \tau)\alpha k_t^{\alpha-1} \tag{8.3a}$$

$$W_t = (1 - \alpha)D_t k_t^{\alpha}, \tag{8.3b}$$

where $k_t \equiv K_t/D_t M_t$. The return to capital is taxed at the constant rate τ. Capital depreciates at the constant rate δ. For simplicity, we take the rate of depreciation to be one. The internationally determined after-tax rate of return on capital is r. Wage income is also taxed at the constant rate τ, but the tax is collected at the household level. The before-tax wage rate paid to a worker is W which, unlike w from previous chapters, incorporates the return to a unit of human capital and the effect of the labor-augmenting productivity index.

Rural Sector

The rural sector produces the same good (denoted by O only for the purpose of helping to keep the two sectors distinct) with a technology that uses land (L) instead of physical capital. For simplicity, we initially assume that rural firms and households face the same tax rate as in the urban sector. Later we consider the more realistic situation, initially discussed in Chap. 6, where taxes are more difficult to collect from the rural sector than they are from the urban sector.

The rural technology is

$$O_t = L_t^{\alpha}\left(\tilde{D}_t F_t\right)^{1-\alpha} \tag{8.4}$$

where F is the labor employed in production and $\tilde{D}$ is the labor productivity index in the rural sector. In keeping with evidence that the labor share of income does not vary with the composition of output over the course of development, we set the land share to be the same as the capital share in the urban sector, α. Similar to the urban sector, the labor productivity index in the traditional sector is determined by

$$\tilde{D}_t = \left(\frac{\tilde{G}_t}{F_t}\right)^{\mu}\left(\tilde{E}_t\right)^{1-\mu} \tag{8.5}$$

where $\tilde{E}_t$ is the technology index in rural production.[6]

The competitive factor price equations for the rental rate of land and the rural wage rate are

$$r_t^L = (1 - \tau)\alpha\left(L_t/\tilde{D}_t F_t\right)^{\alpha-1} \tag{8.6a}$$

[6] Note that we are modeling government services as publically provided private inputs. In some cases, it is more appropriate to treat government services as flowing from impure public goods. We examine this case in Sect. 8.3.

$$\tilde{W}_t = (1 - \alpha)\tilde{D}_t\left(L_t/\tilde{D}_t F_t\right)^{\alpha}, \tag{8.6b}$$

Available land is fixed in the economy, so in equilibrium we must have $L_t = L$ in each period. Given the equilibrium rural wage rate and the fixed amount of land, the allocation of labor to the rural sector, F_t, and the rental rate on land, r_t^L, are given by the competitive factor price equations (8.6a, b).

8.1.2 Households

Households are life-cycle planners that populate the standard overlapping generations model. Households live for two periods; they work only in the first period and then retire in the second period. All households have the same preferences. Household welfare is determined by the consumption of the common good produced in the two sectors, c_{it}, where i denotes the period of life in which the goods are consumed. Households save by purchasing physical capital (s_t) and land (l_t) and then renting them to producers. Households can only work in the sector in which they reside. Unlike in Chaps. 5–7, there is no constraint on hours in the rural sector and land is traded in perfectly competitive markets.

Urban Sector

Household preferences, regardless of location, are given by the following lifetime utility function

$$U_t = u(c_{1t}) + \beta u(c_{2t+1}), \tag{8.7}$$

where u is a strictly concave and differentiable, single-period utility function, and β is the time discount factor.

The single-period budget constraints for the two periods of life of an urban household are

$$c_{1t} + s_t + p_t^L l_t = (1 - \tau)W_t \tag{8.8a}$$

$$c_{2t+1} = Rs_t + \left(r_{t+1}^L + p_{t+1}^L\right)l_t, \tag{8.8b}$$

where p_t^L is the competitive relative price of land and $R \equiv 1 + r - \delta$. The two single-period constraints generate the following lifetime budget constraint,

$$c_{1t} + \frac{c_{2t+1}}{R} = (1 - \tau)W_t, \tag{8.9}$$

with the no-arbitrage condition that determines the equilibrium price of land,

$$p_t^L = \frac{r_{t+1}^L + p_{t+1}^L}{R}. \tag{8.10}$$

Given the competitive factor prices, urban households make life-cycle consumption choices to maximize utility.

Rural Sector

There are two types of rural households. One type chooses to remain in the rural sector, and the second type migrates to the urban sector. Migration is costly. It requires a loss of consumption equal to ω_t (transportation costs, goods left behind, a drop in housing quality, and other moving expenses) and a lost fraction of work-time, $\bar{\omega}$, spent in transit and looking for work in city.[7] The decision to migrate occurs at the beginning of a household's working life and is based on the relative wage opportunities in the two sectors that determine the household's lifetime welfare.

Households that remain in the rural sector maximize utility subject to a lifetime budget constraint based on the after-tax rural wage,

$$\tilde{c}_{1t} + \frac{\tilde{c}_{2t+1}}{R} = (1-\tau)\tilde{W}_t.$$

The second type of rural household migrates to the urban sector. Migrants must bear the time and goods costs associated with migration. They maximize utility subject to a lifetime budget constraint based on the urban wage net of migration costs,

$$\bar{c}_{1t} + \frac{\bar{c}_{2t+1}}{R} = (1-\tau)(1-\bar{\omega})W_t - \omega_t.$$

To assess household welfare in each sector, we use a value function giving the maximum household lifetime utility as a function of the market factor prices. In an open economy, the interest rate is determined exogenously by the international market for capital. We assume the international return to capital is constant, so that maximum utility will vary because of variation in the market wage rate alone. The value function is defined to be $V(X)$, where X stands in for the net wage of the different household types. In some cases, we will resort to the special case of log preferences that we employed heavily in past chapters, where $u(c) = \ln c$. In this case, the value function of a household with net wage X takes the form,

$$V(X) = (1+\beta)\ln\left(\frac{1}{1+\beta}\right) + \beta\ln\beta + (1+\beta)\ln(X) + \beta\ln(1+r).$$

---

[7] The lost work-time associated with migration can also be given a Harris and Todaro (1970) interpretation in that those arriving in the city endure a period of search unemployment.

8.1.3 Demographics

Every period, there will be young and old households of each of the three types. The population of young urban households in each period, N_t^*, is comprised of the children of last period's urban sector natives and the young rural households who choose to migrate

$$N_t^* = nN_{t-1}^* + \varphi_t n\tilde{N}_{t-1} \tag{8.11}$$

where $n - 1$ is the common and exogenous rate of population growth for all households, φ_t is the fraction of young rural households that choose to migrate, and $\tilde{N}_{t-1}$ is the number of rural households last period. The number of rural households in the current period is given by

$$\tilde{N}_t = (1 - \varphi_t)n\tilde{N}_{t-1}. \tag{8.12}$$

The labor supply in each sector equals the number of young households in that sector, $M_t = N_t^*$ and $F_t = \tilde{N}_t$. Assuming a common population growth rate in each sector implies the country's total population size $N_t \equiv N_t^* + \tilde{N}_t$ is exogenous, i.e., independent of the endogenous allocation of the population across the sectors that occurs each period.

8.1.4 Migration in Equilibrium

We primarily consider equilibria where both sectors operate and some movement to the city occurs each period. For these equilibria, the rural households must be indifferent about staying in the rural sector or migrating to the urban sector. To be indifferent about migrating, the value functions must be equal whether the household migrates or not, i.e.,

$$V_t\big((1-\tau)\tilde{W}_t\big) = V_t((1-\tau)(1-\bar{\omega})W_t - \omega_t)$$

or equivalently

$$\tilde{W}_t = (1 - \bar{\omega})W_t - \frac{\omega_t}{1-\tau}. \tag{8.13}$$

Positive migration to the city is needed to satisfy (8.13) when, in the absence of migration, $\tilde{W}_t$ is strictly less than $(1 - \bar{\omega})W_t - \frac{\omega_t}{1-\tau}$.

8.1.5 Government

To examine the possibility of an urban bias in setting policy, we allow urban households to determine the allocation of public services across the two sectors of the economy. Given that all urban households in a given age cohort are identical, the choice of government service allocation can be made by a representative household from the cohort of young households in each period. Only young households care about the allocation of government services because these services affect welfare only by affecting the productivity of labor and wages. The welfare of old households in each period is predetermined by the previous period's wage and the exogenously determined world interest rate.

The government budget constraint confronting the representative urban household in making its fiscal choice is given by

$$G_t + \tilde{G}_t = B_t, \tag{8.14}$$

where B_t is the portion of the total government budget that is allocated to fund government services. In this section, we assume that the value of B_t is exogenous to the model and focus only on the allocation problem. We assume that B_t rises proportionately with the state of technology and the country's population, to capture the effects of an increasing tax base. In Sect. 8.3, we make tax revenue and the budget endogenous.

The representative urban household chooses the allocation of public services to maximize a social welfare function of the form $V_t((1-\tau)W_t) + \upsilon V_t\big((1-\tau)\tilde{W}_t\big)$, subject to (8.14), where υ is a nonnegative weight the policy maker places on the welfare of the rural household.

To focus on the consequences of an urban bias in politics, we assume $0 \le \upsilon \le 1$. The government chooses the allocation of public services taking account the full general equilibrium interactions, in particular, the determinants of the urban wage (8.3b), the link between urban and rural wages given by (8.13), and the effect of the government service allocation on the migration flow to the city, which is indirectly determined by (8.6b).

8.1.6 Efficient Urban Bias

The solution to the government's problem is

$$\tilde{g}_t = \frac{\mu(1-\alpha)}{\alpha + \mu(1-\alpha)} g_t, \tag{8.15}$$

where we define the de-trended, for exogenous technological progress, per worker values of $\tilde{G}_t, G_t$, and B_t as lower case values, that is government services per worker in each sector and the budget available per household, all de-trended by the state of technology.[8] Equation (8.15) determines the optimal mix of government services across sectors. Note that the expression is independent of υ, so politics plays no role in determining the allocation of government services across sectors. There is an unambiguous "urban bias" because government services per capita are smaller in the rural sector, but this is for efficiency reasons.

The fundamental logic for the efficient urban bias starts with the idea that urban wages are solely a function of urban public services per capita, see (8.3b), and not the absolute value of labor as in the rural sector where land is an input. This is true because the private capital–labor ratio is independent of migration flows to the city. As the city becomes more populated, the marginal product of capital rises and attracts private capital into the country to maintain interest rates at the world level. This causes the capital–labor ratio to remain constant, and thus, there is no crowding of private capital that would result in lower wages. Also note that the urban wage determines the rural wage when there is migration across sectors (see 8.13). These two features imply that maximizing government services per capita in the city maximizes wages in both locations.

This logic seems to suggest that rural public services should be set to zero. However, to maximize per capita public services in the city, migration must be limited to some extent by offering public services in the rural sector as well. Thus, the sole purpose of rural public service provision is to control urban crowding leading to the maximization of urban public services for a given fiscal budget.

The role of rural public services in controlling urban crowding can be seen directly by rewriting (8.14) as $g_t\pi_t + \tilde{g}_t(1 - \pi_t) = b_t$. Given the size of the government budget per person, an increase in the fraction of the urban population (π_t) will strain resources when there is an urban bias. The value of π_t is indirectly determined by (8.6b), which expresses the demand for labor in the rural sector as a fraction of the rural population $(1 - \varphi_t)$ that does not leave for the city (see Problem 2). The lower is the provision of government services in the rural sector, the weaker is the demand for rural workers, and the higher is φ_t and π_t. Thus, it is optimal to provide some government services to the rural sector in order to manage the value of π_t in face of an urban bias in government service provision.

The degree of urban bias depends on how much rural government services affect the rural population; the larger the effect, the weaker is the urban bias. The effectiveness of government services in controlling migration depends on the production parameters, μ and α. The larger is the expression $\mu(1 - \alpha)$, the greater is the effect of government services on the marginal product of labor, and labor demand, in the rural sector. A low value of α not only increases the size of the "shift" in the demand for labor, as government services increase, but also reduces the slope of the demand for labor. When the demand for labor has a flatter slope, more workers must be hired in order to drive the marginal product of labor back down to the equilibrium wage rate.

---

[8] For proofs of this result and others in this chapter, see Mourmouras and Rangazas (2013).

The relative wage inequality across sectors is determined by (8.13). The amount of wage inequality that rural households will tolerate depends on the costs of migration relative to the benefit of migration, the urban wage rate. Wage inequality will decrease over time if the urban wage rate increases because it lowers the relative "goods" costs of migration (transportation costs, land or goods left behind, difference in housing costs across sectors, etc.).

Finally, note that the efficient urban bias result depends on the assumption that there is a positive migration flow across sectors. If migration was impossible, or perfectly restricted, then the policy maker's preferences *would* affect the allocation of public services. For example, in the extreme case where the policy maker was only maximizing the preferences of urban households, the entire government budget would be devoted to urban public services because, with migration restrictions, the crowding effects would no longer be an issue.

More generally, with no migration, υ will influence the size of the bias. For example, if consumers have log preferences, the policy solution is $\tilde{g}_t = \frac{\upsilon \pi_t}{1-\pi_t} g_t$, where the extent of the bias depends on the relative cost of providing the services, which are a function of the relative sizes of the urban and rural populations, and on υ.

8.2 Growth and Urbanization

In this section, we consider how various events affect urbanization and growth in the model developed in Sect. 8.1.

8.2.1 Urbanization with Balanced Growth

The economy's dynamics is determined by the exogenous pace of technological progress (E_t) and the extent to which the progress is balancedacross sectors, i.e., the extent to which $\tilde{E}_t$ keeps pace with E_t. Balanced technological progress creates a "pull factor" that increases urbanization but lowers the intensity of productive government services economy-wide. The direct effect of an increase in E_t raises wages, lowers the relative cost of migrating, and reduces wage inequality (see 8.13). However, because an increase in E_t also lowers g_t, the overall effect on inequality is not obvious. One can show that the indirect effect of a lower g_t, only mediates, rather than completely offsets, the direct effect of a higher E_t.

Urbanization caused by balanced technological progress supports the "optimistic" view of urbanization.[9] In this case, urbanization is a natural consequence of progress and increasing opportunity. Some crowding of services results, but the level of wages increase, and wage inequality falls. Here, urbanization is associated with rising worker productivity.

[9] See Bloom and Khanna (2007) for a discussion of the optimistic and pessimistic views of urbanization.

As E_t increases over time, the fraction of the rural population that leaves for the city each period also increases, accelerating the growth in the fraction of the entire population that works and lives in the city. Along the growth path, the urban–rural wage gap becomes smaller. Eventually, the traditional rural sector disappears, as the entire economy converges to the modern urban sector [as in Hansen and Prescott (2002) and Lucas (2004)].

It is important to stress that an increase in technology in the urban sector *only* would not necessarily deliver this favorable outcome. If E_t increases and $\tilde{E}_t$ does not keep pace, a larger migration to the city results. The larger migration may lower g_t enough to offset the direct effect of E_t on urban wages. Balanced technological progress is required to guarantee that urbanization is associated with rising worker productivity and falling wage inequality.

8.2.2 Urbanization Without Balanced Growth

As documented by Fay and Opal (2000), there is a "pessimistic" view of urbanization, one revealed by the concerns of politicians who attempt to limit migration to the city (see the introduction). The pessimistic view is supported by the model when the underlying reasons for urbanization are ones that lower the relative productivity in the rural areas and push people toward the city—for example, a rise in the rural population or relatively slow technological progress in the rural sector. These factors result in crowding and lower g_t, for any given value of E_t. The reduction in government service intensity lowers wages in both sectors and increases wage inequality. Here, urbanization is associated with falling worker productivity.

The intuition about unbalanced technological change that favors the urban sector extends to physical capital inflows. Physical capital favors the urban sector by raising productivity in the city relative to the rural sector. For this reason, relative to its direct impact on urban wages, the effect of physical capital on encouraging migration to the city is large. Thus, the negative effect of reducing government services per worker may be large enough to offset the direct effect on productivity, and urban wages may fall.

When urbanization occurs without growth, there are policies that slow migration and improve the welfare of all households. An example of such a policy would be to direct foreign aid toward the rural sector that is designed to improve the relative state of rural technology by raising $\tilde{E}_t$. Such a policy would lower φ_t and raise g_t. This would result in an increase in government services in both sectors, higher wages in both sectors, and less wage inequality. Thus, directing aid projects to the rural sector will benefit households in both sectors.

It is important to note that, without a feedback of the urban population share on fiscal policy, increasing the level of technology in the rural sector would *not* raise welfare. If g_t were fixed, then improving rural technology would create a Malthusian-type increase in the population of the rural sector that would completely eliminate any productivity gains for an individual worker. It is the fact that lowering the urban population share raises effective government services in the urban sector that reduces wage inequality. The rise in urban government services increases urban wages and limits the population expansion in the rural area, allowing the rural wage to rise as well.

Figures 8.1 and 8.2 give an example of the country's dynamics with and without balanced growth. We consider two economies each with annual population growth rates of 2 %. The population growth lowers rural wages and "pushes" the population toward the urban sector. In one economy, there is balanced technological change leading to 1 % growth in real wages, represented in the figures by the solid line, and in the other economy, there is no technological change, represented by the dashed line. Each period in the model represents 30 years. In the initial period, 20 % of the population is in the urban sector and the rural wage is 80 % of the urban wage. We set $\alpha = \mu = 1/3$, so by (8.15), productive expenditures in the rural sector are 40 % of urban expenditures throughout the economy's development.

Without balanced growth, households are "pushed" into the urban sector by population growth and the wage gap worsens slightly over time. With balanced growth, a "pull" factor is added that increases the rate of urbanization relative to the

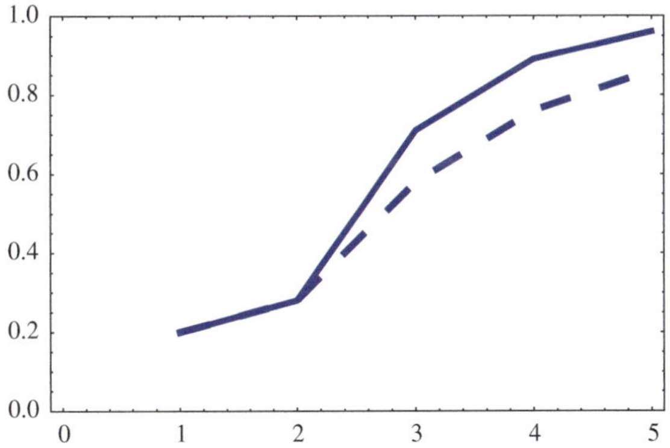

Fig. 8.1 Fraction of population in urban sector. *Notes Solid line* is for economy with 1 % annual growth in *E*, and *dashed line* is for economy with zero growth

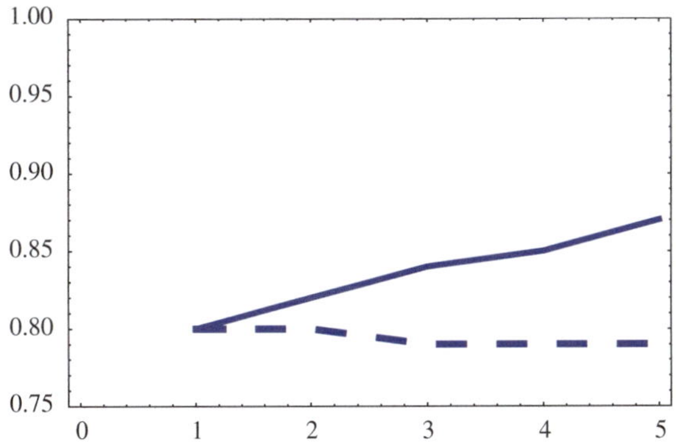

Fig. 8.2 Wage gap—shortfall of rural wages. *Notes Solid line* is for economy with 1 % annual growth in *E*, and *dashed line* is for economy with zero growth

no growth case. After 120 years, the fraction of the population in the urban sector is 96 % compared to 86 % without balanced growth. More importantly, even with modest growth, the rural sector–wage gap narrows significantly to 87 % of the urban wage after four periods (120 years).

8.2.3 Redistributive Urban Bias

It is not in the interest of the policy maker to deviate from the efficient urban bias given by (8.15), even when the weight placed on the welfare of the rural household is zero. However, the government may add to the natural costs of migration by artificially increasing the cost. This is where one would expect to see political debates centered. An increase in ω_t raises g_t and increases productivity and wages in the urban sector. Despite the fact that $\tilde{g}_t$ rises as well, productivity and wages in the rural sectors fall, increasing wage inequality.

Thus, increasing the cost of migration, whether directly due to government policy or not, will lessen urban crowding and give rise to an increase in public services across the economy. However, in the rural sector, the effect of rising public services will not be enough to keep wages from falling as fewer workers choose to migrate because of the higher cost resulting in the crowding of land and lower worker productivity. Thus, the politics of disproportional urban influence in the setting of policy will take the form of raising artificial restrictions on migration or by not taking actions that reduce the natural costs of migration.

8.3 Extensions*

8.3.1 Government Transfers

Our focus has been on productive government spending, largely because of the concerns about the crowding of urban infrastructure that were discussed in the introduction. However, it is natural to ask how the presence of government consumption and transfers may affect the results. We first consider the case where government consumption is a substitute for private consumption (e.g., food and housing subsidies). This case is equivalent to the situation where the government directly provides cash transfers or wage subsidies to households, a common form of alleged favoritism in some developing countries, if the public provision of the private goods is not too large a fraction of the household budget. We will also consider a different situation where the government consumption is not a close substitute for private consumption and thus is very different from government cash transfers to households (e.g., vaccinations that create direct consumption benefits from improved health).

Suppose that the government provides a consumption good to households in each period of life: Q_{1t} and Q_{2t+1} for an urban household of generation t and $\tilde{Q}_{1t}$

and $\tilde{Q}_{2t+1}$ for a rural household of generation t. In the case where the government consumption is a substitute for private consumption, total consumption of good i for the urban household is $\hat{c}_{it} \equiv c_{it} + Q_{it}$ and similarly for the rural household. We will consider the case where the government good provision is not too large so that it is equivalent to a cash transfer or wage subsidy. The case where this is not true, i.e., when the government effectively chooses the consumption level of a good for the household, is similar to the next case we look at where the government consumption good is not a substitute for private consumption.

When the government consumption good is a substitute for private consumption, the urban household's behavior, and similarly for the rural household, can be modeled as maximizing

$$u(\hat{c}_{1t}) + \beta u(\hat{c}_{2t+1})$$

subject to

$$\hat{c}_{1t} + \frac{\hat{c}_{2t+1}}{R} = (1-\tau)W_t + \left(Q_{1t} + \frac{Q_{2t+1}}{R}\right).$$

The timing of when the household receives the consumption good/transfers is irrelevant, so for notational simplicity, we consider the case where the government provides the consumption goods in the first period of life only.

In this situation, the analog to Eq. (8.13), the condition needed to generate partial migration, is

$$(1-\tau)\tilde{W}_t + \varepsilon\tilde{Q}_{1t} = (1-\tau)(1-\bar{\omega})W_t - \omega_t + \varepsilon Q_{1t}.$$

So, differences in government consumption/transfers across the two regions affect the migration choice.

The government's optimization problem, which now involves choosing the detrended government consumption goods q_{1t} and $\tilde{q}_{1t}$, yields the following expression that informs us about urban bias.

$$\frac{q_{1t} + g_t}{\tilde{q}_{1t} + \tilde{g}_t} - 1 = \frac{\alpha}{\mu(1-\alpha)} \frac{\tilde{g}_t}{\tilde{q}_{1t} + \tilde{g}_t}. \tag{8.16}$$

The first thing to notice about (8.16) is that the basic message of the early analysis carries over to this setting; there must be an urban bias, and the weight the government places on the rural household has no bearing on the presence of the bias and no direct effect on the size of the bias. The logic for this result is the same as before. The government should attempt to maximize the welfare of the urban household, which indirectly maximizes the welfare of the rural household when there is a positive migration flow. However, some provision to the rural sector is needed to control urban crowding of both productive consumption services and government consumption.

There are some nuances associated with (8.16) that were not present before. First, the necessary bias is based on *total* government spending in the urban sector relative to the rural sector. It is now possible that there is no bias in the provision of *productive* government inputs. Instead, the government may favor the urban sector in terms of *consumption* good provision and transfer payments. Second, the *size* of the urban bias is inversely related to the *form* of the provision of goods to the rural sector. In particular, the greater is the relative amount of consumption goods provided to the rural sector, the smaller is the total urban bias. Through this avenue the size of the bias may vary with the weight the policy makers place on the rural households. So while the presence of a bias is independent of the weight, the extent of the bias may now vary with the weight.

To see this second point more explicitly, first recognize that under our assumptions, some productive government service provision is needed to operate the rural sector. While this assumption is extreme, it is meant to capture the idea that the return to public investment in production is high when the level of productive services is low—i.e., the return to the provision and maintenance of basic infrastructure such as elementary education and simple roads is high. This means that in raising the quality of life in the rural sector to avoid crowding in the urban sector, the government should start with these basic productive services. However, if the weight that the government places on the rural sector is relatively low, then the government may not go beyond that, i.e., it may choose not to provide consumption goods or transfers to the rural sector so that $\tilde{q}_{1t} = 0$. In this situation, the second expression on the right-hand side of (8.16) is always one and we can solve (8.16) to get an expression that is very similar to (8.15),

$$\tilde{g}_t = \frac{\mu(1-\alpha)}{\alpha + \mu(1-\alpha)}(g_t + q_{1t}).$$

Here, the urban bias is strictly independent of υ, at least over some range of υ and perhaps over the entire range. In addition, the primary way that the government may be viewed as favoring the urban sector is in the provision of government consumption goods and transfers.

However, it is also possible that at a sufficiently high value of υ, but still below one, that the government will provide some consumption goods, so that $\tilde{q}_{1t} > 0$. For this range of υ, the second expression on the right-hand side of (8.16) is always less than one and the size of the urban bias must fall relative to the case when $\tilde{q}_{1t} = 0$. So, while an urban bias must be present for any υ, it is now possible that the size of υ affects the size of the bias.

Next, suppose that the government consumption good is not a perfect substitute for private consumption. In this case, (8.16) remains a necessary condition for the government's optimal policy. However, now the government consumption good may also be viewed as "essential" and thus must always be positive. In this case, the size of the urban bias would vary over the full range of υ.

8.3.2 Endogenous Taxation

To this point, we have analyzed fiscal policy as a pure allocation problem, with an exogenous budget for total government service expenditures. We now show that the presumption of an efficient urban bias becomes stronger if one allows for endogenous tax revenue. For simplicity, we return to the situation where the government is choosing only productive services.

Instead of an exogenous budget, we now assume that the budget for productive government spending is a fixed fraction $\bar{\eta}$ of total taxes collected, $\tau(Y_t + \bar{\sigma}O_t)$. Note that the tax base is endogenously determined because it depends on production from the two sectors and thus on the allocation of labor and productive government services across sectors. In addition, the parameter $\bar{\sigma}$ is bounded between zero and one, taking into account that collecting taxes from the traditional rural sector's tax base may be more difficult than in the modern urban sector.

With a Cobb–Douglas technology, we can write government revenue as

$$\tau\left(\frac{W_t M_t}{1-\alpha} + \frac{\bar{\sigma}\tilde{W}_t F_t}{1-\alpha}\right)$$

As before, wages in both sectors are independent of direct influence from $\tilde{g}_t$. However, now $\tilde{g}_t$ affects the tax base through its influence on φ_t and the relative size of the workforce across rural and urban sectors.

Solving the government's problem gives us the analog to (8.15) when the tax base is endogenous.

$$\tilde{g}_t = \frac{\mu(1-\alpha)}{\alpha + \mu(1-\alpha)}\left[g_t - \frac{\bar{\eta}\tau}{1-\alpha}\left(\frac{W_t - \bar{\sigma}\tilde{W}_t}{E_t}\right)\right] \tag{8.15′}$$

Comparing (8.15′) to (8.15), one can see that, with a wage gap in favor of the urban sector, the efficient urban bias is now stronger (i.e., $\tilde{g}_t$ is now a smaller fraction of g_t). The stronger urban bias results from the fact that an increase in $\tilde{g}_t$ carries an additional cost—a smaller tax base and a loss in tax revenue. An increase in $\tilde{g}_t$ reduces φ_t and increases the relative size of the rural sector. With a wage gap in favor of the urban sector, an increase in the relative size of the rural sector causes the tax base to shrink.

The argument just made would hold even if $\bar{\sigma} = 1$. Allowing for differential ability to collect taxes across sectors further increases the efficient urban bias. In developing countries, it is relatively difficult to tax the traditional sector. The effective tax rate in that sector is less than in the modern urban sector. Assuming that there remains a gap in the pre-tax wages in favor of the urban sector, this adds an additional reason why tax revenue would fall with an increase in $\tilde{g}_t$.

One can go further by substituting (8.15′) back into the government budget constraint to get a complete solution for spending in the two sectors as a function of tax revenue. In particular, the solution for $\tilde{g}_t$ is

$$\tilde{g}_t = \frac{\alpha}{\alpha + \mu(1-\alpha)} \frac{\mu(1-\alpha)}{\pi_t\alpha + \mu(1-\alpha)} \left[\frac{\bar{\eta}\bar{\sigma}\tau}{1-\alpha} \left(\frac{(1-\pi_t)\tilde{W}_t}{E_t} \right) \right]$$

Note that the term outside the square brackets is less than one because $0 \le \pi_t \le 1$. The term in the square brackets gives the tax revenue collected from the rural sector (on a per worker basis and de-trended for growth, as is the case for $\tilde{g}_t$). This means it is optimal for rural government spending per worker to be less than rural taxes collected, i.e., the rural sector must cross-subsidize urban government spending.

To justify rural spending, another dollar spent on the rural sector must create a net revenue gain of more than a dollar by reducing the urban population. This means the urban–rural spending gap must be *greater* than the urban–rural tax collection gap so that, as the urban population falls with an increase in rural spending, a marginal gain in revenue is generated. In other words, some of the rural sector taxes must be used to finance urban spending for there to be a net marginal gain in revenue to the urban sector from an increase in rural sector spending. Since the objective is to maximize urban wages via urban government spending, the rural sector must subsidize the urban sector. In fact, if the rural sector cannot provide net revenue to the government, i.e., $\bar{\sigma} = 0$, then the government should ignore the rural sector, $\tilde{g}_t = 0$ and thereby force everyone into the city.

8.3.3 Impure Public Goods

We have assumed that government services are private goods, which is appropriate for some but not all government services. Here, we consider the case where government services flow from impure public goods.

Suppose now that effective productive government services are generated from impure public goods that are subject to crowding and thus are imperfectly shared by the workforce. As before, we define G_t to be a measure of productive government services in the urban sector, but now, effective services are defined as $g_t = G_t/M_t^{\xi}$, where ξ is a constant parameter that lies between zero and one. The value of ξ determines the degree of crowding of public goods. If $\xi = 0$, then G_t is generated from pure public goods that are not subject to crowding. If $\xi = 1$, then G_t is generated from pure private goods, and to maintain g_t, G_t must rise proportionally with the workforce. Here, we focus on the intermediate case where ξ is between zero and one, i.e., where G_t is generated from impure public goods that are subject to some crowding.

In similar fashion, we define effective government services in the rural sector to be $\tilde{g}_t = \tilde{G}_t/F_t^{\varepsilon}$. Due to its smaller geographic area, the urban sector is assumed to have an advantage in the sharing of the services generated by a given impure public good. The "public" nature of a good is partly a function of its characteristics and partly a function of the population density located around the good. For (i) a given local government public good provided to each sector and (ii) a given population of workers in each sector, the urban sector provides at least as many effective services per worker, i.e., we assume $0 \le \xi < \varepsilon \le 1$. For example, suppose the *same* size road is provided to the urban area and the rural area, and each area contains the *same* total population. It is more likely that a larger fraction of the urban working population lives close enough to the road to use it productively. Thus, there is an efficiency advantage to urbanization that directly stems from the provision of a shared public good.[10] Note that it remains true that an increase in the population in each sector will reduce government services per worker.[11]

Under these assumptions, one can solve the government's problem to get the following equation for efficient allocation of government services

$$\tilde{G}_t/F_t = \frac{\xi\mu(1-\alpha)}{\alpha + \varepsilon\mu(1-\alpha)}(G_t/M_t). \qquad (8.15'')$$

Equation (8.15″) gives the implied relationship between the *observed* government services per worker in the two sectors (found by dividing a measure of the total government services by the population of workers). Recalling that $\xi \le \varepsilon$, the equation indicates that there will always be an observed urban bias in the setting of fiscal policy, $G_t/M_t > \tilde{G}_t/F_t$. In addition to the other features identified under the assumption that government services are private goods, the degree of urban bias also now depends on how advantageous it is to share the impure public goods in the city versus the country—i.e., the lower the value of ξ/ε, the larger is the bias.

More important than the observed bias is the *effective* bias per worker, $\tilde{g}_t/g_t$, a determinant of the relative TFP in the two sectors. The effective bias is given by

$$\tilde{g}_t = \frac{\xi\mu(1-\alpha)}{\alpha + \varepsilon\mu(1-\alpha)} \frac{F_t^{1-\varepsilon}}{M_t^{1-\xi}} g_t.$$

---

[10] Cities may also contain other efficiency advantages such as improved matching between employee and employer and learning spillovers from increased worker interaction (Duranton 2008). Rosenthal and Strange (2004) point out that identifying the precise source of these efficiency advantages is extremely difficult. Moretti (2004a) discusses the difficulty in establishing the presence and magnitude of human capital externalities in cities. Henderson (2010) argues that urbanization per se does not increase growth rates, although growth rates may increase when the population becomes concentrated in very large cities. In Chap. 7, we mentioned evidence suggesting that there are learning externalities related to the average human capital per person in the community where one lives. Moretti (2004b) and Liu (2014) find that the average human capital per worker in a city raises the productivity of firms in the city, especially those that employ high human capital workers. Duraton (2014) reviews the literature and concludes that cities have a positive causal effect on worker productivity.

[11] An increase in the rural population actually reduces government services per worker in the rural sector for two reasons: crowding of the population near the public good and an increase in the population that cannot easily utilize the good.

Note that the effective bias is influenced by the same parameters as the observed bias and, in addition, by the relative population size in the two sectors. We can examine the determinants of the effective bias further by writing out M_t and F_t in terms of demographic Eqs. (8.12) and (8.13), allowing us to rewrite the expression for the effective bias as

$$\tilde{g}_t = \frac{\xi\mu(1-\alpha)}{\alpha + \varepsilon\mu(1-\alpha)} \frac{[(1-\varphi_t)(1-\pi_{t-1})]^{1-\varepsilon}}{[\pi_{t-1} + \varphi_t(1-\pi_{t-1})]^{1-\xi}} \frac{g_t}{N_t^{\varepsilon-\xi}}.$$

For a given φ_t, a larger country population (N_t) increases the effective bias because of the advantage of sharing impure public goods in the city. Furthermore, one can show that an increase in N_t increases φ_t as well, generating a further increase in the urban bias. Thus, as the population of the economy grows in size, the economy becomes more urbanized. During this "structural transformation," the *observed* bias in (8.15″) remains fixed, but the *effective* bias, given above, widens.[12]

8.4 City Size and Development

In a recent article, Henderson (2010) discusses the connection between urbanization and growth. His article also contains interesting thoughts about strategies to deal with the rapid pace of urbanization in many of today's developing economies.

Consistent with Sect. 8.2, Henderson argues that while urbanization and growth have a strong positive correlation, there is not a simple causal effect running from urbanization to growth. The absence of a steadfast positive causal connection is most obvious in the situations where urbanization is actually associated with *falling* wages. This happens when migration to the city is driven by events that cause a drop in the relative productivity of rural workers. When workers are "pushed" to city, there is a crowding of public infrastructure and government services that causes a decline in urban workers' productivity and in wages throughout the economy.

However, Henderson also argues that cities are associated with industry-level economies of scale and knowledge spillovers, features we have ignored, that can generate a rise in worker productivity. To capture these effects, one could write the urban productivity index as

$$D_t = \left(\frac{G_t}{M_t}\right)^{\mu} E_t^{1-\mu} \bar{h}_t^{\sigma_1} M_t^{\sigma_2},$$

[12] Our discussion suggests that an urban bias in the provision of effective government services is guaranteed. This is not the case because if both π_{t-1} and φ_t are small enough, then $[(1-\phi_t)(1-\pi_{t-1})]^{1-\varepsilon}/[\pi_{t-1} + \phi_{t-1}(1-\pi_{t-1})]^{1-\xi}$ could be large enough to make $\tilde{g}_t > g_t$. This situation is more relevant during the early stages of growth when urban crowding is not an issue, and the city would have a small and slow-growing population.

where σ_1 and σ_2 are positive parameters that capture productivity effects associated with living in a city. If we have human capital, as in some of the previous chapters, the term $\bar{h}_t^{\sigma_1}$ would capture the knowledge spillovers flowing from the average human capital of urban workers to the productivity of an individual worker. To capture economies of scale in production, or other urban agglomeration effects such as information flows or job matching, one could also include the term $M_t^{\sigma_2}$. An increase in the size of the urban workforce raises the productivity of the average urban worker.

There is empirical evidence indicating that greater industry size and a higher average human capital in a city cause individual worker productivity to be higher, other things constant. In addition to the advantage of sharing impure local public goods (see Sect. 8.3), these positive productivity effects within concentrated geographic areas explain why the modern sector firms tend to locate in cities. Agglomeration effects based on spatial concentration have the potential to create a causal connection running from urbanization to growth.[13]

Positive agglomeration effects suggest that there may be an optimal city size that maximizes worker productivity. Cities need a certain population size to fully exploit the industry economies and knowledge spillovers. However, these positive benefits may diminish at some point, and the crowding of public infrastructure and services becomes an issue as the population continues to grow. Thus, weighing the benefits and costs of an increasing city population leads to the possibility of an optimal city size.

Empirical work by Henderson and his coauthors finds that there is a concave, hump-shaped relationship between city population and individual worker productivity, confirming the existence of an optimal city size. They also find that the composition of industries within a city matters. The optimal city size is smaller, the higher is the concentration of manufacturing industries. This is consistent with the fact that very large cities tend to have a high fraction of business and professional service industries.

The notion of an optimal city size is relevant in assessing the urbanization strategies in developing countries. Urbanization in today's developing world is both more rapid and more directed by national governments than it was in history. Historically, the typical process of urbanization, as a country's population goes from roughly 15 to 75 % urban, would take more than a century. In many developing countries, the same process of urbanization only takes a few decades.

The rapid pace of urbanization is one of the reasons that governments feel the need to intervene and control the process. China and India are considering the use of policy-based incentives to funnel their rural to urban migration into a relatively small number of megacities: 10–15 cities with average populations of 25–30 million people. This is quite controversial because the empirical work mentioned above suggests that the optimal size of city is much smaller. Thus, the formation of megacities may create a drag on aggregate growth.

[13] Duraton (2014) provides a discussion of the empirical evidence behind different mechanisms through which locating in cities can affect worker productivity. He also discusses the factors that limit worker productivity in developing countries, which is the focus of this chapter and the next section in particular.

8.5 Urbanization Today: New Mechanisms and Consequences

We would argue that most of the theory in this book applies equally well to historical and current development. However, as the last section reveals, there are at least some quantitative differences between historical and current development. Urbanization is occurring much more rapidly in today's developing countries than it did in history. It is also becoming clear that the current rapid rate of urbanization is caused by some forces that were not important in the past. In this section, we discuss these new mechanisms for urbanization. The new mechanisms have important implications for the connection between agriculture and the traditional sector and the connection between urbanization and growth.

8.5.1 Consumption Cities: Urbanization Without Industrialization

In past history, and in many developing countries today, urbanization is closely associated with industrialization and an expanding manufacturing sector. Today, there is an important exception to this familiar pattern. Gollin et al. (2013) find that resource exporters, e.g., oil-exporting countries such as Gabon and Venezuela, have relatively high rates of urbanization despite having relatively low manufacturing sectors.

In the standard urbanization story, the population shifts from agriculture to manufacturing either due to the "pull" of increasing manufacturing wages or the "push" of declining agricultural wages. Instead, Gollin et al. focus on an income effect associated with a rise in rents from natural resources. They find that higher resource rents increase the demand for nontradable urban services—such as restaurant meals, cabs, apartments, and haircuts. The increase in demand raises the relative price of the nontradable services and causes a reallocation of labor to the city to work in the service sector. The reallocation of labor causes cities to grow near locations where the resources are extracted and refined. These are "consumption cities" because they are expanding due to an increase in demand for consumption services rather than an increase in the marginal productivity of urban labor generally.

Gollin et al. use a static four-sector model to articulate the mechanism. Manufacturing, agricultural, and resource goods (natural commodities) are traded in international markets that set their prices. Manufacturing goods and urban services are produced in cities, while agricultural and resource goods are produced in the rural sector. Urban services are nontraded, so their price is determined by domestic market conditions. A rise in the international price of resource goods raises income for countries that export these goods. The increase in income raises demand for all goods, but only the price of urban services rises because other prices are determined internationally. The rise in the relative price of urban services raises the relative wage in the service sector and pulls labor out of other sectors. Even though employment in the manufacturing sector declines, total urban employment can rise because labor is also being pulled out of agriculture. In this situation, an increase in urbanization is associated with a decline in the manufacturing sector.

8.5.2 Mushroom Cities: The Traditional Sector Grows in the City

Another difference between the past and the present is the degree to which urbanization results from population growth *within* cities—what is called "urban natural increase." Jedwab et al. (2014) show that the rapid urbanization of today's developing countries is driven more by natural increase than by the rural-to-urban migration of European history. The urban centers of Europe during industrialization were "killer cities"—with high mortality and low fertility. In contrast, developing countries today largely contain "mushroom cities"—with low mortality and high fertility. They show the resulting difference in the urban natural increase across these two types of cities accounts for most of the difference in the current and historic urbanization rates.

Jedwab et al. also establish that the rapid growth in cities today is correlated with a high proportion of urban residents living in slums, low investment in urban human capital, and a larger informal sector. This scenario suggests that cities in today's developing countries contain a sizeable traditional sector, where households produce in the informal sector, have many children, and do not invest much in education. In the face of the rapid urban natural increase, rural households still continue to move to the city. However, the gaps in living standards between rural households and those living in slums are likely to be small. These household share more similarities than differences. It is best to think of them both as residing and producing in the traditional sector.

8.5.3 Urbanization Without Growth Revisited

Today's developing countries are urbanizing at historically rapid rates. However, their growth rates in worker productivity are, as a group, no different than those of currently rich countries. There is no convergence for most poor countries today (Chap. 7).

The combination of unusually rapid urbanization and mediocre economic growth rates raises doubts about viewing urbanization as an engine of growth. The lack of correlation between growth and urbanization could be due to the weak connection between urbanization and manufacturing for today's developing countries. Today's urbanization is associated more with growing service and informal sectors rather than a robustly expanding manufacturing sector. This pattern also implies a break in the close connection between the urban sector and the modern sector, as today's developing cities often have large slums that have more characteristics in common with the traditional sector.

8.5.4 Slums

Early urbanization, whether in a historical or contemporary development setting, is characterized by areas of poor quality housing and inadequate basic public services, commonly known as "slums." The problem is more severe today than in the past. Currently, 860 million people are living in slums around the world (Marx et al. 2013). Slums are the most dramatic indicators that the crowding of public services in urban areas is a major problem of development. As the theory suggests, if urbanization is predominantly driven by population growth and dire conditions in rural areas, there will be a decline in urban services per worker and wages will fall throughout the economy.

Despite the deplorable conditions in slums, poor urban households worldwide are richer and happier than those that remain in rural areas, at least on average (Glasear 2011). This suggests just how desperate life must be in the countryside of many developing countries. In this situation, aid directed at developing public infrastructure in rural communities would increase productivity throughout the economy by reducing migration flows to the city and raising urban public services per worker.

Marx et al. (2013) argue that slums can cause problems that policy makers do not fully account for. They are particularly concerned with the possibility that slums create intergenerational poverty traps. One can easily see how this could happen. Moving to the city raises wages and family resources. However, living in the slum is a less healthy environment because of the reduced space and overwhelmed public infrastructure that results in generally unsanitary conditions. While, as reported in Chap. 5, the health conditions in rural areas are generally not as good as in cities, there may be city slums where this is not true.

Young children in the family are most susceptible to the disease and illness that an unhealthy environment breeds. Their compromised health could have long-term consequences for their adult productivity because of stunted physical development and impaired ability to learn. While the family as a whole has greater resources in the short run, the next generation may be less productive than workers raised in rural areas. In short, the move to the city was bad for the future generations of family. This could be true even if parents possess intergenerational altruism because the short-term benefits to the current generation of the family may be greater than the cost to the next generation.

An intergenerational poverty trap of this type could easily be ignored by urban elite policy makers. Some aspects of urban crowding, such as crowding of roads and energy provision, lower the productivity of all urban workers. However, if the urban elite live a safe distance from the slums, they will not be exposed to the unhealthy environment created by a crowding of health and sanitation services. As a result, the policy makers will underestimate the full cost of migration to the city and the full benefit of basic public services provided to the slums. Even if the goal is to maximize aggregate economic growth, there will be too little public investment in rural areas and the composition of urban public spending will allocate too few resources to the slums.

8.6 Hukou

Chinese policy provides an interesting example of internal migration restrictions (Meng 2012; Wang and Piesse 2010; and Wang and Weaver 2013). When the Chinese Communist Party rose to power in 1949, no labor mobility between rural and urban sectors was allowed. Rural to urban migration was formally prevented starting in 1955 by a household registration system, known as "Hukou," that established household residency. Those with urban Hukou were given access to high paying jobs and government services. The advantage of rural Hukou was a claim to land use. During the first 30 years of Communist rule, more than 80 % of the population remained in rural areas.

As the Chinese economy was reformed and began to grow in the last quarter of the twentieth century, migration restrictions were relaxed due to the need for labor in the urban manufacturing sector. However, it has been uncommon for a rural person to be granted a permanent urban Hukou. Most migrants to the cities are younger workers who live and work in the cities on a "temporary basis," without access to the government services enjoyed by urban residents. Between 1990 and 1997, rural migrants working in cities increased from 25 to 37 million. By 2009, the number of rural migrant workers quadrupled to reach 145 million.

Due to the strong demand for labor, unemployment for the migrant workers is low and hours worked are high. Migrants work over 60 h per week, which is likely much more than they would have worked in rural settings. The expansion in labor supply and the reallocation of workers to a sector where they are more productive per hour are important reasons for China's continued strong economic growth.

Despite the migration of these temporary workers, large wage gaps remain. There was a threefold per capita income gap favoring urban residents at the end of the twentieth century. The significant work opportunities for the migrants and the large wage gaps both indicate that Chinese labor markets suffer from significant inefficiency due to the persistence of mobility restrictions.

Recently there has been a movement in China to reduce internal migration restrictions and increase the population flow to cities. The primary motivation for the urbanization push is to increase domestic demand for marketed goods. The urbanization push coincides with a desire to eliminate the Hukou system. This raises difficult questions about how to deal with the land rights of potential rural migrants. In some cases, rural residents are forced off their land or given far below market value for the transfer of land to local government authorities. There have been significant charges of "land grabs" by local officials that benefit from reselling the land at market value.

Access to the work opportunities in the city may be enough to compensate younger workers for the loss in their claims to land. It is less clear that this is true for older workers, especially because there is uncertainty about access to government services and pension for the new urban residents. The large migration to the city is straining the capacities of governments to provide the services and benefits that previous urban residents have enjoyed.

8.7 De-urbanization: Past and Present

Many view England, generally recognized as the place where the Industrialization Revolution began, as the nation that was the home of the first modern economy. However, as carefully documented by de Vries and van der Woude (1997), the first modern economy with sustained economic growth may have instead been developed in the Netherlands during the sixteenth and seventeenth centuries. The Dutch economy was not modern in the sense of being industrial, but it was modern in the sense of being built on commerce and trading in domestic and international markets. The early appearance of commerce was fostered by high levels of education in the population, a monetary system, and well-defined and enforced property rights.

Another advanced feature of the Netherland economy was the high percentage of the population living in urban areas. Urbanization was rapid over the sixteenth and seventeenth centuries, see the urban population shares below, followed then by a period of de-urbanization:

1525	31.5 %
1675	45 %
1750	42 %
1795	40 %
1815	38 %

An urbanization rate of 45 % made the Netherlands far and away the most urbanized country in Europe at the end of the seventeenth century. In comparison, England did not achieve an urbanization rate of 40 % until the middle of the nineteenth century. The high rate of urbanization in the Netherlands was associated with a structural transformation of their early economy from one based on traditional agriculture to one based on shipping, ship building, whaling and fishing, brewing, and textiles.

However, what explains the period of de-urbanization that followed? de Vries and van der Woude suggest three reasons. First, exports fell sharply after 1700. This was due to trade wars, in some cases leading to actual wars, and due to the fact that the Dutch began to lose their comparative advantage in ship building and textiles. The Dutch lost their leadership position in these areas as new technologies were being developed in other European countries. Second, the early Industrialization Revolution created a proto-industry in rural areas. Textiles were produced by women and children out of ordinary homes rather than by the more expensive urban craftsmen. Finally, the cities suffered from crowding that created hygienic problems and disease.

The Dutch experience with early urbanization provides indirect evidence for the view that urbanization, especially early in development, is more a by-product of growth rather than a cause of it. When the underlying determinants of growth falter, the wage differential between urban and rural areas shrinks and no longer provides sufficient compensation for the problems associated with urban crowding. As a consequence, urbanization slows or is reversed.

A similar de-urbanization is being forecasted for India today. Just as in many developing countries, India has experienced rapid urbanization since WWII, although about half of its workforce is still in agriculture. There are signs that the labor flow to the cities has now reversed. Growth in the urban manufacturing sector is slowing due to crowding and insufficient infrastructure and due to the high cost of complying with a myriad of labor laws. Crisil, a large economic and business research group headquartered in Mumbai, predicts that a reverse migration of 12 million workers out of the cities and back to relatively low-wage agriculture will take place between 2013 and 2019. Just as in the Dutch Republic of the eighteenth century, if the conditions sustaining economic growth are compromised, and urban crowding is not dealt with, de-urbanization can occur. Urbanization per se is not a sufficiently strong engine for growth to sustain itself.

8.8 Conclusion

Many observers of fiscal policy in developing countries see large disparities in the government's provision of goods and services across regions in favor of urban areas. The most common interpretation of these disparities is that urban households have disproportionate political power that causes fiscal policy to favor them at the expense of rural households. This chapter develops a simple theory of urban bias in the allocation of productive government services suggesting that the common interpretation may not be correct. An urban bias in the provision of government services can be explained by efficiency considerations and it may be the case that the extent of the bias is entirely independent of the weight that policy makers place on urban and rural households. The observed inequities in the provision of government services across rural and urban areas are not necessarily the result of a redistributive urban bias in the politics of developing countries, but rather serve to raise wages throughout the economy.

Our analysis indicates that urban–rural politics is more likely to influence policies that directly affect the cost of migration from rural to urban areas. An increase in the costs associated with rural to urban migration does clearly raise the welfare of urban households at the expense of rural households.

We ignored the intergenerational consequences associated with living in the unhealthy slums of cities in developing countries. Intergenerational consequences of unhealthy slums could create poverty traps that slow economic growth and are worthy of future research. To address the possibility, at least three new features will have to be introduced into the model. First, there must be two types of urban households: One type lives in the slums and one type does not, the urban elite who set the policy. Second, there must be two types of public services: Those that affect the productivity of all urban workers (roads) and those that affect only those living in the slums (public health and sanitation services). Third, the public services provided in the slums must influence the adult human capital of the children living there.

8.9 Exercises

Questions

1. How are the traditional and modern sectors interpreted in this chapter? What is difference between sectors?
2. What is the source of the wage gap between sectors? Write down and explain the equation for the wage gap.
3. Describe the government's behavior. How are the government's preferences modeled? What are the government's constraints and choice variables?
4. Explain why there is an urban bias in government service provision. Why is the urban bias efficient?
5. What is the role of free migration of households across sectors in establishing the efficient urban bias? What happens if there is no migration across sectors?
6. What are "push" and "pull" factors that create migration to the cities? Explain how these factors affect government service provision.
7. How does balanced technological progress across sectors affect the following variables? What happens if the technological progress only occurs in the urban sector?
   (a) urbanization
   (b) government service provision
   (c) wages in each sector
   (d) wage inequality
8. What is a redistributive urban bias? How does an increase in migration restrictions affect the variables in question 7?
9. If the government provides transfers in addition to productive government, services is there still an efficient urban bias?
10. How does accounting for endogenous tax revenue affect the urban bias?
11. If productive government services are provided by impure public goods, such as roads, how does it affect the urban bias?
12. Describe how urbanization in today's developing world differs from the historical urbanization of the USA and Europe. What implications does this have for the application of the dual economy model? For government policy?
13. How can intergenerational effects of living in unhealthy slums cause the allocation of productive government services to rural areas to be lower than the allocation that would maximize economic growth?
14. Discuss some of the issues related to urbanization in China.
15. Make a case for the idea that urbanization causes economic growth. Next, make a case for the idea that urbanization has a neutral or even a negative causal effect on economic growth.
16. Relate the concept of "consumption cities" to the McMillan–Rodrik explanation for the difference between worker productivity growth rates in Asia and Africa (Chap. 5).

Problems

1. Show that $\pi_t = \pi_{t-1} + \varphi_t(1 - \pi_{t-1})$ and $1 - \pi_t = (1 - \varphi_t)(1 - \pi_{t-1})$.
2. Show that one can use (8.6b), along with (8.2), (8.5), and (8.13), to derive the following expression for the fraction of the traditional population that remains in the traditional sector, $1 - \varphi_t = \left\{ \frac{\left[(\tilde{E}_t/E_t)^{1-\mu} (\tilde{g}_t)^{\mu} \right]^{1-\alpha}}{k^{\alpha} g_t^{\mu} (\tilde{W}_t/W_t)} \right\}^{1/\alpha} \frac{L}{n\tilde{N}_{t-1}E_t}$. Use this equation to show $\frac{\partial \varphi_t}{\partial \tilde{g}_t} = -\frac{\mu(1-\alpha)}{\alpha} \frac{1-\varphi_t}{\tilde{g}_t}$.
3. Using the results of Problems 1 and 2, choose $\tilde{g}_t$ and g_t to maximize $V_t((1-\tau)W_t) + \upsilon V_t((1-\tau)\tilde{W}_t)$ subject to $g_t\pi_t + \tilde{g}_t(1-\pi_t) = b_t$. The first-order condition associated with the choice of $\tilde{g}_t$ can be used to derive the efficient urban bias equation given in (8.15).
4. Use (8.13) to argue that technological progress lowers wage inequality.
5. Use (8.2), (8.3b), (8.13), and (8.15), and the government budget constraint, $g_t\pi_t + \tilde{g}_t(1-\pi_t) = b_t$, to argue that migration to the city resulting from push factors, for a given value of E, will reduce wages across the economy.
6. *Extensions*. Write down and carefully explain the urban bias condition when
   (a) the government provides consumption goods and services or transfers in addition to productive services
   (b) tax revenue endogenously depends on the share of the population in the urban area
   (c) productive government inputs are impure public goods
7. In the case where government productive inputs are impure public goods, explain the difference between the "observed" and the "effective" urban bias. How is each affected by population growth?

References

Bates R (1981) Markets and states in tropical Africa. University of California Press, Berkeley

Bezemer D, Headey D (2008) Agriculture, development, and urban bias. World Dev 36 (8):1342–1364

Black D, Henderson V (1999) The theory of urban growth. J Polit Econ 107(2):252–284

Bloom D, Khanna T (2007) Urban revolution. Finance Dev 44(3):8–14

de Vries J, van der Woude A (1997) The first modern economy. Cambridge University Press, New York

Duranton G (2008) From cities to productivity and growth in developing countries. Can J Econ 41 (3):689–736

Duraton G (2014) Growing through cities in developing countries. Policy research working paper 6818. World Bank, Washington, DC

Duranton G, Puga D (2004) Micro-foundations of urban agglomeration economies. In: Henderson V, Thisse J (eds) Handbook of regional science and urban economics, vol 4. North-Holland, Amsterdam

Fay M, Opal C (2000) Urbanization without growth: a not so uncommon phenomenon. World Bank working paper 2412. World bank, Washington, DC

Feler M, Henderson V (2011) Exclusionary policies in urban development: underservicing migrant households in Brazilian cities. J Urban Econ 69(3):253–272

Glaeser E (2011) Triumph of the city: how our greatest invention makes us richer, smarter, greener, healthier, and happier. Penguin Press, New York

Gollin D, Jedwab R, Vollrath D (2013) Urbanization with and without industrialization. University of Houston Department of Economics working paper 2013-290-26

Hansen G, Prescott E (2002) Malthus to Solow. Am Econ Rev 92(4):1205–1217

Harris R, Todaro R (1970) Migration, unemployment, and development: a two-sector analysis. Am Econ Rev 60(1):126–142

Henderson V (1974) The sizes and types of cities. Am Econ Rev 64(4):640–650

Henderson V (2010) Cities and development. J Reg Sci 50(1):515–540

Henderson V, Wang HG (2005) Aspects of rural-urban transformation of countries. J Econ Geogr 5(1):23–42

Jedwab R, Christiaensen L, Gindelsky M (2014) Rural push, urban pull and…urban push? New historical evidence from developing countries. George Washington University Institute for International Economic Policy working paper 2014-04

Lipton M (1977) Why poor people stay poor: urban bias in world development. Harvard University Press, Cambridge

Liu Z (2014) Human capital externalities in cities: evidence from Chinese manufacturing firms. J Econ Geogr 14(3):589–620

Lucas R (2004) Life earnings and rural-urban migration. J Polit Econ 112(1):S29–S59

Majumdar S, Mani A, Mukand S (2004) Politics, information, and the urban bias. J Dev Econ 75 (1):137–165

Marx B, Stoker T, Suri T (2013) The economics of slums in the developing world. J Econ Perspect 27(4):187–210

McCormick B, Wahba J (2003) Did public wage premiums fuel agglomeration in LDCs? J Dev Econ 70(2):349–37

Meng X (2012) Labor market outcomes and reforms in China. J Econ Perspect 26(4):75–102

Moretti E (2004a) Human capital externalities in cities. In: Henderson V, Thisse JF (eds) Handbook of regional and urban economics, vol 4. North Holland, Amsterdam, pp 2243–2291

Moretti E (2004b) Worker's education, spillovers, and productivity: evidence from plant-level production functions. Am Econ Rev 94(3):656–690

Mourmouras A, Rangazas P (2013) Efficient urban bias. J Econ Geogr 13(3):451–471

Rosenthal S, Strange W (2004) Evidence on the nature and sources of agglomeration economies. In: Henderson V, Thisse J (eds) Handbook of regional and urban economics, vol 4. North Holland, Amsterdam

Wang X, Piesse J (2010) Inequality and the urban-rural divide in China: effects of regressive taxation. China World Econ 18(6):36–55

Wang X, Weaver N (2013) Surplus labor and urbanization in China. Eurasian Econ Rev 3(1):84–97

Conclusion 9

In this chapter, we summarize some of the main points we have learned about development and their related policy implications. The points are organized into those related to the *onset of growth* and those related to the *nature of growth* once it begins. We also discuss policy implications and topics for future research.

9.1 The Onset of Growth

We have seen that sustained growth is a very recent phenomena, starting two or three centuries ago for some countries and within the last few decades for many others. The very different timing of the onset of modern growth is the main reason for the divergent standards of living across the world today. This is particularly true because average growth rates remain trendless for long periods of time as economies make the slow transition toward their steady states. With growth rates that are similar at all stages of development, it is not generally true that poorer countries converge or catch up to richer countries. The features of economies that determine the timing of the initial growth take-off are then crucial.

9.1.1 The Appearance of a Modern Sector

In Chap. 4, we present a theory that helps us understand the conditions giving rise to the production in factories that sets the stage for modern growth via the accumulation of physical capital. Before these conditions are met, we can think of the economy as being trapped in a situation where goods are produced using informal traditional methods. The key consideration is whether factories can compete profitably with traditional methods while paying workers at least as much as they make in the traditional sector and capital owners at least what they could earn by owning land. For a given state of technology, the following conditions increase the likelihood that profitable factories will appear.

S. Das et al., *Economic Growth and Development*,
Springer Texts in Business and Economics, DOI 10.1007/978-3-319-14265-4_9

1. *Limited Natural Resources*—Traditional methods rely heavily on direct use of natural resources. Countries that have an abundance of usable land and other easily accessible natural resources will have a productive traditional sector. This leads to relatively high wages and/or high returns to the ownership of the natural resources. High factor prices paid to labor and land means operating factories will be costly. Countries without these resource advantages have cheaper labor and lower required returns to assets that paves the way for a profitable modern sector.
2. *Limited Political Power of Landowners and Traditional Craftsman*—Landowners and craftsmen oppose the competition from factories and seek to prevent their appearance. They support policies that favor the traditional sector and block the formation of large firms by legislating various restrictions, taxes, and regulations in the modern sector. Pro-growth dictators or democratic participation of the general population limit the influence of large landowners and established craftsmen and thereby encourage factory-based production and physical capital formation.
3. *Legal Institutions Protecting Property Rights*—Traditional production relies on informal arrangements between workers, landowners, craftsmen, and customers. In local settings where trading occurs on a small scale between parties that know each other well, these informal arrangements suffice. However, to produce and trade on a larger and more impersonal manner, a legal system that protects property rights is critical substitute for the trust and local information that is present in traditional settings.
4. *Public Infrastructure*—Mechanized factory production and trading at a larger scale requires the provision of public capital inputs such as utilities and roads.

Equation (4.8) from Chap. 4 provides the profit requirement for the appearance of the modern sector. The conditions listed above can be related to Eq. (4.8) as follows: Condition (1) determines the value of $\tilde{A}l^{\alpha}$ in the traditional sector, while (2)–(4) determine the value of A in the modern sector. Given the state of available technology and the country's natural resources, the key is to generate a high level of A. There is no unique way to accomplish this. For example, excellent roads and strong property right protection can offset anti-capital policies supported by large landowners. The sources of A to focus on, in order to get modern growth going, are likely to be country-specific; depending on geography, culture, and political realities.

9.1.2 Poverty Traps and Schooling

Even after modern growth begins, the theory used in this text suggests that schooling of older children may not take off. The schooling poverty trap from Chaps. 3 and 4 is independent of the technological change and capital accumulation associated with modern growth. There is evidence supporting this possibility, as many countries initially experience sustained positive growth without seeing much progress in schooling and literacy across the workforce. The schooling poverty trap is most persistence when (i) there are no significant noneconomic reasons to educate the general population, (ii) the relative productivity of children is high, and (iii) there is a lack of government effort to encourage mass education.

9.2 The Nature of Modern Growth

The theory in Chaps. 5 through 7 identifies and explains some common features of growth as economies begin to develop and modernize. The early period of modern growth is dominated by the structural transformation of the economy as labor moves out of the traditional sector and into the modern sector. The sources of the growth in worker productivity during this initial phase are the underlying technological progress, the expansion in work hours, and the aging of the work force as fertility falls. Work hours expand because the opportunity for working long hours throughout the year is greater in the factories of the modern sector and because families that relocate to the modern sector have fewer children, which allows more time for market work. The decline in fertility also reduces the number of young workers and causes the average age and productivity of the workforce to increase. In some settings, where labor markets are particularly inefficient, there may also be gaps in productivity per hour worked that favor the modern sector. These gaps create an additional source of growthas labor migrates to the modern sector during the structural transformation.

During the early stages of the structural transformation, the accumulation of human and physical capital often does not play a large role in economic growth. The structural transformation itself creates offsetting effects on physical capital intensity in the modern sector. Saving rates rise and fertility falls, which raises capital intensity, but the movement of labor toward the modern sector causes a crowding of the private capital and reduces capital intensity. Schooling often is trapped at low levels or increases very slowly. One reason that some countries created very high growth rates after World War II is that their policies pushed the development of human and physical capital during the early stages of the structural transformation.

In the later stages of development, as fertility continues to fall and the pace of the migration to the modern sector slows, physical capital intensity rises. In addition, schooling of older children accelerates and creates further downward pressure on fertility. During this stage, the growth rates in output per worker increase and then stabilize for many decades. The rise in physical and human capital per worker also cause significant increases in output per hour worked. The long transition, at relatively trendless growth rates, implies that convergence of income across countries can be slow unless lagging countries adopt unusually aggressive pro-growth policies.

The growth over this long transitional period is fueled by events that must eventually come to an end. The end of the structural transformation, the leveling off of the fertility decline, and the prosperity associated with the rise in productivity per hour worked, all cause work hours to fall rather than rise. The rise in the rates of investment in physical and human capital also levels off, leaving the diminishing returns to investment to dominate. These events create growth slowdowns that can only be offset by an increase in technological progress. The prospect of a general growth slowdown, especially for the most developed economies, is a major concern for the twenty-first century.

9.3 Policy Implications

In this section, we summarize some of the main policy implications suggested by the theory.

9.3.1 Domestic Growth Policy

In discussing the conditions needed for the appearance of factory-based production, we mentioned the importance of limiting the influence of those with vested interest in the traditional sector, a legal system that supports formal trading in large markets, and public infrastructure. Of these key elements, we have primarily focused on the importance of investment in productive public infrastructure. For simplicity, many researchers choose to combine public capital, such as roads, with private capital into a single measure of the economy's physical capital stock. This is a very misleading modeling strategy. As in Chaps. 3, 6, and 8, public capital should be modeled as a complement rather than a substitute for private capital. Public capital is an essential input to production that raises the marginal productivity of private capital. This is why growth in the public capital stock is needed to raise TFP, as traditionally measured, paving the way for the emergence of profitable private capital and the modern sector.

As emphasized in Chap. 6, an important by-product of the structural transformation is that economic activity in the modern sector is easier to tax. Thus, the structural transformation naturally increases the economy's capacity to raise tax revenue. An important determinant of the pace of growth is how governments use this capacity. Countries that use the increased revenue for public sector investment will grow faster than those that use it for government consumption and transfers that finance private consumption. Growing governments are often seen as a drag on the economy. However, growth rates need not fall as governments become larger if a significant portion of the increased tax revenue is invested.

Chapter 8 suggests that the *allocation* of public investment is almost as important as the *level* of public investment. As with private capital formation, internal migration to the modern sector crowds the supporting public capital infrastructure. It is optimal for governments to control the pace of migration by investing in public capital that raises productivity and living standards in the traditional sector as well as well as the modern sector. Chapter 8 argues that there is an efficient mix of public investments across sectors that maximizes wages throughout the economy. For various reasons, the efficient mix is biased toward the modern sector, but the traditional sector cannot be ignored.

Apart from public infrastructure investment, in Chaps. 3, 5, and 7, we stress that education of the workforce is critical for accelerating and sustaining economic growth. There is the direct effect of education on the productivity of workers throughout the economy, but there are important indirect effects as well. Increases in human capital speed the structural transformation and reduce fertility, both of which accelerate growth.

We have highlighted the possibility of poverty traps associated with schooling. In environments that generate schooling traps, government action is needed for human capital growth to take place. There are various ways to jump-start the growth, from child labor and compulsory schooling laws to subsidies that replace a portion of the forgone earnings lost to the family when older children attend school. The key is to get schooling going because rising schooling increases the likelihood that schooling will continue to rise, even in the absence of government policies and laws.

9.3.2 International Trade, Capital Mobility, and Foreign Aid

Throughout the text, we have discussed how various types of international activity affect economic growth. In Chap. 3, we found that opening the economy to physical capital inflows significantly speeds up transitional growth. It also raises the effective saving rate of low saving countries leading to greater steady-state capital formation and worker productivity. In addition, opening the economy to capital flows affects the structure of fiscal policy, creating incentives for governments to lower tax rates and to invest a greater fraction of tax revenue in productive public capital. The pro-growth change in fiscal policy provides another reason that opening the economy raises worker productivity and living standards in the long run.

In Chaps. 4 and 6, we found that opening the economy to the international trade of goods can slow the structural transformation for developing economies that have a comparative advantage in the goods produced in the traditional sector. As we discussed at length, there are various reasons why slowing the structural transformation may lower aggregate economic growth. However, while it is possible that aggregate growth may be slowed, the majority of the population may nevertheless be made better-off by the international trade of goods. This is most likely when the growth effects of opening are small, due to the presence of important *domestic* impediments to growth, and when the benefits of growth tend to be concentrated in a relatively small segment of the population.

In Chap. 3, we examined when foreign aid would most likely raise growth and long-run worker productivity. Unconditional budget aid to countries with poor growth records has weak short-run growth effects and no long-run effects on worker productivity. On the other hand, forcing pro-growth fiscal reform is too costly in terms of compensating aid inflows and is likely to be circumvented by uncooperative governments. Aid is more likely to work when the conditions of aid are negotiated and owned by pro-growth governments that have specific ideas about investment projects that are likely to work best in their country.

9.4 Ideas for Future Research

We view the book as an introduction to the integration of the new features of growth theory into a two-sector framework. We hope it provides a foundation for doing further reading and conducting future research on topics where a two-sector approach is important.

Fundamental sources of differences in schooling across traditional and modern sectors should be more thoroughly examined, including the possibility of cultural differences that affect expectations about the benefits of human capital investments. There is evidence of community-level human capital externalities which could reflect the importance of cultural attitudes and informed expectations about the benefits of education. A more detailed analysis of what policies are most effective in raising schooling levels, especially in traditional settings, is needed. We also need a better understanding of how the structural transformation affects average schooling levels in the economy. Does the move to the modern sector generally raise human capital investment in health and education?

Additional work is also needed to identify whether the tradition of keeping land within the family is due to intergenerational preferences or due to the absence of land markets. If the absence of land markets is an important factor that binds labor to the traditional sector, what does it take for land markets to arise and how can the government promote their development?

A more complete study of the structural transformation should include a special focus on the large slums that form in the cities of developing countries. The possibility that slums create poverty traps, associated with poor health environments that impair the development of children, is an important area for further research.

Given concerns about urban crowding, the optimal pace of the structural transformation should be pinned down more precisely. What should the government do to speed up or slow down the structural transformation? Are industrial policies that speed up the structural transformation justified? Should they subsidize all modern industries or are there valid reasons to focus on particular industries? When, if ever, does it make sense to use migration restrictions or agricultural policy to slow down the structural transformation?

We hope that the book has made a case for examining the effects of international trade in dynamic two-sector models. The effects of trade on growth and the welfare of different household types and generations are complex. It is fair to say that we are far from any definitive understanding in this area. The strong case for free trade is predominately driven by results from static models, and we need to examine more carefully when trade is beneficial to developing countries in models that incorporate growth and intergenerational welfare effects.

Index

S. Das et al., *Economic Growth and Development*,
Springer Texts in Business and Economics, DOI 10.1007/978-3-319-14265-4

MIX
Papier aus verantwortungsvollen Quellen
Paper from responsible sources
FSC® C105338

If you have any concerns about our products,
you can contact us on
ProductSafety@springernature.com

In case Publisher is established outside the EU,
the EU authorized representative is:
Springer Nature Customer Service Center GmbH
Europaplatz 3, 69115 Heidelberg, Germany

Printed by Libri Plureos GmbH
in Hamburg, Germany